MY OWN, MY COUNTRY'S TIME

Life must be lived forward;
it can only be understood backwards.

Søren Kierkegaard
Life

My Own,
My Country's Time

A JOURNALIST'S JOURNEY

Vermont Royster

ALGONQUIN BOOKS
1983

ALGONQUIN BOOKS
P. O. Box 2225, Chapel Hill, N. C., 27515-2225

SECOND PRINTING

ISBN 9-912697-02-4

For Bonnie, Eleanor, Heather, and Shelley
Who someday may want to know how it was

CONTENTS

PART SIX: Dixie Again

In which I go home to a different South; find I cannot cut the journalistic cord and am off again to the political hustings and to the troubled places of the world as a commentator of public affairs for the same *Wall Street Journal*.

PART SEVEN: Retrospective

In which from Chapel Hill, North Carolina, where I began, I offer some reflections on the years of my own, my country's time.

Index

ILLUSTRATIONS

BY WAY OF INTRODUCTION

his is in part a journalistic memoir of familiar mold. Except for an interlude of naval service in World War II, I have spent nearly half a century as a journalist, most of the years with *The Wall Street Journal*. As such I have had the good fortune to know, or at least have a journalistic acquaintance with, every president from Franklin Roosevelt to Ronald Reagan.

These were interesting times for a journalist. They began with the New Deal and the political transformation wrought by it which made the Democratic party dominant for years to come. They continued to the years of Ronald Reagan which saw, at least briefly, a counter-revolution in the nation's politics. It was my privilege to have a grandstand seat as these events unfolded. The memories of them are recorded in these pages.

But this is also a personal as well as a journalistic memoir. Recalled are the memories of how it was to grow up in a small Southern town in the years between the First World War and the Great Depression. How it was to be reared in a close-knit family still living in many ways in ante-bellum times. How it was to go forth as an adult into the world in the midst of the depression with a most impractical education, consisting mainly of classical languages drummed into me by a father whose heart remained in antiquity and who was never comfortable in the twentieth century. Indeed, I became a journalist largely because a nodding acquaintance with Euripides hardly prepared me for anything else.

In time I returned to a small Southern town, to teach at the University in Chapel Hill where my father was teaching when I was born.

My lifetime thus embraces not only the depression but four wars, two of them great World Wars, one the most searing to my country since the Civil War. There were also many recessions, repeated periods of inflation, labor riots and race riots, a revolution in manners and morals. In that brief time we have gone from the horse and buggy to the atomic age and the exploration of space, with concomitant changes in society of no less magnitude. All these changes have touched my personal life as well as my journalistic one. Let the young muse upon future shock. I have survived past shock.

Intermingled with this is the story of *The Wall Street Journal*, which I saw grow from a small financial newspaper of about 35,000 circulation to one of the country's great newspapers, with the largest circulation of any newspaper in the United States and published in both Asia and Europe. How that came about, and something of the people who made it possible, is also part of my personal story.

In telling this story I have not followed a strict chronology although there are, as in every man's life, natural divisions between childhood, maturity, and age. I have not resisted, either, the temptation to meander in thought any more than one does in a conversation among friends.

Such, then, are the memories and thoughts here set down of my own, my country's time. If you care to share them, I welcome your company.

In addition to those who were companions on this journey, and who are mentioned herein, there are some who helped me construct it and whom it would be ungracious not to thank.

Warren Phillips, long-time colleague and now Chairman of Dow Jones and Publisher of *The Wall Street Journal*, read the manuscript and corrected factual errors. Matthew Hodgson, fellow Webb School alumnus and Director of the University of North Carolina Press, encouraged me from the beginning and sustained my spirit through many drafts. Dr. Louis D. Rubin, Jr., author and Distinguished Professor of English at the University in Chapel Hill, proved an editor extraordinary, offering valuable suggestions both as to structure and style. My Frances not only lived most of this journey with me but shared the struggle of re-living it.

Chapel Hill, North Carolina   —VERMONT ROYSTER

Prologue

---

*Il faut partir
à point.*

One must begin
at the best place.

—La Fontaine,
Fables

PROLOGUE

t was Friday, May 15, 1936, and Franklin D. Roosevelt was holding his 295th press conference since becoming president of the United States a little over three years earlier. I proudly presented my shiny new press credentials for *The Wall Street Journal* to the guard at the Pennsylvania Avenue gate, walked up the winding driveway, and entered the West Wing of the White House.

In 1936, as for many years afterward, the president's press conferences were held in the Oval Office because, except on special occasions, there were rarely more than thirty or so reporters attending. They were then what the term implies, conferences between the members of the press and the president, not the spectaculars they have since become.

At that time you entered the West Wing directly into a large and cluttered reception room, also oval shaped, with an enormous oak table in the center, used mainly as a repository for coats. Scattered around the periphery of the room were some rather worn chairs available for those waiting to see the president, whether they were as in this case reporters or whether they were congressmen, visiting dignitaries or other government officials. Both the room and the atmosphere were informal.

To your right, just inside the entrance, was a tiny press room. It held no more than a dozen desks for the White House regulars who represented the wire services, *The New York Times*, *The Wall Street Journal*, and the then five Washington newspapers: the *Post*, the *Star*, the *Herald*, the *Times*, and the *News*. There were, of course, no television cameras or crews; even radio mikes weren't allowed at the press conferences.

There was at that time no large White House staff, either. To the left of the reception room was a modest office for Stephen Early, the president's press secretary. Beyond and out of sight were offices for Marvin McIntyre, the president's only other regular aide, and for Marguerite "Missy" Le Hand, his long-time private secretary. There were two other offices designated for executive clerks, and that was all.

By today's standards these were rather primitive working arrangements. That oval waiting room has long since vanished in successive remodelings to make way for scores of new offices for presidential assistants, the overflow being housed in the basement. FDR's swimming pool, then in the passageway from the White House proper to the Oval Office, has been boarded over to make an expansive press room, housing permanent television cameras and lights. Current press secretaries, who now have their own numerous staff, use it for daily "briefings" in which they act as spokesmen for the president, something Steve Early rarely did. Across the street the State Department building has been converted into the Executive Office Building, housing more White House staff than there were on that spring day members of the entire Washington press corps.

But in 1936, all that was far in the future. As I entered the reception room that May afternoon, the reporters were already gathering. They all knew each other and there was an exchange of greetings and gossip. The only two I knew were Claude Mahoney, who kept permanent watch at the White House for *The Wall Street Journal*, and Alfred F. "Mike" Flynn, its senior Washington reporter. As a freshly-minted member of the bureau I felt a bit sheepish. I had had my press credentials no more than a week, and the White House was certainly not my assignment. It took a bit of brashness, I suppose, to push myself forward so quickly. I had done so out of curiosity and, no doubt, an eagerness to feed my ego.

Fred Storm of the United Press stood at the head of the line before the door leading to the inner Oval Office, a position held by virtue of his seniority at the White House and also because he was a huge, hulking man whom it would have been hard to push by. Occasionally he rapped on the door from the reception room and then laughed loudly at his feigned impatience. Someone in the crowd joked, "His Excellency is keeping the press waiting!" But it was all good natured. I stood quietly, wishing I could share in the camaraderie.

Eventually the door opened and we trooped through an outer room into the Oval Office. Although I brought up the rear, we were so few that as we spread out around the desk I was still only a few feet away from the president. He seemed even more impressive close up than in his pictures, larger in shoulders and chest than I had imagined him. As we gathered about the desk he smiled and welcomed us by waving his standard prop, the long, thin cigarette holder.

I was awed. Here I was a duly-accredited Washington correspondent, standing in this historic room in intimate contact with this man who already towered over his political contemporaries.

I was barely a year out of college. And I was twenty-two years old.

The press conference itself was hardly historic. Mr. Roosevelt began by telling us that he was going on the presidential yacht down the Potomac and into Chesapeake Bay to Annapolis, where he would stop overnight. He would be back Sunday night. He might take some papers along with him to be signed, but he didn't look on it as a working weekend. This casual chitchat made it seem less like a working press conference than a social occasion. In fact, it was his informal way of telling the press that "the lid was on" until Monday; there would be no news and the reporters too could relax for the weekend.

After this opening there did follow some desultory questions. The president was asked if he had worked out the details on the proposed Wagner Housing Act. He said no, but that good progress was being made. Someone asked him about a story in the morning paper that he was planning to phase out the Resettlement Administration, one of the emergency New Deal agencies that had been created to give government aid to farmers and other rural families. He replied laughingly that somebody was "writing stories off the wall" again.

He did, however, take several minutes to talk about the good work the Resettlement Administration was doing. About 500,000 families, he said, had been kept off the work relief rolls as a result of low cost RA loans. He also had praise for the agency's educational work, explaining that it taught the lady of the house how to put up vegetables and fruits and the man of the family how to kill their own hogs for winter use. I remember thinking that if farm families had to be taught this by the government they probably didn't belong on a farm anyway. But it was only a passing thought. I was too busy looking around the Oval Office and watching this man who, whether loved or hated, had caught the imagination of the country.

What dominated my first look at him was the impression of

strength, both in physical vigor and inner confidence. Self-confidence radiated from every word and gesture. It was also plain that he was a consummate actor enjoying his place on center stage. There was easy banter with the reporters, several of whom he knew and called by name. There were the familiar mannerisms, the lower jaw jutting out as he clamped the cigarette holder, the head thrown back as he responded to some question, the quick and easy smile. I was not in the least conscious of the fact, though of course I knew it, that he was crippled from the waist down as a result of polio. I do not remember either having then any thoughts about his political ideas or policies. I remember only being overwhelmed by his personality and, I must confess, impressed with myself for being there.

When Fred Storm said, "Thank you, Mr. President," we all trooped out again. The meeting had lasted some twenty minutes, and in retrospect this encounter between an American president and the press seems astonishingly simple, even quaint. Presidential press conferences are now TV events staged with all the panoply of show business in a large auditorium and with a participating cast of more than a hundred reporters.

Size is not the only thing that is different about these meetings. Under the Roosevelt rules we could not quote him directly without special permission; we could only paraphrase what he said and not always that. The president could give us information "for background only" which we could make use of but not attribute to him. And Mr. Roosevelt kept the privilege of going "off the record" entirely when he chose. That meant that he could, and often did, just think out loud, without fear that every word was put indelibly on the record. He could, and sometimes did, misstate himself at first expression as everyone may do in conversation, and then on second thought rephrase his remarks.

There are, no doubt about it, some gains in the way the new technology has altered the manner of doing things. Through television the ordinary citizen today does get a chance to see the president in action and to form some impressions not just by what he says but by his style. His grace under pressure, or his lack of it, is not wholly irrelevant to his performance as our national leader.

But there are some losses amid the gains. Under the glare of television and with each word sent instantly across the country and around the world, a modern president must live in constant fear of the slip-of-the-tongue. A misstated name from a lapse of memory can be an embarrassment. Awkward phraseology on some matter of public import is beyond recall or correction.

One consequence of this is that presidents today try to say no more at a press conference than what might be put as well in a carefully drafted statement. The loss here is to the president, the press, and even to the public. The president has lost an opportunity to be frank and open. The press has lost an opportunity to share his thought processes which, without being the stuff of headlines, nonetheless can help it do a better job of informing the public.

I might add that the president has also lost the opportunity to deal bluntly with the stupid question, not unknown at presidential press conferences. Anyway, I cannot imagine a modern president telling a reporter on television that he had asked a silly question and to go stand in the dunce corner, something President Roosevelt didn't hesitate to do.

But in that long ago spring I had no inkling of the changes time would bring. I was simply overwhelmed by the experience of being only a few feet away from Franklin Roosevelt. With no story to write myself I walked slowly along Pennsylvania Avenue and F street to the National Press Building where the *Journal* had its office. The slow walk gave me time to marvel at the circuitous route which in so short a time had brought me from a small town in Dixie to the White House.

PART ONE

Dixie

If I pick up a book
about a man's life
and it tells me nothing
about his boyhood,
I lay it aside.

—W. R. "Sawney" Webb

DIXIE

Raleigh, North Carolina, lies nearly in the middle of the state, as befits a town which, like Washington, was created and designed to be a political capital. In 1792 a nine-man commission appointed by the legislature purchased Joel Lane's plantation of a thousand acres located near the Wake County Court House. On that land was laid out a new town approximately one square mile, including five public squares and 276 lots of one acre each. In the center would be the Capitol building, from which would radiate four main thoroughfares, the remainder of the streets to form a rectangular grid. This was seven years before David Royster, cabinet maker, came to Raleigh to make furniture for the planned new legislative hall.

Although I bear a New England name, the origin of which is a story in itself, my family had been Southern for seven generations; no member of the family in the direct line ever lived permanently anywhere else.

The first Royster of whom there is a record in America was one Jacob, birth and death dates unknown, who received a patent (or land grant) in Westover Parish, Charles City County, Virginia, in 1682. The next one on record was David, who died in the same county in 1742, sixty years later. Jacob and David were related, though how is not known. It is from this first David that all the Roysters in this country who spell the name this way are, so far as I know, descended. In England the name is usually spelled Royston (we do not know the connection between Jacob and his English forebears), and there is a town of that name not far from London.

His grandson, also David, moved to Granville County, North Carolina, late in the eighteenth century, and it was his great-grandson David who came to Raleigh about 1800.

In those days large families were the rule. The David who came to Raleigh married Susan Sims, and they had twelve children, one still another David and one named James Daniel; he was my great-grandfather. All this makes for a tangled genealogy, spreading the countryside with innumerable cousins. As a small boy I was constantly being introduced to Cousin So-and-So, without it always being clear (then or now) how we were related.

The size of families was the cause of my having my unusual name. James Daniel, my great-grandfather, married Mary Smoothly Ashley and they had eight children. The family tradition is that James, observing the spread of Roysters in the community, decided he didn't want anyone to have to ask his children, "Now, let's see, you are David's child or James's?" He attacked that problem by naming all his children for states.

This was before the late unpleasantness between the states known to history books as the Civil War, so James had no prejudice against Yankee state names. My grandfather was named Vermont Connecticut, which is also, though I no longer advertise it, my own full name. The other boys were Iowa Michigan, Arkansas Delaware, Wisconsin Illinois, and Oregon Minnesota. The girls' names were not quite so outlandish: Louisiana Maryland (who died in infancy), Virginia Carolina, and Georgia Indiana. There was never any doubt thereafter who were the children of James Daniel and Mary Ashley!

The state-name tradition, I should note, was abandoned in the next generation. My father was named Wilbur High and his brother Percy Hoke. I got the name, as a throwback, mainly because my mother so much loved my grandfather that she insisted on naming me for him over my father's protest. Even so, in time the state names became famous throughout the countryside, or maybe notorious is a better word. They have been listed in such diverse places as Ripley's "Believe It or Not" recording of oddities, in the *Saturday Evening Post* and the *Saturday Review*. People still accost me wanting to know the names of my siblings, confusing one generation with another.

It was in my grandfather's house on Hillsborough Street in Raleigh that I was born on the afternoon of April 30, 1914, the first-born of Wilbur High Royster and Olivette James Broadway of Monroe, Louisiana.

At the time my parents were actually living in Chapel Hill, where my father was a young instructor in Latin and Greek at the University. Chapel Hill is only twenty-five miles away, but in those days that meant a full day's journey, and for this momentous event it was thought my mother should come to Raleigh where she could be better cared for than in that tiny village. Although I have only the dimmest memories of it, I lived in Chapel Hill until I was three years old, when my father left teaching to return to Raleigh to help my grandfather in the family business.

Most of my memories, then, are of growing up in Raleigh. In 1920, when I was six years old, the population of Raleigh was less than twenty thousand, and even that figure exaggerates the impression of urbanity. The main streets adjacent to the Capitol had been paved but it would be another decade before this mark of progress could be found on the outlying streets. Morgan Street, where we first lived in a house only a block away from my grandfather's, was still unpaved. Fayetteville Street—the "main street" of the town—retained a small-town atmosphere with its owner-operated groceries, meat markets, and dry-goods stores.

The farmers' market, bustling with produce from surrounding farms, was also on Fayetteville Street only four blocks from the Capitol. The highways leading to and from the town, such as they were, were mainly dirt roads. The first paved road from Raleigh to Chapel Hill was not completed until 1928. The railroad was the main form of transportation.

The memories of growing up in such a town at such a time have now the patina of pages torn from a dusty history book. Although there were automobiles, horses and buggies were no strangers to the streets. There was no television, of course, and radio was a toy novelty; the first one I heard squawked and sputtered, and you marvelled that you heard anything at all. The movies were silent. The phonograph was hand cranked, scratchy, and of uncertain sound. By day children amused themselves as best they could. Evening was the time for being read to until you could read yourself and for being absorbed in a close-knit family.

Sorting out those memories now I realize that this feeling of family belonging, anachronistic as it may be in the modern world, was a major influence on my life and thinking. So was the sense of tradition, born of generations in the South where, at that time, the Civil War was still felt as a palpable tragedy. And so was my father's love of classical languages, to which he introduced me in childhood and which gave me an abiding interest in the antiquity of man's struggle for civilization. They are influences I have not yet escaped.

I have never known anyone from the northern states to whom

the Civil War was anything but an incident in the history books, even though ancestors may have fought in it. Growing up in the South it was different. Because ours was the defeated and occupied land, almost all the adults we knew had some memories of the woes it brought.

My great-grandfather James Daniel had owned a prosperous paper mill near Raleigh, which Sherman's troops burned. One of his sons, Arkansas Delaware, was invalided out of the Confederate Army and was a life-long cripple. Another son, Iowa Michigan, was an English teacher at the University in 1858 (the first of a long line from the family to teach there); he too joined the army and was killed at Gettysburg. A third son, Wisconsin Illinois, was an army surgeon. My grandfather, Vermont Connecticut, only thirteen when the war began, lost his college education because of it.

Another great-grandfather, William Henderson High, had owned a plantation in Wake County. He lost it after the war for want of U.S. money to pay the taxes, and not long afterwards sold it, put his whole family and what possessions he had left into a boxcar, and took them all to California. His daughter Hallie, who later returned to Raleigh, married Vermont and would become my grandmother. She remembered when Sherman's troops took over the plantation house, moving the family into the attic. When for me it was time to say, "Grandmother, tell me a story," it would often be about this four-year-old girl listening to the strange soldiers tramping below her.

Another distant kinsman of mine died of the beau geste. As Sherman's troops entered Raleigh in the spring of 1865, marching up Fayetteville Street in parade order, he rode out in full Confederate uniform to meet them, his back to the Capitol building. When the color guard was in pistol range, he opened fire, shot one of the guards, and took off at a dash. Unfortunately, he got caught in a cul-de-sac and was promptly hanged without the formality of trial.

All these I knew from childhood because they were tales of the olden days, not because my elders wished to inculcate hatred of the Yankees. Actually the lesson taught was something else. Like many North Carolinians James Daniel had opposed secession; in fact, the state voted against it until after Virginia and South Carolina left it an island in the Confederacy. The family attitude which I absorbed was that once your land and your people were menaced you had no choice but to take arms to defend them. It was long a

Southern attitude and accounts for the fact that in subsequent wars Southerners bore arms for the reconstructed Union in disproportionate numbers. Strangely enough, one of my earliest memories was of war, World War I, the first of four wars in my time. I couldn't have been more than four years old, yet I recall vividly a long troop train pausing at the railroad station on its northward journey, myself dressed in a soldier suit complete with campaign hat, my mother in a white Red Cross dress as she served them coffee and sandwiches. All of this may have had something to do with my leaving my wife and small daughter years later to go off to another war.

There were other lessons implicit in my childhood rearing. My grandfather taught me some of them by example. Until I was ten years old, and he died, there was never a day he did not spend some hours with me. When I was very young, he would come in the afternoon to draw me funny pictures and in the evening to read "Old Mother Westwind" or the fairy tales of Hans Christian Andersen. As I grew older he would take me on long walks to feed the squirrels in Capitol Square or to visit the Seaboard Railroad yards where, because he knew all the workmen, I would be allowed to sit in an engine and play at highballing down the tracks. Or perhaps it would be to Pullen Park where there was a swimming pool, a tiny zoo, and a merry-go-round.

When the circus came to town each year we would be up at dawn to watch the animals arrive and the big tent rise. Here too he seemed to know the circus folk from previous visits, and we would join the fat lady and the clowns for lunch. After I was in school he would ask me to read to him. "My old eyes are tired," he would tell me. Without saying so, he was teaching me about the ties that bind the generations.

Gradually I began to learn his story. Seventeen when the war ended, and with the family fortune in ruins, he joined with his crippled brother A. D. to buy on credit a stock of dry goods from a Jewish merchant who saw brighter fields up North. Those first goods sold, my grandfather went to Baltimore to replenish the stock and "rode shotgun" on the freight car bringing them back to Raleigh. In time they shifted to candy manufacturing, sweets being in much demand in the postwar South, and Royster's peanut brittle, stick candy, and "chips" became known throughout the state.

Having little formal education, my grandfather set out to educate himself. This he did by buying complete sets of Shakespeare or Dickens or Walter Scott, starting on page one, volume one, and reading straight through. He also taught himself enough music to play the organ at the Baptist church. All that left an education with many gaps, but few could match him in his knowledge of the literature he had read. When his sons entered Morson's Latin school he learned enough through them to discuss the use of Latin subjunctives.

He would not take himself a wife until he was nearly forty because it never occurred to him that the responsibility for a family lay on anyone's shoulders but his own. In due time, though, he built the house with tall columns where I was born, dreaming that someday his grandchildren would dwell therein with their own children in turn. Changing times have swept away that house, where now sits a Holiday Inn, but his portrait hangs today on my living room wall; that of an old gentleman in high wing collar, a soft white beard, and steel-rimmed spectacles over watery eyes. I hope that as he looks down he draws some comfort from the fact that, despite inheritance taxes many times over, an inheritance from him is helping to educate his great-great-grandchildren. It would please him to know that in his family new generations build on the accumulations of yesterday.

My mother and father also shaped me, though in an entirely different way. To a very young child my mother was like one of those fairy godmothers, beautiful in everyone's eyes, with dark wavy hair set over chiseled features, a creamy complexion and pale blue eyes. She was somewhat distant at first because my daily needs were cared for by Mamie, a large black woman whom I loved dearly and who loved me. But my mother taught me to read and do small sums before I was six, and she filled my head with stories of plantation days in Monroe, Louisiana.

My father at this time was busy managing the candy business to which he had come partly out of family duty, partly out of doubt that teaching Latin and Greek offered much future. He was up early and home late. Yet he loved teaching—in due time he would study law, begin a practice and return in the 1940s to teach law at the University—and he loved his subject. He had met my mother in Boston while doing postgraduate work at Harvard after a year at the American School of Classical Studies in Athens; she was studying piano at the Conservatory in Boston. So it was natural that as soon as I was old enough to talk and read a little he would introduce me to Latin. He taught me the principal parts of Latin verbs before I knew what they meant. A six-year-old can delight in chanting *tango, tangere, tetigi, tactum*. He started me on the formal study of Latin at the age of eight.

My father was also an accomplished amateur musician, playing nearly every instrument somewhat and the cello well. At Harvard he had played in the Pierian Sodality Orchestra and in Raleigh he "moonlighted" in the pit for the traveling musical shows that came through town, one perquisite being free tickets. Later he was to play in the North Carolina Symphony when it was first organized as a semiprofessional orchestra. My mother was a trained pianist. Many nights I lay abed listening to them play together, absorbing Mozart or Chopin. Sometimes there would be what my father called the "sandlot quartet," made up of friends who played the violin or the viola. In those days, with no hifi to listen to, you made your own music.

Among the other influences of my childhood were Mamie, who mothered me, and a black boy a few years older than I, named Skibo, who was part nurse and full-time playmate.

It is hard now to recapture, much less explain to a younger generation, the black-white relationship in that long ago time without being either shocking or falsely sentimental. It was, to be sure, a master-servant relationship better long since ended. But for those of us who grew up under it, it was simply a relationship that existed and one which, for all its evils, fostered closeness and personal affection. To a great extent black and white Southerners had a better understanding of each other and a closer association than in other parts of the country. Of many white liberals in the North on civil rights, whose views I came to share, I knew none who had ever had a close personal relationship with a black. I found that very strange.

Mamie, who stayed with us only a few years, and then Lucinda, who stayed many years until she died, seemed simply part of the family. It was to them I ran to be mothered when I skinned a knee; it was to them especially I ran when I was scolded or spanked by my mother or father. They were solid anchors of my childhood.

They were also women of dignity and pride. Mamie would never let my mother so much as boil water in her kitchen; that was her domain and my mother had to learn her place. This was just as well, since she cooked on an old wood-fired iron stove, the mysteries of which only she understood. I remember once when Mother was especially angry at my younger brother, Lucinda came into the room, eyes flashing and arms akimbo. "Miz Royster, you leave that Tommy alone!" My mother meekly did as she was told.

Yet with Lucinda, as well as with Mamie, my mother had an easy personal relationship of much affection. I recall wintry evenings when my father was working late. Mother and Lucinda would sit opposite in the living room before the fireplace, knitting and chatting while I played on the floor. They were two women doing household chores and enjoying each other's company. Servant Lucinda was, true enough. She was also something else.

So was Skibo to me. We played together from morning to night at being cowboys or locomotive engineers or whatever our fancy called for. While I was still under school age he would take me wandering all over town, to the slaughterhouse, to the black section where he lived and where we would play with his friends. When I was a little older we would play cowboys and Indians with the black children who lived only a block away; our side, the cowboys, was integrated, the other side all black. We fought some fierce battles with make-believe guns.

Life was never boring. For one thing, when I was about four or five I fell in love with my mother, who by this time began to treat me as a child, not a baby. Mornings were devoted to those reading lessons which she made into a delightful game; I learned rapidly because I would do anything to please her. Afterwards she would let me go with her when she went shopping, which meant a walk downtown. She made it a formal promenade, dressed as if she were going calling, which in a way she was because she treated the butcher, the grocer, or the fruit vendor as friends. She would dress me formally, too, with little jacket and tie. I walked the streets proudly then because everywhere we went she made heads turn.

In the afternoons Skibo and I could visit with "Slops," the black man who came to collect our garbage to feed his hogs; he had an ex-circus horse who on command would sit down in the traces. Or on summer days we would run to meet the iceman, who would skim shavings off his big ice blocks to make refreshing snowballs.

Another adventure was to ride with the buttermilk man in his noisy Model T Ford as he made his rounds from our house to my grandmother's. It was real buttermilk in those days, churned by hand and dotted with flecks of butter, not the modern cultured kind. Skibo and I could each easily put away a quart any hot afternoon.

On rainy days when there was nothing else to do, grandmother's was a refuge because she kept a closet full of old Sunday newspaper comic sections; there was Tom Sawyer, Happy Hooligan, the Katzenjammer Kids, all my favorites. When I was a little older she and I had a regular "date" at the Saturday morning movies to see *The Perils of Pauline* or *Eddie Polo in the Circus*, the serial movies that filled the place of today's TV. Finally, there was always the candy factory where my father would let Skibo and me dip our fingers in the chocolate pot or sip the milk from fresh-opened coconuts.

Thus passed my early childhood. Until I started to school I had few friends outside my family, black and white, because there were few boys of my age in the immediate neighborhood and girls went unnoticed. But I had no sense of being lonely, surrounded as I was by so much love and attention.

It was with the school days that troubles began.

*　*　*　*　*

I started in the first grade at the Wiley Public School, a block from my house.

The night before my first day of school when my mother came up to bed she found me still awake from a mixture of excitement and apprehension about the strangeness of the unknown. I was eager to go to this imagined heaven where there would be other children—I had already noticed them leaving school amid much noisy whooping—and where there would be wonderful new things to do. But could I learn all those things others learned? How was it going to be, shut up in a classroom half the day? I remember asking my mother if school and growing up meant that I couldn't play cowboy any more. She said I could but that as I grew up I wouldn't want to and would find other interests.

To which I replied, "But I don't want to *not* want to play cowboy!"

It was, I think now, a revealing remark. For as I look back on those years when I set out boldly to conquer New York, when I rushed eagerly into the competitive thickets of Washington, when I ran off to war, when I went dashing around the world on journalistic forays, I always told myself the attraction was of being engaged in serious business. I suspect, deep down, that much of it was only the allure of romantic adventure, of a grownup still playing cowboy. Even in my age the separation between child and man remains blurred.

That six-year-old learned early, however, that disappointments also come with adventure. I did make new friends. It was the classroom that curdled my enthusiasm. I was no smarter than the other children, but I could already read, write my name, and do simple sums. In school we began with large cards on which were printed the ABCs. The books on which the class spent several days I finished before the day was out. The result was sheer boredom.

By midway in the first year I had been jumped to the third grade. This helped one problem but created another. I was now in a class with children older than I, and at that age a difference of even a year or two is a chasm in terms of both physical and psychological maturity. I only saw my real contemporaries briefly at recess, while I didn't fit in with my classroom companions. The consequences of that were to haunt me the rest of my school days.

That's a perennial educational dilemma for which I know no good solution. It's criminal, I think, to hold back children when they are ready to read, or at any other educational level. Yet the psychologists are right that a young child among older ones, like the ugly duckling of that childhood story, does risk becoming a social misfit. I don't wish to exaggerate, but I certainly became so, at least in part.

This problem, for me, was complicated by other factors. The Southern custom of that time, segregation, meant that going to school separated me from Skibo, who up to then had been a constant companion. I did see him occasionally, but our association could never again be what it was. (Later he left Raleigh and the last I heard of him, during the war years, he was working in Detroit. I have not seen him in sixty years. He holds, nonetheless, a special place in my memory.)

There was also the complication that my brother Tommy was a

frail child, born prematurely in the influenza epidemic of 1919 when the whole family was struck down at once. Thus I suddenly found myself getting less attention at home. I remember crying a lot without knowing why or being able to explain it to anyone.

My father met part of this problem by transferring me when I was eight to St. Nicholas School (later Carolina Academy), a private school run by an Episcopal minister. His daughter, Elizabeth Hughes, had a remarkable gift with children. She started me on the formal study of Latin, which she could make interesting, and in time introduced me to simple algebra and geometry. The school was small enough so that there were no sharp divisions among ages; in fact, as I remember there were no grade levels at all. Each student went at his own pace.

These were happier school years. I made some lifelong friends as well as learning that learning can be fun. Unfortunately this time did not last long, because the school went bankrupt and in 1927 I returned to the public high school.

At thirteen I was not only short of stature—today I am only five feet six inches tall—but also two years younger than my classmates, who were already true teenagers. At school parties and dances I fitted in poorly with either classmates or my age peers. I began to compensate for this by being impertinent and unruly; "smart-aleck" would be the old-fashioned word. I would do things like turn off all the lights in the school building in the midst of a play rehearsal and take delight in the ensuing chaos.

Moreover, my grades collapsed. For the first time I was faced with an angry father and he with a rebellious child.

Total disaster was averted only by activities outside the school. In the summer my father and I would go to the ball park, riding on an open streetcar, to watch the Raleigh Caps struggle in the Piedmont League. One of his cousins, Clifton Beckwith, would let me go hunting with him for squirrels or rabbits. On autumn weekends Jim Thomas (the viola player of the "sandlot quartet") would drive us all to Chapel Hill in his great open touring car to see the football games.

These were all-day excursions, from morning to night. After the game there would be a gathering of kinfolk and friends at the house of Vernon Howell, a bachelor cousin and head of the Pharmacy Department at the University. Our collateral Rocky Mount clan, which included Kay Kyser, later the well-known band leader, would be out in force, and there would be a scattering of other cousins from about the state. I enjoyed these affairs immensely even though I was usually the youngest present.

Impromptu and unannounced visiting was a custom of the times. Often Mother and Lucinda would be challenged by a half-dozen unexpected kin for supper. One morning while Tommy and I were having breakfast we heard a scream from my mother upstairs. Rushing up, we discovered her standing in the door of the guest room staring at Cousin Vernon, who was sitting bolt upright in bed. He had been in Raleigh, needed a place to sleep, found our door unlocked as usual, and had gone quietly upstairs to bed. I don't know who was the most startled at the confrontation, Vernon or mother.

Summers were broken about every other year by a visit to Monroe to see our Louisiana kin. There my mother's stepfather (her own father had died before she was born) had a plantation south of the town on the Ouachita River where, with my cousins Bert and Suzonne Sperry, Tommy and I rode horseback and went camping in the woods. Alex, the plantation's general factotum, taught us how to saddle, how to hitch a team, and even tried to teach me how to plow behind a mule. To me as a child these were glory days.

One summer we returned home via New Orleans, going down the Ouachita, the Red, and the Mississippi on a stern-wheel riverboat. It was a voyage right out of Mark Twain, for along the way the steamboat would stop at farm landings to pick up cargo or passengers, loading them over the huge gangway that dropped down from the bow. On long river reaches the captain, who could have been typecast for *Showboat*, would sometimes let us stand in the wheelhouse watching the river go by.

But the real lifesavers of my preteen years were the arrival of the Charles Cramer Stock Company in Raleigh and my discovery of the Olivia Raney children's library. I have no idea how good these travelling players were, but they opened a whole new world for me. Changing the bill twice a week, they offered everything from bedroom farces like *Up In Mabel's Room* to such melodramas as *The Bat* to their version of *The Merchant of Venice*. I saw every performance at Wednesday and Saturday matinees. When they did

Mrs. Wiggs of The Cabbage Patch I won a part as one of the children and so can claim having been a professional actor, being paid a dollar a performance.

The children's library was a gold mine. There I devoured *Tom Sawyer, Huckleberry Finn* and all the familiar children's books from *Little Women* to *Alice in Wonderland*. It was there that I discovered the G. A. Henty series of historical novels for boys (much of my view of history is colored by them) as well as Kipling and the romances of H. Rider Haggard. Haggard's *She* was especially impressive because its opening chapters contain a supposed ancient manuscript printed first in Greek and then in Latin; novelists of his time did not write down to their readers.

The library held periodic reading contests with a large board on which each contestant's name was inscribed. After each book you read and reported on, your name was moved one notch further on the board. My chief rival, to whom I always came in second, was a dazzling little blonde girl named Nell Joslin. She drove me frantic with her competition.

Some of my reading, to be sure, was what my mother thought "trash," pulp magazines like *Argosy* and cheap paperbound thrillers like *Nick Carter, Detective*. She worried also when I spent sunny afternoons indoors buried in a book. Several times she spoke to my father about this, but he always replied, "If the boy will read, let him read."

My father was right. If I read much of what my mother thought trash, I also read almost anything else put in front of me. I remember devouring H. G. Wells' *Outline of History* as well as *Gulliver's Travels*, neither of which was written for children but both of which made deep impressions. Perhaps if there had been television it would have been different. At least TV is blamed for the complaint that "Johnny can't read," or anyway doesn't read much. If that's true there's more than nostalgia in my remembered pleasures, for books open a world to a child that no other medium can. But I suspect the fault lies less with that technological invention than with the altered values of parents and teachers. If Johnny can't read it's because its pleasures are hidden from him. My own granddaughters, I notice, are inveterate readers, though also TV watchers. That's because they too have grown up in a house where books are many and cherished.

Even so, I wasn't entirely a bookworm. There were no organized sports for youngsters in those days, no Little League, no supervised playgrounds, but I played pickup football or baseball with school friends, using string-wrapped baseballs or footballs patched with old tire inner tubes. There was also the Boy Scouts, which was then still much outdoor-oriented. We went on weekend overnight hikes, learning to box a compass, pitch a tent, and make a fire with flint and steel. Several summers were spent at scout camp. All in all, a rather typical growing up in the semirural, small-town atmosphere of the South in the 1920s. Like my friends, I paid little attention to, and was hardly aware of, what went on in the world beyond. My world revolved around family and friends, one week marked off from another only by Sunday school, which was a time for dressing up; one season marked off from another by the coming of summer.

Then one day, to my surprise, I found myself suddenly interested in girls. If Nell Joslin shook my ego, a dark-haired little girl with snappy eyes stirred other feelings. She was Primrose McPherson, later to become a portrait painter and well-known illustrator of children's books under the simple sobriquet of "Primrose." I was much too shy, though, to be a courtier. Although I once took her to the movies, we spent the whole time in silence because I could think of nothing to say. My other romances were no more successful. In the high school annual my picture is entwined with that of the most popular girl in school, Clara Margaret Grantham, but by the time the yearbook was published she had abandoned me for more dashing companions.

Perhaps it was the arrival of my sister that helped change my mind about girls. Anyway, Saravette—the name is a contraction of Sara and Olivette—was born when I was thirteen and quickly became the center of family attention, including my own. I was too charmed with her to feel any of the resentment I had over the attention to Tommy. That resentment, incidentally, had diminished with time and we had grown closer together despite the five-year difference in ages, largely I suppose because Tommy gave me a rewarding measure of hero-worship.

It was also about this time that I became aware of newspapers and magazines. In addition to the local papers I began to read the *American* and *Liberty*; I even entered some short stories in a *Lib-*

erty contest, to no avail. But it is the *Saturday Evening Post* I best remember. It gave me my first glimpse of the romance of the press.

In its halcyon days the *Post* dripped so much prestige that a boyish salesman like me could be, and was, invited to talk of his sales experience before local civic groups. The audiences were kind, if no doubt amused, and these appearances gave me a sense of self-importance which I associated with being connected, even so distantly, with the publishing world.

The News and Observer, our morning paper, also sowed some seeds for an interest in journalism. I had appointed myself press agent for the high-school football team, and some of the items I sent in were published as notes about injuries, changes in the line-up and the like. One day for some mysterious reason one of these items carried my "byline." The result was dramatic. Suddenly, strapping football players who had never before noticed me began to greet me effusively. That gave me a taste of the power of the press.

I must confess, however, that my reading of the newspaper was confined to the comics and the sports pages, my reading of the *Post* to its stories by Clarence Buddington Kelland or Arthur Train. Articles on world affairs were ignored. I passed through the 1920s oblivious to presidential elections, international disarmament conferences, social changes or economic troubles. I had no premonition that years later I would join the *Post*'s authors' circle, writing just such articles on public issues.

In a sense, then, the more my world changed the more it remained the same. It had expanded beyond the hearth but not beyond the town or the circle of school, family, and friends. It remained a sheltered life. Indeed, looking back, it seems now not only a different time but a different world.

I graduated from the Hugh Morson High School in 1929, aged fifteen, despite obstreperous behavior and poor grades. In those days a high school diploma would get you into the University and I fully expected to go to Chapel Hill in the fall. My father had other ideas.

When he was teaching he had been impressed by the preparation of the boys who came from the Webb School, an old but small school in Bell Buckle, Tennessee. I had heard of it, but not favorably, from some Raleigh boys who had been there. It was reportedly a place of tough scholastic standards and strict discipline. I was not in the mood for either.

My father's announcement that I would go there for two years before Chapel Hill brought an eruption of open rebellion. For days I sulked, sullenly refusing to talk at table or join any family gathering after dinner. I would eat, stalk upstairs, and slam my door. It was a rebellion, however, that could have only one ending, for these were times when parental authority still held sway. Even in my angriest moments it never occurred to me that I could—or should—do anything but what my father told me.

So it was that one day in September 1929 I took the sleeper train to Atlanta, changing there for the train to Nashville which would make an unscheduled flag stop in Bell Buckle.

What I did not know, as I lay awake in my berth watching the green Pullman curtains sway and listening to the click of the rails, was that the next two years would be momentous in my life. They would leave a lasting mark on all that came thereafter.

2

The Webb School was already an anachronism in 1929. It required its students to take four years of Latin and two of Greek in order to graduate.

For the rest, as I was to discover, you studied only history, English literature and composition, mathematics, and—if you wished—physics. No modern languages, no social studies, no current events, and of course no "practical" courses in bookkeeping, business, or carpentry. Its teaching methods were equally old-fashioned. The physics course would make a modern educator's hair curl; there was no laboratory work to heat up rods and measure the coefficient of expansion or to duplicate experiments with falling bodies. Such information you could look up in a book, which was what books are for. But you had the principles of physics drummed into your head, and before you were through Galileo and Newton were old friends. Mathematics meant not simple algebra but trigonometry and the calculus, and this years before "advanced placement" courses in high school were ever thought of.

In all the courses, especially Latin and Greek, you were expected to know and not almost know. It wasn't enough to translate Cicero or Virgil. You had to know the constructions, from the ablative of manner to the ablative absolute, and be able to cite the rule from Allen and Greenough's grammar. In Greek you had to get the diacritical marks right and in English composition you were expected to understand the proper use of the subjunctive.

The rules outside of class were equally quaint. Going from one class to another you were not allowed to stop on the path. A junior couldn't set foot on the grounds surrounding the freshman or senior classrooms, or vice-versa. If you were in the village of an afternoon buying an ice cream soda you had to scurry three blocks away from the railroad station when the Nashville-to-Chattanooga train came roaring through.

All this was a shock to a young boy fresh out of a public high school and accustomed to the freedoms of home. I thought the academic demands outrageous and the rules silly. I was also scornful of the physical facilities. The classrooms were small one-room buildings heated with potbellied stoves. The assembly room—known simply as "the Big Room"—was a huge barnlike building filled with long, hard benches and two of the primitive stoves. I was housed in Mrs. Sturdevant's boardinghouse where a dozen boys were mothered by this buxom widow. It had a privy in the back and the luxury of washing depended on the rainfall caught on the tin roof and drained into a cistern.

No one needed to tell me that Bell Buckle itself, population about five hundred, had changed little since W. R. "Sawney" Webb, a native of North Carolina, moved his school there in 1886. Neither had the school. "Son Will" Webb, chipped from the same block, saw no reason to change anything. He would have no truck with the newfangled educational ideas spawned by John Dewey.

My first encounter with a Webb class foreshadowed the disasters to come. Although I had supposedly read Cicero in high school, a quick examination by Son Will got me assigned to do it over again. There I ran into Webb Follin, no kin to Son Will, a large man with a hooked Roman nose and deep-set eyes that could bore a hole through the lazy, the inattentive, or the ignorant.

The class used the "trapping" system. That is, the boys were lined up on the benches, initially at random. Questioning began with the boy at the head of the line. If he answered correctly he stayed there. If he didn't the next one was asked. If the second one answered it he moved over—in other words "trapped"—the first boy. And so on down the line. A boy who stayed in the head place through a whole class then moved to the bottom and started his climb back to the top. It made for a very simple way of grading; you were measured by your progress—or lack of it—up the ladder.

On that first day I was, by luck of the draw, about halfway down the line. I don't remember now the question put to me except that it had something to do with compound verbs. Anyway, I missed it.

But I will never forget the answer of Maurel Richards to whom the question was next put. "Verbs compounded with *ad, ante, con, in, inter, ob, post, prae, pro, super* and some with *circum*," he responded promptly, "admit the dative of the indirect object."

Webb Follin stared at me from under his beetle brows. "The first thing you have to do, Vermont," he said, "is learn the rules."

From not knowing the rules, at least precisely, by the end of the first week I was at the bottom of the class.

There were similar disasters in trig, history, and English composition. For example, in English composition this same Webb Follin would assign us to write a composition of, say, 368 words, which meant 368 words, neither one more nor one less. Idiotic. What possible difference could one word or less make? Or the assignment would be to write a page of pure dialogue; no "he said angrily" or "he answered quietly." You had to show mood by the dialogue written. Once the assignment was to write pure description, no action or dialogue. I described the view from my bedroom window with the sun rising over the Tennessee hills. That phrase was red-pencilled. The sun was moving, so said Follin, and that was action.

I was also very quickly in disciplinary trouble with all those silly rules I saw no point to. It seemed as though every few days I was in Son Will's office for some mortal sin like stopping to look at a squirrel while going from Latin to Greek class.

When those first grades came at Christmas, beautifully timed to arrive while I was home on holiday, I had barely passed anything, and a note from Son Will said my attitude needed some improving. I spent most of that holiday unhappily begging not to be sent back. I had had enough of that nonsense.

But the word from my father was that I was there, and there I was going to stay. So there I stayed, fuming all the way back on the long train trip.

In the event, however, the trauma of that first term at Webb proved a salutary one. I could not believe that my all-A classmates such as Maurel Richards, Langdon Taylor, or Mallory Harwell were really smarter than I. Injured pride drove me to show them. In the winter term, moreover, there were fewer schoolyard distractions from football or other outdoor lures. My roommate was Bruce Shepherd, who was conscientious about homework and burned the midnight oil. He was a good example and helpful in other ways because as an "old boy" he knew the kind of thing that would be demanded of us in class the next day. Between Bruce and my new-found pride I began to study not only harder but more successfully.

By this time I had also noticed that the all-A students were privileged fellows. They were exempt from all those out-of-classroom rules. They could (and did) lord it over their fellows, stopping wherever they pleased and casually finishing their sodas while others fled the village before the oncoming train. That was one way Sawney Webb had devised to put a premium upon academic excellence. At Webb the scholars, not the athletes, were the big boys on the schoolgrounds.

As a result, my performance, if not my attitude, changed quickly. When grading time came at the end of the winter term, lo and behold—to the astonishment of everyone, including myself—there was my name on the list of those making an A in every course.

I thought that a remarkable achievement. Indeed, I was so impressed with myself that I had an attack of hubris, and the result of that overweening pride was that the following semester I slipped from that exalted perch. Having been humbled again by that lesson, however, I did thereafter manage to keep a place near the top of the class among formidable competitors. Maurel and Langdon, as I recall, managed straight A's for four full years.

If such a school at such a time seemed already out of date, it was in its beginnings both radical and experimental. Not so much in its curriculum, for ever since the earliest American prep schools—Andover in 1778, Exeter in 1781—the studies had leaned heavily on classical languages, borrowing their basic curriculum from the English "public" schools. Rather, what made Sawney Webb an educational radical for his time was his attitude toward the school and the boys who came there.

The post-Civil War period was a flourishing time for prep

schools; in the East they sprang up everywhere. But these were seeded in a time and place of prosperity. There the new mercantile and banking classes were being born, and as they grew prosperous they looked to England for the models of the schools to which to send their sons. They were good models and they resulted in exceedingly good schools. But the very prosperity that made them bloom tended to make them schools for the sons of the rich.

The post-Civil War South was something else. In the South of 1886 there were few rich. So when Sawney Webb founded his school time and circumstance put a different cast upon it. Like the Eastern schools it was, of course, elitist in outlook for Sawney intended it as a place to educate those who would go on to college and become leaders in the South. But Sawney was more interested in the boys themselves than in the material wealth of their families.

Once to a shy boy embarrassed by his family's poverty and lack of education, Sawney remarked, "I want you to go into the world and pedigree your ancestors."

Because his own education, like that of so many other Southerners, had been interrupted, he put a high value on education itself and felt contempt for anything shoddy about the process, whether on the part of the teacher or the pupil. He knew how hard a good education was to come by and what a difference it could make in a man's life. He meant the boys to earn it and to value it.

Because his aim was to develop leaders he put much emphasis also on teaching moral values, on striving to build character. There was chapel service every morning where one or the other of the teachers gave a brief lecture. They were for the most part built around the copybook maxims of honesty, integrity, pride in work well done, decency in personal conduct, and a sense of responsibility to one's self and to one's fellows. They would, I am sure, fall quaintly upon the ears of today's youth brought up on the theory that they shouldn't be "indoctrinated" but left to find, somehow, their own moral values.

Thus at Webb the slow-learner was met with much patience. The lazy-learner with none at all. Every boy was expected to do the very best that he could. If you got an A, you knew you deserved it; the grading system wasn't "relative." Sometimes in some classes there would be no A's at all. I remember one math class, later on, in which everybody got an A, because I made it and was still at the foot of the class.

Slowly, very slowly, the school began to seduce me. Greek was taught by Annie Whiteside—"Miss Annie" to generations of Webb boys until she left to become Dean of Students at Randolph-Macon Woman's College—and she was one of those teachers who loved her subject and could communicate her enthusiasm. In the first year we read Xenophon's *Anabasis*, full of enough military marching to and fro to interest young boys. It was in the second year, though, when we came to Homer's *Iliad* that I began to feel the full beauty and power of the language. We read it aloud as poetry, and even today many of Homer's phrases still echo in my mind. The sound of Apollo's silver bow. The black, angry eyes of Agamemnon. Achilles weeping by the boundless sea.

Yet, curiously, within all that formal discipline there was also enormous freedom. You were free to do your own work on your own time at your own pace as long as you did it. Afternoons were free to do with what you would, play football, walk in the woods, or whatever. On pleasant days there might be declared a sudden holiday, yours to spend as you wished.

In the classrooms there was also freedom within the discipline. Several times, being in a rebellious mood, I used Webb Follin's essay assignments to criticize not only his own teaching methods but the "formalism" of the whole Webb curriculum. My writing style might set his editorial pen whirling; never once did my criticism draw his ire. The school did not intend to stifle either the boys' minds or their spirits.

"Before I imprison innocent children," Sawney once said, "I would quit the profession of teaching. . . . A child ought to love to go to school."

Not all of them loved it, to be sure. Some were sent home because they couldn't make it; some fled because they couldn't take it. Son Will, a small man not much taller than I and rather portly, wasn't as cantankerous as his father was reputed to have been, but once aroused he could be formidable to a young boy. I was always a little afraid of him, even at his Sunday afternoon at-homes when he tried to be friendly and relaxed. I can't say I always loved everything about the school myself. What difference did it make, so I grumbled, if I confused an ablative with an accusative after a Latin preposition? It seemed to me a bit useless to sit in Bell Buckle, Tennessee, computing with trigonometry the height of the Egyptian pyramids. It was years later, when I became a journalist, before I saw any sense in being forced to put my thoughts into an arbitrary number of words.

Yet for all that, I came to find the school an exciting place. For one thing, not all was classroom drudgery. With the encouragement of Miss Sadie Frizzel, who taught piano, some of us put together a reasonably respectable orchestra to play the popular tunes of the day. Bennett Geer, who played the violin, was our leader and we played every Saturday night at the school movies in the Big Room. I doubled in brass, after my fashion, on both the trumpet and the trombone. Since all the sports were intramural nearly every boy had a chance to participate; despite my size I even got to play football and baseball.

So I have a mélange of memories. Recalling them now in tranquility I have difficulty in taking their measure. If the school was already an anachronism in 1929, it could not exist at all today in such a form. To survive it had to change, as indeed it has. Returning many years later I found new buildings to alter its physical aspect; the students are housed in comfortable dormitories, the Big Room has given way to a modern auditorium, the long hard benches and the potbellied stoves have yielded to progress. Greek is gone now, as are those silly schoolyard rules, and Latin is optional; you can substitute a modern language. Girl boarders have intruded on its once masculine world; the only girl in my time was a lonely day student. Radio, television, and changing times have made the monasterial life of my day forevermore impossible. Those who shared its isolation, cut off almost entirely from the outside world, had an experience never to be repeated.

I will not weep for all of that. Two years in that cloistered atmosphere had some drawbacks in terms of social maturity, as I was shortly to find out. As for that Latin and Greek I have forgotten most of it, and today I could not compute the height of the pyramids. Even so, to think these later-day changes outmode the Webbs, father and son, mistakes the mannerisms for the manner. The schoolmaker's art remains the same. "Learn one thing at a time," Sawney said, "that's all Solomon could do," which is not a bad description of programmed learning, to use the modern phrase. "Great masses of students," he also said, "tend to become a machine with lesson hearers and no teachers"—a remark that ought to be appreciated by students today complaining about the vast, impersonal nature of our modern educational system.

Even those seemingly silly rules had a method in their manner-
ism. Webb Follin, by then himself the headmaster, explained it to
me long afterwards.

"Young people are naturally rebellious," he told me, "and sometimes the brighter the more so. Whatever the rules, they will try to
get around them. But they must learn to live with rules, whatever
they are, if they are to live in the world. So we just made up some
arbitrary rules to teach discipline. They were innocuous enough so
that if they were violated no great harm was done and the punish-
ments were mild. We gave the boys a safe outlet for their rebellion.
For many boys those rules saved us from much worse misbehavior."

Neither Sawney nor Son Will pretended, either, that an ability
to read the *Aeneid* or the *Iliad* was necessary for the practical
world, although an acquaintance with them is not without its
value. If nothing else, they give a sense of history, of the antiquity
of man's search for civilization. More than that, Latin and Greek
give to young minds a sense of the structure of language itself,
which makes their own easier to master. But most of all Sawney
and Son Will saw Latin and Greek as tools for toughening young
minds. Cleverness and a gift of gab will not get you through Cicer-
onian syntax, especially if you are required to know and not almost know. Their aim in education, put simply, was the cultivation
of excellence, to stretch young minds.

Thomas Huxley once wrote that the most valuable result of all
education is the ability to make yourself do what you have to do
whether you like it or not. Son Will would have agreed, with the
proviso that you not only do it but do it to the best of your ability.
The aim of his school was "to develop those powers of the mind
which tend to distinguish rather than reduce to a 'contemptible
dead level.'" That aim, it seems to me, is no less pertinent to today's more complex world.

Not everyone who graduated was a top student by any measure.
But the school was elitist in the sense that its ambition, whether
always realized or not, was to make the most of every boy's potential, to stretch his reach as far as possible. That did indeed mean
setting a goal in the classroom beyond the lowest common denominator.

That view of public education—that it can be both elitist and
egalitarian at the same time—seems now to be as anachronistic
as Webb's curriculum was even then. But if the school's reach

exceeded my grasp I am no less grateful. Nor do I, in retrospect, begrudge those monasterial years. They gave me a quiet and undisturbed time for growing up in a place where learning was valued for learning's sake, something not irrelevant to the years that followed.

*   *   *   *   *

A different kind of shock awaited me at Chapel Hill.

For one thing, there were more than seven hundred in the entering freshman class in the fall of 1931. As we milled around in the registration hall of the corrugated steel shell known locally as the "Tin Can," I was overwhelmed by the sheer numbers. In Raleigh and at Webb, whatever pains I suffered I was at least a known person. Here for the moment I was just another number to be called to sign up for this class or that. Aside from the required courses, such as freshman English, I myself had to pick and choose from among the scholastic wares with only the barest of guidance from a young registration counsellor impatient to get on to the next number. I had at this point not the slightest idea of what I wanted from a college education, so I took the easy way out. I signed up for Latin and Greek, having noticed that even in some advanced courses I would be merely repeating what I had studied at Webb.

It's true that in the previous summer my father had offered some suggestions about what courses to take. But they consisted of such comments as, "Well, you ought to take Bully Bernard and Horace Williams." Or: "Sign up for Johnny Booker, surely, and maybe Froggy Wilson. Try to get into one of George Coffin Taylor's classes, or Dougald MacMillan's."

I had heard of most of these people but I wasn't always sure of what they taught.

"What difference does it make?" my father replied. "Take a good teacher just because he's a good teacher. Doesn't much matter what he teaches."

As things turned out, I did take courses under a number of them and my father proved to be right. Although I have forgotten nearly everything I learned in their classes—indeed, I've forgotten most of what I learned in any of my classes—I have never forgotten good teachers. But for the immediate purpose of freshman registration these weren't very helpful suggestions. I ended up in freshman English, a history course, and one each in Latin and Greek. In such accidental fashion are destinies sometimes decided.

The second shock was to discover that nobody at the University cared when I went to bed, when I got up, what I did with my time, or, in fact, cared very much whether I went to class at all.

But the biggest shock was in the classroom. For a survivor of Webb Follin's assaults, freshman English was ridiculous, and because this was before the day of advance placement tests, it took me several weeks to persuade the department I was up to the nineteenth-century novel or the romantic poets; I didn't tell anyone I had already read quite a bit in both fields. In Latin I discovered that for the most part all you had to do was translate and that everybody was using "ponies," those interlinear translations which were taboo at Bell Buckle. As for grammar I made quite a splash, and unwittingly got myself branded as a show-off, by frequently quoting verbatim some rule or other from Allen and Greenough.

All this sudden freedom, coupled with the discovery that I wasn't going to have to work too hard, took some adjusting to. Perhaps not surprisingly the adjustment took the form of bringing out my latent brashness. I set out to make myself noticed among the faceless seven hundred. Some of the ways I chose now make me wince.

I was living in Old West, one of the original University buildings which was then a dormitory, and sent my clothes to be washed at the University laundry, a service covered by our lodging fees. My socks kept coming back with holes in them. Finding this outrageous, I marched myself across the square to confront Dr. Frank Graham, the University president. Why not, I thought, take the matter to the top?

A few minutes after giving his secretary my name I was ushered into his office. Dr. Frank knew who I was, being an old friend of my father. He shook hands, bade me sit in a chair beside his desk, and said, "I'm glad to see you, Vermont. What can I do for you?"

By way of answer, I bent down, took off my right shoe and put my foot on his desk, waggling my big toe through the hole in my sock.

I explained this was what his laundry was doing to me.

I don't know what Dr. Frank thought of this behavior, but he looked at me quietly for a few moments. Then he reached into his wallet, pulled out a dollar bill and handed it to me.

"Use this," he said, "to buy yourself some new socks."

I was completely undone. All I could think of was to mutter some kind of apology, return the dollar, and sheepishly depart. This was my first encounter with him as a person, and it was an incident to tell what manner of man he was.

Dr. Frank, as he was always called, was to become famous as the man who made the University at Chapel Hill one of the leading intellectual centers in the South and one respected all over the country. He was later to become a United States senator and an important figure in the U.S. delegation to the United Nations. But his real claim to fame was the impression he made on every student who came within his ken. In this instance, for example, he showed no irritation toward a bumptious freshman; instinctively, he found the reaction which cut me down to size. Over the next four years I was to have other clashes with Dr. Frank, but with each one my admiration for him grew until it ended in a lifetime friendship.

Unfortunately this same incident shows what manner of young man I was at seventeen. I wish I could say that Dr. Frank, with one gesture, cured me of fractious behavior. But I continued to be brassy and not a little arrogant, possibly because deep inside I was uncertain and insecure at being thrust from a sheltered life into this new less structured milieu. There was also the complicating factor of my family's long association with the University, which created a compulsion to do something—anything—to make my presence there known.

For over a hundred years, since Iowa Michigan went off to get killed at Gettysburg, some member of my family has taught there in every generation. Besides my father, there were James Finch Royster, professor of English and Dean of the Graduate School, and Hubert Royster in the early Medical School, both sons of Wisconsin Illinois. Vernon Howell, son of Virginia Carolina, founded the Pharmacy School. My father's brother Percy had also taught there as an instructor of physics. Innumerable cousins from 1856 onwards have gone to Chapel Hill. I was the latest in a long parade. That made a heavy burden.

It was thus in searching about for a niche that I found *The Daily Tar Heel*, the student newspaper, and the Carolina Playmakers, the theatrical group.

I knew I could never make a splash as a college politician; my manner had a way of alienating many of my fellows. But I liked to write and I could do so well by college standards. In those days the Playmakers wrote their own plays, gave most of them experimental productions and full productions to the better ones. Acting also brought out the natural ham in me. With the encouragement of Frederick Koch, the flamboyant head of the department, and Samuel Seldon, the quiet but more thorough teacher, I wrote several plays. Two of them were given full productions. I also played many parts, mostly for some reason "character" parts of old men. The theater was not to be my future but the Playmakers did get me some campus attention.

That future I found, accidentally, on *The Daily Tar Heel*. The *Tar Heel*, founded in the early 1890s, was a strictly independent student enterprise unconnected with the University administration. Many who worked on it were journalism majors, but even Oscar Coffin, head of the department, had no authority over the paper. Its staff was open to all. Without any professional supervision or guidance, the journalistic quality varied from year to year. Those who worked on it learned by doing and it was a marvelous laboratory for young journalists. Being free of authority it could be bold in both its news columns and editorial expressions, and if at times this led it to be sophomoric it also meant that it could be a powerful influence on the campus. Authority might sometimes be annoyed, but it had to pay attention.

Over the years it had become a breeding ground for future journalists. Among those who worked on it in my time were Clifton Daniel, later chief Washington correspondent and managing editor of *The New York Times*; Walter Terry, dance critic for the *Herald Tribune*; James Daniel, senior editor for the *Reader's Digest*; Robert Mason, editor of the *Norfolk Virginian-Pilot*; Don Shoemaker, editor of the *Miami Herald*; and Robert Ruark, syndicated columnist and author of *Something of Value* and other novels. A number besides myself later served on *The Wall Street Journal*. George B. Bryant, Jr., was my predecessor as chief of its Washington bureau, and Albert Clark was a successor.

My first assignment as a freshman was a "beat" consisting of some University offices of secondary importance as news sources. Most of the time they had none although I daily made myself obnoxious badgering secretaries and office heads.

Out of this frustration I cast about for other things to do. I found the print shop, where the *Tar Heel* was printed on an old flatbed press, a fascinating place. There I learned to run a Linotype and to read type upside-down-and-backwards, the way it appeared in the galleys. Before long I was one of the night assistant editors who saw the copy through the final production stages.

It was on one of those nights that I got my first glimpse of the delight newspaper people take in disasters.

We were just beginning to lock up the paper when someone rushed in to announce there had been a hold-up and shooting on Franklin Street. What followed was right out of the Hecht-MacArthur play, *The Front Page*. We stopped the press and rushed with glee to find out what had happened. It turned out that several men had robbed a local store and jumped into a get-away car. A policeman then commandeered a student's car, a Cadillac owned by Ashby Penn, and took off in pursuit.

They overtook the robbers a short way out of town and there ensued a gun fight in which Ashby was shot. Chortling with excitement we remade the front page and gave the story banner treatment. A "death watch" was set up at the hospital and a stakeout at the police station. We kept the story going over the next few days until Ashby recovered and police tracked down the gunmen. They were Chicago gangsters caught short of money on their way to Florida who thought they could easily knock over a small-town shop. That added an extra dash of spice to the story and we all agreed we hadn't had so much fun in years.

Unfortunately such dramatic stories were rare in Chapel Hill. So I began to seek other things to write about that weren't on anyone else's assignment sheet.

By default of others I appointed myself the paper's music critic. This involved writing not only about student productions, but also about visiting professional artists: Amelita Galli-Curci, the opera singer; Albert Spalding and Fritz Kreisler, violinists; Josef Lhevinne, pianist, and others. Naturally I was uninhibited by any modesty in my critical judgments.

I complained that Spalding's opening selection from Debussy was one scarcely suitable for an introduction to University students. "While lively in tempo and calling upon the dexterity of the artist for its proper execution, it lacked the softness of theme more appreciated by the untrained ear." My own ear, of course, being quite trained! Madame Galli-Curci I found rather "old in voice" (she was forty-four), and I thought Lhevinne not up to Rachmaninoff. As for Kreisler I approved only of his performance of his own *Caprice Viennois*; "it was in this number that Kreisler became Kreisler." So much for Brahms and Mozart, also on his program!

The young, full of self-esteem and confident judgments, can be both preposterous and cruel critics.

I was not long content, however, with being a cloistered critic and began to seek out visiting celebrities for interviews, beginning with the visiting musicians but gradually widening my net. Some of my questions were unusual. I led Madame Galli-Curci to remark, "I am a strong advocate of sports and athletics." I doubt if any other interviewer over her long career drew from her this unexpected thought.

Lawrence Tibbett, the great Metropolitan baritone, I found "exuberantly friendly." Katherine Cornell, touring in *The Barretts of Wimpole Street*, waxed enthusiastic about what was then called "little theater" and is now known as "community theater." Maude Adams, playing Portia to Otis Skinner's Shylock, charmed me as "Peter Pan grown up." Such interviews were exciting for a young college student, and what struck me most about them was that I had only to announce I was from the campus newspaper and the doors opened. Not just with show business people, either. Norman Thomas took time to tell me "capitalism is on its way out," and George Washington Carver, the black chemist, to explain his work with peanuts. It was all very heady.

Meanwhile, I was also going to class.

Thanks to Webb I coasted my first two years, taking Latin and Greek as "crip" courses to boost my grade average. English and history, and even economics, posed no problems. Nor did the math as far as I went. The only annoyance was physics because here there was required lab work for such things as measuring the coefficient of expansion for metals. I eventually resolved that by looking up what the figures ought to be and then adjusting my data accordingly. I trust any reprisals from this confession of fudging are now barred by the statute of limitations.

Along the way I met some teachers to be fondly remembered. The teacher-adversary I delighted in most, though he usually bested me, was Dr. William Bernard, known to all as Bully Bernard, under whom I read both the *Iliad* and the New Testament in Greek. Readers of Thomas Wolfe's *Look Homeward, Angel* will be familiar with him as Buck Benson, who taught Eugene Gant in World War I days. He was by now a man considerably older and no longer a bachelor, but he retained a dandified manner, wearing high wing collars and wide, outlandish ties. He wore his shirt sleeves longer than the current fashion and he had a habit of stretching his arm out in a wide sweep so that an expanse of white showed beneath his cuff.

The temptation for me to be a show-off in Greek was irresistible, but Bully would not be bullied. If I was laboring some correct and obvious point, he would simply watch me with his large, sleepy eyes until I had finished; then he would go on as if I hadn't interrupted him.

If I made a slip, however, the lightning struck. "Ah, yes, Mr. Royster," he might say, letting his arm sweep around in a circle. "But I would have thought a man of *your* scholarly attainments"—here he would pause to let the barb sink in—"would have recognized here Homer's use of the dative of advantage."

Johnny Booker was a Victorian in love with Victorian poetry. Dougald MacMillan was as biting as the Alexander Pope he taught. Richmond P. Bond was far more perky and interesting than the nineteenth-century novels he made me read. George Coffin Taylor spent little time probing the psychology of Hamlet or Macbeth, but he was a frustrated actor who transmitted his enthusiasm for the language of Shakespeare.

Then there was Horace Williams, professor of philosophy— or so it said in the catalogue. By my time he had already been on the faculty for forty years and what he really taught was Horace Williams. A short man with hawk eyes and oversized ears, he too has been immortalized by Thomas Wolfe as Vergil Weldon. No one who ever took his course mislabeled "logic" ever escaped unmarked. The study of formal logic he thought a waste of time. "Not once have I heard an intelligent thought derived from the formal syllogism," he would say. His approach was to challenge you on the simplest, most obvious statement, and his method was Socratic. In this he could be infuriating, but his aim was to force you to define your terms and not to think you had grasped an intellectual concept merely because you had given it a name.

It was a method to make iconoclasts of the young because before he was through almost every accepted idea of religion, philosophy, politics had been put into the crucible. "Orthodoxy," he would say, "has the advantage of definiteness. Truth is not so easily pinned down." Naturally this got him into trouble around the state for corrupting the young.

Horace Williams taught me two things that remain with me yet. There's fun to be had in challenging any idea; later I was to be labeled a "conservative" when in fact I was a radical smashing away at the prevalent political orthodoxies miscalled "liberal." Secondly, he taught me that it's only by challenging every idea that you can be sure of what you think, for then you know why you think what you think.

If Horace Williams was corrupting me, other things were also changing me. At home I found much altered. The depression was at its nadir, and my father was having financial problems. He had owned stock in one of the failed banks, and in those days a bank stockholder had "double liability"—he not only lost his investment but was liable for an equal amount to help pay off depositors. My father had by then studied law, passed the bar and was trying, in his middle age, to begin a law practice and at the same time to keep the candy manufacturing business afloat. He managed, including paying off that bank stock debt, but only at great emotional cost. My mother, meanwhile, had begun to grow deaf; in a few years it was almost impossible to talk to her without shouting, making the simplest conversation sound like an argument. Tommy was off at Webb. Saravette was now growing into a young lady with her own life to lead. Home still drew me on weekends and holidays but it was no longer what it had been.

By my junior year even these visits were less frequent. One reason for this was that in the summer of 1931, between Webb and Chapel Hill, some friends and I had spent the Fourth of July at Morehead City, a resort town on the Carolina coast. There at a dance I had met Frances Claypoole from New Bern, a petite young girl with light brown hair, an oval face and the largest deep brown eyes I had ever seen. I was seventeen, she sixteen.

She changed a great many things. For the first two years she went to St. Mary's College in Raleigh, which got me home on weekends but only as a fleeting visitor in my own house. I also began to have her to college dances, which opened a social life I had not known before. In my junior year she transferred to the Woman's College of the University of Greensboro. Thereafter Greensboro, not Raleigh, beckoned me on weekends.

I can't say it was a case of true love always running smooth. As teenagers will, we had our fallings out, mostly because she became at times impatient with the way I tried to monopolize her. She would occasionally date others if only to show her independence. Yet we were always drawn back together again, and on my part there was never a doubt of my feelings. She gave me something I badly needed, a confidence in myself as a person as distinguished from the false self-confidence that lurked behind my brassy manner. As the years passed, she gave me also a loyalty undiminished in either triumph or disaster. That Fourth of July proved the beginning of a story not yet ended.

Meanwhile I was growing weary of the classroom. Thanks to those "crip" courses in classical languages I had made Phi Beta Kappa in my junior year; that accomplished, I lost interest in my courses. To hasten graduation I went to summer school in 1934, which was even more boring. The only thing that kept up my interest in Chapel Hill was the *Tar Heel*.

By this time I had shifted from reporting to editorial writing. That broadened my horizons because we thought there was nothing untoward in delivering our opinions on any subject under the sun— the depression, the New Deal, German politics, communism, or whatever. It was particularly intoxicating to have carte blanche to lay into Dr. Frank and the University administration, which I did with gusto. Because I approved of the New Deal, spoke kindly of Norman Thomas, quoted from Karl Marx, and viewed the University administration with scorn, I was soon marked as a campus radical. I minded not, so long as people paid attention.

One incident I remember involved the Music Department, which had managed to appoint a chairman who, it turned out, had none of the degrees he claimed to have had. He was quietly fired during a summer recess, but of course we found out about it and made it front-page news in the *Tar Heel*. I accompanied this with a fierce editorial holding it up as "typical of the incompetence of the administration."

That brought another encounter with Dr. Frank which again proved his character. Seeing him later at some gathering I tried to avoid him, but he sought me out, came over and put his arm around me. "That was a pretty rough editorial, Vermont," he said. Then after a pause he added, "But I guess we deserved it." Few victims of later editorial wrath knew so well how to score with a soft answer.

My friends and I were trouble for Dr. Frank in other ways. One year that marvelous musical drama *The Green Pastures* played an engagement in Chapel Hill. Drawn by Marc Connelly from the short stories of Roark Bradford, it offered a series of biblical stories as they might have been told by a Negro preacher in days gone by. Naturally it had an all-black cast headed by Richard B. Harrison, a man of commanding mien who played "De Lawd." It had had a long Broadway run and we of the Playmaker crowd were overwhelmed by it. So after the performance we invited the principals to a cast party, a joyous affair that went on well into the morning. Inevitably the news of this got around and soon was the topic of gossip about the students at Chapel Hill "entertaining niggers." Dr. Frank, as usual, stood up to the fire. A truly remarkable man.

But he would soon be relieved of one troublemaker. By January of my senior year I was about to be retired from *Tar Heel* duties and all my course work for my degree had been completed. There was nothing any longer to hold me in Chapel Hill. So I arranged to get my degree in absentia and left.

The next few weeks were a trial to me and my family. A degree in classical languages hardly prepared me for anything practical. I knew nothing of business, had no interest in law or medicine. I had the vague idea, born of my experience on the *Tar Heel*, that I might like to be a journalist, but I had no idea how to start. The *News and Observer* professed no interest in my talents. I just sat around the house and moped, to my own and my family's frustration. One life had ended and I knew not how to begin another.

Then came one of those accidents of timing that have so often changed my life. An elderly lady visiting Raleigh needed someone to drive her back North in her car. She offered to pay my expenses up and back. I seized upon the escape. I told my father I would like to spend a few days in New York while I was away, and he gave me fifty dollars. What I did not tell my parents, or Frances either, was that I had no intention of coming back.

For one thing, I was restless and eager to see something of the world north of the Mason-Dixon Line, to break out of the cocoon of family and Dixie in which I had lived so comfortably but which had begun to suffocate me.

For another, I was full of romantic notions about Times Square, Greenwich Village, the Algonquin Roundtable, of O. O. McIntyre, Franklin P. Adams, Dorothy Parker, Alexander Woollcott. I knew about all those newspapers, the *Times*, the *Herald Tribune*, the *Sun*, the *News*, the *Mirror*, the *Post*, the *American*, the *Evening Journal*, and the *World Telegram*. No one had yet called New York the Big Apple, but I knew it was the place where everything happened, the mecca of all newspapermen, the glory place for Heywood Broun, Walter Winchell, Stanley Walker, Lucius Beebe, Westbrook Pegler. I believed the myth that it could all be conquered with pluck and a little bit of luck. I didn't know how I would manage, but manage I intended to do.

So one rainy March morning in 1935 we set out, my lady passenger and I. I could not see what lay ahead, but my head was a jumble of memories. Of Skibo and the buttermilk man, of that first journey out to Bell Buckle, of Morehead on the Fourth of July, of the *Tar Heel* and the Playmakers, of the way it had been in that house, warm and loving and secure, surrounded by Tommy and Saravette, by a mother not yet grown deaf, by a father not yet harassed by the woes of the depression.

We headed north away from home. Except for brief visits I was not to come back again for thirty-five years.

Interlude

BAGHDAD ON THE SUBWAY

Around lay the city,
like a ragged purple dream,
the wonderful, enchanting,
bewildering . . . great city.

—O. Henry,
"A Tempered Dream"

 stood in the middle of Grand Central Station a few days later, having left my passenger in Connecticut, with fifty dollars in my pocket and no idea where to go or what to do but full of excitement and the confidence of youth.

The first problem was lodging. I checked my suitcase, bought the *Times*, and pored over the rooms-for-rent classified. Greenwich Village, the one area I had heard of, seemed too expensive. I made a list of several places uptown, braved my first venture on the subway, and set out to explore. By late afternoon I had settled in desperation on a tiny cubicle in a converted apartment house on upper Broadway near 104th Street. It was not much larger than a Pullman roomette, containing a bed, a table and one straight chair; the bath was down the hall and was shared by five other tenants. But it was clean and it cost only five dollars a week.

The next problem was how to eat. Although in 1935 fifty dollars was a lot of money, it wouldn't last forever. The next day I was up early and hit several employment agencies but received no encouragement. On the way back to my room late in the day I passed a cafeteria near Sherman Square with a "Boy Wanted" sign in the window. Five minutes later I had a job cleaning off tables and helping carry supplies from the storeroom to the kitchen. The pay was

ten dollars a week and two meals a day. Not exactly the job a Phi
Beta Kappa classical scholar would dream of, but it was pleasant
enough, the food was plentiful, and the boss, a man named Nick,
was impressed enough to say that in time I might be promoted to
behind the counter.

Two days. If I hadn't conquered the city, I had at least burrowed
into it. With food, lodging, and ten dollars a week spending money
I was ready for the fray.

Disillusionment came quickly. Although I had some letters of
recommendation from North Carolina newsmen, they proved no
"open sesame" to the city's journalistic portals. At the *Times* I did
talk to some ancient fellow (or so he seemed to me) who said
he would put me on their waiting list for copy boys, which is
where they started even graduates from the Columbia School of
Journalism.

The only other place where I got by the Cerberus who guarded
the newsrooms was at the *Daily Mirror*, the raucous Hearst tabloid trying to compete with the more successful *Daily News*. At
that time the *Mirror's* managing editor was Stanley Walker, the
famed former city editor at the *Herald Tribune*, who'd been hired
away from his old paper by, I presume, a packet of money. One of
my letters of introduction was from Robert Madry, director of the
UNC News Bureau and an old Walker colleague. That got me received, and Walker listened courteously to my story. After hearing
about Webb School, the *Daily Tar Heel*, and my classical education, he looked at me and said quietly, "Son, you don't want to
work for the *Daily Mirror*!" Since he left a year later (for *The New
Yorker* magazine) I gather he didn't want to, either. Today, if not
then, I can put down his rejection as a disguised good turn. But
that was the beginning of months of discouragement.

By midsummer I did escape from clearing off tables at my Broadway cafeteria. I got a job as a messenger for the Commercial National Bank, a small bank on lower Wall Street now merged out of
existence.

Here the pay was fifteen dollars a week, which I soon found less
real pay than the busboy's job since now I had to buy my meals.
The other messengers—"runners" as we were called—were, like
myself, recent college graduates who in those depression years had
to start at the bottom. You didn't turn up your nose at any kind

of job. But the newspaper job I was seeking remained far out of reach although I continued my importunings with monotonous regularity.

Nonetheless, if they were discouraging months they were interesting ones as I explored the byways of the city. New York has always been an exciting place for the young.

In retrospect, indeed, one of the more astonishing things is how safe New York seemed in those days. At twenty-one you're not inclined to get off work, eat dinner, and go to bed. Some nights I would go to a local movie house, most of which ran double-features. Other nights to a neighborhood bar where you could nurse a ten-cent beer and watch the comings and goings. Many times, though, I would take the subway, that marvelous bargain for a nickel, and get off at some random stop to walk the Village or the Bowery. Sometimes I would spend an evening just walking around Times Square, even then a bit garish but not the shabby place it has become. What astonishes me now is that whether alone, or with some of my new found friends from the bank, I never felt the slightest sense of danger. Even Harlem was not out of bounds in those days. The September night Joe Louis beat Max Baer several of us wandered up and down 125th Street in the small hours of the morning, arousing no more than a few catcalls from the black celebrants.

The contrast with today remains a puzzle. Why should there be less violence in the streets in those depression days when there was more real cause for muggings and purse snatchings than in later, more prosperous times?

Altogether, then, it was neither a lonely nor a boring life. In addition to new friends at the bank, Chapel Hill classmates began to drift into town by midsummer—some were just passing through, some stayed awhile—and they shared the rent for a new two-room apartment on Sixty-ninth Street just west of Broadway. There with the help of two of them, Carl Thompson and Don Pope, fellow veterans of *The Daily Tar Heel*, there was born and briefly survived The Metropolitan News Service, complete with fancy stationery and a cable address. We dreamed of creating a correspondence bureau for out-of-town newspapers. We did indeed sell a few stories about folks-from-home either visiting or living in New York. One of them I still treasure, a profile for *The News and Ob-*

server of Eugenia Rawls, a Chapel Hill contemporary just beginning her long stage career in Lillian Hellman's *The Children's Hour*. But we never got enough assignments and the venture died of dollar malnutrition.

I also had some kin to attach to. A great-uncle, Gavin High, now retired, had worked for the *Sun* for many years and so understood my newspaper interest; he and his wife fed me many free meals. A young doctor cousin, Chauncey Royster, was interning at New York Hospital. He and his wife were as poor as I, but they gave bring-your-own parties and it was through them that I met Thomas Wolfe, author of *Look Homeward, Angel* and Chapel Hill's most famous graduate. A tall, gangling, awkward fellow, he lived up to his reputation by dominating any gathering with his nonstop talking.

Such friends aside, the city itself offered its own endless fascinations, not all of them nocturnal. On Saturday mornings you could take in the Radio City Music Hall for a quarter if you made it before one o'clock. If you felt like splurging a couple of dollars, you could get last minute tickets to Broadway shows, taking the luck of the draw at an agency for unsold tickets in the underground maze beneath Times Square. With a little diligence you could find small, Italian cafés where you could get a four-course meal for seventy-five cents. With a little patience at standing in line you could hear the Metropolitan Opera for a dollar. When your pocketbook was squeezed for eating money, there was always the Automat.

This was, of course, in the midst of the depression, and for many people the city was a place of hardship and despair. Many had lost good jobs and now had crafts or professions which offered them no opportunities. A familiar sight was the neighborhood employment office with a crowd of men outside looking at the posted signs for dishwashers, short-order cooks, janitors, or one-day laborers. Some of the men would be in coats and ties which had obviously seen better days, and for them it must have been depressing to stand on the sidewalk and wonder if they should take what came or keep hoping for better days again. For the middle aged and up there was nothing romantic about the depression.

But it is characteristic of youth that the world begins when they first take notice of it, and, having no other measure, they take it for what it is. I wasn't aware of being poorly paid at fifteen dollars a week; that was the going rate and I accepted it as being normal. In the same way youth of a later time would not think of two hundred dollars a week as extravagant, nor coffee at three dollars a pound exorbitant. I bought it at fifteen cents a pound and thought it not cheap.

At any rate I had a job and by that fall had been promoted from runner to stock transfer clerk at $18.50. For all I knew my future lay in banking, as it did for many of those one-time messengers, some of whom went on to successful careers in that field. So it might have been for me except for a happenstance.

One day on my third or fourth visit to the office of the New York News Association, known as "City News," a cooperative venture of the many New York papers for covering the routine of the city, I was offered a temporary job. Pop Henderson (I don't remember his full name) explained that one of the younger men had to go to the hospital for an operation. He would let me fill in for two weeks, maybe three. After that, he would see what he could do but he couldn't promise anything.

A real dilemma. If my present job wasn't exciting, it was at least steady. The City News job might lead nowhere. I accepted on the spot.

The City News's function on the local scale was much like that of the Associated Press on a larger scale. That is, it was responsible for covering the police precincts, night court, run-of-the-mill fires and so forth for all the city papers. For much of this kind of news the papers would simply choose what they wanted from the City News file distributed to them by teletype. If an important or spectacular story broke they would be alerted and could then, if they wished, send a staffer to provide them with their own story. Those who worked for City News fell into two groups, the eager young with good legs and a few old-timers who stayed in the office to rewrite stories from the information phoned in. Some of the younger ones had in fact gone on to regular jobs with the *Times* or the *Trib*. So it was, or so I thought, at least a foot in the journalistic door.

The job, as it turned out, was not spectacular. Much of the time I stayed in the office, running copy from the rewrite men to the teletype wire room, occasionally being given a chance to write a brief and unimportant item myself. Mostly, though, I was simply a "gofer"—the one sent for coffee or sandwiches for the older hands. My working hours were from four in the afternoon until one in the morning. The pay, incidentally, was fifteen dollars a week. I was going backwards.

But it was interesting and I learned a lot. Following the various stories that passed through the office gave me an idea of what went on in the city that I would not otherwise have had. A few times I was sent to fill in for a regular at the precinct station on West Sixty-eighth Street; I remember a Captain Marxhausen who was helpful to a neophyte. Occasionally I was sent to keep watch on night court on Center Street, where I got a different education from the parade of whores, pimps, drunks, muggers, and domestic brawlers of both sexes. To a young man who had lived a sheltered Southern life they were fascinating.

Suddenly it all came to an end. The person I was substituting for had the bad grace to get well. Pop Henderson was kind about it and promised to rehire me if he had the opportunity. All the same, I was out of a job.

It was a bleak period. I was ashamed to go back to the bank, and it was depressing to think of being again a cafeteria busboy. I didn't have the nerve to write anyone at home what had happened; my family was already upset that I had left the bank, offering what they considered a respectable opportunity. I knew my little capital hoard, the remnants of that original fifty dollars, wouldn't last long. It wouldn't have lasted as long as it did except for the un-expected kindness I encountered. I was allowed to miss nearly a month's rent without being thrown out. A genial Irishman named Kelly, who ran a neighborhood bar nearby on a Broadway corner, let me put some meals on the cuff. The city, I discovered, wasn't always cold and unfriendly, at least in the depression years.

Then one raw February day in passing by a newsstand I noticed a copy of *The Wall Street Journal*.

I had of course seen the paper while I was working in the bank but I had paid little attention, thinking it a paper full of stuff about stocks and bonds, about which I knew nothing and cared little. That day for the first time it crossed my mind that it was at least a newspaper and one I hadn't importuned. So I took the subway to the Wall Street stop and walked around the corner to 44 Broad Street, a small building where the *Journal* had its office. The lobby

With my mother, Olivette Broadway
Royster, Raleigh, 1915.

Fourth birthday celebration,
Monroe, Louisiana, 1918, with
cousin Bert Sperry.

Three Royster generations,
Raleigh, 1922: my grandfather,
Vermont C. Royster I (*seated*),
and my father,
Wilbur H. Royster (*standing*).

From the *Oak Leaf*, Hugh Morson High School yearbook, Raleigh, N.C., 1929.
The school band: Vermont Royster, French horn virtuoso,
top row, fourth from right.

Miss Frances Claypoole, of
New Bern, N.C., 1931.

Snapshot of a working seaman,
SS Lehigh, summer of 1932,
on trip to Europe.

The President and Mrs. Roosevelt
request the pleasure of the company of
Mr and Mrs. Royster
at a reception to be held at
The White House
Thursday evening, February the third
nineteen hundred and thirty-eight
at nine o'clock

Invitation from President and Mrs. Franklin Delano
Roosevelt to reception at White House, Washington,
1938.

Cousin James ("Kay") Kyser, then a nationally famous band leader,
with my father (*in straw hat*), Raleigh Airport, about 1940.

Shortly before entering active
duty as ensign,
U.S. Naval Reserve, Washington,
1941—*photo by Harris & Ewing.*

My brother Tommy, 2d Lt., U.S.
Marine Corps, Clearwater, Fla.,
1941—*photo by J. A. Ogg.*

The *USS Jack Miller*, still in wartime camouflage, Okinawa, 1945.

Aboard the *USS Jack Miller*, Ulithi atoll, Caroline Islands, June 8, 1945, with Lt. (jg) Dota C. Brown, who has just been awarded the Silver Star medal for valor during the landings at Peleliu.

Back home from the Navy, with Eleanor (*top*) and Bonnie.

Bonnie Royster confronting her first birthday cake, at her grandparents' home in Raleigh, 1944. Her father was away at sea.

Eleanor Royster, age 5.

Barney Kilgore—*photograph courtesy of The Wall Street Journal.*

William Grimes

Buren McCormack

Joseph Evans

Photographs this page courtesy of The Wall Street Journal.

directory said the newsroom was on the third floor. I took the elevator and got off by the little reception desk where visitors were supposed to stop.

For some reason there was no guardian at the gate. I walked into the newsroom and saw in one corner a glassed-off room, obviously the office of the boss. Without saying anything to anybody I crossed the room and stood in the doorway.

A slightly built man with glasses and speckled hair sat behind the desk, bent over a typewriter. After a moment he saw me, pushed his glasses up on his forehead, and asked rather gruffly, "What do you want?"

I said I wanted a job.

He stared at me and said, "Oh, you do, do you? And what can you do?"

It was not quite the response I expected. I looked around the office, which was much cluttered with copy paper strewn around the floor, and replied, "Well, if you will give me a broom I'll sweep up this office."

It was an impudent reply I immediately regretted. But he just sat there, staring. Then to my surprise he said, "What else can you do? You ever worked on a newspaper?"

I took this as an invitation, walked over to his desk and began pouring out my life story—about City News, the bank, the busboy job, *The Daily Tar Heel*, the classical education—all in a desperate monologue. I thought I had glimpsed at least a glimmer of interest and felt this was my last chance to get any sort of newspaper job in New York.

I'm not too clear on the rest of the conversation, but after awhile he interrupted me. "I'll give you a temporary job," he said. "And then we'll see."

Another temporary job! I had been in New York a year. Was this the way it was always going to be, bouncing from job to job? Had I been foolish to think I could come to the big city and conquer it? Should I give up and go home? I said I'd take it.

He told me to report the next morning at eight o'clock to a man named Eddie Costenbader. I recrossed the city room, nodded to the guardian now back at his desk as if I belonged there, which now I did. It might not be much of a newspaper but it was a newspaper. The next time I applied at the *Sun* or the *World-Telegram* I would at least have something to talk about. I might, after all, someday make it to a good paper!

The man behind that desk was William Henry Grimes, the *Journal*'s managing editor. For the next twenty-two years he was to be my patron, guide, irritant, teacher, obstacle, and friend. He told me long afterwards that what caught his attention that afternoon was my very brashness about the broom. What finally persuaded him to give me a try on so brief an encounter was that I asked no questions about the job or what it paid. If I wanted it that bad, he thought, he'd take a chance.

As it turned out the job paid fifteen dollars a week—I was beginning to think there was some sort of a conspiracy to fix wages— and at first it wasn't much of a job either.

Eddie Costenbader, to whom I dutifully reported the next morning, ran the Dow Jones News Service. Widely known as the "broad tape," it supplies a ticker news service to banks, brokerage houses and similar firms about corporate news, stock market developments, the doings of Congress and the various Washington agencies, as well as foreign news of business or economic import. In those days the News Service provided the bulk of the revenue for Dow Jones, the parent company. The *Journal* then had no more than about 35,000 circulation, mostly in the New York financial area with a sprinkling in Washington and some on the West Coast from an edition printed in San Francisco.

There was also at that time a competitive ticker service. Since with this kind of news, time is of the essence, it was important to keep track of what was carried on the competitive wire and when. The New York Stock Exchange next door had both services and someone was stationed there to follow the other ticker, log news items down to the quarter-minute, and alert the News Service desk of any story it did not have. That was my job.

It was boring but had a disguised blessing. Following the ticker all day gave an overview of the day's news and you quickly learned to judge the most important news. It thus made a good starting place. I was to languish there for several weeks, goaded to pay attention by Costenbader, an exceedingly gruff editor who constantly preached the importance of speed and who railed at me for imagined daydreaming.

It wasn't until mid-March that I saw Bill Grimes again. That happened late one afternoon as I was bringing my daily timesheet to the News Service desk. He passed me in the corridor, then turned around and tapped me on the shoulder, shoving his glasses up on his forehead.

"Would you like to go to Washington?" he abruptly asked.

I said I would.

"When can you go?"

I looked at my watch. "It'll take me half an hour to get home," I said. "Twenty minutes to pack and another half-hour to Penn station. Give me two hours."

"Report to Bernard Kilgore tomorrow in the Washington office," he said, and just as abruptly turned away.

I didn't know it at the time, but he had already offered the job to several of the younger men with more seniority than I. Some had turned him down, some said they wanted to think it over after asking what the job was and what it paid. Years later I would understand Grimes' quick decision to send me. As an editor it's frustrating to offer a young person a promotion and to be met with a flurry of doubts, questions, uncertainties about accepting it, as if it might contain some hidden trick. In this case I had, unwittingly, again impressed the boss, something he was to remember.

When I broke the news to Costenbader he growled something about Grimes's idiocy, but I made the six o'clock train to Washington and that night lodged in luxury at the Willard Hotel, revelling in my first expense account travel. The next morning I crossed Fourteenth Street to the National Press Building and was waiting outside the office door before anyone else showed up. It was March 25, 1936.

Once more, though, my job was a lowly one. I was put to work taking telephone dictation from the reporters scattered about town and helping Kenneth Kramer, the copy desk chief, edit copy for the News Service wire and sometimes rewriting it later for the paper. Repackaging the same news, I learned, was a Dow Jones habit, one it continues even today. It makes efficient use of the reporting staff.

After a few weeks Ken Kramer began to send me out occasionally to fill in for some absent reporter or to cover a less important press conference when no one else was available. This led to Charlie Sterner, the office general factotum, putting in for my press credentials, which I was to use for the first time at that Roosevelt press conference.

I was now officially a Washington correspondent, however low in the hierarchy, and I was dizzy with excitement. I could hardly believe that I had come so far from those beginnings back in Dixie.

PART TWO

Washington

Young and in the press
and in Washington . . .
was there ever such a bright
and shining world?

And will we ever again
know anything like it?

—Allen Drury,
Anna Hastings

WASHINGTON

Henry Wallace was a most attractive man. It was a long time before I concluded he wasn't very smart.

When I first encountered him in the fall of 1936 he had been Roosevelt's secretary of agriculture throughout the first term, always a man around whom controversy swirled. He was anathema to conservatives, businessmen, and to much of the urban population, the "man who slaughtered little pigs." But he was a popular figure to most of the nation's farmers, who thought him a savior come to deliver them from the abyss of the depression. Among the intellectuals gathered around FDR—dubbed collectively the "brain trust"—he was rated one of the brighter stars in the New Deal constellation.

In person he seemed to me to fit none of these images. At forty-eight he was a good-looking man of medium height with well-formed features except for a nose a bit overlarge for his face and slightly skewed to the right. In formal appearances he was well groomed. In relaxed moments a shock of hair often fell down over his face, making him look somewhat like a serious-minded Will Rogers; both retained the appearance of country boys come to the big city, Rogers from Oklahoma, Wallace from Iowa. In Henry Wallace this corn-shucks air was accompanied by a soft voice, at least in casual conversation, tinged with a Midwestern accent.

At his press conferences, usually rather sparsely attended, he seemed professorial, as if he were trying to instruct the reporters in the intricacies of agricultural economics and his own visionary plans for resolving the plight of the farmers. It was hard for me to picture him as either a horned villain or as an inspired Moses. He just seemed an ordinary, plain, and on the whole likeable man who was trying to find a reasonable way to deal with an intractable problem.

But then when I was assigned to cover him for *The Wall Street Journal* I knew little about Henry Wallace and nothing at all about agricultural economics.

I fell heir to that assignment, along with the Commerce Department with which it was coupled by our office organization, because John Hazard had left the *Journal* to become the agricultural expert for *Kiplinger's Washington Letter*, and I was handy. It wasn't the choicest assignment, at least in comparison with covering Congress or the financial area of the Treasury and the Federal Reserve Board. Nonetheless I welcomed it. Having my own beat gave me a more recognized status as a Washington correspondent, and I assumed that it meant Kenneth Kramer, who ran the copy desk, and Bernard Kilgore, the bureau chief, thought well enough of me to trust me with something more than being an occasional fill-in man for other reporters. Now I would be in daily competition with the rival business news service which competed with the Dow Jones service, with the regular wire agencies, with the local Washington papers and, most importantly, with *The New York Times*.

I knew what tobacco looked like because it was a major crop in North Carolina. I knew what cotton looked like, how it was grown and picked, because I had picked it on my step-grandfather's plantation in Louisiana. An ear of corn was at least recognizable. But I had never seen a grain of wheat or barley. The "dust bowl" I had only read about or glimpsed in brief shots on the movie newsreels. The lone economics course I had taken at Chapel Hill had nothing in it about corn-hog ratios or the complexities of farm price "parities." As far as agriculture was concerned I was an untutored town boy.

All the same, I decided to tackle the assignment with vigor. This suggested, first of all, a cram course in the New Deal agriculture laws including the second Agricultural Adjustment Act (the first had been declared unconstitutional by the Supreme Court) and the Soil Conservation Act, as well as in Henry Wallace's own theories. For that I turned to a young man named Milton Eisenhower, who was director of information services, to Sam Bledsoe, the knowledgeable press officer, and to Mordecai Ezekiel, the secretary's economic advisor. They loaded me with pamphlets and speeches, copies of congressional testimony and the like. Much of it was like learning to read Greek.

It also meant, or so I thought, learning something about the politics of agriculture. One way to do this, I decided, was to talk to Senator Ellison "Cotton Ed" Smith of South Carolina, chairman of the Agriculture Committee. Cotton Ed had been in the Senate since 1909, was himself a farmer, had helped write most of the agriculture legislation, and was one of those on the Hill to whom even FDR had to listen. He was also a fellow-Southerner.

It was a good idea in theory. In practice it was a fiasco.

By identifying myself as a *Journal* reporter I got to see him, but in a few minutes it was clear I had been hasty. I didn't even know the right questions to ask. He was surprised to find himself dealing with a youthful neophyte. He was a crusty character, the very archetypical Southern senator. He quickly sent me packing.

The next thing I knew I got a call from Barney Kilgore. It seems that Cotton Ed had asked Alfred "Mike" Flynn, our man covering the Senate, who this kid was who annoyed him with silly questions. Mike complained to Barney about my poaching on his terrain and irritating his sources. Barney asked me what was the big idea.

I carefully explained to him my rationale for approaching the senator and went on to say I thought it might be well also for me to talk to Representative Marvin Jones of Texas, chairman of the House Agriculture Committee.

Barney's answer was curt. "You're getting awful big for your britches awful quick."

Thus chastened I decided to stick to my last, at least for the time being. My daily schedule became a brief stop around ten in the morning at the Commerce Department press room to look over the "handouts" prepared overnight. The Commerce Department then, and to a large extent now, was mainly a statistical gathering organization with little involvement in political policy matters. With rare exceptions—the chief one being Herbert Hoover, who somehow managed to use it as a springboard to the presidency— the incumbent secretary, though a member of the cabinet, has not had a large voice in the economic policies of the administration. This was certainly true of Daniel Roper, the secretary in 1936, one of the most colorless men I ever met in public life. I can't recall anything he ever said at a press conference that made front page news anywhere. I would rummage through the handouts for some small item of news worth a paragraph or so, some foreign trade figures perhaps. Then a brief walk down Fourteenth Street to the Agriculture Department.

Most of the news there on most days was also pretty much routine. But agriculture policy was in a state of ferment. There was frequently news of importance to the commodity markets (crop reports, for example), and if you wandered around talking to enough people you could come up with what are known in the trade as "dope" stories, ideas that were being considered or talked about. Not all of them came to fruition but they could nonetheless make good one day's reading. Within the press room coterie there was a lot of competition in digging them out.

My chief competition on "spot" news—news that had to go out on the ticker promptly—was Central News, the official name of the rival business news service although for some reason it was always referred to around the office as "Tammany." Eddie Costenbader had drilled into me the importance of speed and I quickly learned to dictate a story from a few notes or from a glance at a handout without sitting down to the typewriter. It was a skill to come in handy in the years ahead.

On digging out situation stories the competition was mainly from Ovid Martin of the Associated Press, then just beginning a long career that would make him the doyen of agriculture reporters, and from Felix Belair of *The New York Times*—Felix especially, since our New York office subscribed to the AP service but of course didn't see the *Times* until Felix's stories were in print. In the early days I got many a "call-back" on his stories, a message from New York saying "*Times* says this morning. . . ." Irritating fellow, Felix Belair.

It was a long time, then, before the New York office began to recognize my sterling qualities. Not until May of the following spring did I get my first byline. That had some unexpected twists.

The story in brief said, "The possibility of abandoning the sugar quota system under the Jones-Costigan Act is being considered in certain quarters here, it was learned yesterday." That would be a major change in agriculture policy affecting domestic growers of both cane and beet sugar, the refiners, and of course ultimately the consumers. Foreign sugar growers, particularly those in Cuba, could produce and sell sugar cheaper than domestic growers. This had resulted in a quota system on imports. Because of the importance of any change, the word came from New York in the late afternoon that my story would lead the paper the next day—and how did I want my byline?

I sent back "Vermont Connecticut Royster"—there, I thought, was a byline to attract attention! The chief of the New York copy desk at that time was William F. Kerby, subsequently better known as president of Dow Jones & Company. He sent back a message, "Byline requested won't fit. Will use initials." Then he got the initials backwards, and so my first signed story in the *Journal* was by "C. V. Royster." Such is the bumpy road to glory!

As it turned out, the story was wrong too. Well, not exactly. Abandoning the sugar quotas was being "considered," but in fact they weren't abandoned. Sometime later Barney punctured my balloon by remarking, "That story of yours is still exclusive. Why?"

But it had one good effect. It brought me to the attention of Henry Wallace and led to my getting to know him better. In the late spring of 1937 he made a trip to Canada for some discussion with the Canadian agriculture minister about cooperation in wheat planting and marketing. I persuaded the New York office to let me go along and Wallace agreed. As it turned out, I was the only reporter along because Felix Belair dropped out.

In those days cabinet officers did not travel in great style. The secretary and I shared the same Pullman car, he in a drawing room, I in my lower berth. There being only the two of us we had drinks in the barcar and dinner together on the overnight train from Washington to Montreal.

I quickly found out that Wallace wasn't much on casual chit-chat. But he had an almost mystical feeling about farming and the importance of agriculture in the progress of civilization. On that topic he blossomed.

Wallace had originally been a Republican, his father having served as agriculture secretary under Presidents Harding and Coolidge. Henry had served as editor of *Wallace's Farmer*, founded by his father, and had worked out the first corn-hog price ratios which indicated the probable course of markets for both the commodity and livestock. He had begun during those years advocating some government action to regulate farm production and to put some minimum supports under farm prices, which had been depressed long before the economic depression became general. This led to his appointment by Roosevelt.

The original New Deal farm program had been to support farm prices at an officially determined "parity" price by paying farmers not to produce on all of their acreage; they were to be paid for "soil conservation." This failed to halt overproduction because many farmers increased their yield per acre, keeping the market price below parity. Enter then Wallace's visionary idea of an "ever normal" granary, a concept borrowed from the biblical story of Joseph and his brothers, that of storing food in the seven fat years against the seven lean years. The government would take over the surplus, store it, and lend farmers money for it. In later years when production was down, farmers would theoretically redeem their crops and sell them at a time when prices would be higher. The "ever normal granary" program thus had a rational, even religious underpinning. At the same time it also fitted the political needs of the time, keeping farm prices up. That made Wallace seem for a time both a visionary and a practical man, politically speaking.

The Canadian trip produced only a routine story for me. It strengthened my acquaintance with him, however, and listening to his espousal of the ever normal granary gave me a glimpse into the visionary, or mystical, side of him that was to be his undoing. I was to be startled when, in 1940, FDR picked him for vice-president, and not at all surprised when four years later he was dumped. He was too much a mystical visionary to be a practical politician in a broader field.

In fact, intellectually speaking, I thought him not very stable. He had begun, for example, adamantly opposed to recognition of the Soviet Union. He ended up being beguiled by its Marxist socialism in which he saw a vision to match his own. When he made a try for the presidency himself in 1948, he was the preferred candidate of the American Communist party. I attributed this to his naiveté. He was too easily influenced by some of the extreme left-wingers, some of them actual Communists, who surrounded him.

Henry Wallace's last public service was, ironically, as secretary of commerce. He would have been a misfit there in any case, a square peg in a round hole. As it was, he was a disaster. It was almost as if he had succumbed to delusions of grandeur, thinking because he had been FDR's vice-president he could sound off at will on foreign policy. Truman had no choice but to fire him from that job too. After that he faded from public view.

He was not, I'm afraid, a very smart man. He had learned nothing about politics or the ways of the world in more than a dozen years at the center of government. But I felt sorry for him. I always personally liked the man.

*   *   *   *   *

Harold Ickes was also an attractive man, though in a different way. Along with my Agriculture and Commerce beats I had temporarily inherited the Interior Department, of which he was secretary, when Carlton Skinner was beguiled into government service— which was to lead in time to his becoming, among other things, governor of Guam.

This shifting around of reporters occurred frequently. The *Journal* of those days wasn't the familiar one of today. Not only was its circulation small, in size it ran no more than sixteen to twenty pages. It also had then a varied makeup (including pictures) like other papers. The predominant coverage was still business and financial. But with the coming of the New Deal it had greatly enlarged its Washington bureau; there were usually a dozen or so reporters on the staff besides Barney, making our bureau larger than that of the *Herald-Tribune* but smaller than the *Times*. Even so, we were always shorthanded because we had to cover for the Dow Jones News Service as well as for the paper. Juggling staff assignments, Ken Kramer must have felt much like Tom Sawyer's uncle trying to stop seven rat holes with six plugs. The result was an informal organization, which was an advantage to me in those early years.

Eugene Duffield, our resident intellectual, was well-anchored at the Treasury and Federal Reserve. Kermit Sloan was a fixture at the Interstate Commerce Commission as was William Raymond at the Securities and Exchange Commission, both major news sources for us and requiring special expertise. Claude Mahoney was tied to the White House. Mike Flynn, the senior reporter, covered the Senate and George B. Bryant, Jr., the House. The rest of us floated from one thing to another as personnel and demands changed. That made it a lot more fun.

Interior was one of the fun places just because of Ickes. He enjoyed his public reputation as the "old curmudgeon," earned because he took swipes at everyone including his cabinet colleagues. Privately, among the press corps, he was also often referred to as Donald Duck. There was nothing handsome about him; he was already in his sixties with a weather-beaten face. But he had not only a sharp tongue but a witty one.

He was likewise a great in-fighter. Historically the Interior Department had been a rather dull place, compiled of such things as the Office of Indian Affairs, the Geological Survey, the Bureau of

Mines, the Alaska Railroad, and St. Elizabeth's Hospital, colloquially referred to as the place for "crazies." Ickes had hardly been installed before he set out to corral some of the special New Deal relief-spending agencies, like the Civil Works Administration and the Public Works Administration, which he did. Stirring this alphabetical soup led to a running feud with Harry Hopkins, head of the Federal Emergency Relief Administration and later of the Works Progress Administration. Many of these agencies, or at least their roles, bounced back and forth between Hopkins and Ickes. It was hard enough to keep track of them as a reporter. The public never did.

Ickes was another ex-Republican (he had helped run Charles Evans Hughes's campaign for the presidency in 1916) who had come to the Roosevelt administration via the old Progressive party. His varied career had embraced being a Chicago newspaper reporter before the turn of the century, a doughboy in the First World War, a lawyer, a gadabout in Chicago civic affairs, which included being chairman of something called The People's Traction League.

Most of the hard news from the Interior Department came in the form of mimeographed announcements, the award of this or that contract for public works construction or this or that relief grant to some local community. The reporters delighted in his press conferences because he was usually good for a quote, most of them pungent.

On Huey Long: "The trouble with Senator Long is that he is suffering from halitosis of the intellect." On Alf Landon: "Landon is the poor man's Hoover." On Thomas Dewey: "I see where Dewey has thrown his diapers into the ring." On Wendell Willkie: "The Barefoot Boy from Wall Street."

Ickes was one of that small band of original New Deal cabinet officers who were still around when Roosevelt died. By then in his seventies, he was more crotchety than ever, and he and Harry Truman didn't hit it off well together. Even so, Old Harold got in a final quip when he resigned in 1946. His parting shot at Truman was "I don't like government by crony."

Harry Hopkins, the other half of that early feud, was a different breed. He was tall, lanky, almost a walking cadaver. I never thought he would last through Roosevelt's second term, much less imagined that in the third term he would become FDR's right-hand man during World War II. He struck me as being very smart, in the sense of being shrewd, but also as too intense and solemn. He did show flashes of humor, but it was nearly always sardonic, even tinged with cynicism.

He was controversial from the beginning because the whole work relief program was controversial. I felt that he was sincere in his arguments for the program and honest in handling the millions that passed through his hands. But this cynicism showed through when he said—or anyway, what Arthur Krock said he said—that the Roosevelt program was to "tax and tax, spend and spend, elect and elect." His role appears better in history than it did to me at the time.

Throughout 1936 and most of 1937, however, my main beat continued to be Agriculture and Commerce. My other activities were add-ons, sometimes assigned by Ken Kramer, sometimes undertaken on my own as a matter of curiosity. This multiple activity wasn't onerous. In journalism, as in the army, there is much hurry-up-and-wait, with hours during the day when there is really not much duty to be done. When the opportunity presented I would use this time to drop in on other press conferences, those of Secretary of Labor Frances Perkins, for example, or Postmaster General James Farley. The only agencies I missed entirely (thank the Lord!) were the ICC and the SEC.

Frances Perkins left me unimpressed. So did Jim Farley in some ways, but at least he was interesting. A large, genial man, his main function was not policy but politics. At his press conferences a few desultory moments would be spent on Post Office affairs, about which he knew little and didn't seem to care. Then someone would ask a political question and Big Jim would entertain us for an hour talking about his favorite subject.

Years later he gave me a lesson in a politician's artful trick. We were table neighbors at some luncheon in the Waldorf-Astoria ballroom and people came by in droves to speak to him. Each time he stuck out his hand and said, "I'm Jim Farley." When he finally sat down, I asked him with amusement if he really thought there was anyone in this vast room who didn't know who he was.

"I guess most of them do," he said. "But I've a great reputation for remembering names. I won it by learning that if I would first give my name the other fellow would almost always respond by giving his, and thereafter I could call him by name. He'd think I remembered it all along." I might add that I've tried the Farley gambit myself many times since then and have found it remarkably successful.

I also began during this time serving as backup man at Roosevelt's press conferences. Since we needed fast coverage for the News Service wire, the usual practice was for Barney or perhaps Mike Flynn to station himself at the rear of the Oval Office for a rush to the telephone to dictate. I would work my way forward in the press group, as near to FDR's desk as I could get, taking notes also to fill in any gaps in the story. This had its advantages. It gave me a good closeup view of the president, and gradually he began at least to recognize my face.

Then in the late spring of 1937 I got another add-on assignment, to cover the newly created Maritime Commission. I drew it largely, I think, simply because it was housed in the Commerce Building. There I encountered one of the more fascinating men I was to meet in those early years, Joseph P. Kennedy.

All I knew about Joe Kennedy was that he had made a potful of money as a banker, movie tycoon and stock market speculator, and that he had been the first chairman of the Securities and Exchange Commission. When he got that job some people, especially the more liberal New Dealers, thought it a case of putting the fox to watch the chickens. But he had fooled everybody. He proved a tough policeman on the securities markets (because he knew all the angles, I suppose) and an able administrator. At the same time he had also managed to earn the respect of the business community by restraining the other, more radical commissioners and staff.

The Maritime Commission was another new venture. Created by Congress in 1936, it was assigned the task to revitalize our decrepit merchant marine. At first it was welcomed by the ship operators, thinking it would be a soft touch because Congress planned to vote it millions to subsidize shipbuilding and ship operations. They too got fooled.

When I first saw Joe Kennedy he was a tall man in his late forties already beginning to grow slightly portly, with a receding hairline over large round horn-rimmed glasses, and he exuded energy. It was clear from the beginning that he had nothing but scorn for the majority of the ship operators, whom he considered incompetent. When he was off-the-record this view was expressed in earthy language.

Under the old shipping laws American flag vessels had received large subsidies for carrying mail, the sums having little or no connection with the mail carried or the quality of service rendered. The companies laid claim to back subsidies amounting to more than seventy million dollars. The first thing Joe Kennedy did, using the iron fist, was to settle these claims for less than one million. He also cut in half the amount of operating subsidies that had been paid under the old system.

He then let it be known that the commission would not subsidize inefficiency and poor management; to get any subsidies the companies had to meet government specifications in both building and operating their ships. He also proposed that no company receiving subsidies could pay an executive more than twenty-five thousand dollars a year. That threat wasn't carried out, but it shook the industry to its roots.

Kennedy did something else unheard of. FDR had sent Congress a bill providing for a $160 million shipbuilding program. Kennedy startled the House Appropriations Committee by asking them *not* to vote the money. To do so, he said, might set up pressures to spend the money before the commission had decided how best to spend it.

He startled the operators by laying into them about the working conditions of seamen, something that struck a responsive chord with me. In the summer of 1932 my Chapel Hill roommate Hoke Pollock and I had worked our way abroad on an old World War I freighter, the *SS Lehigh*. Since we were young and our jobs temporary, we didn't too much mind the bad working conditions, but bad they were. The crew was housed as many as a dozen to one compartment. There were no showers, only a couple of hoses for washing, one for salt water, one for fresh water. Clothes had to be washed in a bucket. The food was badly prepared and sloppily served; the latter had even led to a fight between me and one of the messmen.

But of course this aspect of Kennedy's criticism seemed to be playing into the hands of Harry Bridges, the firebrand union organizer, and got Kennedy branded as being "soft" on radical labor.

On the other hand, he was outspoken in his demands for "discipline" on American ships and proposed training schools for seamen under the Coast Guard. To Bridges and his associates "discipline" was a fighting word. Kennedy was caught in a crossfire, though he was right on both points.

Looking back on it, Kennedy performed no miracles, although his new subsidy formula, for both shipbuilding and operations, was a considerable improvement over the old system. Forty years later the American merchant marine was to find itself in as bad a shape as it was in the 1930s. It is still a sick industry. But that Joe Kennedy gave it a valiant try there can be no doubt. He was a quintessential Boston Irishman, which means that he grew up being snubbed by the old families of Back Bay Brahmins. This seeded in him an internal drive to "show 'em," first by making a lot of money—which he did in movies, whiskey, and other free-wheeling enterprises—and then by proving himself in politics. The fact that some of the businessmen he had to deal with, first at the SEC and then at the Maritime Commission, looked down on him socially added to his toughness. He had to be better at what he did than anybody else. He took these jobs seriously, was gulled by nobody, worked at them prodigiously. His Irishness was to prove a handicap when Roosevelt, in a strange decision, appointed him ambassador to Britain. But that internal drive, born of being Boston Irish, he transmitted to his sons John and Robert who were to make even greater impressions on their times. In my brief contact with him I came to have enormous respect for this Kennedy founding father.

*   *   *   *   *

Another among the fascinating personalities I ran across in those early years was Wendell Willkie.

Willkie at that time was head of Commonwealth and Southern, a utility holding company, and he was engaged in a duel with the Tennessee Valley Authority, headed by David Lilienthal. The TVA was a huge project to develop the water resources of the rivers in the Tennessee Valley, ostensibly to combine conservation, flood control and hydroelectric power. In fact, its hydroelectric program soon became dominant, and this was supposed to provide a "yardstick" for measuring the efficiency of private power companies and the fairness of their rates.

Willkie, a small-town Hoosier turned city lawyer, had already come into some prominence as spokesman for the industry in the long drawn-out fight over the Public Utilities Holding Bill, ultimately passed. But the immediate issue with Lilienthal was the TVA plan to bypass private utility operating companies in distributing its electric power. It was encouraging municipalities to buy up local power companies, using the right of eminent domain if necessary, or to build distribution systems of their own. The fight over this TVA program had begun as far back as 1934. Willkie was now proposing that TVA limit its public power distribution to a restricted area and, beyond that, sell its power to private companies.

It was an argument to go on for years; eventually C & S sold its operating companies to TVA. My involvement in it as a reporter was brief. There was a series of discussion meetings between Willkie and Lilienthal, and I along with other reporters would wait for them to break up and then try to pry some information out of Willkie as to what progress, if any, had been made. It was a boring assignment and rarely resulted in more than a paragraph or two for the paper.

But late one afternoon after an all-day session a weary Willkie invited some of us to join him in his room at the Carlton Hotel. There he took off his coat, offered us a drink, slumped down in a chair in his usual disheveled fashion, and began to talk. It was the nature of the talk that surprised me.

It began, naturally enough, with the immediate issue between himself and Lilienthal. Unlike most businessmen involved in a dispute with government, Willkie managed to present his side of the case without sounding like a neanderthal businessman just defending a special interest. He did this by treating the issue as an important philosophical one about the nature of government and the role of private economic activity in American society. Then as he talked on he began to range even farther afield from the immediate dispute, talking about the various ways of organizing society from ancient times to the present.

He was sometimes rambling—this wasn't a press conference but what would have been called in my college days a "bull session"—yet he was always coherent, and the amount of knowledge he displayed about history, philosophy, and economics was astounding. Since it was not an occasion for taking notes I can't recall in detail anything he said. But all of us there that evening were impressed. He showed himself a man of wide-ranging interests and rare articulateness. Here, obviously, was a combination of the intellectual and the practical man of action.

I had not a glimmer at the time that these qualities would project him into center stage in national politics, culminating in his winning the Republican nomination for president. I was even surprised when it did happen because successful presidential candidates aren't usually cut from that bolt; Woodrow Wilson was probably the only one who came close to the same combination. The difference was that Wilson, or so he appears in the history books, was on the pedantic side and, I suspect, a little dull, while Willkie seemed a brilliant shooting star. In the end, as shooting stars will, he burned himself out. But as I left the hotel room that night I knew I had crossed paths with an exciting and exceptional man.

Of course, excluding possibly Henry Wallace, I never got to know any of these people well. For one thing, I was very young, too uncertain as to how much I could presume on a journalistic acquaintance. For another, the *Journal* itself did not then stand high in Washington prestige. With its tiny circulation of around thirty-five thousand it wasn't in the class, as far as politicians were concerned, with such papers as *The New York Times*, the *Herald-Tribune*, the *Chicago Tribune*, with circulations numbered in the hundreds of thousands. We did have a large bureau for a paper of such size because of the importance of Washington news to our specialized, small audience, but never enough reporters to keep every "beat" permanently manned. This kept me, as the youngest reporter, flitting from one place to another with too little time anywhere to establish myself other than at the Agriculture Department.

On the other hand I was getting a broad exposure to New Deal Washington in a way I could not have done working for, say, the Associated Press or the *Times*. They were too departmentalized; anyway, I wouldn't have had much chance to work in Washington for either, at my youthful age. At the *Journal* we were all younger than average because the bureau had expanded rapidly since 1932 with the growing importance of governmental news to the business community. Before that, the *Journal* had managed with a two-man bureau; Charlie Sterner, who was an inside man, was the only one whose service reached back into the 1920s. Barney Kilgore, our bureau chief, was only twenty-eight in 1936.

Barney and Ken Kramer were both Hoosiers, schoolmates at De Pauw University in Greencastle, Indiana; indeed, a great many of the *Journal* staff at that time were from Indiana. Barney had joined the *Journal* fresh out of college in 1929, had served as a reporter and copy editor in New York and as news editor of the small edition printed in San Francisco, before being sent to Washington as bureau chief only a few months before my arrival as the bureau's youngest member. He was able, brilliant, imaginative, and mature beyond his years, clearly marked even then as a young man on the way to the top.

After three years I was by no means a star, either among Washington reporters generally or the *Journal*'s in particular. But I had managed to establish myself with both Barney and Ken as a competent reporter. I was no longer worried about the lapsing of that "temporary" job Bill Grimes had given me. I was even trusted for a time with the financial beat (Treasury and Federal Reserve) when Gene Duffield left. That got me acqainted with Henry Morgenthau and Marriner Eccles, the latter of whom I was to know better later on.

As a result I was both having fun and gaining invaluable experience. I no longer felt timid in the presence of either my journalistic elders or these famous headline personalities I encountered in my duties. I was growing up, and one reason for that was that at last I had gotten married. I was twenty-three, my Frances twenty-two.

2

I attended my first White House reception in the winter of 1938, proudly resplendent in white-tie-and-tails and with my young bride in a trousseau evening gown on my arm.

The Roosevelts had established a custom of having a series of receptions during the social season for the judiciary, the diplomatic corps, the Congress, and similar parts of the Washington establishment. At each of these a few newspaper people were included, chosen by lot as far as I could tell. By now I had an asterisk by my name in the press listing of the *Congressional Directory* indicating that I had a wife; there was a different marking for those who, in the *Directory*'s quaint wording, had "other ladies with them." Anyway, our invitation to the reception was hand-delivered to our tiny apartment on Nineteenth Street, just behind where the Washington Hilton now stands. It read: "The President and Mrs. Roosevelt request the pleasure of the company of Mr. and Mrs. Royster. . . ." The invitation itself was engraved, with our names written in old-fashioned calligraphy. Frances and I were as excited as children at Christmas.

These were formal occasions. We rode to the South Entrance of the White House in a taxi to be greeted by a squad of young military attachés in dress uniforms and were directed upstairs to the main floor. The President and Mrs. Roosevelt received in the Blue Room, the receiving line stretching through the East Room into the North Foyer. It must have been tiring for the president, strapped into his leg braces, but he and Mrs. Roosevelt greeted each guest graciously. Afterwards there was punch and dancing to the Marine Band.

The formality would have made these very dull affairs, except that it was, after all, the White House, and one could, depending on the occasion, catch a glimpse of Chief Justice Charles Evans Hughes, Speaker of the House William Bankhead, or some beribboned foreign ambassador.

The Roosevelts also held an informal "At home" once a year for the members of the press, then small enough in number so that all could be accommodated. These were much more fun for both of us. There was no receiving line, but President Roosevelt would be in a chair at one end of the East Room, available to anyone who wished to speak to him. Eleanor would bestir herself with the energy of a cruise-ship social director to liven up the party, which she did. It was at one of these that I had my one and only personal conversation with FDR.

I went up to him at his chair to pay my respects. He asked me about my name, recalling that Vermont was one of the two states voting against him in 1936. I explained that I was a Southerner born-and-bred and told him the origin of the state names.

He asked me what the other names were. I told him.

At this he threw back his head and burst into laughter. He said that with a name like that I ought to use all of it, like Kennesaw Mountain Landis.

End of conversation.

In a later time and clime Frances and I would have gotten married much sooner. We had, in that antique phrase, "gone together" all during our college years. She had visited me once in New York, several times in Washington. But I was still imbued with my grandfather's old-fashioned idea that a man didn't take a wife until he could support her. I was by now making twenty-five dollars a week and also writing occasional pieces for *Barron's*, the weekly financial magazine published by Dow Jones, for which the editor, Tom Phelps, paid fifty dollars, or twice my regular salary. Unfortunately I could not find enough subjects to make these sales regular, and altogether there wasn't enough money for the two of us, even in the depression.

It was Frances who cut the gordian knot. By now she was working as a secretary in the Resettlement Administration in Raleigh and had her Civil Service rating. She was confident she could get a job somewhere in Washington.

So we were married on June 5, 1937, in New Bern in a formal Episcopal church ceremony on one of the hottest nights on record.

We had a splendid honeymoon, thanks to the then practice of newspapers accepting hotel ads in return for "due bills," redeemable for rooms. Barney arranged for me to use the *Journal's* due bill at the Ambassador Hotel on Park Avenue in New York. We therefore lodged in high style, although since the due bill didn't cover food we ate at Child's or the Automat. Even so, we returned to New Bern broke and I would have had to borrow money from my new father-in-law to get back to Washington had it not been for the timely arrival of one of those *Barron's* checks.

As it was, we began our married life in low estate, one room on the third floor of a rooming house in Riggs Place, already a rather run-down section of town. We had a bedroom and an unusual combination kitchen and bath; that is, the kitchen had no sink and we had to wash the dishes in the bathtub. Not too long afterwards, however, I got a raise to thirty dollars and Frances got a job in the State Department at thirty-five dollars. Thus rolling in money, we moved to that two-room apartment on Nineteenth Street.

It was about this time that I was transferred from my varied collection of downtown beats to Capitol Hill, where I was assigned both to cover the Supreme Court and to serve as "swingman" on the congressional beat. This time I was welcomed by Mike Flynn, if for no other reason because I relieved him of the Supreme Court chore.

The Supreme Court and Congress could be matched together because of their physical proximity and because most of the Court work was done during the summertime. That work was a bit of a chore, or at least quite different from the usual type of reporting. It consisted mainly of slugging through the briefs filed with the Court on upcoming cases and writing up "dummies" so that when decisions were handed down in the fall they could be handled quickly on the News Wire. These dummies would read something like this: "The Supreme Court today (affirmed) (overruled) the lower court decision in the case of. . . ." They would then go on to describe briefly the nature of the case and what the lower court had decided. On decision day—then always on Mondays—someone would be stationed in the courtroom to send the decisions down a tube to be in a small telephone cubicle in the basement. There I had a direct line to the office and by glancing at the final order on the last page could dictate a bulletin without delay.

In short, covering the Supreme Court involved something more like library work at school rather than the familiar and more exciting type of reporting where you talked to people to learn things. You didn't wander into a justice's office to discuss a pending case with him.

Nonetheless, I enjoyed it—within limits. And it was to lead to my first job offer outside of the *Journal*.

Since my legal knowledge was minimal, the assignment had called for another self-assigned cram course. In the Court library I began reading up on constitutional law and even went so far as to buy for myself Edward Corwin's monumental annotated analysis of "The Constitution of the United States" published by the Library of Congress. After some time of this I began immodestly writing "second day" interpretative stories about the more important cases, drawing on both the majority and minority opinions (there were usually both) and setting them against past Court rulings.

One day I received a note from Arthur Krock, head of the *Times* bureau, complimenting me on one of the articles and suggesting I drop by to see him. I did so and found him flattering, although a little surprised to discover that I didn't hold a law degree. We discussed the possibility of my working for the *Times*, which interested me at first because the *Times* was then much more prestigious than the *Journal*. But it was soon clear that he was interested only in having me work on legal stories, not for general assignment. That meant, in practice, that I would have been second man to Lewis Wood, the *Times'* long-time Supreme Court reporter.

It sounded too confining compared to my work on the *Journal* and I decided to stay where I was. Since then, though, I have often wondered what would have happened if I had followed through with Mr. Krock. On the whole, I am content.

Covering Congress was an entirely different matter. As the senior man Mike Flynn covered the Senate while the House was the domain of George B. Bryant, Jr. As "swing" man I would move back and forth as the occasion demanded, covering routine committee meetings and in general helping both of them when they couldn't be two places at once. My morning routine was to take a look at the scheduled committee meetings, check with Mike, and then go where he thought I might be most useful.

Once more I was a "new boy." Aside from Senator Smith, I knew few of the senators or congressmen even by sight, and Cotton Ed I now preferred to avoid when possible. In the beginning I found myself handicapped by the fact that I was young, and being short with a round, boyish face, looked even younger. This was to give me some embarrassing moments.

One day, for example, I was assigned to wait outside the House Ways and Means Committee, which was holding an executive session on a tax bill. The chairman of that committee was Representative Robert L. Doughton, more informally known as "Muley" Doughton. He was a rather large man with an influence even larger, having been in Congress since 1911. He was also a fellow Tar Heel with a broad Southern drawl, but I was to find that didn't help me any.

On this particular day a small group of reporters hung around the committee room until, late in the afternoon, Muley Doughton came out to tell us whatever he wanted to say about what went on. After he made his remarks, the questions started and mine were rather persistent.

A few minutes of this and he suddenly turned to me. "Who are you?" he asked.

I threw out my chest and said I was Royster of *The Wall Street Journal*.

He slowly looked me up and down from his height.

"When," he drawled, "did *The Wall Street Journal* start hiring adolescents?"

It was devastating. My colleagues roared with laughter. It was a story that quickly spread and for weeks afterwards I had to listen to amused—but not to me funny—remarks along the lines of the *Journal's* kindergarten. It did get me known in the press gallery, but I could have done without that kind of notoriety.

*   *   *   *   *

Despite such incidents I was enjoying myself and broadening my knowledge of the ways of Washington.

For one thing, I had two good teachers. Mike Flynn was the storybook Irishman, with a charm that came naturally from his easy, outgoing manner. He knew every senator and, what's more, every senator knew him. To follow Mike around was an education in itself. When we met a senator strolling in the hall, Mike would stop him and ask about some legislative matter in which he was involved. The questioning was never heavy-handed, almost casual, but more times than not he would come away with some news-worthy quote or a different slant on some bill working its way through a committee. Although Mike was not the best writer, he was one of the two or three best reporters I've ever met.

George Bryant was also a good reporter, but in an entirely dif-ferent way and with a different manner. George was a hulk of a man, a Tar Heel who had preceded me by a few years at Cha-pel Hill, and he kept his Southern accent. This was especially effec-tive with the many Southern congressmen who had been in Con-gress for years and who by now held key positions as Speaker, as party leaders, or as chairmen of the most important committees. As Southerners will, George would spend some time in casual conversation—passing the time of day, as it were—and you were hardly aware when the talk shifted to what George really had on his mind. Later you realized he had extracted a lot of information.

There were others too in the press gallery who served as excellent models for a young reporter. Douglas Cornell and Edward Haakinson of the Associated Press were real pros, as was Sandor "Sandy" Klein of United Press. At one time or another events on the Hill would attract Thomas Stokes of Scripps-Howard, by then more commentator than straight reporter, or the UP's Harrison Salisbury or Richard Strout of the *Christian Science Monitor*. But the one who intrigued me most was Turner Catledge of the *Times*.

Turner was by then the *Times*'s chief man at the Capitol. He would arrive in the Senate Press Gallery around noon and spend most of the afternoon stretched out on one of the big leather couches, seemingly doing nothing except "holding court" with other reporters passing by. Around five or so in the afternoon he would vanish. Then the next morning on the *Times*'s front page would be a long Catledge story on the main developments of the day—clear, readable and full of details that had somehow escaped me, and most of the other reporters for that matter. From Turner I learned there was no necessary correlation between energy expended and results achieved. Or, to turn a copybook maxim upside down, the virtues of laziness.

Covering Congress also helped me in that the work wasn't specialized, as it inevitably was downtown. Sooner or later every public issue, whether dealing with Agriculture or Interior or the Treasury, found its way to the Hill. It was there that the basic laws were passed and it was from there the money came. The result was that one day I might be covering a tax hearing and on the next a meeting of the Senate Commerce Committee. Congress, I found, was the crossroad where all the forces affecting government met. And that got me interested in politics.

I had been only on the periphery of the 1936 presidential campaign. I did spend a few hours at the Democratic convention because it was in Philadelphia, only a few hours away, but my trip was strictly unofficial and on my own. Although I don't think Barney approved, he did get me a one-day ticket to the hall. In so brief an exposure all I came away with was the sense of excitement at these quadrennial exhibitions, a feeling I still retain even though the changing nature of politics has made them not the decisive factor they once were in nominating a presidential candidate. Television and the proliferation of state primaries have changed all that. During the rest of that 1936 campaign Barney was our lone political reporter, and a shrewd one he was. By getting away from the candidates and just travelling the countryside (a practice I was to adopt later) he foresaw FDR's big victory, the *Literary Digest* poll notwithstanding.

By 1938, however, the 1940 campaign was already underway. It had been precipitated the year before when President Roosevelt launched his move to remake the Supreme Court, quickly dubbed the "court-packing" plan. He had been having a running battle with the Court, which had declared many of his early measures unconstitutional, and even though it had upheld more recent laws the Court remained a political obstacle. Fresh from that sweeping victory in 1936 the president flung down the gauntlet before the Court. Technically all he asked was an increase in the number of justices coupled with an attractive retirement program to persuade some of the older justices to step aside. But the true purpose—to remake the Court to his own liking—couldn't be disguised.

In retrospect the Court plan was doomed to defeat; FDR had overreached himself. The chief consequence of it was that he gave the Republicans a good political issue. Strangely enough, FDR compounded this by a fight with Senate Democrats over the majority leadership; most Democrats wanted Senator Pat Harrison of Mississippi, but Roosevelt forced them to take Alben Barkley of Kentucky. It was a pyrrhic victory. Barkley won by only one vote, and together these two events ended FDR's sure control of Congress. As Harold Ickes noted, "Everything on the Hill now seems to be at sixes and sevens."

Even more strangely for a man of FDR's political acumen he compounded his troubles by attempting to purge critics from within his own party during the 1938 congressional elections, men such as Senators George of Georgia and Tydings of Maryland. This too was a debacle for Roosevelt.

As far as I was concerned all this only added to the excitement of being a Capitol reporter. Even though I was the bureau's "third man" on the Hill I gradually had occasion to meet and talk with most of the key men of that time. Perhaps it is only an illusion of memory but it seems to me that Congress today lacks the colorful characters of yesteryear, however able the current incumbents may be. It would be hard to find a match today for the likes of Tom Connally of Texas, with his flowing mane; or Theodore Bilbo, firebrand populist from Mississippi; the crusty Carter Glass from Virginia; the tough outspoken William Borah of Idaho, constant foe of FDR's foreign policy. William Bankhead of Alabama not only acted like but looked like a Speaker of the House. The majority leader in the House was Sam Rayburn of Texas, and the minority leader peppery Joe Martin of Massachusetts, both in time to serve as Speakers.

At that time the Speaker, the party leaders, and the committee chairmen were strong enough, politically and personally, to govern the Congress. Usually it was enough to talk to a handful of people to know what the Congress was going to do on some particular bill. It was the kind of political discipline later to be much criticized, but at least it meant that things could get done, not always true in the anarchy of the post-Vietnam and post-Watergate years. Even though I was very junior I remember two occasions when I managed to get included in one of Vice-President Garner's informal gatherings to "strike a blow for freedom," Garner's phrase for hauling out the bourbon bottle and discussing matters at hand. These gatherings were completely off-the-record, but nowhere else could you get such a feel for the sense of Congress.

Vice-President Garner, incidentally, had little sympathy with the band of New Dealers around Roosevelt, a feeling mutually shared. A Texan, he had been chosen initially to balance the ticket in 1932. For a time he had presidential ambitions, but by 1940 he was ready to step aside as vice-president, not only because of age (he was seventy-two), but because he had had enough of FDR and the New Deal. It must have galled him, however, that he was replaced by Henry Wallace, a man for whom he held no great affection, political or otherwise.

It was in the spring of 1938 that I drew an assignment that was to have considerable effect on my standing within *The Wall Street Journal*. With the country in another recessionary period despite all the New Deal programs, Roosevelt asked Congress to launch an investigation of the alleged concentration of economic power in American industry. Congress responded with alacrity and the result was the Temporary National Economic Committee, drawn from both House and Senate and chaired by Senator Joseph O'Mahoney of Wyoming.

What followed was one of those long and interminable hearings which accomplish very little but give Congress a chance to haul before it the leaders of industry and pillory them with the aim of making them political scapegoats for whatever ails the economy, in those days recession, in more recent times inflation.

Because the topic and the roster of witnesses the hearings were of particular news interest to the *Journal*. Day after day I sat through the hearings and was rewarded the next day by two or even three columns of space in the paper. These stories began to attract attention both within and without the bureau, and I got complimentary notes from Bill Grimes and, once, one from K. C. Hogate, then president of the company and the *Journal*'s publisher. I was beginning to feel that I was on my way to carving a niche as a Washington reporter.

Meanwhile my private life was also changing. In that first bachelor year my Washington social life consisted largely of hanging around the office late, then going out for drinks and dinner with some of my younger colleagues. I had too little money to spend on girls even if I were of a mind to. Now I was adjusting to married life, and Frances was adjusting to being married to a newspaperman, a life a bit different from that she had known in New Bern or Raleigh.

Some of it was exciting for her, such as invitations to the White House and the fact that when the King and Queen of Great Britain paid a state visit I could get her tickets to the honored guest box at the Capitol reception. Other things took a bit more adjusting. For one, she worked from eight-thirty in the morning to four-thirty in the afternoon. I hardly ever went to work before ten o'clock and stayed there "until." Supper was not always on schedule.

As a young couple we also began to exchange social visits with other young-marrieds, within and without the bureau. These were mostly enjoyable, but sometimes they held surprises. One Sunday morning, for instance, we were invited to a picnic breakfast in Rock Creek Park by some journalistic friends. We arrived at their house about nine o'clock, sans breakfast, to be greeted by a pitcher of martinis, something not on the morning menu at home in New Bern. Before we could get away other friends of our hosts dropped by. The pitcher was filled and refilled and it was nearly noon before we got to the park and breakfast. The result of this alcoholic morning was a crisis. When I finally got Frances home, reeling, she wept that "if this is the way newspapermen live, I can't take it!"

Happily that adventure wasn't repeated and we gradually settled into a more sedate social life, although still an interesting one because on occasion our dinner companions would include a senator or congressman. It was at one such dinner that I first met a new senator from Ohio, Robert Taft, who had just taken his seat in January 1939.

Later, of course, he was to become a national figure, "Mr. Republican" and a presidential candidate. In Washington he was already attracting more attention than an ordinary freshman senator. In part this was simply because he was the son of former President William Howard Taft, but also because he was a Republican elected from Ohio, where labor unions, with their strong Democratic ties, held sway. After World War II I would get to know him better, but my first impression foreshadowed later ones. A product of both Yale and Harvard (law school at the latter), he was obviously intelligent, able, and articulate. He also struck me as rather plodding and pedestrian.

There were also some nonpolitical diversions in those years. My Rocky Mount cousin, Kay Kyser, had become a popular big band leader, and we shared the backstage festivities when his Kollege of Musical Knowledge played the local theaters. Frances' brother Stanley was a midshipman at the Naval Academy and this meant excursions to Annapolis and also to Army-Navy football games. We were also now a bit more prosperous (my pay had risen to seventy-five dollars a week), so we could move to a small but comfortable rented house on NW Thirty-second Street and could afford play evenings at the National Theater. We splurged on a new Chevrolet and began to talk of starting a family.

All in all, the future looked bright. But, scarcely noticed at first, the clouds of war were gathering over Europe and the Far East. They were soon to change Washington, the country and, most dramatically, our personal lives.

3

World War II began on September 1, 1939—that's what it says in the history books.

In the summer weeks preceding that fateful Nazi invasion of Poland those of us covering Congress were preoccupied with following the various appropriation bills (Roosevelt had proposed spending nine billion dollars in the coming fiscal year), with the fate of the president's government reorganization plan (it was approved, regrouping some fifty administrative agencies), and with a series of amendments to the Social Security Act (they advanced the date for starting old-age benefits to January 1, 1940). The most controversial piece of legislation that summer was the Hatch Act, an outgrowth of election scandals involving the WPA, which would prohibit federal government workers from participating actively in political campaigns.

But the war clouds had been gathering for at least four years. Mussolini had invaded Ethiopia in 1935. Hitler had occupied the Rhineland in 1936. The Spanish Civil War broke out in 1937. And in 1938, following the Munich Conference with British Prime Minister Chamberlain, Hitler absorbed Czechoslovakia into the Third Reich—assuring, said Mr. Chamberlain, "peace for our time."

In the Far East the Sino-Japanese War had begun in July 1937, and in December of that year the first shots were fired between the United States and Japan when the *USS Panay* was sunk (in a mistake, said Japan) by Japanese bombers. Within Japan the "war party" was gaining ascendancy after the assassination of former Premier Saito. In the fall of 1936 Japan had signed a mutual defense agreement (the Anti-Comintern Pact) with Germany.

September 1939 only confirmed what had long been underway, a war between two worlds.

The response to all this, at least up to that fateful September, was simply the feeling both in the country and in Congress that here were once more foreign wars that we ought to keep out of. The Neutrality Act of 1935, approved by Roosevelt, established the country's official posture; the sale of arms to any belligerents was prohibited. In my first three years in Washington everything I wrote about dealt with the country's domestic problems. I read about foreign affairs, of course, but they left my work as a reporter untouched. Until Munich they seemed remote from my personal affairs also; I was too engrossed in establishing my journalistic career and beginning a new life as a married man.

The Nazi invasion of Poland was a thunderbolt that altered American politics forever; from that day to this the United States has not been able to avoid the rest of the world. It's a cliché in journalism that come Judgement Day a message will arrive from the home office, "Get Congressional reaction." It was no different that September. For the first time I found myself scurrying to probe the congressional mood on a war beyond the seas, especially in the Senate. I found much sympathy for the Allies, no one openly favoring intervention, and many outspoken against any U.S. involvement.

Two days after the invasion President Roosevelt declared "this nation will remain a neutral nation," although he added he could not expect every American to remain neutral in thought as well. On September fifth our neutrality was officially proclaimed. "As long as it remains within my power," said the president, "there will be no blackout of peace in the United States."

In the Senate there was loud applause from Wheeler of Montana, Vandenberg of Michigan, Hiram Johnson of California, and most of all from Borah of Idaho. Bill Borah had been in the Senate since 1907 and had an unbroken record of opposing any American military involvement abroad. He had been opposed to America's entrance into World War I, and after the war was one of that "little band of willful men" who blocked American membership in the League of Nations. By now in his seventies he had a craggy face and was crustier than ever. A Republican, he was ranking minority member of the Foreign Relations Committee and a voice to be reckoned with. Encountered in the corridor, or called out from the Senate floor, he was always good for a quote which minced no words about his view that the U.S. ought to keep out of these wars too. In fact, until September he still refused to believe that there would be a European war.

Not long before, he had been one of a group of senators invited to the White House to hear Roosevelt's concern about the war clouds. Borah's response, shared with reporters afterwards, was that "all this hysteria is manufactured and artificial." He was also reported to have told Secretary of State Hull that he had sources of information he regarded as "more reliable than those of the State Department."

With the knowledge of hindsight the old man can be dismissed as muleheaded, even as in his dotage. But at the time he was by no means alone in isolationism, and he was not a man to be ignored. Roosevelt could not ignore him because, although a Republican, he had strongly supported most New Deal measures. I have to admit that I was impressed by him when he spoke in that authoritative manner of his. At least you had to respect him as a senator who always spoke his mind whether or not it was in tune with the prevailing political policy.

However that may be, the events of that September changed the emphasis of my reporting on Capitol Hill. Domestic matters, while remaining important, began to be overshadowed by foreign affairs and national defense issues.

One reason for this was that the president, up to now equivocal in his political stance about the war threat, had himself begun to change his mind as well as his heart.

Still, he moved gingerly. His first move was to ask the Congress to remove the arms embargo provision of the first Neutrality Act and to authorize "cash and carry" export of arms and munitions to belligerent powers. That was supposed to help the Allies because in practice most of the arms sales would be to Britain and France, both at that time better able financially to buy them and to ship them across the Atlantic than Nazi Germany. The change was approved by comfortable margins in both House and Senate, although in the mysterious ways of Washington the bill was labelled "The Neutrality Act of 1939."

FDR's gingerliness—or maybe craftiness is the better word— began to be reflected in his press conferences, to which I now returned occasionally under the pretense that it would help me in my reporting on the Hill. At these Roosevelt's posture would shift back and forth, though ever so gently, between the promise of neutrality and the hint of a stronger U.S. role. At one I remember he was asked point-blank if he thought we could stay out of the war. His reply was only that he "hoped so" and that he would make every effort to do so. Yet at another, when the topic was Navy moves to protect our territorial waters, he was asked how far our territorial waters extended. His ambiguous reply this time was "as far as U.S. interests require them to go."

If Roosevelt was equivocal, so too, I think, were the American people at that time. Without doubt they were anti-Nazi and their sympathies were with the Poles, the French, and the British. On the other hand the prospect of being embroiled again in a shooting war of European origin was frightening; hardly anybody then was paying much attention to Japan and the Far East. The stay-out-of-it mood was strengthened by the fact that once the Nazi blitz-krieg had smashed Poland months of quiet settled over the western front. It was Borah, I think, who invented the phrase "phony war." Anyway, he used it repeatedly.

Besides, wasn't the German army now facing the impregnable Maginot Line, built by the French after World War I against just such a contingency, and the combined military power of both France and Britain? Hitler now faced something more formidable than the ragtag Polish army. What was there to worry?

That complacency came to an abrupt end in 1940, first with the Nazi invasion of Norway which the British navy was unable to halt, and then with the eruption of the German army through the Netherlands, Belgium, and finally France, which neither the Maginot Line nor the combined British-French armies could stop. The war in Europe could no longer be ignored, or even be treated as something remote from our interests, by the president, the Congress or the country. A few voices began to speak cautiously of aid to the Allies.

In this progression of events President Roosevelt was never more than a half step ahead of the country. In his 1939 budget message, after Munich, he had asked for a small increase in military spending. He raised the amount further in his 1940 budget message, following in May with a supplemental request, bringing the total to a little more than three billion dollars. But that was enough to change, among other things, my journalistic duties on the Hill.

Until 1939 the *Journal* had paid little attention to the War and Navy Departments except for occasional notices of contracts let. By mid-1939 I found myself covering the military committees of Congress, the Military and Naval Committees in the Senate, and the Military Affairs Committee in the House. By 1940 they took up much of my time. I became in effect the *Journal*'s military affairs correspondent, such as I was.

The two Senate committees (the War and Navy Departments were then separate) were headed by Morris Sheppard of Texas for the Army and David Walsh of Massachusetts for the Navy. In the House the chairman of the single committee was Andrew May of Kentucky. With the possible exception of Senator Walsh none was impressive. Neither was Secretary of the Navy Claude Swanson, an aging (nearly eighty) ex-senator, or Secretary of War Harry Woodring, a banker and former governor of Kansas. Both were soon to be replaced.

The people who interested me were the military men who came to testify. Most of their testimony was behind closed doors as the committees met in executive session; no one then thought it strange that some governmental matters, especially military ones, should be considered in private. But we reporters did get a chance to chat with them afterwards and, on the whole, they were remarkably open and frank. General Malin Craig, the Army chief of staff, was rather restrained and formal, but there was a young brigadier, George C. Marshall, who was more forthright and willing to talk about the deficiencies of the army. There was a major general of the Air Corps, Henry Arnold, known to his associates as "Hap," who was eager to convince everybody of the importance of the air arm. There was also a gruff admiral, William Leahy, then chief of Naval Operations, who spoke up for sea power.

Most of the people I had met in government up to then—Wallace, Ickes, Hopkins, the collection of congressmen—were essentially amateurs in their particular jobs; or, if you prefer to be kind, generalists. What impressed me about these military men was that while they might lack breadth of interest they were professionals, confident of their specialized knowledge. Perhaps I was being taken in, but they seemed to know what they were talking about.

It was in this new assignment that I began to write occasionally what are called in the trade "backgrounders" or "news analysis" articles, largely because spot news was spasmodic. In retrospect, they weren't exactly brilliant, but they did lead to my being asked by New York to do a series on the outlook for the rearmament program. The program was ambitious, a lot of money was being spent on it, but how successful would it be? How long would it take industry to gear up? How long would it take to build all those ships and planes Roosevelt was talking about?

These articles, published at irregular intervals, were well received by the New York editors. But one of them was to lead to the first skirmish in what was to become, for me, a running war with the U.S. Navy.

In the summer of 1939, even before Hitler's Polish sweep, I had decided to seek a reserve commission in the line of the Navy. This was before the Navy began to commission reservists wholesale, but I had discovered an obscure regulation which said that any college graduate could be commissioned after an examination in such subjects as gunnery, navigation, seamanship and Navy regulations. A reluctant four-striper (captain) in the department finally agreed to let me take the exam. I found a young Naval Academy graduate to tutor me, crammed as if I were back in Webb School, and a few months later passed. The Navy then had little choice but to commission me.

Mine was a decision I cannot explain even now, and certainly not defend. Here I was launched on a promising career, married to a wife I loved very much and with a family on the way. By becoming a reserve officer I risked it all if the nation went to war. I rationalized the decision by telling myself that, if the war came, I would be drafted or otherwise called to service anyway, quite possibly in the infantry. This way I would steal a march on other civilians. All this was, I fear, pure rationalization. Frances' brother Stanley had just graduated from Annapolis. Tommy, freshly out of the University at Chapel Hill, was already in the Marine reserve program. I was a bit jealous. I was fond of quoting Oliver Wendell Holmes's remark that one avoided the actions and passions of one's time at the peril of being judged not to have lived. I was also fascinated by ships and the sea, had been ever since reading Henty and spending a summer on a freighter. And deep down, I suspect, was the small boy still hankering "to play cowboy."

In the event it was to prove a cruel decision in its effects on my family and one that very nearly spoiled my journalistic career. But its first effect was to get me embroiled in a "conflict of interest" dispute with the Navy Department.

One of the *Journal* articles in that defense series dealt with building battleships and in particular with the time-absorbing problem of building armor plate and forging 16-inch guns. To explain it required giving some technical details. A few days after it appeared I got a call from the Navy.

There I was confronted by two stern officers, a captain and a commander, who wanted to know why I was using information I was privy to as a reserve officer for a newspaper article that cast doubt on the efficacy of the rearmament program.

I explained that I had used no such information. In fact, none of the material I had studied or had access to dealt in any way with this type of information. All of it, I said, had come out of the *Encyclopedia Britannica*, and I was able to show them volume and page. I did this, I'm afraid, not too diplomatically. I had not yet learned the proper manners for a junior officer.

That might have been the end of it except that Drew Pearson heard about it and included a short account of it in his syndicated column "The Washington Merry-Go-Round." That made me around the department, not too happily, probably the best known reserve ensign in the entire Navy.

Fortunately the admirals on Constitution Avenue had other and more important things to worry about. So did I as a journalist, for the curtain was rising on the 1940 presidential election and that was to prove more than a one-day skirmish.

4

As the 1940 presidential campaign year opened, one thing was clear. The "war issue" was going to dominate its politics. Domestic affairs—public attitudes towards the New Deal and the reaction to what had been labelled the Roosevelt recession—would play their part, but they would be overshadowed by the question of whether the country could, or should, stay out of the war. This meant, at the time, the European war. The danger in the Far East had not yet registered strongly in the public mind, or even in that of official Washington.

One thing, however, was very unclear. What would FDR do? Would he, or would he not, run again?

The Constitution permitted him to do so; there was as yet no Twenty-second Amendment. But there was an established tradition, reaching back to George Washington, that no president served more than two terms. No previous incumbent had even tried to challenge the tradition. On the other hand, no previous president had dominated his times as thoroughly as Roosevelt did the 1930s. Always a figure of controversy, he had nonetheless won in 1936 in an unprecedented landslide. While his personal popularity and his mastery of Congress had slipped somewhat, he remained the preeminent political figure. He had also showed himself a man who sometimes delighted in flouting precedent. Would he challenge this one?

Historians probing that period with access to intimate conversations in the White House have concluded that Roosevelt himself was long of uncertain mind about what he would do. "Roosevelt," writes James MacGregor Burns in his biography *The Lion and The Fox*, "was not one to make a vital political decision years or even months in advance and then stick to his decision through thick and thin. . . . [He] was genuinely unsure of his desires."

Neither I nor any other reporter of that time, however, had the benefit of the historical archives. Nor the benefit of hindsight as to what happened in that 1940 election. We were involved in nothing more than a guessing game, both as to what Roosevelt would do and what effect the "third term" issue would have on the outcome if he did run. Whether or not FDR knew what he was going to do, he enjoyed encouraging that guessing game. If nothing else it enabled him, in that phrase Lyndon Johnson was later fond of using, to keep his options open.

The result was "dope" stories galore. Many were based on the impressions the president left on a parade of visitors who had talked to him. The problem was that different visitors came away with different impressions of the president's intentions. However, others were written, as FDR might have himself put it, "off the wall."

I even essayed such a story myself. I was emboldened to try it because by this time I had established myself well enough as a reporter and had been encouraged to write background and analysis pieces on the defense program. I didn't intend it as a news story based on fact but as a kind of "think" piece to run on the editorial page or somewhere inside the paper, the way some of Barney's political pieces were handled.

The gist of it was that Roosevelt would run for a third term. It was founded on nothing more than intuition, a feeling reaching back to that very first Roosevelt press conference in the spring of 1936. What had impressed me then—and nothing since had altered the impression—was the man's supreme self-confidence and the obvious enjoyment he took in being center stage, in being president. In short, his ego. I found it hard to believe such a man would quietly step aside, especially at a moment in history when the American presidency would be at the vortex of world affairs. Nothing would deter him, I thought, so long as he saw a chance to win, and I suspected he had enough self-confidence to believe that he could.

The copy for that story has long since been lost, so I cannot say whether that view was skillfully or awkwardly presented. Probably it was overwritten. It was my first venture in expressing my opinions with no supporting "facts," and it may have read like a sophomoric exercise for the *Tar Heel*. In any event, it was destined never to see the light of day. Barney read it and dropped it in the wastebasket. His only comment was that I was still pretty big for my britches. Not until Bill Grimes killed a similar exercise in "writing off the wall" on the eve of the 1948 election was I again to feel so put down. Or, afterwards, so regretful.

But at the moment it seemed only a minor setback. I really didn't expect to be a pundit, and anyway there was enough else going on to occupy both my mind and my time.

For one thing, our first daughter was born in March 1940. She was named Frances after her mother and her grandmother, but, following a tradition for alternate generations, to avoid confusion she is called Bonnie. Her arrival meant new responsibilities but also new delights. Despite today's professed attitude toward having children, different as it is from what used to be, I doubt if there is anything more exciting for a young couple than the arrival of their first born. It changed both our lives. Shortly before, Frances had left the State Department and was thereafter to be mother and housewife until the war forced her again temporarily to seek a job. If she has regretted that domestic role, I am not aware of it.

That day—it was March 27—is frozen in memory. I had taken Frances to the hospital around breakfast time. I hung around the office for awhile and then wandered over to the Treasury press room, a block away, where a strange card game called "pitch" was underway. At that time the press room walls were lined with nude pictures—very risqué for that day (Secretary Snyder later had them removed)—and it was among them I got the word I had a new daughter. I rushed over to the hospital to stare through a large glass window at this red, squirmy little thing we had produced together. I found that all the clichés are true.

At home we converted our small dining room into a nursery and I altered my habits by arising early to watch Frances bathe and feed her, and sometimes, timidly, giving bottle and bath myself. I got adept enough at that and changing diapers so that one summer weekend I let Frances and her mother take a holiday in New York for the World's Fair while I played nursemaid. They returned to find me exhausted because I had slept little, getting up a half-dozen times each night to be sure all was well. If only I had continued to be as good a father as I began!

My journalistic life continued exciting. Notwithstanding that one rebuff from Barney I was now involved in covering events that were in the mainstream of the day's news, the growing military preparedness program under the shadow of war and the repercussions all this was having on the presidential campaign.

It was fascinating to watch Roosevelt skirt some very tricky shoals. On the one hand he seemed to be encouraging other Democrats to come forward as if the nomination were wide open. At one time or another he seemed to be giving his blessing to Secretary of State Hull, Big Jim Farley, former Governor Paul McNutt of Indiana (now head of the newly established Federal Security Agency), Governor Lehman of New York, Henry Wallace, Attorney General Robert Jackson, and his Senate leader, Alben Barkley. Or so, at least, each in turn was given to think. At the same time he was careful never to close the door on his own candidacy.

In many ways it was a sort of cat-and-mouse game, each hopeful being given a little free run before being headed off and before any ran too far. It was cruel for those so treated. It was also skillful politics. The more the field got crowded, with none able to become a clear front-runner, the easier it was for Roosevelt to position himself to step in commandingly.

The war in Europe, and the U.S. policy toward it, also presented some dangerous rocks to navigate, especially if Roosevelt was to be the candidate come November. A delicate touch was required to give aid to beleaguered Britain, to steer a safe course through French politics after the fall of France, while at the same time showing a determination to keep us out of the war. Given the public mood, Roosevelt had to run—if he ran—not as a war leader but as the leader who had and could avoid it.

Early in the year, before the Nazi invasion of Norway, he made an effort to line up some Republican support for a bipartisan foreign policy. It was premature. Senator Charles McNary of Oregon, the minority leader of the Senate, and Representative Joe Martin,

Republican leader in the House, both rebuffed him. They told reporters they viewed it as a stratagem to entangle the Republicans in the administration's policies without letting them play any part in forming those policies. Joe Martin, especially, thought it a ploy to undercut Republican criticism in the coming election. These suspicions, no doubt, were correct.

After Norway and the Nazi blitz through France the president moved more boldly. It was then, in a personal appearance before Congress, that he asked a billion dollars extra for defense and announced the goal of building fifty thousand new planes a year. Once again FDR was reading the public mood shrewdly. The military disasters for France and Britain hadn't invoked much support for aiding these countries by entering the war ourselves. The impression of unstoppable Nazi military power had, however, scared the country. The public, and therefore the Congress, was ready to support a major U.S. rearmament effort.

The president rallied this support with a fireside radio chat in mid-May in which he said that it was no time for panic but that it was a "high duty, a noble task" to build our defenses against any mistaken Axis notion that the U.S. would knuckle under to its ambitions. It was rearmament to prevent our involvement in war, so ran his theme.

This posed a neat problem for Senator McNary, Representative Martin, and other Republicans on the Hill. They had to try to picture the president as being too aggressive, even reckless, yet they dared not reject his rearmament program out of hand. Joe Martin went around grumbling about being caught between the devil and the deep.

In spite of that, a reporter could find considerable optimism among congressional Republicans about the forthcoming election. As they saw it, Roosevelt might well run aground on one or another of the war shoals. If he didn't run, there was no Democratic candidate of equal stature. If he did, the prospect was he would divide the Democrats, and the Republicans would have both the war issue and the "third term" issue. In addition, there was a recession underway and signs of public disenchantment with the New Deal.

The Democrats, after two terms in the White House, had failed to restore prosperity. There were some ten million unemployed.

Business was in a slump; the recent spurt of arms orders hadn't had time to spread its effect through the economy. The middle class, as well as the business community, was unhappy. On the left, labor was grumbling, particularly John L. Lewis, who was a magnificent grumbler. On the extreme left, the Communists and their intellectual sympathizers had turned against FDR after the Hitler-Stalin accord had temporarily put Germany and the Soviet Union on the same side.

There was also the feeling that some potentially attractive candidates were emerging in the Republican ranks. The front-runner was Thomas E. Dewey, the youthful crime-busting district attorney in New York, whom I had not met but who had caught the public imagination. There were two candidates from the congressional ranks, both of whom I had met, Senator Vandenberg of Michigan and the relative newcomer Senator Robert A. Taft of Ohio. Out on the fringes—far out on the fringes as 1940 opened— was my old acquaintance, the shooting star from Commonwealth and Southern, Wendell Willkie.

Both Vandenberg and Taft were leaders of the "peace bloc" and had become its chief spokesmen since the death of Bill Borah early in the year. Vandenberg, so far as I could tell, lacked the ambitious drive necessary to be president. Taft had the ambition (his father had been president) but he was still not too well known to the general public, and he was, besides, a rather strange, aloof figure, lacking what later was to be called charisma.

My own favorite was Willkie, in part because of my encounters with him, in greater part because most of his political ideas matched my own at that time. He was not a reactionary opposing every New Deal reform. He seemed to feel, as I did, that much of it was necessary given the time and the circumstances. If, in the next forty years, the momentum of many of these programs, including especially the deficit-spending habits, were to run wild, as I was to think they did, that still did not mean they were misplaced in the beginning. The Securities and Exchange Commission, for all that it began to act idiotically in its age, was an example. Reform and regulation of the securities markets were overdue in the early 1930s.

Nor was Willkie an isolationist. He didn't advocate direct U.S. intervention in the war but he was in favor of measures to assist

Britain and France. So was I. In late 1939 I had written an article, submitted to *Harper's* under the title "Peace It's Wonderful?" It was rejected, but it expressed my view that while peace is indeed wonderful there comes a point where it is not worth the price. Peace is easy to achieve. Britain could have had it from Hitler in 1939, as we today can with the Soviet Union. All that is necessary is for a peace-loving nation to submit to the demands of an aggressor. In 1939 and 1940, I thought, that would have meant yielding the western world to barbarism. The question was, Was peace worth such a price?

Willkie, of course, won the nomination in one of the strangest political conventions of modern times. Dewey and Taft ran out of steam. The rumpled, hoarse-voiced but articulate Willkie had that charisma they lacked; he won on the sixth ballot.

In retrospect, the Democratic convention in Chicago was a put-up show. The Democrats had no real choice except Roosevelt, and though he continued to play coy he was renominated on the first ballot. His political skill had been reaffirmed earlier when, on the eve of the Republican convention, he persuaded Henry L. Stimson and Frank Knox, Republicans both, to be secretary of war and secretary of the navy, respectively. Naturally, other Republicans cried "foul" and tried to excommunicate these apostates, but they had been outfoxed.

Also in retrospect, the election was a foregone conclusion. Willkie, shining star though he was, had no political experience whatever and his campaign was a shambles. Roosevelt made another dramatic move early in the campaign, swapping fifty old destroyers for naval base privileges from Britain in such places as Bermuda, just off the American coast. It was aid without intervention and even Willkie—at least at first—couldn't quarrel with it. Roosevelt didn't repeat his 1936 landslide, but he won by a comfortable margin as the Republican shooting star burned himself out. The only real surprise was his choice of Henry Wallace as vice-president, which startled me and shook the Democratic professionals to their roots. Even that, though, was good politics at the moment. Wallace was a favorite not only among farmers, whose votes were important, but in the liberal-left intellectual community. He also proved, surprisingly, to be a good campaigner.

Thus freed by the election from immediate political pressures,

Roosevelt moved boldly and quickly on the home war front. In September, after much debate, Congress had finally approved the first peacetime compulsory military service program in our history. It provided for a draft of young men to serve for a year's military training, its announced aim being not to enlarge the permanent army but to provide a cadre of trained soldiers "in case of emergency." Roosevelt used the draft as an excuse to call up some National Guard and Naval Reserve units, also for a year's active duty. His justification was that these reservists, exempt from the draft as such, should not be privileged. They should serve their year too if others were to be called.

One of those units called to active duty was the Naval Reserve unit of the District of Columbia.

* * * * *

Upon hearing the news I made a beeline for the Navy Department. This I had not expected, thinking that I would be called only when—or if—the country went to war. I asked for an exemption on the grounds that I had a wife and child, the same sort of exemption being at the time open to potential draftees. I was told that I could apply for a deferment, if not an exemption, but politely reminded that it would have to "go through channels." I was also told that in general it was not the policy to defer officers except in cases of extreme hardship.

I made the application and waited. I never heard anything from it, and presumably that letter is still floating around somewhere in the yellowing personnel files of the department.

That was in November and my reporting date was January 1. Frances and I had no choice now but to begin closing our lovely little house on Thirty-second Street and ship our small collection of furniture to New Bern. Alone in Washington, Frances could not work and also care for a new baby. An ensign's pay at that time, set for newly minted officers from the Academy who weren't permitted to marry, was barely two thousand dollars. It was not enough. Her parents, Jesse and Bonnie Claypoole, had agreed to take in my family for the year.

Thus one day in late December we packed our personal things in our new Chevrolet and headed south with our Bonnie quietly asleep in the back seat. We would spent Christmas in North Carolina before I returned to Washington on New Year's Day to report for duty.

It was a melancholy Christmas. I had established at least the beginnings of a career in work I enjoyed and for which I had talent. Frances and I both enjoyed our new domesticity, the little house in which we could close ourselves off as in a sanctuary. She took pleasure in the nest building, I in having it to come home to. We relished, too, the modest prosperity which had replaced that early third-floor walk up with the bathtub serving as a kitchen sink. Our nine-months-old Bonnie was a delight. There was something else. The nearly three years of marriage had deepened the relation between us; it had passed beyond youthful romance into a bonding we both knew was durable. There had been between us not even those little frictions which seem to mark the early years of many marriages. We shared a mutual happiness and, altogether, bright hopes for the future.

Now, with a rash gesture, I had blown it all. There was no escape from the trap I had laid for us both. All those romantic notions, all those brave words about sharing the action and passion of my time, had come back to haunt me. The guilt feelings were not only for myself but for Frances, who would suffer most, and for her parents who would have to squeeze another family into their home. What they thought I could only guess. But Frances never whimpered or complained. Bonnie, I hoped, was too little to notice. As for myself, I was deeply depressed.

There were only two small compensations. The *Journal* had given me a leave of absence, promising me my job when I returned. And as I took the overnight train from Raleigh to Washington, I consoled myself with the fact that my tour of duty was only for one year. Or so I thought.

Interlude

WAR AT SEA

Forsan et haec olim
meminisse juvabit.

Someday, with luck,
even these times
will be remembered
with pleasure.

> —Virgil,
> Aeneas to his crew
> in the midst of
> a storm

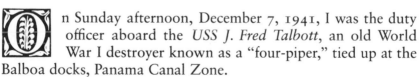n Sunday afternoon, December 7, 1941, I was the duty officer aboard the *USS J. Fred Talbott*, an old World War I destroyer known as a "four-piper," tied up at the Balboa docks, Panama Canal Zone.

In fact I was the only officer on board. The others, including the captain and the executive officer, were ashore enjoying a pleasant holiday after a week of routine maneuvering exercises in the Bay of Panama. Some of them no doubt were sipping mint juleps on the veranda of the Tivoli Hotel under the slowly revolving big-bladed electric fans. Two-thirds of the crew were also ashore, possibly enjoying the more exciting pleasures of Panama City.

On board the tropical heat and humidity were oppressive even with the portholes open. Sweat rolled down my face, chest, arms, and legs. I was sitting at the wardroom table in my skivies, my cap and a rather rumpled uniform on a chair nearby. I was writing a letter to Frances, whom I had not seen in nearly a year, about the happy prospect that in a few short weeks my year's tour of duty would be over. I was writing of a grand reunion and of seeing my Bonnie again, now a year and a half old and already walking.

A little after 1330 (1:30 P.M. civilian time) the duty radioman stuck his head in the door and said something was going on at Pearl Harbor, judging by the radio traffic. I wearily told him to keep monitoring and let me know if it was anything interesting.

About 1400 he came flying down the ladder from the radio shack and burst into the wardroom as if the devil were after him. He handed me the radio-file clipboard with a message on top.

It read: AIR RAID PEARL HARBOR X THIS IS NOT A DRILL.

It had been sent by Cincpac (commander-in-chief, Pacific Fleet) and forwarded by Navy radio Washington, information to all ships and stations. It had to be true. But I stared at it in disbelief.

The radioman and I were both paralyzed. I wiped some of the sweat off my face with a handkerchief trying to clear my head. Any such air raid had to come from the Japanese. The thought flashed through my mind that if the Japs had raided Pearl Harbor we might be next at the Canal. Obviously I should do something. But what?

I sent the radioman back to follow the traffic. In this situation it was unlikely any of the messages would need officer decoding; I put on my uniform and went out to the gangway. There I sent a messenger for the chief machinist's mate on duty. In about five minutes he arrived, sleepy-eyed and a bit grumpy at having been awakened from a nap. I told him to fire up the boilers and prepare to get underway.

He started to balk at such an unusual order from the most junior officer on the ship. I told him there was a war on and to get cracking. I was beginning to feel the authority suddenly thrust upon me.

I knew with our ancient boilers it would take an hour to get up steam unless we wanted to risk damage to the tubes, and possibly an explosion. So I next crossed over to the USS Borie, a sister ship tied up alongside flying the flag of our division commander. Several other duty officers were collected on her deck. Most, like myself, were ensigns, the lowest commissioned officer. The senior among us was a lieutenant, junior grade. We held a "council of war" and decided the best thing was to get underway and away from the docks.

I returned to my ship exhilarated. Navy regulations were quite clear that in the absence of the captain the senior officer on board was in command. That was me. I had visions of getting the ship underway myself, steaming out to meet the foe at thirty knots, undoubtedly winning a Navy Cross or something, posthumously or otherwise.

It was not to be. Word had already come from below that with the crew available we could only fire-up two boilers, giving us at most twenty knots. It also took longer than an hour to raise steam. In the meantime Lieutenant John Foster, our engineering officer, showed up, followed by Lieutenant Shallus Kirk, the executive officer. Some crew members also began to straggle aboard, alerted by announcements in all the movie houses, and elsewhere rounded up by the shore patrol.

So it was nearly 1600 by the time we cast off the lines and backed into the turning basin. As we straightened out for the channel a motor-whaleboat hove in sight with Lieutenant Commander C. M. Jensen, our captain, frantically waving. He scrambled up the portside ladder and came to the bridge still in his civilian sportswear.

Then we headed out into Panama Bay, turned right for Cape Mala and the open Pacific beyond. It was ridiculous. The *J. Fred*, built in 1918, was armed with old four-inch World War I guns that had to be aimed and ranged individually by eye, and they couldn't be elevated high enough for aircraft even if we had any antiaircraft shells for them, which we didn't. For the rest we had only a battery of infantry fifty-millimeter machine guns that couldn't have hit a plane at a thousand feet. We had no radar, not even any echo-ranging sound gear (sonar) to detect submarines. Neither had our sister ships. It was as absurd as the Charge of the Light Brigade.

Fortunately we found nothing but an empty ocean. If there were U.S. fighter planes anywhere, we never saw any. The Japs had missed their chance. If they had the ships and the wit they could have bombed the locks with impunity and put the Canal out of commission for months.

All that night and the next day our division of old destroyers steamed nervously but aimlessly well out to sea. Then we got orders to return at best speed and transit the Canal to the Caribbean side. There had been reports of German submarines in the area.

Normally a Canal transit takes seven to eight hours, deep water to deep water. When we reached the entrance we found that all other shipping had been cleared away; the locks were set for our transit, and we tore through it like epsom salts in a matter of four hours, hitting twenty knots in the cuts and sending sweeping waves on the banks from our wake. It was a record transit up to then and may still be.

We found nothing on the Caribbean side, either, save one lone freighter on innocent business. It all proved much excitement about nothing, though in fairness to those directing the operation there was no way they could be sure of that.

So it was a week before I could visit the ship's office, find a typewriter and write a letter to the Bureau of Navigation, which then handled officer personnel. Since there had been no general directive from Washington about the one-year service people, I thought I would at least try, citing my original orders, for a request to be transferred to inactive duty. By this time, however, I understood about going through channels. I took it with me to Captain Jensen for forwarding with his appropriate endorsement.

Captain Jensen looked at me as if I were crazy, which I probably was. Anyway, he quietly tore up the letter. That was strictly contrary to regulations but I knew a protest was futile. Although I never got any official extension of my one-year orders, I was in for the duration.

*   *   *   *   *

On the morning of Saturday, September 19, 1945, I sat on the bridge of the *USS Jack Miller* steaming northward from Okinawa. The sea was calm, the weather balmy. Off to starboard was the western peninsula that sticks out from the Japanese Island of Kyushu. In the morning sunshine it was lovely to look at, peaceful and quiet.

The *Jack Miller* bore little resemblance to the *J. Fred Talbott* except that both were the destroyer type designed to shepherd convoys, hunt out submarines, screen the larger ships of the fleet, serve as scouting pickets, or run the many errands admirals can think up for a navy at sea. The *Jack Miller*, built in 1943, was one of the newer design of escort destroyers. Manned by twelve to fourteen officers and a crew of two hundred, she was armed with two double purpose (air and surface) five-inch guns in her main battery, two twin forty-millimeter antiaircraft guns, a dozen twenty-millimeters and three torpedo tubes. Aft were two racks of depth charges and forward was the latest antisubmarine weapon, a "hedgehog" of ahead-firing projectiles that exploded only on contact. Powered by two Westinghouse geared turbines, steam fed by two Babcock and Wilcox superheated boilers, she could cruise comfortably at twenty-three knots and with a little coaxing turn up twenty-five or twenty-six knots. Her cruising range at most economical speed was better than five thousand miles. Below the bridge was a small but efficient combat information center, its plotting board fed by two radars and the latest underwater echo-ranging (sonar) gear for tracking enemy air, surface or submarine ships.

Not exactly a match for the newest fleet destroyers which had double the main battery armament and could turn up thirty to thirty-five knots, she was capable all the same of giving a good account of herself in action, as her sister ships had done in the North Atlantic and with Admiral Sprague's carriers in the Battle off Samar. The *Jack Miller* herself had survived weeks on the Okinawa picket line against kamikaze planes as well as two typhoons, proving herself also a good sea boat.

This Saturday morning she was bent on a different kind of duty in company with the *USS Marathon*, a troop-carrying attack transport. We were to rescue American prisoners of war. The bridge clock showed a little before 0800 when Lieutenant C. W. McKnight, the ship's executive officer and navigator, came up to me.

"Captain, if those new charts are correct that buoy up ahead marks the entrance to Nagasaki channel."

The seabuoy was clearly visible to the naked eye. Off to the right, through the binoculars, I could also see several smaller buoys outlining the channel into the harbor.

"Very well, Bill," I said. "We'll go to general quarters."

In a few moments the AHOOGA-AHOOGA-AHOOGA of the alarm sounded throughout the ship. Before it had stopped the bridge telephone talker was already ticking off the reports. "Number one gun manned and ready." "Engine room manned and ready." "Damage control manned and ready." The crew had obviously anticipated the general quarters. We must be setting a record for manning all stations.

I was pleased by that, but I also felt a bit foolish. The Japanese had announced their surrender on August 10, one day after the second atomic bomb was dropped on Nagasaki. American advance troops had landed in Japan in late August and the official surrender had been signed aboard the *USS Missouri* on September 2.

But there had been wild rumors that some militant Japanese officers, including some of the kamikaze pilots who had been suicidally hyped up, were refusing to accept the Emperor's edict of surrender. I was uncertain what reception we would find in Nagasaki where we were to pick up the American prisoners. I couldn't be sure either that the channel had been fully swept clear of Japanese mines. A little caution seemed in order, having the ship "buttoned up" and guns at the ready.

It proved an unnecessary caution. A small American minesweeper was there before us and came out to the seabuoy to serve as pilot vessel. By 0830 we were standing into the harbor, speed five knots, and any tension we had felt gave way to curiosity. A shore signal station exchanged call signs by blinking light in formal fashion. By 0912 we were anchored in seventeen fathoms in Nagasaki Ko, the inner harbor. As far as we could see all was quiet; from the ship's bridge there were no signs of the atomic bomb's devastation, or of any hostility from the few anchored Japanese ships.

A short while later Bill McKnight and I, both wearing sidearms, took the gig into the dock. We were met by a junior Japanese naval officer who bowed and saluted us impassively and took us to a small building which housed the dockmaster. There our reception was punctilious. One officer spoke a little English and there was a U.S. Marine (naturally the Marines got there first) who seemed to understand a little Japanese or at least knew what they were trying to say. We were told that a POW train would arrive at the station sometime after noon. Meanwhile, would we like to take a tour? It gave me an eerie feeling, as if to the Japanese we were casual tourists come to see the sights, not conquerers come to occupy their land. I found it hard to equate these smiling, courteous—even obsequious—men with the fierce, even cruel, foe with whom we had been at war for four years. The transformation was too sudden. I could not take it in.

A small jeeplike car with a Japanese driver took us on a bumpy road from the harbor to the city proper, or what was left of it. The city of Nagasaki sits in a natural amphitheater surrounded by high hills which hide it from the neighboring countryside. As we rounded one of the hills the view of the amphitheater suddenly opened up. The view made us gasp.

Much more has been written about Hiroshima, which I have not seen, but the sight of Nagasaki was enough to tell me instantly that the weapons I had known, destructive as they were, were primitive bows and arrows in the new age. The face of war would never be the same. Looking down the vista of the amphitheater to the other end of the city all you could see was rubble with, now and then, a standing stone or concrete pillar or some twisted steel beams that had once been a building's framework. The street we were on, which ran through the middle of the city, had been cleared enough for our car to pass. On each side the houses were flat. Here and there was a working party searching through the debris for undiscovered bodies. Old men, old women, and children—except for some soldiers we saw few people in middle adult years—were picking through the jumble of clothes, broken walls, and smashed furniture, their faces expressionless. We did not know at the time, of course, what these survivors had ahead of them in the way of delayed radioactive effects, nor did we realize that the bomb which had destroyed the city was itself a primitive weapon of the new age. We could see plainly enough, however, the devastation wrought by this one bomb in a matter of minutes. That was enough.

We stayed in the city only a half-hour and drove back to the dock in silence. Neither Bill nor I could think of anything to say.

It was late in the afternoon when the American POW train arrived. All of this group was ambulatory; the others would come later. Some of them seemed in reasonably good physical condition, some walked with difficulty; all had gaunt, drawn faces. I stood on the platform and saluted them incessantly, not knowing what else to do. Only a few returned the salute. Most of them simply stared back with vacant gazes, as if not quite comprehending what was happening. On the platform they were sorted out by some gentle Marine MPs, two doctors from the *Marathon*, and their own officers. It was late in the evening before the forty we would take aboard the *Jack Miller* were fed and bedded down in the bunks our crew gave up for them. Many, as I learned later, couldn't sleep, and the ship's pharmacist's mate was busy administering to the most restless of them.

One of our group was a Navy doctor from Florida who had been in prison camp a few miles south of Nagasaki. The day after the bomb hit, so he told us, the Japanese had asked the American camp doctors to come to the city and help out, which they did, but without of course having any idea of what they were dealing with. They treated the survivors for ordinary burns as best they could. He pressed us for news, especially for medical information, but there was little we could tell him.

The next morning, Sunday the sixteenth, we got underway to return to Okinawa where our passengers could be better attended to. As the ship turned in the harbor Japanese officers on the dock came to attention, and as we reentered the channel I saw that the signal station was now flying an American flag alongside the Rising Sun.

It has been three years and ten months since that Sunday in Panama, four years and nine months since I left Frances in North Carolina to go to sea.

*   *   *   *   *

All of those nearly five years had been spent at sea except for brief periods when I was between ship assignments. Even those periods allowed little time for leave, never more than a week or ten days, because I was involved either in commissioning new construction or attending naval schools at Key West or Miami. I never had the luxury of shore duty. As a result Frances and I had to snatch what time we could together, a few days in Miami or Boston, a few weeks in New Orleans or Norfolk, living in such drab and temporary quarters as we could scrounge on a junior officer's pay. Twice we went eighteen months without seeing each other. This was even harder on her than on me, for I at least had the excitement of the war, life at sea, and the challenge the Navy presented to civilian sailors. In those respects ours wasn't a unique story. It was repeated with variations by thousands, hundreds of thousands, of my generation who went off to fight that war in faraway places.

Before the war was over the temporary civilian-warriors became the backbone of our armed forces, land, sea, and air. Many were to acquire the skills of professionals in arms, as sergeants, chief petty officers, lieutenants, commanders, colonels, and in a few cases even generals or admirals. In my own case I was to go from the rawest reserve ensign to warship commanding officer, as the distinction between reserve and regular vanished for the duration. Had it not, the war would not have ended as soon as it did.

But that was not the case a year before Pearl Harbor. When I reported for duty aboard the *J. Fred Talbott* in January 1941, our reserve group from Washington were oddities. Captain Jensen (in the Navy every ship's commanding officer is called captain, although Jensen's rank was lieutenant-commander) did not quite know what to expect from us. Except for Lieutenant John Foster, the engineering officer, Jensen's ship had been denuded of regular personnel, officers, and crew. Two of the reserves had attended the Naval Academy although they had never before served on active duty; the other officers were graduates of ROTC programs at civilian colleges. So they had at least some familiarity with customs and regulations. I had none except what I had read in books. And thus began what might well be called "my war with the Navy."

When Captain Jensen inquired, somewhat dubiously, what qualifications I had, I said I'd passed exams in seamanship, gunnery, and navigation. He asked if I knew anything about engineering. I said, "Nothing at all, sir." In that case, he replied, "as of now you are the assistant engineering officer of the ship."

Obviously a madman. I stormed back to my cabin denouncing the stupidity of the Navy mind that would put me to work at the one thing I had no qualifications for and no aptitude for. I stormed even more when Lieutenant Foster put me in charge of a boiler room and directed me to crawl around the below-deck spaces and draw a sketch of the ship's steam lines, useful, he said, for damage control purposes. But I really cursed the Navy and all its works when I discovered the ship's plans already included these steam lines. I was no happier when Foster made me read the boiler and engine-room manuals designed for chief petty officers and then grilled me on them like a schoolboy.

It was a long time, I'm afraid, before I had sense enough to be grateful to Captain Jensen. For the eighteen months I spent on the old *J. Fred* he force-fed me, no doubt trying to make up for the madness of the Navy in ever having commissioned me in the first place. I was to serve sequentially as assistant engineering officer, torpedo officer, assistant gunnery officer, communications officer, assistant navigator, and even the wardroom mess officer. All this in addition to my regular watch officer duties, first as junior officer of the deck and then OOD at sea. It was not until in the course of time I came to command my own ships, from subchasers to an escort destroyer, that I appreciated what that "madman" did for me. Pity, I never got to tell Captain Jensen so.

After Pearl Harbor the *J. Fred Talbott* spent some weary months escorting convoys from Panama to Guantanamo or San Juan. I hope those merchant seamen drew some comfort from seeing their escort of old four-pipers weaving to and fro on their flanks. Unknown to them, however, we offered little else. Without underwater echo-ranging gear we had no way of detecting submarines until they made their presence known with a torpedo into a freighter as we shepherded our group through Mona Passage or the Jamaica Channel. Then we could only scurry about helplessly. But for those of us learning the ways of war and the sea it taught much in a hurry. With darkened ships and no radar a young watch officer had responsibilities unknown in a newsroom. Captain Jensen would be on ready-call in his night cabin, but often in the darkness decisions could not wait on him.

Two memories of that apprentice time remain vivid.

One is a night of Stygian blackness and pouring rain when I was OOD trying to keep station on the port quarter of a convoy barely visible periodically. I would close in until I could see the nearest ship, then veer out for some five minutes before turning back until again I could see the ship. Returning from one such outward swing no ship could be found, though I kept searching. The convoy was lost. I called Captain Jensen, who immediately returned us to the base course and speed while we awaited the dawn. Then we found ourselves on the *starboard* quarter of the convoy; we had somehow passed safely across it. Jensen's remark to me was his favorite expletive, "Holy Spotballs!" I was surprised he didn't take me off the watch list.

The other is of a hurricane that caught us northbound in the Caribbean, my first experience in such a storm. I remember staggering about the wallowing ship, praying that the thin hull plates, some of them twenty years old, would hold together as huge waves battered against us sweeping the decks, violently seasick for my first and only time. What the man felt who had all the responsibility for our safety, Captain Jensen, I would not understand until many years later in the Western Pacific.

Nor could I appreciate until later the value of both experiences.

In the summer of 1942 I was sent to the subchaser training school in Miami and thereafter commanded successively two of the 125-foot wooden subchasers being hurriedly built to fill the convoy escort gaps. After commissioning the second one and taking it through "shakedown," I was given one of the larger "PC boats," 175-feet, steel-hulled, diesel-powered, equipped with sonar and radar, and armed with a three-inch gun, forty- and twenty-millimeter antiaircraft guns. They carried the ahead-firing rockets (hedgehogs) as well as depth charges. With four to five officers and a crew of seventy-five, they were smart little ships with good sea-keeping qualities and provisioned for weeks at sea. Now I really felt like a "commanding officer" of a true seagoing warship.

The *PC-1262* was based at Staten Island, New York. From there we ran some convoys south to Puerto Rico or Guantanamo, but most of the time, happily for me, we weren't in formations but on detached duty far at sea and free from constant signals. The theory was we'd be so positioned in the Atlantic we could quickly respond to reports of German submarines as part of a "hunter-killer" force.

There was lots of hunting as we went dashing about the ocean, sometimes joining up with other ASW forces, in response to sub reports. But no killing, except perhaps for some unfortunate fish that gave back echoes on the sonar. For the rest, endless days of cruising in good weather and in foul. I loved it.

It was just after I left the *PC 1262* that Tommy was killed— November 22, 1943—in the invasion of Tarawa. Tommy the premature baby, the sickly child. Tommy-tag-along of our growing up years. But unlike me he had inherited the family good looks, the dark hair, the brown eyes under long eyelashes, and he was a head taller than I. Unlike me also, he'd grown into an athlete, running track, no doubt spurred to overcome his frail beginning. It was this spur, I'm sure, that led him to join the toughest branch, the Marines, long before I joined the Navy. Unlike me also, he was an extrovert, an outgoing young man who made friends easily and quickly. He was my mother's favorite. Like me, however, he had married a youthful sweetheart, Eleanor Badger of Raleigh, with never a look elsewhere. They had only a brief married life before he was ordered to the Pacific. Now he was dead at twenty-four.

At Tarawa he captained an amtrac company of the 2nd Amphibious Battalion. Somehow he led his amtrac safely across that reef that wrought so much havoc on D-day. He survived the landing only to be blown up by a mine on the last day of battle while bringing up ammunition from the beachhead. Robert Sherrod, the *Time-Life* correspondent there, noted his grave, with a cross already erected over it by men of his company. Afterwards my father decided to leave him on his island, unable to bear the emotion of homecoming for his body. He lies there still. My mother and father, like so many others of fallen soldiers, never got over it. And I have never forgotten.

My next assignment was as executive officer on the *USS La-Prade*, then under construction, sister ship to the *Jack Miller*. A bit of a comedown (number two isn't like being number one), but this new class of DEs were impressive ships. Although well equipped for antisub work, they were designed for more than merchant convoying. In the Pacific, where we were destined, they also operated with "baby" carriers, served as antiaircraft screening ships and accompanied landing forces. This assignment meant I'd have a month at the Norfolk Naval Base, where it was my job as exec to get the crew organized and trained. That would give me some time with Frances and Bonnie.

Norfolk was not as attractive as New Orleans had been when during the commissioning of the *USS PC-1262* we had spent some weeks there, but any place we could all be together was rare and welcome. Although Frances would later spend a few days with me in Boston when the *LaPrade* after shakedown had some maintenance work at the Navy Yard (a memorable visit because nine months later our second daughter Eleanor was born), the Norfolk interlude would prove the last time the whole family would be together until after V-J day. C'est la guerre.

From Boston the *LaPrade* headed for Panama, San Diego, Pearl, and the Western Pacific. For me it was a new and different kind of duty, operating with fleet units rather than merchant convoys. I remained with the *LaPrade* until, in the fall of 1944, I received surprise orders to relieve the commanding officer of the *Jack Miller*. That began the last and in many ways the most interesting phase of my naval interlude, from the Palau Islands to Okinawa to Nagasaki.

*   *   *   *   *

Until this point my wartime adventures had been not so much with the enemy as with the sea and the Navy itself. In the Caribbean and the Atlantic the potential for danger, and the sense of danger, were ever present, but in fact I had never met an enemy submarine, ship, or aircraft. What I had encountered were two hurricanes, much stormy weather on the North Atlantic, and some unhappy admirals.

With my first command, that wooden subchaser, I managed to lose a whole convoy between Galveston and New Orleans one night in a torrential downpour. Due to a confusion of signals the convoy changed course without my knowledge, and at that time I had no radar. The result was that the convoy went one way, I another. The admiral in charge of the Gulf Sea frontier—or at least his aides—voiced some disapproval.

Then with the *PC-1262* I ran into a Miami Beach causeway which proved immovable and put the ship into drydock. For that I got a "long green board"—a board of investigation, that is. Fortunately the investigation disclosed a mechanical failure, so that the ship couldn't reverse engines in spite of all my frantic orders. Acquitted, therefore, but with the incident still on my record.

My most famous—or infamous—encounter with the Navy came when I was exec on the *LaPrade*. I am, so far as I know, the only officer to stand naked on the quarterdeck while being dressed down by an admiral.

It happened this way: we had arrived at Pearl Harbor for a one-day turnaround which involved loading tons of stores before proceeding to Ulithi atoll. Early that morning (July 26, 1944) we received notice from ComDesPac (Commander Destroyers Pacific Fleet) that the commander-in-chief, President Roosevelt, would be arriving at 1300 on the *USS Baltimore* for a conference with Nimitz and MacArthur. All vessels would man the rail, crews in white, to salute the president.

Carl Fellows, my skipper, cheerfully told me to "carry on" and took off for the officers club. I "turned to" all hands in work clothes to load stores until 1130 when I sent them to chow down, scrub, and shift into whites. Meanwhile I put the officer-of-the-deck, a young ensign, in whites. A little before noon I was showering when the ensign stuck his head in the door and said there was an admiral on the quarterdeck to see me. I told him to show the admiral into the wardroom, offer him some coffee and say I'd be there in a few minutes.

Less than a minute later the shaking ensign returned and said, "Mr. Royster, that admiral wants to see you *right now!*"

I grabbed a towel, picked up my cap on the way through the wardroom to the deck and, still dripping suds, saluted. The first question was whether we had received the all-ships notice. I said yes sir. The second question was, where was the captain? When I said ashore, I was curtly informed that both the captain and I were to report to ComDesPac's office at 1400 to explain our failure to carry out orders.

As matters turned out, the *Baltimore* didn't dock until 1500 (three o'clock) by which time the crew of the *LaPrade* was in whites manning the rail as directed. A four-striper came by to check us out but his good report didn't alter the admiral's mood. He lit into Captain Fellows, not me, but when Carl tried to explain that I was a competent officer, had in fact carried out the orders, and had been recommended for a command of my own, the admiral replied, "Never while I'm Comdespac."

My performance on the quarterdeck, incidentally, had been observed by the goggle-eyed crews of the *LaPrade* and two destroyers alongside. Happily no one thought to take a picture, but I was the talk of the base, or at least that part of it where destroyer-men gathered. Even now I get letters from people who remember.

So you can see why I was surprised by those orders to command the *Jack Miller*. But by that time, as I learned later, there had been a change in admirals at destroyer headquarters.

I proudly took command in December 1944 and would stay with the ship until she was laid up a year later in San Diego. In between there would be different kinds of adventures.

*   *   *   *   *

It may be difficult to believe, especially by those whose war experience came later in Korea and Vietnam, but there was a curious sense of guilt among many of us at this war far from home. There certainly was with me. Frances was always cheerful in her letters but I knew that those at home were rationed on meat, on butter, on many other necessities. I knew that even now with a lieutenant commander's pay she couldn't have made ends meet had she not gone back to work as a secretary. It could not have been easy either for Jesse and Bon Claypoole to have to squeeze in their daughter and granddaughter, although I never heard from them any recriminations. The guilt was that, in the Navy at least, we lived well except briefly when we missed a rendezvous with the heavily laden supply ships, good steaks, for instance, were no rarity in our mess for officers or crew. I couldn't avoid the feeling that, by joining the Navy in a spirit of adventurousness, I had somehow shirked my responsibility for my wife and daughter.

The truth is, whatever that says about me, I enjoyed the Navy, especially after I left the old *J. Fred* behind. There is no job in the world, bar none, that can match being commanding officer of a Navy ship in wartime. You are your own boss in a way that no commander of a battalion or even a regiment can be in the land forces. Admirals can send you orders to go here or there, do this or do that; how you do it is your own affair. Within the ship you are a little dictator, made so by Navy regulations and the fact that your ship is an island all its own. If I said "left rudder" the *Jack Miller* went left, no questions raised. As captain I had only to push a button for coffee or a sandwich at any hour, day or night. No meal in the wardroom would start until I was present unless I gave permission. If I left the bridge and stepped out of officer country, someone would call "attention on deck" and all would stay at attention until I said, "Carry on!" It was heady enough to give me understanding of how power, even in small doses, can corrupt.

The price of power, of course, is responsibility. A ship captain's daily working hours, even in wartime, aren't onerous in number. A well-crewed ship for the most part runs itself, and what administration is needed falls on the executive officer. On many days the captain can doze in his bridge chair, or lie abed if he prefers. It's when something happens—an enemy alert, a fleet maneuver, a storm or some other emergency—that a captain "earns his pay," in the navy saying. Then it is that lives and the safety of the ship depend on whether he says go right or go left. The tension can be as great (at least for me) at times when the captain stands quietly on the wing of the bridge and lets the watch officer maneuver the ship. Day or night, nothing relieves the captain of his responsibility.

I enjoyed all that part too. Though there were times when the tension put knots in the pit of my stomach, even that could be exhilarating. There was a challenge in working as plane guard for carriers, mostly skippered by inconsiderate captains who never told their escort what they were going to do next. To put your ship alongside a huge tanker, or perhaps a carrier, and keep her there with the sea roaring between the ships while you suckle fuel oil across the narrow gap is a harrowing experience. Afterwards come the sense of accomplishment and the pride that your tension (you hope) didn't show to the crew.

The same is true in the dark of a night running down an underwater sound contact or watching radar "bogeys" turn into kamikazes. It's also true in the midst of a typhoon.

The first of the vicious typhoons occurred in December 1944, wreaking havoc on Halsey's Third Fleet, sinking three destroyers, severely damaging others, with a loss of eight hundred lives. I missed that because I was far to the south, in Kossol Roads, Palau, assuming command of the *Jack Miller*. The second major one, in June 1945, was a different matter.

We were then part of the screening force for the Support Groups under Rear Admiral Donald Beary, which included tankers and supply ships for the Okinawa force, again under Halsey's overall command. On June 4, while fueling operations were underway, the sea had been heavy with increasing winds. A number of fuel lines ruptured as destroyers tried desperately to keep closed-up to their suckling mothers. Fueling was suspended and early the following morning course was changed to due north, then westerly, unhappily leading directly toward the storm center. This time no ships were sunk, but the *John Rodgers* lost steering and wallowed helplessly for hours; *Maddox* reported rolling sixty degrees, almost on her beam. The cruiser *Pittsburgh* lost her bow.

Although many have tried, no one can convey to landsmen the fury of a cyclonic storm at sea. Waves rise fifty to sixty feet from crest to trough, towering over a destroyer's bridge, with wind velocities more than seventy miles an hour. To add to the maneuvering problem, wind and sea may come from different directions. Early in the morning of the fifth, though I didn't know it at the time, we passed through the eye of the storm and the signal came to "proceed independently," meaning each captain should do what he thought best to save his ship.

For the first time I could sympathize with Captain Jensen those years ago in our Caribbean hurricane. Storms I had met before, but nothing like this. Hour by hour I knew little to do but slow down to bare steerageway and pray that those distant shipbuilders had built strong and true. Because rain shut out visibility from our open bridge, I spent most of my time in CIC watching the radar plot because no ship was keeping formation and I was as fearful of collision with a neighbor as of the sea itself.

Doctrine at the time was to meet the sea head-on, a sound principle for heavy merchant ships or battleships. But at the time the sea was on our port quarter. Question: To turn around or not? I elected to keep the sea on the quarter, terrified of the effect of a huge beam sea while turning. That proved the best decision. A sister ship that did try to reverse course had her port side stove in, topside near the radio room. Our only damage was to the motor whaleboat riding in davits. Since good fortune attended, I look on it now as a memorable adventure. But not then.

Later I learned that Admiral Halsey was severely reprimanded for want of respect for the sea; Admiral Nimitz reminded him his two typhoons caused more damage to the fleet than any enemy action since the Battle of Savo Island. Halsey wasn't the "hero" to his ship captains that he was to the public at home. Most of us thought Admiral Spruance, who alternated in fleet command, the more levelheaded and capable commander.

As it turned out, we would have one more skirmish with a typhoon in August at Okinawa. The *Jack Miller* was anchored in the east harbor, known by then as Buckner Bay, when we got sudden orders to get underway and proceed to sea. We had to leave an officer and two crewmen ashore while we headed eastward around the southern tip of Okinawa into the China Sea. This time the crew ashore fared worse than we; the high winds swept away a Quonset hut in which they had taken refuge. We had a rough two days amid scattering ships but this time we were on the fringes of the storm out of the most perilous seas.

Yet those times, too, could afterward be remembered with the pleasure that comes from perils surmounted. War is a tragedy for the dead and the maimed, for those at home who loved them when they were young and whole. But for those who survive, terrible though it may be to say so, the experience is not only unforgettable but also, for many, unmatched by what life delivers thereafter. Just sit and listen while old soldiers and sailors of my war gather. They come with their wives and their walking canes, and their eyes light up as they talk of how it was. That from generation to generation, from the soldiers of Napoleon to the veterans of Normandy or Okinawa, war can so move men—that is its true terror.

*   *   *   *   *

For the "small boys" on the Okinawa picket line—the Navy's affectionate terms for all the destroyer-type ships—the nights of July 1945 were quieter than most. The heaviest attacks from Japanese suicide planes—the kamikazes—had occurred in April through June as Japan tried desperately to halt the American invasion of the Ryukyus, so close to her heartland. On land Okinawa itself had been declared "secured" by the end of June, meaning that organized resistance had been overcome though sporadic fighting continued. Nonetheless the young and mostly untrained Japanese pilots weren't ready to quit, and they continued their one-way flights to death right up to the day of surrender.

The *Jack Miller* had been on and off Okinawa since May on daylight forays escorting a lone tanker or some LSTs. The kamikazes came mostly at night, and then we would be anchored in one of the harbors, Kerama Retto or Buckner Bay, shielded by American night fighters. Frequently there would be an "airflash red," and we could hear the sound of gunfire and the voice radio crackling with action reports as we followed the "bogeys" on radar. Half the night would be spent at general quarters, but we were never attacked.

So it wasn't until July, when we were assigned regular picket duty to fill depleted ranks, that we first directly encountered Japanese planes. The first time we were attacked, the kamikaze was just a bright spot on the radar; the plane itself we never saw in the darkness, although it passed across our bow and dropped one bomb. About 0200 on a later night we had a closer call. This time the plane dropped several bombs off our stern (the after-gun crew counted three to four explosions) and passed over headed toward

In full dress for opening night at the
Metropolitan Opera, New York City,
1959.

Frances Royster, 1959—*photo
by Edward Thayer Monroe.*

Dinner at the Istanbul-Hilton, Istanbul, Turkey, 1959.

THE WHITE HOUSE

WASHINGTON

June 3, 1960.

PERSONAL AND CONFIDENTIAL

Dear Mr. Royster:

Rarely if ever have I found so much to command my approbation and applause as did your editorial page of June first. The article by Henry M. Wriston and the editorial entitled "The Pursuit of Unhappiness" are unusual, timely, and tightly reasoned.

For some reason, possibly just ignorance, I have never been a regular reader of your newspaper. But I assure you that if it makes a habit of producing articles of this value, I shall make it my business to see it regularly.

Sincerely,

Dwight D. Eisenhower

Mr. Vermont Royster,
Editor,
THE WALL STREET JOURNAL,
44 Broad Street,
New York, New York.

PERSONAL AND CONFIDENTIAL

Letter from President Dwight D. Eisenhower, June 3, 1960.

Chess match with Russian friend aboard boat on the Volga River, USSR, June 1962.

Dancing with a "Georgia Belle," wife of a local Soviet journalist, Tbilisi, USSR, July 1962.

Meeting with Chairman Khrushchev, Moscow, 1962. *Left to right:* Paul Miller, Vermont Royster, Lee Hills, interpreter, Khrushchev.

At the White House, August 2, 1962. *Left to right:* Walker Stone, Paul Miller,
President John F. Kennedy, Lee Hills, Vermont Royster
—*photo by United Press International.*

Telecast, "CBS Reports," June 3, 1963. Discussing tax cut with economist
Walter Heller (*at table, right*). Harry Reasoner (*center*) is moderator.

Editor at work in *Wall Street Journal* office—*photo by Marvin Koner*.

With President Lyndon B. Johnson and Alan L. Otten (*left*) at the White House, 1964.

The trawler yacht *Covenant III* at Morehead City, N.C.

Caught in an argumentative mood, Center for Strategic Studies, Georgetown University, Washington, 1978, with former Secretary of the Treasury Henry C. Fowler (*center*).

With Vice Premier Keng Piao, Peking, People's Republic of China, 1978
—*photo by Gordon R. Converse, Christian Science Monitor.*

Expressing thanks to entertainment troop from the Sixth Tank Division, Peking, 1978.

"The Thinker," 1972—*photo by Andy Howell, Charlotte Observer.*

On the bridge of the *SS President Monroe*, in Pacific Ocean, 1977—*photo by P. Barrett.*

the island. We saw the plane when it was about two thousand yards abeam, but as far as we could tell our guns left it unscathed, although a few minutes later there was another big explosion in its direction with a ball of fire on the empty ocean.

The *Jack Miller* had a simple fire-control system to direct all of her antiaircraft fire but, unlike the systems on fleet destroyers, it wasn't connected to the radar. You had to be able to see the target, and I wouldn't give a "commence firing" until we could. That would only pinpoint our position better, something I didn't welcome.

Again in the early morning of August 6 (it must have been about the same time the *Enola Gay* was taking off for her flight to Hiroshima) there were air raids from the north, approximately ten to eleven planes which scattered. We were illuminated by three flares, which made firing possible, but if we were the target we were missed.

On August 10 the Japanese decided to surrender, and on the fifteenth General MacArthur directed all their armed forces to lay down their arms. There were a few more desultory raids (on August 13 the *LaGrange* was bombed), but for the *Jack Miller* the shooting was over.

There hadn't been much of it for us. Through most of the spring as the preparation for Okinawa went forward we were attached to the support force which kept well out to sea, carrying supplies for the Fifth and then the Third Fleet; they were the same ships, only the fleet number changed as Admirals Spruance and Halsey swapped jobs. Once a task unit we were with was shadowed by two Japanese patrol craft, but they never closed to gun range.

The only other time we came under fire was early in the Okinawa operation when, calmly cruising down the side of the island, I was startled to see two shell splashes on the landward beam. We started dodging, but so far as I could tell the Jap battery wasn't serious. Anyway, it made no effort to correct fire and follow up. Our own firing before Okinawa was limited to an afternoon's shore bombardment on Orukuizo Island, one of the Palau Islands, back in February. We lobbed twenty-four five-inch shells· and about one hundred forty-millimeter shells at what was reportedly an artillery battery annoying our ground troops. Lots of fire and smoke, but real damage done unknown.

Such was my war, from Panama to V-J day. Altogether, five years at sea; some excitement, much boredom, no glory. After that came Nagasaki, one more trip to Japan to pick up American prisoners at Sasebo, and then the long voyage home—Guam, Pearl, and San Diego.

*   *   *   *   *

On that voyage for the first time we had the whole of Escort Division Sixty-five in company—the *Strauss*, the *Corbesier*, the *Conklin*, the *McCoy Reynolds*, and my former ship, the *LaPrade*, now with a new skipper. We were back in the peacetime Navy, steaming in line abreast with running lights and the novelty of nighttime movies on the stern.

It was a lazy time. No more sunrise general quarters, no more sudden shattering of the AHOOGA-AHOOGA-AHOOGA in the middle of the night—only a few drills during the day, more for form than anything else; the crew as well as I knew we were headed for mothballs. I had almost nothing to do but read, remember, and wonder about the uncertain future.

The memories reached back to the beginnings when the Navy could spare only a few ancient four-pipers, without proper guns or gear, to shepherd merchant convoys through sub-infested waters. That contrasted with a day in the spring of 1945 when, as the *Jack Miller* awaited its turn for a tanker, the sea around me was full of ships as far as the eye could see, an armada such as there had never been and would never be again. There would be, I supposed, a role for the Navy in the next war—but not for such a Navy as this. The atom bomb had changed everything. Whatever else it meant, it meant never again so many ships gathered so close together to be obliterated in one stroke. It would be a Navy of ships, perhaps, but not of a fleet at sea.

Mingled in were special memories of the old *J. Fred*, my first ship, and those who served with me. I lost track of some of them. But Captain Jensen went on to command a squadron of destroyers. Shallus Kirk and Robert Winkle, already lieutenants then, rose to be four-stripe captains. Samuel Spencer, once and future lawyer, was in command of the escort destroyer *Oberrender* when she was sunk at Okinawa. Ulysses Brooks Carter (Nick Carter, naturally), my cabin mate, stayed with the *J. Fred* when she was converted to a fast transport and rose to command; he lost her stern to a kamikaze when he zigged instead of zagged. Altogether the Navy was well served by that little band.

Meanwhile, much had changed at home. My brother Tommy had been killed. My father, aging, was not well. Frances' father, Jesse, had died, and so I would never have a chance to tell him of my gratitude for sheltering my family. Bonnie was now five years old, with a father who could only be a dim memory. I had a new daughter, Eleanor, six months old, whom I had never seen.

What would the homecoming be like? As between Frances and myself I had no worries; we had known each other so long, shared so much, there would be no unravelled seams as we rejoined our lives together. With Bonnie I was less certain; I had lost the bonding years. With Eleanor I could only wait and see.

The great uneasiness was over returning to civilian life. Barney Kilgore had said my job was waiting. But how would I fit into it after five years? For the moment I felt myself a naval officer, not a journalist, but that career was over and I wasn't sure how well I could pick up the other. It would be like beginning all over again.

These were not unusual feelings. There were more than fifteen million of us coming home to the same uncertainties; we could only be thankful we weren't among the million who were returning wounded or wouldn't return at all. We could hardly be cheered by the talk of troubles, economic and otherwise, that would come with demobilization.

San Diego gave us a ceremonial welcome. Two weeks later I took my last walk down the *Jack Miller*'s gangway, saluted the colors and paused for a last look. She still looked fit and ready for sea, a beautiful ship.

Riding the train on the slow trip across the continent I had no idea what the future might be. But there was one thing nobody could ever take away from me. I had had the honor of commanding a ship in the last of the world's great navies.

PART THREE

Washington Again

People only leave Washington
by way of the box—
ballot or coffin.

—Claiborne Pell, United States
Senator from Rhode Island

WASHINGTON AGAIN

he Washington of 1946 bore little resemblance to the Washington I had left in 1940.

When I had covered Capitol Hill in prewar days I had barely been aware of Harry Truman, a relatively junior and generally undistinguished senator. He chaired no committee and served on only one of major importance, Appropriations, where he was well down the seniority list. I had spoken to him once or twice but I thought of him, if at all, as a rather unprepossessing product of old-fashioned machine politics, the Pendergast machine in Kansas City. He registered low on my memory scale. Now he was president of the United States.

I knew, of course, that he had been chosen as Roosevelt's vice-president in 1944 when Henry Wallace—not to my surprise—had been dropped. I gathered this was largely because of Senator Truman's investigation of war industries, though I was hazy on the details. Roosevelt's death had come while I was at sea in the Western Pacific and I had wondered what sort of president Harry Truman would make, but I had been too busy to give it much thought.

Many other familiar faces were gone or had changed jobs, to be replaced by others. Former Senator James Byrnes was secretary of state. Robert Patterson was secretary of war; James Forrestal, secretary of the navy; Tom Clark, attorney general. Clinton Anderson sat in Henry Wallace's old seat at Agriculture while Wallace— to my astonishment—was secretary of commerce. Henry Morgenthau would soon be replaced by Fred Vinson at the Treasury. Except for Wallace, the new faces were more or less strangers to me; Patterson, Anderson, and Forrestal I knew not at all. Harold Ickes was still at the Interior Department, as curmudgeonly as ever, but he wouldn't be for long.

The government structure had also undergone many changes. Gone were the old familiar agencies, WPA, PWA, and the like. Now I would have to grapple with the Office of War Mobilization and Conversion, the Office of Emergency Management, the Wage

Stabilization Board, and the Office of Price Administration. They in turn, along with President Truman, had to grapple with new problems. When I had gone to sea the country was still in the grip of the depression even after seven years of the New Deal; government efforts had been aimed at creating jobs, raising prices and wages. The war solved the job problem. Its aftermath, as a result of the huge spending, was the problem of holding down prices and wages. A heretofore almost unknown word had appeared in the political vocabulary: inflation.

Much had also changed at the *Journal*. Barney Kilgore had gone to New York, first as managing editor and then as vice-president and in effect the company's acting president. Bill Grimes was now the paper's editor. Bill Kerby, he who got my byline initials backwards, had moved up first to managing editor and then to executive editor. The current managing editor was a young man about my age, Buren McCormack, who had been a banking reporter in my earlier time.

The Washington bureau was almost completely new. Out of a staff of twelve, only two old-timers remained, Charlie Sterner, the perennial fixture as office business manager, and George Bryant, my old Hill colleague who was now chief of the bureau. The *Journal*, as promised, gave me my job back. But I found myself amid strangers while the stay-at-homes, as I saw it, had moved upwards and onwards during the war. Even those who had left the *Journal*, like Ken Kramer, had switched to better jobs elsewhere as the Washington press corps (including radio and magazines) had multiplied. The list of names in the *Congressional Directory* took up twice as many pages.

Thus, as with many thousands of others, mine was a discouraging homecoming. For those who had gone to war very young there were compensations; colleges all over the country were jammed with veterans who could finish their education at government expense. For those of us older, who had spent some years working before the war and already had families, it was different. We all had the feeling that we had lost years out of our career; in my case it was five years, the early five years so important for building a career foundation. It was hard for me to see where I was going with so many of my stay-at-home contemporaries already filling the higher posts. The truth is all of us home from the war were frightened by the problem of picking up the threads of civilian life again. The movie *The Best Years of Our Lives* spoke eloquently for us. Many had left relatively modest positions in civilian life, had in the Army or Navy gained responsibility and authority. It was hard to go back. It was discouraging for me to become again just another reporter after having commanded a ship at sea. Besides, I was flat broke. For months I had to live in a Washington rooming house while Frances and the girls remained in New Bern. My "civies" were navy blues with the gold stripes removed. I could afford nothing else. Now I had to start all over again.

Not all among us could make the adjustment; some succumbed to drink, others just drifted. It would have been more difficult for me had it not been for Frances. She was no longer the teenager who had captivated me, nor even the young wife and mother I left behind in 1940. Though still trim of figure, large brown eyes dominating a piquant face, she was a mature woman who for five years had had to cope by herself with all the home problems. Fortunately for me, we had behind us fifteen years for love to grow, nearly a decade of marriage which had survived the separations. Out of those eyes shown patience, understanding, and trust. If my homecoming was troubled, she made it nonetheless one of warmth and welcome. That made possible not only my transition from war to peace but all that came thereafter.

Of course I too had changed. I was now nearly thirty-two years old, and if I as a journalist was no longer "a young man of promise," I was myself more mature and had acquired a new self-confidence. For one thing, I was no longer awestruck by the politically famous, cabinet officers, senators, or presidents. My views of the world, including my political views, were also different.

I had become disillusioned with the man I had earlier so much admired, FDR. I was shocked by the blunders, as I saw them, he had made in shaping the postwar world. Here I and millions of others had spent those best years of our lives—and many, like Tommy, had lost their lives—to defeat the Axis powers in the belief that it would end the barbarism that had threatened to engulf the world. As to the rightness of that cause I had no doubts and was proud of my small part in it. But we had won that struggle at such a cost only to find, once again, that we had lost the peace.

I needed only to look at the map. Despite the warning of Churchill and others, Roosevelt had arranged the division of Germany; worse, his plan left Berlin itself divided and sitting like an island in the midst of the Russian army. Beyond that, Roosevelt had delivered half of Europe to the Soviet Union. In the Far East he had acquiesced in the division of Korea, been so beguiled by Chiang Kai-shek that he had delivered China to Chairman Mao. I was not so prescient as to foresee it would take a generation to repair that China damage or that Roosevelt's peace plans would soon lead to other armed clashes. I could see, even amid the euphoria of victory, the seeds of trouble. I didn't think history would forgive Franklin Roosevelt his postwar decisions, nor has it.

For the present, Truman was caught in a double-bind. He could not alter the decisions made at Yalta when he himself met Stalin at Potsdam. Domestically he could not resist the political pressures to dismantle the armed forces; a war-weary people wanted their soldiers home. By midsummer 1946 the once most powerful army in the world had been reduced to barely three divisions in any kind of combat readiness. The Navy still had ships, but they were at half-complement, as I knew from bringing the *Jack Miller* back to San Diego the previous fall. So many of her crew had already been discharged that she couldn't have fought a destroyer from the Honduran navy. Even so, demobilization didn't go fast enough to satisfy the civilian soldiers or their families.

Demobilization was only one of the controversies swirling around the new president. A nation that had spent four years of wartime austerity had had enough. Returning veterans (myself included) were disgruntled by the housing shortage; almost no new housing had been built from 1941 to 1946. Consumers who had been forced to save during the war for want of anything to buy now felt that money burning holes in their pockets. There was a rising clamor for a quick return to production of civilian goods, which couldn't have been satisfied even if Truman had a clear policy for doing it, which he didn't. Such goods as were available were sky-high in price compared to prewar standards. That made price controls another explosive issue. As is always the case with inflation, the choice was keeping nominal prices down with controls, thus driving goods to the black market, or letting the prices rise. Either choice meant political troubles.

This eruption of postwar impatience also led to strikes everywhere. Early 1946 saw a strike at Western Union so you couldn't send a telegram, at Western Electric which kept the phone company from meeting new demands, among meat packers, among auto workers, to mention only a few. On a visit to the *Journal*'s New York office in late February it seemed to me as if there were picket signs everywhere. Some estimates put the number of people out of work because of strikes at more than a million and a half.

*   *   *   *   *

My first view of the man at the center of this vortex, of Harry Truman as president, came at a press conference that winter of 1946. As with that first Roosevelt press conference ten years earlier, I was there unofficially. George Bryant, my new bureau chief, covered it. I went out of curiosity.

I can't remember now the date or what transpired. I do remember coming away with two strong impressions. The first, naturally, was the contrast between this man and Roosevelt, or at least the Roosevelt I remembered. Truman didn't exude the same sense of self-confidence and strength. He was still in his period of humility, being almost apologetic at times. The other impression, perhaps seemingly contradictory, was the difference between Harry Truman as president and Truman the relatively obscure senator of 1939 or 1940. He wasn't yet the figure he was to become, but for all that air of humility a new feistiness showed through. Many of his answers to questions were short sentences, sometimes just a yes or a no, uttered in a quick, curt manner. It would be awhile before I could really think of him as president, and even longer before I came to have a grudging admiration for him.

Meanwhile, George had assigned me to the Treasury and the Federal Reserve Board. It was an important assignment in the bureau, but for me it was still going-around-again. I had covered these at least briefly five years earlier.

There was nothing else to do, however, except to tackle the assignment with as much energy as I could muster, to show the paper (and myself) that I was still a competent reporter. That wasn't easy at first because sitting around press rooms seemed a tame comedown after the excitement of a wartime command.

There was another difficulty. I was baffled at first by the *Journal*'s change of format and its way of handling the news. Barney

Kilgore had banished most "spot news" from the front page except for the two-column "What's News" summary. His idea was to make the *Journal*'s front page different from any other newspaper, distinctive both in appearance and in content. Each day the makeup would be the same, regardless of the day's news. The two outside columns, right and left, would be devoted to situation stories developed in depth. They could be tied to the day's immediate news, but they did not have to be; they could deal instead with some current development in business, government, or foreign affairs in which the background would be thoroughly explored, the aim being to make news developments more understandable to the reader. There would be no pictures used and the front page headlines would always be only one-column wide.

Basically that's the format now so familiar to *Journal* readers. But at the time not even Barney was clear what constituted a "leader," as those two major stories were called around the shop. Certainly the staff wasn't. There was a great deal of improvisation, and there were days when it was a scramble for the New York editors to find stories that fit this ill-defined specification. No one realized, except perhaps Barney in his dreams, that what was being done would mark the beginning of the first national newspaper, to be in time the paper with the largest circulation in the country. It would be several years before the paper reached even a hundred thousand circulation.

Nonetheless, if "interpretative" stories or something of that kind was what Kilgore wanted, I would try to supply them. I began to importune Secretary Vinson at the Treasury and Federal Reserve Chairman Marriner Eccles for visits, explaining that I didn't so much want an "interview" for the record as a visit "just for conversation" that would inform me and that I might make use of on my own. Sometimes I succeeded.

Fred Vinson was a big man with a craggy face over a deep wattle. A native of Kentucky, he had served in Congress off-and-on from 1923 to 1938; later he had been a federal judge and director of the Office of War Mobilization before President Truman, an old friend, appointed him treasury secretary. In Congress he had been considered an expert on taxes and fiscal policy. His manner was courtly, his speech measured and marked by something of a drawl. This manner and appearance made him an impressive figure.

At the Treasury he played a major role in launching the World Bank and the International Monetary Fund. The World Bank and the IMF had been designed at the Bretton Woods conference during the war, the first to be an international lending agency and the latter a sort of regulator of international currencies. Both were activated in 1946 at another conference in Savannah, Georgia, which I was sent to cover and which in the event affected my relations with Vinson and my standing in the *Journal*.

Until Savannah my relations with Vinson had been somewhat distant but pleasant enough. At that conference, as it turned out, there wasn't much real news in the formal communiqués. So I wrote some background pieces explaining the functions of the new agencies, which the New York editors liked and ran in full. Also, in talking with the delegates informally around the swimming pool or at cocktail time I found that many of them from the smaller countries, particularly in Latin America, were ruffled by what they thought the high-handed manner of Harry White, the assistant secretary who played a prominent part at Bretton Woods as well as at Savannah. These delegates grumbled that they were little more than rubber stamps for the U.S. I thought their disgruntlement made an interesting story from an otherwise dull conference.

Secretary Vinson didn't think so. Neither did Harry White or Will Clayton, the State Department's representative at the conference. Vinson, White and Clayton all let me know their opinions quite forcefully. The confrontation, as sometimes happens to reporters, was a step forward in my relationship with Vinson. At least thereafter he paid me more attention. It was also my introduction to Harry Dexter White, later to be a controversial figure accused of being a spy (today the word would be "mole") for the Soviet Union.

From my first meeting with Harry White I thought he must be a man of ability because he certainly didn't rise on his personality; he simply wasn't an attractive person. I thought him arrogant. But he rose pretty far, leaving the Treasury to become executive director of the Monetary Fund he had helped create. When he was accused of being part of the Alger Hiss–Whittaker Chambers Communist apparatus I was surprised, even though the evidence for it was strong. He just didn't seem to have the smoothness you'd expect from an infiltrator, at least as they are portrayed in spy novels.

The truth about White will probably never be known because he died (possibly a suicide) while his investigation was still pending.

My relations with Marriner Eccles at the Fed, while prickly at times, remained generally cordial. Eccles was a Mormon banker from Utah, formerly president of the First National Bank of Ogden. Since he had never been actively involved in politics, I'm not quite sure why FDR picked him in 1936 to chair the Reserve Board except that Eccles thought little of the Eastern "banking establishment" and neither did Roosevelt. During the depression he'd opposed the Hoover monetary policies, which he thought too restraining. During the thirties he was an "easy money" man, though later he was to advocate more restraint and ultimately to clash with President Truman over monetary policy.

Eccles could be sharp-spoken, and this led to an amusing encounter. I had an appointment with him one afternoon and Bill Grimes had picked that morning to write a highly critical editorial about Fed policy in general and Eccles' role in particular. That sort of thing often happens to Washington reporters.

I knew Eccles was in a bad mood the moment I entered his office. Before I could ask a question, or even say "good morning," he lashed out at me. I tried to explain I wasn't responsible for the *Journal*'s editorial opinions—in fact, as is the wont of Washington reporters, I did the best I could to disown my editor. But Eccles wouldn't be turned aside.

"Of course I personally don't care what *The Wall Street Journal* says," he began, with a wave of dismissal. "Nobody pays any attention to its reactionary opinions. I don't think many of its readers even bother to read the editorials. I don't. I know Grimes and his views haven't changed since the Coolidge administration."

He went on this vein at some length, repeatedly avowing his disinterest in anything the *Journal* had to say about anything.

Then there came a pause in the diatribe. He leaned forward in his chair and pounded the desk until his paperweight bounced.

"But it makes me *so goddam mad*!" he exploded.

After he calmed down, we went on talking about whatever we were talking about, and quite pleasantly. His explosive remark, however, was a dead giveaway. He wouldn't have cared if he really thought nobody paid any attention to the *Journal*. That gave me a clue to the paper's growing influence. I was also intrigued for the first time by the possibilities of exercising influence and getting attention through editorial comments, as distinguished from news reporting.

Actually I thought Bill Grimes a little unfair to Eccles. I agreed with his criticism of an "easy money" policy at a time of inflationary pressures; what was unfair was to blame all that on Eccles. The Truman administration, indeed most of Washington, was still fighting the depression, the memory of which was to linger long.

Perhaps it was because I had been away and come back that I saw the country's situation in a different light from those who had remained there, which included most of the nation's political leaders. Or perhaps it was only that I was older than when I viewed most of the New Deal policies with some enthusiasm. Whatever the reason, my attitude toward Washington political orthodoxy was now far more skeptical.

During the 1930s I thought, and I still think, much of the New Deal program well-advised. Some of its reforms, such as those of the Securities and Exchange Commission, were overdue. There was logic in Wallace's "ever normal granary" concept even if its political motivation was simply to raise farm prices. I favored the New Deal labor reforms. I also favored, or at least didn't object to, the deficit financing of the government's budget; "pump priming" was the catch-phrase of the time.

But all that was in a different time and circumstance. The war's demands on industry had done what none of the New Deal programs did, end the depression. War financing—deficit financing in spades—had vastly multiplied the money and credit in the economy, all of which was now chasing a shortage of goods. In that time and circumstance it made no sense whatever to continue governmental deficit financing or for the Federal Reserve to continue an "easy money" policy. On that score, Bill Grimes was right.

What he didn't know was that Marriner Eccles was already beginning to have some doubts about continuing an "easy money" policy past its time, or at least was beginning to have some questions about it. These doubts were but mildly expressed, and he would never put them "on the record." I recall wondering at the time whether he was "putting me on." Possibly, although it would not be long before Eccles would clash with the president and the then secretary of the treasury, John Snyder, over this issue.

In any event I was developing workable relations with Vinson and Eccles, and it was a personal blow when Vinson was appointed chief justice late in 1946. Snyder, whatever his merits, was colorless and, I think, a bit fearful of the press. But most of the information a reporter gathers comes from the second-tier officials anyway, and not infrequently from those further down the hierarchy. One of the more helpful at the Treasury was Archibald Wiggins, the undersecretary, a South Carolina banker; he was a short, thin man with ears of a size to match those of Jumbo, the flying elephant, but he was knowledgeable and friendly. So was James Webb, assistant to the undersecretary and later director of the budget and administrator of NASA. Of other board members at the Fed, the most knowledgeable was M. S. Szymczak, though I could neither pronounce nor spell his name.

I was doing a creditable job, I thought, of covering the financial beat, and the experience was to be of great help in later years. Nonetheless, I was frustrated at being thus restricted; there was much going on elsewhere in Washington which was outside my official beat. So once more, as in the prewar days, I began to drop in on press conferences elsewhere, including the White House.

Truman's press secretary at that time was Charles Ross, formerly correspondent for the *St. Louis Post-Dispatch*. Although in prewar years I had been very junior and Charlie already well established and well recognized around Washington, I had known him slightly. As White House secretary he disappointed some of his former colleagues because he wasn't a good administrator and the mechanics of the press office didn't always run smoothly. Like Truman, he was from Independence, Missouri, and no doubt there was a touch of that cronyism about his appointment for which Truman was to become noted. But I found him a good press secretary; in manner he was courtly to all and friendly to me. He had the confidence of the president and he inaugurated the practice of holding his own briefings, thus creating the new job of White House spokesman. He was much more relaxed with reporters than Steve Early had been, or at least than Early had appeared to me.

One afternoon I spent a good part of an hour with Ross, and he proved both helpful and perceptive in his view of the man he worked for. He didn't deny (although he didn't emphasize) Truman's deficiencies, his insecurities in the job that he had fallen heir to, his tendency to make too-quick decisions and his habit of talking too freely off-the-cuff. That was smart of Ross because it made the rest of what he had to say more believable.

He told me I was going to be surprised at the difference in Truman given another year in office and the time for the shadow of FDR to fade somewhat. He made one observation I remember especially, for it applies not only to Truman but to others after him. Some men come to power and grow, he said, and some do not. Truman, he insisted, was a "grower." In Ross's view Truman had been growing ever since he came to the Senate, continued to grow and would continue in the future.

Ross was right about the surprises to come, though perhaps not in the way he intended the remark. Truman never ceased to surprise people, even long after he left the White House, and I never got over the surprises he sprang. Before he left office he was to do—and say—many things I thought wrong, at times outrageous, and for which I would criticize him when my opinions began to penetrate the *Journal*'s columns. I would withdraw none of them today. He had a poor grasp of economics and continued to think in 1930s terms. He was also impetuous and cocky, although I think this disguised uncertainty. But if you take the *whole* of his presidency it stands up remarkably well beside some of his successors. The Marshall Plan and his gutsy reaction to the Soviet's Berlin blockade, those two alone assure him a respected place in the history books.

That, though, is getting ahead of the story. The immediate effect of that spring afternoon with Charlie Ross was to increase my dissatisfaction with being hemmed in on the financial beat and to whet my appetite for a chance to cover other aspects of Washington. I felt that as a junior reporter covering Capitol Hill in 1939 I had more room for freewheeling than I did now. The war was barely six months past and already U.S.-Soviet relations were strained; foreign affairs remained very much in the news. Truman, so I gathered, had been suspicious of Stalin as far back as the Potsdam Conference, although of necessity he had to follow the lines formed by Roosevelt. Domestically, the Truman honeymoon was obviously ending as the administration wrestled with the unprecedented problems of inflation. The wartime moratorium on politics was no more. The Republican opposition was stirring again; the

Congress was getting restless. Everywhere things were popping, and most of them were beyond my journalistic purview. Despite the fact that I had an assignment the paper considered a major one, I was discouraged.

Then in midsummer 1946 came one of those happenstances that altered everything. George Bryant decided to leave the *Journal* to take a job with Kiplinger's *Washington Letter*. A few days later I was called to New York to see Bill Grimes and Barney. They told me I would take over as chief of the bureau. I was naturally pleased, but the only part of the conversation I remember was Barney's remark, "Now maybe the britches will be big enough for you!"

2

I first met Tom Dewey in 1947 on his Duchess County farm. It wasn't a private visit for an interview. The governor was holding a "nonpolitical" open house intended only for reporters from New York State newspapers, and I had pushed my way into the gathering. Having heard about it, I called James Haggerty, his press aide, and asked to be included. He was reluctant but finally gave his okay, and so I joined a dozen or so reporters in a bus to drive out and "see the farm," which was the occasion's announced purpose. I went because while the governor wasn't yet an "official" presidential candidate—that announcement wouldn't come until the following January—everybody knew he was not only a candidate, but the most likely Republican nominee in 1948. I simply wanted to have a look at this man about whom I had heard so much.

It was a curious afternoon. The weather was balmy and we were in the country, but Dewey met us dressed in a business suit. After we had a chance to freshen-up from our journey he led us on a tour. By this time he had removed his jacket but he still had on a white shirt and a tie and was wearing black city-type shoes. He wore this costume through the manure-covered fields. I couldn't judge the place as a farm, although it gave the impression of being well-kept. My remembered impression is of a "squire's place," the sort of show farm that would be owned by a well-to-do citizen of the gentry. It did have a spectacular view. On one side the trees had been cut away to expose a broad expanse of lawn and, beyond, the rolling hills.

I found Tom Dewey an equally curious personality. He was a little taller than I—about five feet seven or eight inches, I would guess—but he seemed shorter than that. Perhaps that was because he was slight of frame, but I thought it was the moustache; I have always felt that moustaches were for the tall, lanky and suave. Dewey was none of these. They tend to make short men look a little comic, like Charlie Chaplin. That's why Clare Boothe Luce's remark was so cutting when she called Dewey "the little man on the wedding cake."

That barb lay in the future. All I thought at the time, as I recall, was that the man was rather stiff in manner.

Clare's wisecrack was a bit unfair to Dewey. A native of Michigan, he had acquired a reputation as a sharp, intelligent lawyer in private practice in New York. In 1933 he had been elected district attorney for the Southern District of New York and in 1935 had been named special prosecutor to investigate organized crime. His success in that role brought him national attention, and in 1942 he was elected governor of New York. He proved an able governor and this brought more national attention. He was reelected twice, which suggests not only some political savvy but also some general political appeal.

Dewey had been a candidate for the Republican nomination in 1940, losing out to the charismatic Willkie. In 1944, when he won the nomination, he lost to Roosevelt, but that election being in the middle of the war, the loss brought no stigma. In fact, the war notwithstanding, he had run Roosevelt a closer race than any of his previous opponents. As the 1948 campaign approached Dewey was the clear front-runner.

If there was any national political conversation that afternoon I don't remember it. There was some talk between the governor and the local reporters about New York State affairs, about which I was not well informed. I contented myself with observing.

That visit was a consequence of, and one of the things I enjoyed about, my new job as chief of the *Journal*'s Washington bureau. It automatically made me the paper's main political reporter, and I had been fascinated with politics and politicians ever since I got a taste of politics covering the Capitol in the late 1930s.

I can't go as far as Will Rogers and say I never met a man I didn't like, politicians included. I can say I never met a successful politician who wasn't interesting, and most of them have likeable qualities. This isn't surprising when you think about it. Dewey was stiff, Nixon more so. Robert Taft was aloof and distant, Eisenhower very much the commanding general even when he was at Columbia and in the White House. Adlai Stevenson was often vague and Bobby Kennedy abrasive, unlike his brother Jack. But no man (or woman either) gets very far in politics without having something about him that appeals to a large number of people. For a journalist, anyway, that gives all politicians a special fascination.

Politics, though, wasn't the only attraction about being head of the bureau. I now had the administrative responsibility for a staff of twelve reporters, a sizeable bureau for the time, and for the whole of the Washington report. The office I took over was a good one. George had had staffing problems during the war but he had gradually found first-class young reporters. Three of them—Ellis Haller, Albert Clark, and Alan Otten—were to be among my successors as bureau chief. Three of them were women—Alice Estill, Shirley Scheibla, and Mildred Diefenderfer, among the few women to work for the *Journal* anywhere in those days. All were able reporters. Among the others Frank Bourgholzer, like some other *Journal* staffers of the time, was to become a national TV reporter. Just before he left, George had hired Carl Thompson, my senior roommate at Chapel Hill and a fellow worker on *The Daily Tar Heel*, to fill Ken Kramer's old slot as head of the copy desk. With Carl, Al Clark, and Shirley Scheibla, we had a bit of a Tar Heel coterie.

In the hierarchy of Washington journalism there is a considerable difference between being a reporter, even on a major newspaper, and the head of a bureau. In part it's a matter of status in a status-minded town. In the *Congressional Directory* your name leads the list of correspondents, the others usually following by seniority. This often brings invitations to embassy receptions or luncheons with cabinet officers who want to talk informally about current matters. A bureau chief is apt to get a little better attention when he seeks a meeting with department heads or other influential administration officials.

You also have a little extra status with your peer group. In time I came to know well Paul Miller, head of the Associated Press in Washington, Lyle Wilson of United Press, Walker Stone of Scripps-

Howard, Bert Andrews of the *Herald-Tribune*. Other good friends of those days included Phelps Adams of the New York *Sun*, Gould Lincoln of the *Washington Star*, Eddie Folliard of *The Washington Post*. It was then that I met James Reston of *The New York Times*, not yet quite so famous, who was to become a lifetime friend.

I also got acquainted with Mark Sullivan. Then an old man, he was part of my youth; at Chapel Hill I had absorbed his *Our Times*, those volumes of informal history of America from the turn of the century to the midtwenties. Though not scholarly in the academic sense, they were wide-ranging in subject matter and remain a valuable source for anyone interested in the politics, mores, or fashions of those years. I found him personally gracious and journalistically thought-provoking.

The older man who awed me most, however, was Walter Lippmann, then at the height of his intellectual power and influence. In his column of commentary he could at times seem didactic, even pompous, and he was later to be criticized for repeated shifts in his views. Nonetheless he brought to journalism something rare among journalists, a disciplined mind and a pen of stylistic power that made him always stimulating to read. The only one who came close to him was Arthur Krock of *The New York Times*, whom I continued to see from time to time though I always continued to address him as "Mr. Krock"—as, so I gathered, did those who worked with him.

There was, then, I confess, a certain headiness in my new position. But what I liked about it most was that I was no longer confined to any particular "beat." I had a license to roam at will. True, I had to be careful not to interfere with the job of any of the reporters, not to usurp a story from any of them. But if I wanted to talk to some senator or cabinet officer I felt free to do so. I could follow the main flow of the news wherever it went. It was all grist for the mill. And fun.

There were, to be sure, other problems. Dealing with Buren McCormack, the managing editor, gave me an understanding of the personal frictions that had driven George Bryant to go elsewhere, something that puzzled me when I first heard about it. Mac was a good, solid newsman. His attention to detail was meticulous; he worked late reading galley proofs of almost every story with a sharp eye for sloppy style or fuzzy expression, especially with regard to technical terms. He sought good, clear writing. The *Journal* owes him much of its reputation for thorough reporting and, I think, some of the best journalistic writing in any daily paper. Nothing was too trivial for his eye or for an effort to make it better.

But in his very virtues lay problems for those who worked under him. His meticulousness could at times be picayune and he was almost impossible to argue with. He thus drove George frantic, as he was to do others, including myself. Possibly the feeling was mutual because George too had a low boiling point. In any event, no great persuasive effort had been made to keep George. That was a loss to the *Journal*, as his subsequent career showed. After a brief time with Kiplinger he went on to become the Washington editor of all McGraw-Hill publications.

George told me his irritations with Mac were the chief cause of his departure, and it didn't take long for me to understand why. Although I didn't know it then, this was the beginning of years of personality clashes and rivalries with Mac that were to last through both our careers with the paper. Nonetheless, I respected Mac's journalistic abilities and the Navy had accustomed me to frictions with "authority." Perhaps I had more patience than George, but in any event I was enjoying my new job too much— and, I doubt not, was too confident of my own abilities—to let problems with a managing editor spoil the fun.

These were interesting times to be a newspaperman. Harry Truman had come to office with a reservoir of good will, as do all presidents suddenly thrust into that office. By 1946 much of that reservoir was exhausted. His popularity fell rapidly. By 1948, the election year, Gallup reported that only 39 percent of the people approved of his presidency. Part of this was due to Truman's ineptness; much more to the times themselves. It was a period of much unrest. People were weary of the war and not a little frightened by the belligerency of our one-time ally the Soviet Union, which threatened another. On the home front many of them were weary of the New Deal.

One example of the changing domestic mood: When the Wagner labor act had been passed in 1935 creating the National Labor Relations Board and establishing the right of unions to organize, there was wide public support for union labor. The epidemic of strikes after the war with all its disruptive effects shifted public sentiment.

I suspect that the true inspirer of the Taft-Hartley Act of 1947 was not Senator Robert Taft but John L. Lewis. In April of 1946 Lewis had called some half million coal miners off the job, spreading slow industrial chaos. Truman seized the mines, but in November Lewis called another strike, this time against the government and in defiance of a court injunction against striking. Truman took him to court and the United Mine Workers were fined $3.5 million. Labor union leaders were aghast but the public, take it all in all, approved. It was a sign that people thought organized labor was overreaching itself in power.

John L. Lewis, the man thus humbled, was not a man to take easily to humility. A son of Welsh immigrants, he had gone to work in the coal mines as a teenager, cutting short his formal education. He educated himself by reading, especially Shakespeare, and worked his way up the union ranks the hard way. Once at the top he fought with everybody: Franklin Roosevelt, his fellow union leaders (he opposed FDR's third term and in 1942 pulled the UMW out of the CIO), the courts, and Harry Truman. A bulky man with flowing locks, shaggy eyebrows, and out-thrust chin, he was also a frustrated actor who liked to declaim in overblown rhetoric.

This made him a delight, whatever else he was, to newspapermen because he made good copy. At his press conferences he kept reporters scribbling. On the eve of World War II he called the draft a prelude "to dictatorship and fascism." He labeled his fellow labor leader Walter Reuther "a pseudo-intellectual nitwit." He thought Vice-President Garner a "whiskey-drinking, poker-playing, evil old man." Of Truman's views of the president's legal authority he snorted, "What does Truman know about the legality of anything?" As I recall it, he was the first one to tag the Taft-Hartley Act a "slave-labor law."

Another dramatic Truman clash with labor was the railroad strike of 1946. The railroads, at that time the nation's transportation artery, had been shut down by two of their operating unions, threatening to strangle the country. That made Truman fighting mad. He seized the railroads as he did the coal mines, meatpacking houses, New York tugboats and strikebound oil refineries. This time, however, he took an unprecedented step. He proposed to draft all the rail strikers into the army. At a press conference Truman put his views succinctly: "Whenever strikes against the government are legal, the government will ceast to exist."

The showdown came on a Saturday in May. Carl Thompson and I had gone to the Capitol where Truman was to address the Congress personally. The press gallery of the House was packed, the tension high. While Truman was sitting in Speaker Rayburn's office the rail brotherhoods surrendered; they called off the strike on Truman's terms. Truman did not get the word, however, until he was nearly through with his speech when a note from Clark Clifford was handed to him. Truman ended by dramatically announcing that the strike was over.

Congress nonetheless went forward with the legislation that would give the president such military drafting power. The House quickly passed a bill overwhelmingly. In the Senate majority leader Alben Barkley asked unanimous consent to bring the bill up out of order. At that point a lone senator rose to object. He was Robert A. Taft.

The aftermath was an odd twist of affairs. For Senator Taft, the man who stopped Congress from being emotionally carried away, became viewed as the enemy of labor because he later fathered legislation to put some carefully considered restrictions on unions, such as bans on the closed shop and "secondary boycotts." Truman, the man who asked such extreme action against union strikers, became praised as the friend of labor.

I had met Senator Taft socially at a dinner party shortly after he came to the Senate back in 1939. During the war years I followed his emergence as a national figure with at most a casual interest. In the years from 1946 into the 1950s I was to see much of him. Once I made a trip with him to Chicago, unaccompanied by other reporters, when he appeared on a public affairs radio program, "The Chicago Roundtable." I saw him several times in the preludes to the 1948 Republican convention and followed him around in his Ohio campaign for reelection to the Senate in 1950. I liked the man but I found him strange. He had a most unusual personality for a politician to rise high in national attention—restrained, cool, aloof, not unfriendly, but never outgoing. He rarely displayed the slightest sign of a sense of humor, especially about himself.

An incident that came much later may illustrate his unusual manner. During that 1950 campaign in Ohio, he was invited to speak to a grammar school class as he swirled through a small town in the southern part of the state. He accepted and was greeted by a teacher all-a-twitter who explained to the class the privilege it had in hearing from one of the candidates and a man of national renown.

Taft acknowledged the introduction with a nod of his head. Then he stepped forward, bellied up to the teacher's desk with one hand in his trouser's pocket, and launched into his standard campaign speech on the farm program.

The pupils may have been impressed, but they had not the slightest idea what he was talking about. The solemn Taft had not the slightest idea that the speech might be inappropriate. Doris Fleeson, a Washington syndicated columnist, and I were sitting in the back of the room. We agreed afterwards it was a ridiculous performance, and yet there was something warming about a man who would do it because he took his politics and his ideas seriously.

But to return to 1946. There were other fronts to engage the president's attention as the off-year congressional elections approached. Abroad clouds were already gathering that had an ominous look. And at home there was the "beefsteak war."

On June 30 price controls expired. There had been a wrangle over a bill to extend them, passed by Congress but vetoed by Truman because of amendments that would have permitted price ceilings to reflect rising costs. A second bill was passed, stronger in some ways but containing a provision that livestock controls could not be reimposed before August 20. There was thus a gap in meat controls, into which Truman would tumble.

What happened this was: Prior to June 30 meat, especially beef, practically disappeared from grocery shelves. Between June 30 and August 20 meat reemerged, although at higher prices. When controls were slapped back on, meat disappeared again except in the black market.

The *Journal* was full of horror stories about the black market, using a technique other papers found hard to duplicate—the "round up," based on reporting from all around the country; the *Journal* could do this because it had the largest number of domestic bureaus of any paper. In Washington we were writing about the consternation the meat shortage was causing in administration circles. By late September and early October we were trying to find out what, if anything, the administration planned to do about it.

Truman's advisers were clearly divided. On the one hand the liberals, led by Henry Wallace, who was still in the cabinet, urged the president to keep the controls, arguing that the price rises from removing them would be bad both economically and politically. On the other hand Democratic professional politicians, including many in Congress, were warning the president, "no meat, no votes."

I was busy badgering Charlie Ross and Dr. John Steelman, one of the president's economic advisers, to get some clue. No luck. I had the feeling they were stalling me, but more likely they just didn't know. I doubt if Truman himself knew until the last minute. Confusion seemed to reign everywhere.

The upshot was that in mid-October, less than a month before the congressional elections, the president suddenly gave in. "There is only one remedy left," he said. "That is to remove controls." I wrote in the *Journal* that the president had "slaughtered meat controls to get more meat." It did get more meat. It also, naturally, got higher prices than before. And by then it got few—if any—votes.

The president and the country were caught in a dilemma that would face the country repeatedly in the years ahead, notably in the oil shortage of the 1970s. Controlled prices, if they are below what would be the market level, produce shortages, black markets, and chaos. Removing controls removes the shortages because it simultaneously increases supply and decreases demand. But inevitably prices rise to the level they would have reached without controls. Truman would have been better advised, I think, to have let them all expire on June 30 so things could have settled down before the election. The worse choice was the on-again-off-again course actually followed.

Parenthetically I might note that Truman learned nothing from this experience. The whole mess was to be repeated again during the Korean War.

I have to admit that, as a newspaperman, I revelled in the confusion. It may not have been good for the country but it made good copy, just as that shoot-out in Chapel Hill years before had made good copy for the *Tar Heel*. One of journalism's unfortunate characteristics is that bad news writes and reads better than good news. Although I had only been bureau chief for a few months, I had already begun writing commentary pieces occasionally, many of which appeared on the editorial page. And there wasn't much good news to write about.

Certainly not on the foreign affairs front. Almost every day the tension between the Soviet Union and its former Western allies seemed to draw tighter. So had the tension within the administration on policy. Churchill, who was more far-seeing than most, had made his famous "Iron Curtain" speech in early March. Truman was asked if he endorsed it. The president's reply was both waffling and inaccurate. He said he believed in free speech and Churchill could say what he wished, and then added gratuitously that he "didn't know what would be in the speech" beforehand. Every newspaperman knew, however, that texts of the speech had been widely circulated on the train taking Churchill and Truman to Fulton, Missouri.

Truman's attitude toward the Soviet Union had already been hardening, with much justification. Stalin's postwar actions had made it pretty clear that as far as he was concerned the Russian-occupied parts of Europe would remain in Russian hands. The prospect of a permanently divided Europe was beginning to emerge. Mr. Churchill, then, was really only saying out loud what Truman was beginning to think. And just by sponsoring the speech, Truman invited the interpretation that he shared those views.

Press commentary on Churchill was generally favorable and, I think, so was the public reaction. But Truman was caught in a bind. Whatever credit there was in forthrightness went to Churchill. When Stalin replied belligerently, whatever fears were aroused of war possibilities reacted against Truman.

Anyway, the result of all these developments, foreign and domestic, was that in November 1946 the Republicans made sweeping gains, capturing control of both the House and the Senate for the first time since 1928. To all Truman's other woes was now added the fact that the opposition party held a majority in Congress. Since traditionally such midterm congressional swings foreshadowed defeat for the incumbent president's party, like most other political writers I began to write about the ill-omens for the Democrats in 1948.

That election, incidentally, brought some new members to Congress whom I'm afraid I didn't notice much at the time: Richard Nixon from California and John Kennedy from Massachusetts in the House, and an ex-marine from Wisconsin to the Senate, Joseph McCarthy. Sitting in the House press gallery when Congress convened in January 1947, however, I paid attention to what President Truman said in his State of the Union speech and to Congress' reaction to it.

Truman tried to make a conciliatory speech. He endorsed a housing bill sponsored by Senator Taft. He even asked for some modification in the labor law, such as a ban on "secondary boycotts," and he suggested a bipartisan commission to study management-labor relations. He made no sweeping call for additional legislation of the New Deal variety. But the Republicans had been invigorated by the election results and weren't in a conciliatory mood. They quickly launched an attack on Truman's budget and started planning tax cuts. What was to become the tougher Taft-Hartley labor law began its way through Congress. The new Speaker of the House, Joe Martin, remarked after the speech that this year—1947—the legislative agenda would be set by Congress, not by the president.

Meanwhile, on the president's political left another group was forming—including such people as John Kenneth Galbraith, Arthur Schlesinger, Jr., young Franklin Roosevelt, and Mayor Hubert Humphrey of Minneapolis. In their view Truman was backsliding on the New Deal, the final straw probably being the firing of Henry Wallace, last of the original FDR cabinet, just before the election because he implied Truman was too anti-Soviet. "We must not let our Russian policy be influenced," Wallace had said, "by those who want war with Russia." That group was the beginning of the Americans for Democratic Action, which was to play an important role in the future.

As I saw it, Truman was being caught in a crossfire between right and left which was dangerous and could be fatal to his reelection. At least it was clear that in January of 1947 the lines were already being formed for the presidential campaign of 1948.

*   *   *   *   *

It was a crowded year, 1947, and the memories tumble so one upon the other that I have difficulty in sorting them out. It was the year of Marshall's failed mission in China and the beginning of decades of recrimination; of the announcement of the Truman

Doctrine; of the launching of the Marshall Plan; of the first stir-
rings of the "Berlin question"; and of rumblings in Korea, both
the seeds of future crises. On the domestic front, 1947 saw passage
of the Taft-Hartley Act over Truman's veto; the approval by Congress of the Twenty-second Constitutional Amendment to limit
presidents to two terms; Secretary Byrne's departure; the reorganization of the military into a single Defense Department; the beginnings of the civil rights disputes that would climax in 1948;
the Communists-in-government issue that was to lead to Senator
McCarthy.

It was also, for me, the first full year as head of the *Journal*'s
Washington bureau with the promise it offered for my journalistic
career.

By this time I had had up-close looks at the two leading Republican contenders for 1948, Tom Dewey and Robert Taft. I had also,
though I didn't at the time realize its significance, a long acquaintance with one of the two men who would make that 1948 election
a political quadrille, Henry Wallace. But aside from casual encounters in prewar days I had seen President Truman only at his
formal press conferences.

I was soon to get a better look at him, if not in private at least in
a more informal way.

Truman had continued the Roosevelt custom of regular White
House receptions as well as irregular at-homes. The first one
Frances and I attended was in late December 1946, with others to
follow the next year. It was at one of these that I had a chance for a
few minutes' talk with the president.

Truman, of course, was not anchored to a receiving line or to a
chair as was the crippled Roosevelt. It was Truman's habit, once
these affairs were underway, to walk about, greet his guests, and
pause now and then for conversation. Oddly enough, he was rarely
surrounded by any great crowd on these walks, either out of people's timidity at approaching the president or possibly out of uneasiness over how to talk to a man with so many political troubles.

I was inhibited by neither. So on one of these occasions I walked
up to the president and introduced myself. I was rather hoping that
he would ask me the origin of my name. Then I would tell him,
and like FDR he would put back his head and roar with laughter.
But he didn't; the remembered past is seldom repeated. Instead I

made some polite inquiries as to how he was feeling, which he took, I suppose, as referring to his political health. Anyway, he replied "fine" and added with a grin, "I never trouble trouble."

We chatted in this vein briefly before he walked on. I remember thinking that indeed, for a man in so much political trouble, he seemed remarkably chipper. As he walked away I noticed that he walked ramrod stiff, as if in imagination he was still Captain Truman, Battery D, 139th Field Artillery. I should have recognized it as a clue to what came thereafter.

It was on a similar occasion that I got a glimpse of his reaction to pomp and circumstance. Carl Thompson and his wife, Mary, had gone to the White House with us, and when it came time to leave Mary said she had to say good-bye. I explained to her that this wasn't necessary at the White House and wasn't expected. If everybody did that, I remarked, the Trumans would never get to bed.

But she insisted and we went wandering around until we found the president, who was all alone. Mary went up to him and said, "Mr. President, I just want to thank you for a very nice party."

Truman looked startled, staring at her for a moment from behind those thick-lensed glasses.

Then he shook hands and said, "*I* thank *you*. Nobody here has ever said that to me before!"

Later I got another view of the president, also in a group but this time in a group of newspaper people. It was in connection with a meeting of the American Society of Newspaper Editors at which he appeared. I wasn't then a member of ASNE but went along as Bill Grimes's guest. What we saw was a foretaste of the way Truman would campaign in the summer and fall of 1948.

President Truman, like President Carter after him, was not very good at reading a prepared speech. He came across stilted because his voice lacked the rhythm of vocal speech and was so lacking in modulation that it was a monotone. Sometimes he stumbled over words, possibly because of eyesight problems. The result was that the emphasis was often in the wrong place, diminishing the force of whatever he had to say. There was also, no doubt, the fact that these prepared speeches, though expressing Truman's ideas, were written by someone else. They weren't necessarily his own words.

This time I heard him deliver a speech off-the-cuff for the first time. It revealed an entirely different Truman as speaker. He was clear and forceful. The cadence was that of the spoken word, not the written one. I thought him much more effective. He must have thought so too, because more and more thereafter he abandoned manuscript reading for "just talking."

For a president of the United States this involves some risk. There is always the danger of the misspoken phrase or a want of precision that can lead to misinterpretation. Truman frequently succumbed to this kind of foot-in-mouth disease at his press conferences; Charlie Ross and later Joe Short, his press secretaries, were kept busy putting out "clarification statements." Thus informal speech isn't suitable for State-of-the-Union messages and other times when precision is important. But for Truman it worked well, as we were to discover, on the political campaign trail.

That doesn't mean that at these times Truman hadn't thought ahead of time about what he was going to say. As Mark Twain observed, "The secret of a good impromptu speech is careful preparation." It only means that Truman then relied on inspiration for the actual words.

As 1947 wore on I was engrossed as a journalistic observer in most of the events of the year. The only matter I stayed completely clear of was the fight over the unification of the armed services; I thought my Navy service might unconsciously affect anything I wrote. I couldn't help thinking, though, it was typically Washington that in the end "unification" resulted in three separate armed forces instead of two, the Air Corps of the Army becoming the independent Air Force.

Early in January the long-rumored rift between Truman and Secretary Byrnes resulted in Byrnes's resignation (I always thought it more a personality clash than a policy one) and the appointment of General of the Army George Marshall as secretary of state. I had not seen Marshall since he was a brigadier testifying before Congress in 1940. Now I found him much more restrained and distant; I never got to know him well, but I always was, and still am, an admirer. He had just returned from his abortive mission to negotiate peaceful cooperation between the Kuomintang and the Communists in China. That was the beginning of the long, acrimonious argument over the question, Who lost China? It was to wreck the careers of a number of honorable men.

The correct answer is that no American "lost" China. It was lost, if that is the word, by Chiang Kai-shek, an obstinate man who lacked the political vision to match his courage. Nonetheless, the Communist takeover in China sowed some seeds for what was to become the McCarthy witch-hunt.

Those seeds were nourished by the unfortunate fact that there were indeed some in high government places who were Communist sympathizers and/or party members and who thought this allegiance overrode any allegiance to their own country. Alger Hiss was certainly one of those and Harry Dexter White possibly so. I did not think so in the beginning; to me it was inconceivable. Of Harry White, as mentioned, I had seen a good deal. Hiss I knew hardly at all except as a nice, clean-cut young man who had served in the Agriculture Department and as director of the Office of Special Political Affairs in the prewar State Department. I had met his eventual accuser, Whitaker Chambers, who impressed me as a good journalist but not in any other way.

Truman created the Temporary Commission on Employee Loyalty just after the 1946 election. In the following March he issued an executive order on procedures for the administration of a loyalty program for government employees. It required a "loyalty investigation" of every person entering government service. The attorney general was to draw up a list of allegedly subversive organizations.

That was enough to unleash J. Parnell Thomas, chairman of the House Committee on Un-American Activities, and in time to lead to Senator McCarthy. That there was cause for concern—meriting some careful, thoughtful investigation—does not make it less a pity that the concern should turn into hysteria that was to affect, and infect, politics for a long time to come.

The other events that were to dominate that year, aside from the continuing battle over Taft-Hartley, were the growing civil rights movement and President Truman's launching of the "Truman Doctrine," one prong of which was to evolve into the Marshall Plan for rebuilding Western Europe and the other into the policy of "containment," that is, the resistance of Communist expansion anywhere in the world.

What became the Truman Doctrine didn't spring full-blown, or anyway wasn't so recognized at its birth. I remember that when Truman went before Congress in mid-March to ask for aid to

Greece and Turkey against Communist influence, the press gallery was so crowded that I had to stand in the rear; the story belonged to Al Clark, now filling Mike Flynn's old job as senior Capitol reporter. That proposal was controversial in itself, but the president's speech also contained a sentence fraught with other consequences, that henceforth it would be American policy "to support free peoples who are resisting subjugation." The full implications of this sweeping statement—which would in time lead first to Korea and ultimately to Vietnam—weren't immediately apparent. I recall only Bill Grimes in the *Journal* and Lippmann in his column who saw that sentence as an open-ended commitment.

These were indeed turbulent times; the events of that one year alone have occupied a pride of historians. But as for myself, I was simply enjoying it all immensely. Indeed, what stands out in memory now is not so much the great events themselves as the people who played their roles, big and small.

Congress continued to fascinate me for its larger-than-life characters. Senator Wherry of Nebraska, the Republican whip, was a master of the malapropism. I still recall with delight his referring to Southeast Asia as "Indigo China" and of his comment that Truman was "sugar-coating red ink." Vandenberg, now elevated to the role of statesman because of his cooperation with Roosevelt on foreign policy, still managed to look like the ex-editor he was, portly, jowled and cigar smoking. The Southern contingent remained not only powerful but colorful. My own state, North Carolina, contributed Senator Clyde Hoey, attired in gray trousers and a swallow-tailed coat. Representative Rankin of Mississippi, a forthright bigot on racial matters, was a treasury of Shakespearian quotations. And there was always Senator Connally of Texas with his stentorian speaking voice which rose to oratorical heights—or depths—when he had a bit of bourbon under his belt. These were not men easy to forget.

Downtown there was less color. I learned early to bypass Treasury Secretary Snyder and to cultivate instead Undersecretary Wiggins, the skinny small-town banker with the big ears. At Interior, Carlton Skinner, former *Wall Street Journal* reporter, was director of information and even gave out some. Undersecretary Dean Acheson at the State Department was more communicative than George Marshall. Oscar "Jack" Ewing, acting Democratic national chairman, was a good source of political chitchat.

One day I got an irate call from Averell Harriman, perennial Democratic officeholder, then secretary of commerce. It seems that one of the *Journal's* subscription salesmen got to see him by announcing himself simply as being from the *Journal* and then once inside delivered his sales pitch to the astonished secretary. I had to admire the salesman for his initiative, but now it was my turn to complain to Kilgore that somebody was being "too big for his britches." Shades of Cotton Ed Smith! The incident did, however, give me a chance to call on Harriman in the role of pacifier.

At the White House I liked John Steelman, formerly a sociology professor and by now Truman's right-hand man, much as Sherman Adams would be under Eisenhower. The budget director was Jimmy Webb, formerly at the Treasury and a fellow Tar Heel. He was always as candid as a budget director can be.

John Steelman was particularly helpful, although as it turned out his helpfulness wasn't always just to me alone. By now he was in effect the president's chief of staff as well as one of his leading economic advisers. In 1947 the Republicans, with the bit in their teeth, passed a tax reduction bill. To Truman and his advisers it seemed lopsided, giving percentage-wise bigger cuts to higher income people than to those of lower income. There was much talk of a veto, but a presidential veto of any tax cut measure was almost unheard of and, in the orthodox political view, dangerous.

I had been following the running argument at the White House and as the day approached when Truman had to either approve, veto, or let the bill become law without his signature, my nervousness increased. It was not a story the *Journal* would like to be beaten on.

Late one afternoon Steelman called and told me Truman's decision. So I wrote a story saying, flat out, "President Truman today will veto the tax cut bill." Either, I thought, I had a scoop or I had best head for the briar patch. The *Journal* gave it good play the next morning.

It turned out to be right. The only trouble was that Steelman, or somebody else, also told the *Times*. So my exclusive wasn't. Better, though, I consoled myself in my disappointment, than being scooped.

So that year wore on. At home, too, things were looking up. Bonnie was doing well in school and making new friends; Eleanor had found playmates in the neighborhood. Frances and I were both enjoying our new house, bought with a VA loan, and our growing social life. Professionally I had also begun to spread my wings beyond the *Journal*. After several rejections I had cracked the *Saturday Evening Post* with the help of Hugh Morrow, then in its Washington office, later to be Nelson Rockefeller's press secretary. I sold them two articles, one on the effects of the postwar inflation and taxes on industrial workers and the middle class, the other a profile of Marriner Eccles. Both the money and the extra recognition they gave me were welcome.

All in all, the omens were good. I was looking forward to the 1948 election in which I was to be in charge of the *Journal*'s coverage. I didn't anticipate what turns that campaign would take nor that, by then, my life would be once more altered.

3

In 1948 both political conventions met in Philadelphia, the Republicans in June, the Democrats in July. I was, as expected, in charge of the *Journal*'s coverage, but from an anomalous position.

One day early in 1948 I received a call from Bill Kerby saying that Bill Grimes was ill and asking if I would come to New York to help out on the editorial page. There was no choice but to accept. I owed Grimes much and I had already written some editorials on Washington matters, such as the president's budget, so I couldn't plead want of experience. Thus for several weeks I commuted between Washington and New York, developing a split journalistic personality, one half political reporter, one half editorial commentator. I didn't mind it as temporary duty, although it made home life difficult, because it gave me a chance to get better acquainted with my New York colleagues. Bill Grimes wasn't in the office but I saw a lot of Barney, Kerby, and McCormack.

This duty done I returned to Washington. A few weeks later, however, I had another call, this time from Grimes himself. He was pleased with my editorial writing, he said, and wanted me to come to New York and join the staff. This was an entirely different matter. My bureau job was the most satisfactory and rewarding one I had had; I thought then, and I think now, it's the best job on the paper except for being the editor. I was just beginning to build a reputation within the paper, with official Washington and, most important of all, among my colleagues. Newspaper Washington is a close-knit, socially conservative society. Reputations aren't established overnight no matter how able the newcomer. I had no desire to leave all that.

To move posed problems at home as well. My family was just beginning to put down roots and Frances was in no mood to be uprooted again after all that wartime hopping about. I was caught on the horns of the proverbial dilemma. To accept would spoil a bright present. To decline would probably cut me off from rising within the *Journal*.

At first I declined, deciding that I would be willing to accept being only a Washington staffer, taking my chances that I could build a reputation on that. But the more I thought about it the more I wavered. I had gotten where I was by accepting each opportunity that presented itself, from the day I became a cafeteria busboy until the day Grimes first sent me to Washington. Was it wise to act differently?

The consequence was that after further talks with New York I agreed. The offer included what seemed to me a large boost in salary and the title of associate editor. Under Grimes, so I was told, I would be in charge of the editorial page and be one of the chief spokesmen of the paper's views.

On his part Grimes agreed that I would continue, at least for the time being, as the *Journal*'s chief political writer. Ellis Haller, who would succeed me, was a good newsman; he was then the editor in the bureau dealing with the in-depth "leaders" we offered to New York. He was probably better than I as an administrator, but at the time he had had little experience reporting on politics.

So despite the technical change in my position, by mid-June I was ensconced in the Bellevue Stratford Hotel in Philadelphia getting ready for the Republicans. The front-runners for the nomination were Taft and Dewey but there were some possible "favorite sons," Vandenberg, Governor Warren of California, and a man who was to become a fixture of GOP conventions, Harold Stassen. Sometimes referred to irreverently as "Childe Harold," he had been governor of Minnesota in 1938 at thirty-one. He had a good war record, serving on Halsey's staff in the Pacific. His Godkin lectures at Harvard had attracted much attention; he had also been the keynoter at the 1940 convention. So he had some credentials. He added to them by winning primaries in Wisconsin and Nebraska.

I met Stassen for the first time on the eve of the convention. I found him personable and articulate. His political ideas at that time could be best described as middle-of-the-road, somewhat more conservative than Dewey but less so than Taft. He had to be taken seriously.

This was before the days of the ubiquitous TV cameras although those newfangled instruments were present. That meant for newspapers much more detailed coverage of preconvention maneuvering as well as of floor fights than would later be the case. For us it also meant fast coverage on spot developments for the News Service wire. As a result I took a larger staff to Philadelphia than the *Journal* had previously used. We set up our "command post" in the paper's small Philadelphia bureau and both there and at the convention hall had direct teletype wires to New York.

Dewey arrived with the largest delegate count. It was quickly apparent he also had the best organized team, under the direction of Herbert Brownell, a no-nonsense lawyer from New York. Taft's organization was enthusiastic but inept. Dewey led on the first ballot but was short a hundred votes needed to win. The horse-trading began.

This was also before the combination of television and the proliferation of state primaries could settle a nomination before a convention met. Conventions were the place where the contending forces all joined for the first time and the delegates actually chose the nominee. There was, therefore, much courting of delegates by the rivals, mixed in with some arm-twisting, and reporters scurried about to find out who was doing what to whom.

On the second ballot both Taft and Dewey gained but Dewey gained the most. In midstream Governors Driscoll of New Jersey and Bradford of Massachusetts, as well as Senator Kem of Missouri, were cajoled or propelled to swing from Taft to Dewey. Taft won no major new allegiance. By this time the outcome was clear. Taft withdrew, followed by Stassen, and Dewey won on the third ballot. Governor Warren of California was tapped for the vice-presidential spot to balance the ticket geographically.

None of this took very long. It was a businesslike convention and the delegates left convinced that they had in fact nominated the next president of the United States.

The Democratic convention the next month was something else

again. It was a three-ring circus from beginning to end and therefore much more exciting for those in the press contingent.

The first free-for-all was over the platform, ordinarily a thing
not of much consequence but this year to play a major role. Truman got most of what he wanted from the platform committee on
repeal of Taft-Hartley, Marshall Plan support, and aid to Israel.
He failed to get his way on a more liberal but not extreme civil
rights plank, which was to prove fateful.

There was a bitter running fight between the ADA (Americans
for Democratic Action) group led by Mayor Hubert Humphrey,
now a candidate for senator in Minnesota, and a small but diehard
group of Southerners. The ADA wanted a strong civil rights platform, asking a federal guarantee of clearly defined civil rights. The
Southerners opposed it. Both sides rejected, for different reasons, a
compromise Truman proposal. A bitter fight followed on the floor
which the liberals won, but at the cost of splitting the convention.

Then came a second damaging fight over seating the Mississippi
delegation, that of the "regular" Mississippi Democrats being opposed by the ADA because it came instructed to bolt if the more
conservative civil rights plank was rejected. Following the acceptance of the liberal civil rights plank sponsored by the ADA, Mississippi walked out of the convention, followed by a number of
other delegates from Alabama.

The tension of all this in-fighting was heightened by the fact that
a heat wave had hit Philadelphia and the jammed hall wasn't air
conditioned. Periodically during the night's fight a voice would
drone over the loudspeakers, "the temperature in the hall is now *a
hundred and four degrees!*" We were all—delegates, news people
and audience—drenched in sweat.

My first impression of Hubert Humphrey, gained in an impromptu gathering with some of the press, was of a likeable, voluble man who enjoyed a fight for fight's sake but who was also sincere in his battle for a stronger civil rights plank. He seemed at
times a bit immature, which no doubt he then was, but a man who
given floor speaking privileges could make a rousing speech. He
did so shortly on the convention floor with a speech on civil rights
that put him in the national spotlight.

Truman obviously had his troubles. But he also had his strengths.
He was president and incumbents are rarely dumped for renomi-

nation by their own party. Sam Rayburn and Alben Barkley, among others, warned against it.

The climax of all this came on the night of June fourteenth and the early morning of the fifteenth. Despite all the fighting, Truman received 947 ½ votes on the long first ballot, enough to win. But of the Southern votes he got only thirteen, all of them from my home state of North Carolina. There was too much bitterness for the convention to give him the usual gesture of making it unanimous. Alben Barkley, aged seventy-one, was picked for vice-president.

The voting over, we waited for Harry. Confident of winning the nomination, he had been sitting backstage talking with Sam Rayburn, Barkley, and other friends. It was in the wee hours of the morning, with such television audience as existed at that time long abed, that he came out to face a weary and discouraged Democratic party in convention assembled.

He made it an electric moment. Speaking with only a few notes, the way he spoke best, he proudly dwelt on the Democratic administration's record and gave the Republican Congress what-for. At the end came the surprise. He was calling Congress back into session on July 26. He would give that Republican Congress a chance to act on aid to education, on housing, on civil rights, on a national health program, on an increased minimum wage and an extension of Society Security, all of which the Republicans professed to favor.

"If there is any reality in the Republican platform," he said, "we ought to get some action. . . . They can do this job in fifteen days if they want to do it. They will still have time to go out and run for office!"

The convention erupted in pandemonium. The applause was spontaneous, long, and enthusiastic. Captain Truman had rallied the troops.

Jonathan Daniels of the Raleigh *News and Observer*, who was sitting beside me, slapped me hard on the back. "Harry just won the election," he said.

I didn't believe him.

*   *   *   *   *

The 1948 presidential election holds a major place in political history books because Harry Truman confounded politicians of both parties, all of the press, and the practitioners of the new art of polling. By election day even Jonathan Daniels was surprised to find that his instinct had been right.

The heralders of a Dewey victory weren't without reason. Although Truman had won renomination his party was badly split. The Southern Democrats, walking out of the convention over the civil rights issue, met in Birmingham in mid-July and nominated Governor Strom Thurmond of South Carolina as candidate for the newly formed States Rights party, soon to be dubbed the "Dixie-crats." They had no illusions about winning the presidency for Thurmond; their strategy was to win all, or most, of the 127 electoral votes from the states of the former Confederacy and thus deny the election to either Truman or Dewey. This could throw the election into the House of Representatives. There, with each state having one vote regardless of population, the Southerners would be in a strong position to bargain for "states rights" with both candidates. Meanwhile, another dissident Democratic group gathered in Philadelphia, borrowed the old name of the Progressive party, and nominated Henry Wallace. Under the slogan "Peace, Freedom, and Abundance" the new Progressives opposed the Marshall Plan, the draft, the military buildup; they advocated destruction of all the atom bomb stockpile, the breaking up of big businesses, and closer cooperation with the Soviet Union. These weren't exclusively Communist ideas but they were close enough so that Wallace was endorsed by the American Communist party. Truman had cannons to both left and right, catching him in a crossfire.

Following all this, I developed something of a split personality, professionally speaking. Technically I was now attached to the New York office as an editorial writer. In spirit I was still a Washington reporter and I held Grimes to his promise that I would not be office-bound, despite his constant grumbling. Of course I had to leave much of the day-by-day coverage of the campaign—covering the candidates' speeches, much of their travels on whistle-stop trains—to others in the Washington bureau, notably Al Clark, who was emerging himself as a good political reporter. Nonetheless, I was able to break away for political safaris on my own. On these I borrowed a leaf from Barney Kilgore's political manual which he had developed back in the 1936 campaign. That is, I would sneak time to travel the country, at places chosen more or less at random, talking to people about their views of the candidates, the issues of the day or whatever else was on their minds.

In addition to such random travels, I kept a list of many party officials on the local level, Democrats and Republicans, who would presumably be familiar with political sentiment in their areas. I visited as many as I could and used the long distance phone to talk to others.

Doing so, I began to notice something interesting but the full significance of which, I'm sorry to say, escaped me. People who were for Dewey were for him because of intellectual reasons; they would recite all the troubles of the country, especially economic ones, and ascribe them to Truman and to the Democrats, whom they thought too long in power. There wasn't much enthusiasm for Dewey personally. On the other hand those for Truman were personal admirers, often saying they were for him "in spite of" this or that. They liked his "spunk."

There was another oddity I didn't pay enough attention to. Frequently when talking to local politicians I'd hear them say Truman was doing pretty well in their own districts even though they expected Dewey to carry the state. There was a difference, then, between their assessment of the situation where they had personal knowledge and their view of the "broader picture." In retrospect this difference was explained by the enormous influence of the Gallup poll, which continued to show Dewey leading nationally, and generally by a wide margin.

The influence of the polls was especially strong in Washington, where the special session of Congress was proceeding about as everyone expected. Truman tossed it an agenda of social and other legislation that would have been a big order for a regular, full-length session. In the eleven days of the special session Congress managed to pass a housing bill, to which the Republicans were already committed, adopt two of Truman's anti-inflation proposals, and approve a sixty-five million dollar loan to the United Nations. An effort to pass Truman's new civil rights bill ran into a filibuster by Southern senators, all Democrats, and died. The general verdict on Capitol Hill was that all this wouldn't affect the election one way or another. Senator Taft, with whom I talked, was irate at what he called the president's "cheap politics" and predicted it would backfire on Truman. The people, he said, would see through it.

Altogether, Truman seemed to have enough troubles. The two

Democratic splinter groups—the Dixicrats and the Wallace Progressives—would each subtract from Truman however many votes either got, or so it seemed. In late summer, prices on the New York Stock Exchange had taken a big tumble, attributed by brokers to the special session of Congress and the situation in Europe from the Soviet blockade of West Berlin. In Dayton, Ohio, police skirmished with tear gas against rioting strikers; indeed, there were strikes all over. Inflation caused General Motors to raise its car prices by 8 percent, the major steel companies to raise their prices by $2.50 a ton. In New York the nickel subway vanished forever. The Bureau of Labor Statistics reported the cost-of-living was now 171 percent above the 1939 level, with food prices more than 214 percent higher than prewar.

The Republicans, naturally, blamed all this on Truman. Dewey ran his campaign with dignified aplomb, already acting presidential. Herbert Brownell, caught for a moment in New York, explained that Dewey didn't want to do or say anything that would haunt him after he was president. His problem, Brownell said, wasn't in winning but in being able to govern when he was elected.

Truman, on the other hand, launched a whirlwind campaign. I can't begin to remember how many speeches he made between September and November, but their number piled up and they were spread all over the country. He truly "whistle-stopped" by train, with no station platform crowd too small for him to pause and give the Republicans hell. He was Harry Truman at his feistiest.

Over all these domestic questions hung the problem of Berlin. In late June the Russians had closed all land access to the city in defiance of the wartime agreements. President Truman rejected a direct confrontation but launched an airlift to supply West Berlin. The Republicans favored a strong anti-Soviet position but could, and did, criticize the Truman response, which they called a makeshift. The Wallaceites argued that the U.S. should withdraw all its Berlin forces "in a search for peace." Their slogan was "Wallace or war." The public, so far as anyone could discover, was of mixed mind. There was a strong "stand-up-to-the-Russians" feeling but also a fear that inept handling by the president could lead to another war.

The rest of the campaign need not be labored; it's an oft-told tale. But the final Dewey rally in Madison Square Garden on the eve of the election is worth a footnote, if only because it introduces my mother as a political prophet.

She was visiting us in New York and I got her a ticket to give her a glimpse of big-time politics. It was the usual large last-minute rally, and as we left I asked her what she thought. "That man can't win," she said. Amused, I asked her why she thought so. "Because," she replied, "this was supposed to be a victory rally and there was almost no excitement when Dewey entered and spoke." Sad to say, I dismissed her prophecy.

There was nothing left for me to do now but write the customary wrap-up piece to appear in the *Journal* the Monday before the election. I brooded over it long. I had no reason to challenge the prediction of the Gallup poll and others that Dewey would win handsomely, nor would I have had the nerve to do so. Yet I was haunted by the puzzle I had found in my travels and noticed by my mother at Madison Square Garden, the contrast between the enthusiasm among those favoring Truman and the want of it for Tom Dewey. How to note that puzzle without making myself look foolish after Dewey was elected?

So I sat down and wrote a piece, the opening of which I will never forget: "By all the polls and portents, Thomas E. Dewey will be the next president of the United States. But it's hard to see why."

I then went on to say Dewey's win would be because the voters were weary of all the postwar troubles and thought the Truman performance poor, confusing, and uncertain. I added, though, that Dewey would be a president beginning his term with less popular appeal on his election day than any president in memory.

Bill Grimes killed the piece. The reason he gave was that it was based on nothing more than my own personal feeling—he knew I had never really "cottoned" to Dewey as a person—and that it would be read as a gratuitous slap at the new president. It would reflect on the paper and do me no good when I had to write about the new administration.

I was irritated at the time. But I wasn't crushed until afterwards. I thought then, and I still do, that in the stunned aftermath of Truman's victory it would have looked more prophetic than it actually was and might have made me a candidate for a Pulitzer Prize.

There was some small recompense, however. In 1948 there were none of these huge computers which with electrifying speed tell us the winner before bedtime of election night. On the *Journal* we planned an all-night vigil with many replates of the front page as the raw votes were counted, and I was in charge of the election coverage. Dewey did take a strong early lead, but I had just enough of a gnawing uncertainty to avoid the blunder of the *Chicago Tribune* which early proclaimed Dewey the next president. We still hadn't committed ourselves on a winner when the last of the replates left the press in the early morning hours. It wasn't until nine-thirty the next morning, Wednesday, that the issue was settled, and Dewey didn't concede until eleven o'clock.

That Truman victory, incidentally, wasn't quite as sweeping as folklore remembers it. He was in fact a minority president in terms of the popular vote, the first since Woodrow Wilson in 1912. He did carry the electoral college with 303 votes to 228 for Dewey and Thurmond combined. Wallace, though polling a million popular votes, got none in the electoral college.

All the same, 'twas a famous victory. Harry Truman had staggered all the experts—Gallup, Roper, the professional politicians and, not least, the journalistic craft. He would probably have won by a larger margin had not Wallace and Thurmond between them siphoned off more than two million votes.

*   *   *   *   *

I've been journalistically involved in every presidential election since. Several have been as interesting, never one I have enjoyed as much. Thereafter the main responsibility for the *Journal*'s political coverage, which continued to expand, would be in the hands of successive Washington bureau chiefs. Whether at conventions or, sometimes, out on the hustings, I would feel as if I were a supernumerary. I thus ended my Washington years with regret.

But before they ended entirely I would have one more meeting with a president, this time an ex-president. For it was during the Washington to New York commuting period when I was still a political reporter as well as an editorial writer that I met former President Herbert Hoover, whom President Truman had asked to head a newly formed commission on reorganization of the federal government.

My preconceptions of Hoover were largely formed in the early 1930s when he was held responsible for the Great Depression or at least for failure in dealing with it. To Democratic propagandists he made a handy villain. So my impression was of an inept if not un-intelligent man who didn't take the depression seriously and was rather heartless toward the unemployed and others who suffered from it. This impression had been modified somewhat by reading of his work as food administrator during the First World War and his extraordinary postwar efforts at feeding the war-torn countries, especially Russia. This had won him wide respect as a man of vision and compassion. To the world before 1929 he was the "Great Engineer" and had won the presidency handily over Al Smith.

I had also by now some sympathy for him because I knew of his shoddy treatment by Roosevelt. In that long interregnum in 1933 between election and inauguration of the new president (inauguration day in those days fell in March) Hoover wanted to close the banks but felt he was too discredited to do so without at least the tacit approval of President-elect Roosevelt. Roosevelt refused any support, then closed the banks himself immediately after taking office. There was something sad too in the way Roosevelt left the former president on inauguration night to go unnoticed to the railroad station to catch a train to New York and exile. This without even Secret Service protection for a man then hated by millions of people. Nonetheless, I still had a stereotyped picture of Hoover.

I was young at the time, with no sense of being an observer in the making of history. I can find nowhere any notes from that meeting, and the published result of it was no more than a pro forma editorial saying Hoover was well-equipped to study government reorganization and that Truman had done well to choose him for the task.

But that meeting is still vivid in memory. Hoover received me in a large and comfortable office in the Waldorf Towers, where he had lived quietly for years. His manner was gracious, though he must have been surprised at the youth of his interviewer from *The Wall Street Journal*. He was then in his seventies. He looked exactly like his pictures, portly, round of face with heavy jowls, formally dressed with his familiar stiff white collars. Formality also marked the beginning of our conversation.

Asked what shape his recommendations might take, he reminded me there were other members of the commission; they would make a lengthy study, and he could not forecast the result. No news there.

Then gradually he began to talk about government in general

and its propensity to both grow and sprawl. I remember his remarking that when he came to the White House in 1929 he thought it already too big. He also reminded me that when Roosevelt was campaigning in 1932 one of his complaints was excessive spending by the Hoover administration and his promise that he would reduce it. If there was any bitterness in this recollection, I didn't detect it. What was plain, however, was his gratitude toward Truman for giving him this chance to come out of exile.

That was about all there was to the meeting. I left, though, with a different impression of the man as a person of insight into the nature of government and as a man of ability. I didn't change my opinion, and haven't since, that in 1932 he was the wrong man for the presidency, if for no other reason because he lacked the presence to give the country confidence. I had a new picture of him as a man of character who had been undone by the times. I remain thankful I had the opportunity for even so brief a visit.

*   *   *   *   *

Ahead of me, however, lay new adventures. Some would be unhappy ones, and at one point my career seemed to fall into an abyss. Yet in time I found that shifting to New York and to the editorial page opened new horizons. And one of these was the chance to be a more active participant in making *The Wall Street Journal* a truly national newspaper.

PART FOUR

New York, the Beginning

An institution
is the lengthened shadow
of one man.

—Ralph Waldo Emerson,
Essays, First Series

NEW YORK, THE BEGINNING

I

n the summer of 1956 I sat in the Cow Palace outside San
Francisco where the Republicans had gathered to re-
nominate Dwight Eisenhower for president and where
Harold Stassen was trying to dissuade them from renominating
Richard Nixon for vice-president.

Since every newsman knew what was going to happen, the renomination of both Eisenhower and Nixon, there wasn't a lot of
suspense over the outcome. Like my colleagues on other papers I
was both amused by and grateful to Stassen; at least he provided
us something to write about. So it was that late one afternoon I
went down to the *Journal*'s subterranean workroom in the Cow
Palace and wrote a bit of commentary. The subject of that article is
of no interest now. What is of interest is its journey from my typewriter to readers the next day in New York, California, Illinois,
or Texas.

The article written, I handed it to a teletype operator in our
workroom who sent it by direct wire to the *Journal*'s editorial
headquarters in New York, a procedure being followed by hundreds of other correspondents for other newspapers across the
country. The difference was that about an hour later when I walked
into the downtown office of the *Journal* in San Francisco I was
handed a galley proof in type of the article I had just written. In
the meantime it had travelled three thousand miles across the continent to New York, been edited for any vagaries in my spelling,
had a headline written for it, and then sent three thousand miles
back across the continent to our printing plant in San Francisco.
At the same time the article had been sent to *Journal* printing
plants in Chicago, Washington and Dallas.

It was a dramatic illustration of what had happened to that
small newspaper I had joined twenty years earlier. When I had
temporarily left it to go to war its circulation was 32,600. When I
returned five years later the circulation had crept back to 50,000,
about what it was before the depression hit. Now, in 1956, it was

more than 300,000. Even more impressive, it was now published each night in five plants strategically located across the country. Because the type was set automatically from punched tape, the news and editorial copy from each of these plants was the same (including, I might note, the same typographical errors when they occurred). For the first time it really hit home to me that *The Wall Street Journal* was on its way to becoming what it has long since become, the country's largest circulation daily and only national newspaper, with the same paper delivered on the same day to readers as far apart as Portland, Oregon, and Portland, Maine. I had no doubt any longer that a dream would be fulfilled.

That dream was already in the mind of Bernard Kilgore when, those years ago, he had been the chief of the *Journal*'s Washington bureau. In the bull sessions around the office he used to talk about it. His basic idea was simple. Most news in most newspapers, including prestigious ones like *The New York Times*, was primarily local or regional, with an overlay of national and international news of major importance which filled only a relatively small part of the "news hole." Business news, too, tended to be regional. Major newspapers like the *Times* carried the stock exchange quotations and some news of the larger and more important companies, such as earnings reports, dividends, and the like. Some also carried news of companies in their circulation area. Smaller newspapers did not do even this much.

The Wall Street Journal of that time, although specializing in business news, tended to take a narrow view of it, or so Barney would say. For example, we already had a Pacific Coast edition, begun in 1929, but it was then separately edited by the San Francisco staff. The editors there had access to all the same news, including that from the Dow Jones News Service, but they made their own selections of what to use and they added news they thought of special interest to West Coast businessmen. In short, there were two newspapers of the same name a continent apart, but they were different. A reader in California might or might not see the same news as the *Journal*'s reader in New York.

In the late evening hours of those early years when the work was done in the Washington bureau some of us would sit around hashing over the day's news while engaging in a bit of poker or a curious card game known as "coon-can," usually with a bottle somewhere in evidence. There Barney would argue that the two *Journal* editions should be the same, with stories selected for their broad national interest or importance. His theme was that, of all the areas of news, business and things that affected business, such as government actions or international developments, were the most universal in interest to readers across the country. Even sports, he would say, couldn't match it. New York papers might give all the scores but their readers were mainly interested in the Yankees, Dodgers or Giants, all then New York teams. West Coast papers concentrated on the football teams of Stanford or UCLA. And so on.

I must confess I wasn't as impressed by all of this as I should have been. Nor were most of the others who heard Barney's ideas. What he was saying—that the country needed a "national" newspaper, and that business-related news could be the foundation of it—flew in the face of every orthodox idea about newspapers in a country as large and diverse as ours. England, a small country, might have nationally circulated newspapers. Not the United States. Even if it were possible to design one, how would you get it printed and distributed each day across so vast a land?

Barney himself wasn't too sure about that. Certainly there would be technical problems, but even in 1936 we had two publishing plants, one on each coast, which was a beginning. Barney didn't have too clear an idea, either, what kind of paper such a national newspaper should be. He only said, vaguely, that it should be "different" from other papers. Different in format and play of the news. Anyone who lived in Richmond, Virginia, had to take the *Times-Dispatch* to keep up with things in that area; so readers in Des Moines, Iowa, would need the *Register*. The *Wall Street Journal* couldn't take away their readers. To succeed it would have to appeal as each reader's "second newspaper," one with a business base and a national and international outlook, thus offering something not available in the local press.

Now that the *Journal* has proved the point it all seems obvious. It wasn't then, nor would it be for years to come. Many people played their parts in the making of the modern *Wall Street Journal*; imaginative editors, first of all, but also technical people in the printing trades, able people in merchandising, circulation, and advertising, people too often overlooked when the success of the paper is recalled. Nonetheless, it all began with a dream and without the dreamer it would not be.

When I first met Barney Kilgore, in 1936, he was twenty-seven years old, my senior by only five years. He was a Hoosier, born in Albany, Indiana, son of a railroad man. He graduated from DePauw University in Greencastle, where he was editor of the student newspaper, and he talked his way onto the *Journal* in 1929, in part because the then company president, Kenneth C. Hogate, was also a DePauw graduate. There he was quickly marked as a young man of promise. He rose rapidly as reporter, copy editor, news editor of that San Francisco edition and as a financial columnist before being picked to head the Washington bureau, the youngest chief of a sizeable bureau in the capital.

In appearance he was of medium height, stockily built, with dark hair (already showing signs of forehead baldness), good features and a soft voice. He was then a bachelor and something of a ladies' man. He struck me as having an unusual combination of shyness and that quality called "command presence," even for one so youthful. The shyness showed in a neck "tic" which he never completely overcame and which became more pronounced when he became tense. He was also an able journalist, a good and lucid writer, and he took the trouble to study and understand what he was writing about. Among his peers he quickly became known as a good explainer of the new, and sometimes esoteric, programs of the New Deal. On one occasion during what was known as the "gold crisis" President Roosevelt told questioners at a press conference "to read Barney Kilgore" if they wanted to understand it.

He was also ambitious. An illustrative incident is his manner of getting himself elected to the famous Gridiron Club, a relatively closed society of old-time newspapermen in Washington. He did it by making a list of all the members and then in organized fashion inviting them each to lunch or to dinner at the rather sumptuous apartment he had rented. That way he bypassed a number of other hopefuls. He also set out to broaden his public recognition by writing for magazines of more general circulation; for a number of years he was a regular contributor to *Today Magazine*, a forerunner of *Newsweek*. On late afternoons he would often sit down at Ken Kramer's desk and read all the copy filed for the day, with an eagle eye for an obscure phrase or something that needed better explanation. I know, for I was frequently the target of his quiet but firm comments. He was properly deferential to New York, but when he thought the editors there had mishandled a story he let them know what he thought. This naturally raised his stature with the Washington staff.

In 1941, shortly after I had left for the Navy, Barney was called to New York as managing editor to succeed Grimes, who had been named editor. Almost at once he began trying to remake the paper. In 1943 "Casey" Hogate suffered a severe heart attack and the Barron family, then proprietors of Dow Jones, cast about for someone to serve as general manager. The post was first offered to Grimes, who declined on the grounds that he didn't want the responsibility and headaches of business management. He recommended Kilgore, although Barney was many years his junior. So that year Barney was named vice-president and general manager, and from then on the destiny of the company and the paper was in his hands because Hogate never recovered sufficiently to be active on a daily basis. In 1945 Barney was made president, but that was a change in title only.

*   *   *   *   *

The company and the newspaper the management of which Barney inherited had its beginnings in 1882 when Charles Dow, then thirty-one years old, persuaded two friends, Edward T. Jones and Charles Bergstresser, to join him in founding a financial news service for private clients. Their first venture was the publication of a series of "slips," delivered by hand several times during the day, containing the latest news on the stock market and other financial developments. This was the forerunner of the Dow Jones News Service, known today as the "broad tape." Originally those "slips" were handwritten; later they were set in type in a small print shop. This proved so successful that still later they decided to reprint them all in late afternoon using a newspaper format. So on July 8, 1889, the first issue of *The Wall Street Journal*, a small four-page pamphlet, was printed on an old Campbell press and distributed to a few hundred readers within a carrier-boy's walk of the corner of Broad and Wall Streets.

The story of those early years belongs to the formal history of the paper and the company well told by Lloyd Wendt (Rand

McNally). Suffice it to say here that Jones dropped out early, leaving the enterprise to Dow and Bergstresser. Charlie Dow, the chief initiator of the project, was the more experienced newsman of the three. A Connecticut farm boy, he had been a reporter on papers in Springfield, Massachusetts, and Providence, Rhode Island, before joining the New York *Mail*, a paper long since vanished. In those years he learned to write simply and forcefully, a skill that stood him in good stead when he struck out on his own as a reporter of business affairs. He once wrote in his newspaper: "Nobody who plants corn digs up the kernels in a day or two to see if the corn has sprouted, but in stocks most people want to open an account at noon and get their profits before night." Another observation of his led to what later became known as the "Dow theory" of stock market movements, though I suspect he would have disowned the precision claimed by those who later formalized it as a means of prophecy. "The market," he wrote, "is always to be considered as having three movements, all going at the same time. The first is the narrow movement from day to day. The second is the short swing from two weeks to a month or more. The third is the main movement covering at least four years in its duration."

Dow died in 1902 and the company and the newspaper passed to another New England newspaperman, Clarence Walker Barron, who was to put a stamp on both that would last to this day.

By all accounts Clarence Barron was an eccentric personality. His education didn't extend beyond the English High School in Boston but he was to become a major publisher, a friend of the famous and the important, an author of several books, a rich man who believed in spending his money to live well. He was small in height, and judging from his portraits and recollections of those who knew him, as round as he was tall. He soaked up information like a sponge and disgorged it in nonstop fashion to a platoon of male secretaries, one of whom had to follow him everywhere, even into the men's room. Out of all that dictation came his best known book, *They Told Barron*, and one still fertile in raw material for historians of the first third of the twentieth century. Under Barron the circulation of the *Journal* grew from about seven thousand (there are no accurate records of the early years) to fifty thousand during the 1920s. In terms of prestige and influence it was larger than its circulation.

Barron had already founded two local financial newspapers, one in Boston and one in Philadelphia. The addition of the *Journal* put him in the three major financial cities of that era. Although in time the *Journal* overshadowed the other papers, Barron kept the others alive, partly as a concession to local pride and partly, no doubt, to help defray the cost of news bureaus in those important cities. One of his major innovations was to interlock the news gathering so that each of the three could draw on the resources of the other. This was to be the foundation of what is today the largest number of domestic news bureaus of any newspaper.

To this nucleus of the present day company Barron added a weekly financial magazine in 1921 and the Pacific Coast edition of the *Journal* in 1929. Both also got off to shaky starts, the Pacific Coast edition being launched on the eve of the stock market crash a year after Barron's death in 1928. Both showed, however, that "C. W." had visions of broader horizons.

It was in the early 1920s that "Casey" Hogate (DePauw, 1918) joined the *Journal* as manager of its Detroit bureau after having been a reporter there and in Cleveland. A big, bluff man, Hogate could match Barron in stubbornness as well as ability. The paper's folklore is rich in tales of their personal encounters after Hogate became managing editor in 1923. One, which I hope is not apocryphal, is of the two of them on Barron's yacht, arguing. Neither would speak directly to the other. So Barron's secretary acted as go-between. "Tell Mr. Hogate. . . ," and the secretary would trot from stern to bow. "Tell Mr. Barron. . . ," and back would go the messenger. I suspect both enjoyed the game. Anyway, Hogate became the company's general manager and, by the time I arrived, its president.

The depression was a near-disaster for Barron's little empire. For a time there seemed to be no economic place for a newspaper specializing in business and finance; Wall Street was in disfavor and few people had any money. The circulation of the *Journal*, New York and San Francisco editions combined, sank to 28,000. That the paper and company survived is due to the juggling skills of Hogate and the patient determination of Jane Bancroft, Barron's daughter, who refused to surrender. By the mid-1930s *Journal* circulation had barely recrossed the 30,000 mark; the company's succor lay only in the Dow Jones News Service, which retained most of its brokerage house customers. No wonder I thought of the *Journal*, in 1936, as a temporary stopping place.

But Hogate had done a number of things which in retrospect would lead to a better future. For one, he recognized early the new importance of Washington to *Journal* readers with the arrival of the New Deal. He hired Grimes away from the United Press to head an enlarged capital bureau and shortly thereafter brought him to New York as managing editor. Washington news became one of the paper's strong points with its readers. Hogate also bought out that rival news service which had occupied my attention in my apprentice days in the "comparison room." Both operations were then so small that no one even thought about the antitrust laws, but the merger strengthened the survivor. And Hogate also, of course, hired that other young DePauw graduate, Barney Kilgore.

*   *   *   *   *

When Kilgore arrived in New York, a few months before Pearl Harbor, he first set about remaking the San Francisco edition in the image of the New York paper so that readers on both coasts would get the same news handled the same way. All readers would thus be treated alike. But the doing of it proved difficult.

First of all, there were technical problems. It was possible to send San Francisco all the copy scheduled for the New York edition via teletype. But there the copy had to be reset in type by hand on Linotypes, using hot metal. That was slow and meant variations in line-lengths and spacing between lines, which in turn meant that a story which filled, say, exactly a column in New York might be more or less in San Francisco. Then the advertising content of each paper was different. Each had ads that were local. Even when a national advertiser wanted to use both editions there would be a time delay between an ad's appearance in New York and San Francisco unless copy was delivered well in advance, especially if the copy contained art work. There was no practical way at the time to send that kind of material by wire with sufficient clarity for reproduction. That applied also to news pictures.

So one necessary step was to eliminate pictures if the makeup of the two editions was to be the same. It was also necessary to devise a simple, fairly standard makeup which could be explained to an editor in San Francisco with a brief message. In practice these problems led to what is now a familiar feature of the modern *Journal*: no pictures and a standardized front page makeup with no headlines more than one column wide. Today with facsimile transmissions it would be possible to use pictures and have as varied a makeup as other papers, but the invention that necessity mothered proved an advantage. With rare exceptions the practice forced on the paper is continued; it's one of the things that makes the *Journal* look unique.

To the technical problems were added some human ones. New York editors were quite happy with the idea of making the two editions alike, since it gave them better control over the whole paper. The San Francisco editors, naturally, felt otherwise. They would lose their autonomy, and instead of being editors making their own decisions they would be merely technicians carrying out orders from New York. Bureaucratic resistance to change isn't limited to government. But the San Francisco editors also had an argument not easily refuted. What of the local or regional news of especial interest to West Coast readers? Every other newspaper in the world paid special attention to the news of its own region. Why should the *Journal* fly in the face of all experience?

In the event, these human problems proved as knotty as the technical ones. Long after Kilgore had succeeded in persuading (browbeating) the San Francisco editors into compliance, at least as far as major stories and the front page were concerned, he had to allow them several columns inside the paper for regional news. It would be years before everyone would be convinced that the *Journal* should be truly national in its news presentation, giving exactly the same news to every reader everywhere with no allowance for regional differences.

Meanwhile, Barney had another little problem to wrestle with. He had talked much of how the *Journal* should be different from other papers not only in appearance or even in the "play" of stories (that is, where they would be put in the paper) but also in content. If the paper should have "different" stories, what kind? What kind of stories were there, in fact, that other newspapers didn't deal with one way or another? Finally, how could the paper establish itself as being national in scope as well as distribution, how could it pretend to be anything more than a trade publication, if it banished from its front page the president's press conference or whatever was the day's major development?

Part of the solution lay in a feature already in the paper. During the Hogate years it had begun giving front-page space to a display headed "What's News." It led the main news of business and finance, followed by a summary of general news and an index to the paper as space permitted. This "What's News" feature was gradually transformed. Taking up two columns on the front page, it devoted the left-hand column to business and finance and the right-hand to general national and world news. As time passed, more manpower and attention were devoted to these two summary columns and soon they bore little resemblance to the "news briefs" carried by other papers. They became carefully crafted compressions of the major news, the work of two full-time writers who did nothing else and whose work was supervised by both the news editor and the managing editor. They soon thus performed two functions. They gave the reader a concise, organized summary of all the main news he could at the time find nowhere else. And they thereby relieved the editors of the necessity of putting the president's press conference story on page one; it would be at the top of the page under "What's News" anyway. The other columns could be used for other matters.

But for what? There then began the groping, which was to go on for years, as to what the *Journal* could offer on the front-page showcase that would be different, would be interesting and useful to its readers, and yet would not change the basic character of the paper as one concentrating on business and economic news and the developments in politics and foreign affairs which impinged on the economy.

The *Journal*, then as now, was a six-column paper. Two of the front-page columns were devoted to "What's News." Back in the 1930s Barney had persuaded New York to accept a weekly column called the "Washington Wire" which would permit the staff in a dozen or so items to offer some behind-the-scenes news from the capital. The information was gathered from the staff at a weekly meeting, the available material selected by Barney and then written by a single writer (Ken Kramer originally) to give it a unified style. It was well received by the readers and had by this time become a Friday fixture. As managing editor Barney began to experiment with similar columns in other news areas; eventually the

"Business Bulletin" and others evolved until there was one a day. Thus three of the six front-page columns became fixed in format.

That left the two outside columns and one in the middle. For the outside columns experiments began with stories that would not be pegged to the immediate news of yesterday except in rare cases but would nonetheless deal with current developments as, for example, in housing, retail sales, overseas political trends or whatever. But there was at the time no clear idea, in Barney's mind or anyone else's, of how to find and develop these stories, and therefore of how to tell the staff what was desired. The formula, if that's the word, was a long time gestating; it has undergone sea-changes over the years. What to do with that sixth column in the middle of the page, day in and day out, was to prove even more vexing. Today's front page didn't spring, like Aphrodite, full-blown from the sea.

Barney, once he became general manager, was also confronted with a business decision. During World War II and for some time thereafter the supply of newsprint was rationed. With its small circulation the *Journal* had a low base, so it was a struggle to find every extra ton. When some was found, the question was what to do with it. Use it for extra ads, which would bring the most immediate rewards at a time when advertising space was at a premium, or use it to expand circulation? Barney shrewdly opted for circulation, choosing a long-term rather than a short-term view. As a result of all this, combined with the growing interest of businessmen in "news they could use," circulation climbed slowly but steadily from its prewar level, though it still remained small in the number of its subscribers if not in their characteristics as leaders in business, government, labor and the professions.

This, then, was *The Wall Street Journal* I had returned to after five years in the service. Much was the same but more seemed to be different and, as I've mentioned, I had some adjusting to do. I did have the advantage, however, of those long-ago "bull sessions" in which Barney had talked out some of his dreams. Up to this point I had had nothing to do with helping give them shape. Any role I was to play would not begin until, reluctantly, I left Washington for New York.

2

When I ended my career as a political reporter in Washington and became permanently attached to the New York office, the editorial staff of the *Journal* consisted only of Bill Grimes, Frederick Korsmeyer, and myself. I had been given the title of associate editor, which Fred did not have, and was told that I would be second in authority to Grimes. Under Grimes I was to be responsible on a day-to-day basis for the paper's editorial page, the word "page" being then a misnomer since it involved only two columns. When he was absent I would be responsible for stating the paper's editorial position on current issues. As Grimes put it, I would be trusted "not to get the paper in any trouble" by contradicting established policies. There was a small problem initially because no one had bothered to tell Fred, a much older man and a *Journal* veteran, of my authority, a vagueness I was to learn was typical of Grimes. I had also been led to think, if somewhat vaguely, that I might inherit Grimes's mantle "someday." This was supposed to assuage my disappointment at leaving Washington and becoming an anonymous editorial writer.

My difficulties with Korsmeyer were to be resolved in time, though they taxed my diplomacy, largely because of a growing mutual respect. But I also had to feel my way through some vagueness in the relationship to and among my other new colleagues, none of whom I knew well except Barney. In those days lines of authority were everywhere a bit fuzzy.

Grimes himself, as the "old man" of the shop, was the head of both the news and editorial departments. Even Barney paid him deference. But Barney was president of the company and had no intention of relinquishing his control of the paper, content-wise or otherwise, since he was bent on remaking it. That made for an unusual relationship.

Grimes was frequently skeptical of Barney's ideas for the "new" *Journal*, especially when he launched out on his expansion program which was to give us printing plants in other places. But his respect for Barney was high; he had, after all, recommended him for his present job and voluntarily settled for a secondary position. In practice Grimes would state his objections, if he had any, and then ultimately defer to Barney's judgment. It was an odd arrangement, but it "worked" because both men were determined that it would.

Meanwhile, as I watched this relationship, I was getting better acquainted with my new colleagues.

First of all, there was Grimes himself. He had hired me, sent me to Washington and brought me back. Yet I had in fact seen little of him close-up. A short man of slight build, no taller than I, he bore an odd resemblance to Harry Truman. With his glasses on his forehead, where they frequently were, his face had a slightly popeyed appearance. He often spoke in cryptic phrases, full of lacunae which you were left to fill in, a difficulty compounded by the fact that he also spoke so softly he was hard to hear. I can remember his mentioning to me ideas he had for editorials which when spoken made no sense but when written were clear, logical, and persuasive. He communicated best by typewriter.

That was surprising, for he had little formal education, and as far as I can remember he never read a book. But in his early experience as a reporter in Ohio he had learned the construction of the simple English sentence, and in his years with the United Press in Washington he had acquired a self-education in politics and government. He had a quick mind and was endowed with good common sense which he could bring to bear on seemingly abstruse philosophical issues. In his writing he reminded me much of an untutored artist who without formal training can attack a block of marble and hew from it a thing of beauty. He well deserved the Pulitzer Prize he won for editorial writing in 1946, the first to come to the *Journal*.

Over the years our personal relationship was to oscillate puzzlingly between affection and estrangement; he was to prove for me both mentor and obstacle. But from him I learned much and to him I am much in debt.

Among others of my new colleagues I established a quick affinity with William F. Kerby, the one-time copy editor who got my first byline wrong and who was now the paper's executive editor. Bill Kerby was also short of stature, somewhat pudgy and with a gimpy leg (as a result of polio) which gave him a kind of rolling gait. Bill didn't have Barney's imagination, but better than anyone else he understood what Barney was dreaming of and he was adept at carrying out Kilgore's ideas. In my first days as an editorial writer he edited my copy and was by far the best copy editor I ever encountered. He was skilled at helping a writer say what the writer wanted to say, though not himself an outstanding writer.

There was not quite the same affinity with Buren McCormack,

the managing editor with whom I had had some frictions as Washington bureau chief. But now that I was not directly under him we got along well enough. Mac was another Hoosier, incidentally, and DePauw graduate, one of a coterie on the *Journal* that came to be known as the "Indiana mafia." Others of that group besides Barney included Robert Feemster, top man on the advertising and circulation side, and Robert Bottorff, then on the West Coast. Both of these were to be key people in the *Journal*'s future.

Mac, Kerby and Barney were the regulars at a daily "coffee clatch," to which I was now admitted. At that time the *Journal* had an open newsroom, no partitions between desks, no private offices even for Mac and Kerby. (Grimes and Kilgore had private offices but they were on a different floor.) Mac and Kerby had desks opposite each other at the end of the long room; I had been installed a few feet from Kerby but within hearing distance of anyone Bill was talking with. When I needed a secretary I shared his.

It was in this corner that the coffee clatch met about ten o'clock each morning to review the day's paper, brainstorm ideas for new stories or, sometimes, just pass the time in idle talk. If there was anything in those informal days that could have passed for an idea center, or policy committee, that was it. It was also, as I was to learn, a constant source of gossip for the news staffers, who speculated what we were talking about.

Barney almost always arrived with a well-marked copy of the day's issue. He lived in Princeton, which was a long commute, and he used the train time to read the paper in its entirety, marking with a red pencil every typo, misspelled word, awkward phrase, or obscurity. I began to realize what made Mac so "finicky" about the Washington copy. Many of the stories that would later develop into "leaders," the name we'd given those two stories on the outside columns of the front page, originated at these meetings.

Grimes never attended these meetings. He rarely arrived in the office before noon. By then, though, he had not only read the *Journal*, but the *Times* and the *Herald-Tribune*. He was also an inveterate reader of the opinion magazines, such as the *Nation* and the *New Republic*, and of the innumerable pamphlets on public issues that poured into the office. Most of the latter were propaganda for special interest groups, but they sparked ideas if only in disagreement. So on arrival he would be full of thoughts for his daily comments.

In the beginning Grimes wrote most of the main editorials for the day. Fred and I would supply one, or perhaps two, to fill out the editorial columns. It wasn't onerous work, and this may have contributed to Barney's view that I was lazy. But the leisurely pace, so much in contrast with my Washington days, gave me a chance to study Grimes's technique, which I did as diligently as in a classroom. Although he may have been untutored in any formal way, he had a natural sense of organization. His editorials had a clear beginning, middle, and end and he took care to say not only what he thought but why, a rarity among editorial writers. With him an editorial became a small essay.

I did not try to imitate his style, which was informal and full of homely analogies. I was, I suppose, more "literary." But gradually I absorbed from him a sense of form for the short essay, and it wasn't long before I was writing editorials he thought worth occupying the top spot for the day. Not infrequently Barney would compliment Grimes on some editorial only to find that I had written it.

All in all I was beginning to feel comfortable in my new job though regretting the excitement of Washington. Both Grimes and Barney seemed pleased with my work; when Grimes was away no one bothered me. On such days I was in effect the paper's editorial voice, and I thought I could foresee the time when I would succeed to the editor's chair. At least there was no one else around, Korsmeyer being too old, who looked like an heir apparent.

And then disaster struck.

*   *   *   *   *

It happened this way:

One afternoon in mid-1950 Grimes stopped by my desk, as was his wont late in the day, to read proofs on the next day's editorials. Having done so, he passed them back to me without comment or correction.

Then he said, casually, that Buren McCormack would be joining the editorial staff. That alone was a surprise. Mac had never written an editorial in his life and, so far as I could see, had neither the type of mind nor the writing skill for that particular craft. What followed was a shock indeed. Since Mac was senior to me in point of service on the paper, Grimes said he would have the title of *senior* associate editor and would be in charge.

I was stunned. I felt as Harry Truman once did, that the sun and the stars and the moon had fallen on me, but unlike the Truman case I was not being lifted up but being hit over the head by them. In a trice all my great expectations vanished.

My first thought was of the terrible mistake I had made in coming to New York. Barely a year and a half earlier I had held one of the best positions on the paper, indeed one of the best journalism jobs around, chief of the *Journal*'s Washington bureau. It was a job that offered almost endless opportunities for being in the center of great events, for acquiring a reputation among my colleagues, for building a durable career. I had thrown it all away by listening to Bill Grimes's blandishments.

This was followed by a sense of outrage. Those blandishments had been empty words. I had been betrayed. In no way could I think, or did he say, that I was being superseded because my work was unsatisfactory. I knew, and he knew, that I had performed well. I had not only been betrayed but betrayed by a man for whom, a moment before, my heart had been full of admiration, gratitude, and affection.

As a matter of fact, when I stammered out some words from my first anger, Grimes, strangely surprised at my reaction, tried to assure me that this was no reflection on my work and hadn't been so intended. He could only give some feeble explanation that Mac needed more varied experience. Mac had been in the managing editor's job for four years and it was time for him to move on. Henry Gemmill was to be the new managing editor.

In that, as I was to discover, lay the true explanation. Grimes and Barney wanted to make Henry managing editor; for good reason, I think. That left the question what to do with Mac. It was almost as an afterthought that the editorial page occurred to them as a place to move him. They felt they could hardly put him under me, considering his past service and my relative newness in New York. So they created this new post with barely a moment's reflection in advance on what my reaction might be. That made the move not only cruel but thoughtless.

My next thought was, What should I do?

My immediate instinct was to quit on the spot. Had I been younger or the circumstances different, that is what I would have done. But by now I had given hostages to fortune. I had a wife and two children who were dependent on me. I had, moreover, up-rooted them from a place where they were happy and myself from a place where I might have had a better chance to find another job on a different newspaper. Now I could not take chances. The thought of putting Frances once again through hardships or uncertainty was abhorrent to me. The responsibility for my family lay upon my shoulders.

I picked up my coat, without saying anything further, and left Grimes sitting silently in his chair. For one of the few times in my life I went across the street to Eberlin's bar, the *Journal* hangout, and fortified myself with a drink against the night's homecoming. Joe Guilfoyle, one of my older and better friends on the staff, was there and asked me what was the matter. I told him. He quietly picked up my bar check.

I can't remember what I said to Frances when I got home. I only remember that we had supper with the children as if nothing had happened and that when we went up to bed I wept. I could only think that all the hopes I brought with me to New York for my career lay in ashes. It was a bitter night.

The next morning I went to see Barney in his eyrie on the top floor. I told him, as calmly as I could, exactly how I felt. I said I wasn't going to do anything rash; I wouldn't childishly pick up my marbles and go home. But I explained that I thought in all fairness he ought to know I no longer felt bound by any loyalty to the paper. I would take the first decent job offer.

My relation with Barney was quite different from that with Grimes. There was, of course, none of the feeling of the younger man for an older father-figure. Barney and I were contemporaries; he was only five years older. I had worked closely with him for four years in Washington. He too had been, and still was, a young man with ambition. He was easier to talk to because he could understand my feelings.

He explained that he couldn't change the decision, but he was sympathetic and tried also to assure me that I had a bright future with the paper. What, he asked, did I want to do? I said that eventually I wanted Grimes's job. This made him gulp, but he spared me any further remarks about the size of my britches. Although the meeting resolved nothing, I was glad to get my feelings off my chest.

Meanwhile I had begun to think out what I would do. First, I would write my pieces as before. Beyond that, I would withdraw from any responsibility for putting out the page. Mac could write his own editorials. I would offer no thoughts either about his or Fred's copy. Next I would try to use the excuse of having an extra writer at hand to break away from the office now and then for special pieces; the need of an editorial writer to get out of the office would be a good argument. Finally, I would cast my net far and wide for another job.

It proved to be the best course. Mac, as I suspected, turned out to be a pedestrian editorial writer. It must not have taken Grimes long to realize this, for one day he asked me why I didn't help out more with idea and writing suggestions as I had done before.

I looked at him as expressionless a face as I could muster. "That's not my job anymore," I told him. He made no reply.

What followed was a strange year, an agonizing one. It came at a time when my situation at home was also depressing. Frances and I had not solved our housing problem after our move to New York. We were living in a rented house in a not-too-pleasant area of Queens where there was a difficult school situation for the girls. Frances had been having a bad time physically, in the hospital twice in a matter of months. Even without the troubles in the office it would have been an unhappy time. The wreckage of my career hopes, as I saw it then, deepened my depression. Only the fact that Frances, as she always did, absorbed the rude changes with grace and loyalty made it bearable. She spoke more confidence in me than I had in myself.

As for the changes wrought in the office, I could in no way begrudge Henry Gemmill his promotion to managing editor. Henry had worked with me briefly in the Washington bureau on my return from the war and had, even then, been marked as a superb writer. In fact, he had preceded me to New York for the job of "leader" editor, the man in charge of those two main front-page stories and so second in importance to McCormack as managing editor. I knew he would bring to the managing editor's job new qualities of imagination. That meant, of course, that he now emerged as a new rival, but I liked him and admired him.

Mac, to his credit, went out of the way to be conciliatory now that he was, once again, my boss. When I broached my idea of getting out of the office occasionally, he was receptive. Nonetheless, the return of friction between us was inevitable, compounded now by the fact that he was an obstacle to my own ambitions which I saw no way to get around.

The first escape from that trap in which I found myself came with the Korean War.

* * * * *

On that dramatic June Sunday when hostilities began we were vacationing in a cottage we had rented on Point Lookout, Long Island. Monday morning I had a call from Kerby who asked if I could go to Washington to take temporary charge of the bureau because Ellis Haller, then the bureau chief, was away.

Landing in Washington I tried all my old sources at the White House, elsewhere in the administration and on Capitol Hill, to find out what was happening. Among those who would talk, it was plain none knew very much about what came next. Possibly, Truman himself didn't know much except that he had made a decision "not to let the Communists get away with" their invasion of South Korea.

The only thing at all clear was that the Pentagon wasn't prepared for fighting on the Korean peninsula. As far back as 1947 the Joint Chiefs of Staff had agreed South Korea wasn't worth fighting for, and in the winter of 1950 Secretary of State Acheson had publicly said the Asian continent was outside the line of major U.S. defense interests, a speech that may well have emboldened the North Koreans.

On Tuesday Truman asked the United Nations to condemn the invasion, which it did, with the Russians for some reason abstaining from a vote. On Capitol Hill Truman's announcement that he would therefore provide naval and air support for South Korean troops was received with near-unanimous approval. Only one man stood publicly and loudly against the day's emotions. That was, once more, Robert Taft.

On Wednesday, June 28, the South Korean capital fell to the invaders. On Thursday, at a jam-packed press conference, Truman insisted "we are not at war." In the following question period someone (I don't remember who) asked if it could be called a "police action." Truman said, "Yes, that is exactly what it amounts to." And so a 1984-type "newspeak" phrase entered our political vocabulary.

Once more Washington was in a state of confusion and, once more, I was enjoying the excitement. All this time I had been trying to collect my thoughts. That Thursday afternoon after Truman's press conference I sat down to pull them together and wrote a piece for the Friday paper. I decided to call Korea a war, which it was.

"The Truman administration," I began, "got into the Korean war in a moment of inspiration and now it is relying on perspiration to get us through."

I went on to say the president made his momentous decision to fight in Korea as a "calculated risk." Then: "But so quickly was it made, his advisers are only now just beginning to calculate all the risks. . . . Each new decision is sweated out as another new decision is forced upon them. . . . The decision [to fight] was as much a surprise to the president's closest advisers, diplomatic and military, as it was to the public. The haste in which it was made obviously precluded any but the most rudimentary calculations about the moves ahead on the complex chessboard."

Up to this point what I wrote was simply an assessment, as best I could gather it, of what had happened and what practical problems it posed. But now I injected a personal point of view, which Grimes let stand, by offering my own thoughts.

"War itself is so big a problem it sweeps little problems away. But the mire of a half-war makes all decisions difficult.

"How much blood and tears is Korea worth? Do we make a token effort or do we go all-out for this remote peninsula? Do we send ground troops and risk another Bataan in a second gamble to back the first gamble?

"Korea is worth nothing except as a symbol. We went into this shooting war to wage a political fight against the Russians. Today it looks like the shrewd Russians may ignore the challenge, neither backing down nor [themselves] openly fighting. . . .

"Thus we may be drawn deeper into a war against a little man who isn't there. Are we willing to expend the wealth of lives and material that may be necessary to win a prize of uncertain value? But, having committed ourselves this far, can we afford to quit?"

It was not a piece well received in Washington. Nor, for that matter, among *Journal* readers. We were all to forget it later, but initially the Korean intervention had wide public support. Governor Dewey, still titular head of the Republican party, endorsed it. So editorially did most of the nation's newspapers. To my astonishment even Grimes decided to support the Truman move.

Nonetheless, the piece was not only prophetic, it was also to have an effect on future turns in my career.

For one thing it let me escape the editorial sanctum, now become oppressive. It led me back to the political hustings for the 1950 congressional elections. Neither Grimes nor Mac tried to stay me. It also attracted enough attention to lead in time to an escape route from the trap that entangled me on the *Journal*.

Reporting congressional elections poses different problems from a presidential campaign. There is no central focus; every congressional district is different in its political crosscurrents, making it difficult to measure national trends. Yet it seemed to me that this year, 1950, there would be a central question that would affect all the political races, namely the Korean War. Therefore I set out not so much to write about individual races as to try to measure the public's temper about the war and its accompanying economic problems. I decided just to prowl the country. That did give me some insights into the mood of that uneasy summer, a chance to renew my acquaintance with Senator Taft and to introduce me to another fascinating political character, Everett Dirksen.

I flew to St. Louis, rented a car, and began a meandering journey through Illinois, Missouri, Kansas, and then into Ohio. The first part of it I built around route U.S. 40, not yet a four-lane interstate but still a main cross-continental highway. In Missouri I branched off to visit towns like Montgomery City, Mexico, Centralia, Pilot Grove, and Odessa. There I searched out local business people, farmers, newspaper editors if there were any. I got myself invited to Rotary Club luncheons, 4-H Club meetings, church suppers or any place I could find gatherings of people.

At Lawrence, Kansas, just for one example, the farmers who came to the Underwood feed and grain store had heard much about Korea and didn't like much of what they had heard. That first euphoria had passed. At a barbecue picnic one of them said, "One time or other we made a mistake. Either we shouldn't have gotten out of Korea in the first place or we shouldn't have gone back." Others worried about the talk of price controls again and were uneasy about the prospects of renewed inflation.

There was a curious ambivalence toward Truman himself. People seemed worried about his ability to deal with the war and its problems without quarreling with his basic decision to fight there. There was little that summer to foreshadow the widespread disillusionment that was to come.

The feeling grew on me, and I so wrote, that we would not see a repetition of 1946 when the Republicans swept the congressional elections, but that there could be, all the same, large GOP gains. So I decided to take a closer look at two key states, Illinois and Ohio.

In Ohio the labor unions were going all out to defeat Senator Taft, author of that hated "slave-labor law." It was a rough campaign. A hint that the unions would fail came one afternoon in Akron. Taft was visiting a machine tool plant where every workman wore a "Jumping Joe" Ferguson button for the Democratic candidates. As Taft walked through the plant, several other reporters and I hung back to talk to the workers after Taft had passed. Asked what they thought of the senator, many volunteered that they "liked the man." A few recalled that his father had been president and thought he might be too. Plainly the outward buttons and their inward feelings weren't always the same. Taft carried the state handily.

In Illinois the important race was between Democratic Senator Scott Lucas, the majority leader of the Senate, and an upstart Republican, Representative Everett McKinley Dirksen. Lucas, because of his established position in the Senate, had the apparent advantage. It did him no good against the flamboyant Dirksen.

I saw why one day in southern Illinois. Dirksen had swept through Pinckneyville, Murphysboro, Cairo, until late in the day he came to Vienna. There under the hot summer sun was a gathering of farmers, the men in shirt-sleeves and galluses, the women in bright printed dresses. Dirksen roared into town in a cloud of dust, an evangelist come to wrestle with the Democratic devil. As the afternoon wore on, off came Dirksen's coat, his tie slipped from his collar, his hair became ruffled—it was, after all, a powerful devil he was fighting. He took his audience to old Vienna, to Czechoslovakia, to Poland, to Korea and China—the Communists hadn't won any of these places, he said; they'd been given away by the

Democrats led by Truman and Scott Lucas. By the time dusk came and the people were ready for the fish fry, he had an audience as aroused as at a Holy Roller's revival.

It was, I suppose, pure demagoguery, but no more so than Truman's "give 'em hell" speeches against the Republicans in 1948. Looking for some way to frame the account I hit upon comparing it to the story of Gideon slaying the Midianites. It made a good story, and one result of it was the beginning of a long acquaintance with one of the spellbinding orators of the decade ahead.

That story and others from these political hustings drew some attention on the *Journal* and elsewhere. They had something to do with the next break in my up-and-down journalistic career.

*   *   *   *   *

That break came before the year was out. I had a call from Paul Miller, whom I had known when he headed the Associated Press bureau in Washington. Paul is a tall, handsome man, and even then he had more the bearing of a diplomat or a man-of-affairs than the working newspaper reporter which he had been for the AP since 1932. Now he was right-hand man to Frank Gannett, founder of the newspaper chain that bears his name. Paul said Mr. Gannett and he would like to talk to me. Could I come to Rochester, headquarters of the company?

All during this upsetting year I'd been looking for job opportunities. I had tried the New York papers, meeting some encouragement but no immediate offers. I'd approached several newspaper syndicates and had one proposal. I'd also had an offer from the *Saturday Evening Post*, where by now I knew Ben Hibbs, the editor, and one of his main assistants, Arthur Baum. But these offers from the syndicate and from the *Post* involved what are best described as "Hollywood contracts." That is, each offered me a year's salary guarantee with options for renewal each year; their options, not mine. They were tempting but not overwhelming. I risked being out of work a year later, stranded in Queens with no financial resources to fall back on. That risk was too much to ask of my family.

So Paul's call came at an opportune moment. I spent two days in Rochester talking to Mr. Gannett and him. I was offered a job with their Rochester paper, flagship of the chain, at a 30 percent increase over my *Journal* salary along with the prospect I would soon be editor.

I went home to think about it and talk it over with Frances. She was willing to move again, even eager considering the circumstances. I was on the verge of accepting when I got a phone call from Barney.

Unknown to me, Paul, ever the diplomat, had called Barney ahead of time to say he was thinking about making me a proposal. So I went up to see Barney and told him what it was, and he asked what I was going to do. I replied that given the situation at the *Journal* I didn't see what I could do but accept. He reminded me I could meet disappointments with Gannett too; promises didn't always work out.

"Yes," I said, "but with one important difference. I will have no emotional investment there as I do here. No matter what happens at Gannett I won't have the feeling of being betrayed by people I have long trusted."

There was a pause, each of us occupied with our own thoughts. Then he said he thought I had talent the paper needed and he didn't want me to leave. He would top the Gannett offer by immediately increasing my salary by half-again.

I acknowledged that as both generous and flattering. It would still leave me, though, in my uncomfortable position. Barney's neck tic became more pronounced and he said he would try to think of something to do about that, perhaps finding me a different job.

There was a long silence.

After a time he got up, said he would count on my staying and I could count on him, if I'd have a little patience, to resolve my job problem. I had known Barney a long time. I felt there was nothing I could do but agree.

In early 1951 an announcement came that Kerby had been elected vice-president of Dow Jones and Mac would succeed him as executive editor. I would be senior associate editor, taking Mac's old title, although there was then no other associate editor for me to be senior to.

Thus I was restored to my former estate with a sizeable pay increase. How all this was arranged with Grimes I don't know, but on the day of the announcement and afterwards he treated me as if the past year had never happened. It took no more than that day for our old relationship to be renewed.

I was not to be dethroned again. There would in time, though, be other cases of friction as ambitious people, all of about the same age, bumped against each other in the growing company.

3

From its earliest days as a four-page paper *The Wall Street Journal* kept a small corner for the editor's observations on topics of interest. Dow, the first editor, confined his comments largely to the stock market and financial affairs affecting it. William Peter Hamilton, an Englishman who was editor under Barron, enlarged the area of subject matter to include broader economic questions; he was widely read for his trenchant opinions. But it was Thomas F. Woodlock who most shaped the future scope of the *Journal*'s editorial columns.

Woodlock was an Irishman, a Catholic, a linguist, and a scholar with a philosophic turn of mind. He worked for the *Journal* briefly in Dow's time, drifted off into business and government service as a member of the Interstate Commerce Commission. He returned to the paper as a commentator in 1930. He was still there when I joined the paper in 1936, and his regular column "Thinking It Over" continued until his death during World War II. It was in this period that the paper's columns began to blossom with essays on Plato or John Stuart Mill and with thoughtful examinations of the issues of the day against a background of the principles on which Western thought had developed. He stretched the intellectual dimensions of the editorial columns and laid the foundation for an editorial policy that would rest on a moral and philosophic base.

Woodlock, though, could be frustrating for readers with less education than his. He "wrote down" to none. He was instrumental in introducing to America the thoughts of the Spanish philosopher Ortega y Gasset, frequently by quoting from *The Revolt of the Masses* without bothering to translate. If he thought a Latin or French phrase expressed an idea best, he would use it and leave the reader to search out its meaning.

Woodlock and Grimes overlapped each other for a few years as the paper's editorial commentators and they complemented each other. Grimes too had a philosophic mind. He too wrote about current issues from a base of general principles. But his style was simpler. His presentations of ideas were straightforward, analogies and illustrative stories in the Lincoln fashion replacing literary or learned allusions. Both men were to influence my own ideas and the expression of them.

Editorial writing, or commentary on public affairs, is a peculiar occupation. The writer is perforce called upon to deal with many topics and issues on which he is not, and cannot be, an expert. One day he is writing about taxes, on another some complicated economic argument, and on the next about foreign policy, perhaps involving some distant and relatively unfamiliar part of the world. He must find something to say, sensible he hopes, about all these things. I have often said that any journalist who comes to deal with the world beyond the police court beat, and especially one asked to comment upon what happens in it, is by the nature of his job a "professional amateur." He is rarely an expert on anything but he is forced to learn a little about many things—economics, law, science, government, sociology, and so forth.

Furthermore, unlike the writer of monographs or essays in magazines he must be able to compress his thoughts into a few words, often no more than three hundred or four hundred and rarely more than eight hundred. Yet if his comments are to be worth reading the compression cannot lose sight of the basic principles involved nor of the line of the argument.

This helps explain why the general level of editorial writing, or commentary, is so mediocre. Most journalists come to it because they have been good reporters, and it is assumed that because they are knowledgeable about, let us say, government or foreign affairs they will have opinions worth listening to. Sometimes it's true, often not. Many a good reporter has been ruined by asking him to think.

Nonetheless, the journalistic commentator, whatever his skill, has some credentials not understood by those who ask that frequent question, "What gives you the right to sound off on anything—and everything—that happens in Washington or the world?" It is that following the news is his full-time occupation. A lawyer, doctor, businessman or carpenter can be just as capable of judging public affairs; any one of them may be smarter than the professional commentator. But they have their daily occupation with all its demands on their time and attention. An editorial writer's only justification before his audience is that he does all day what every citizen does, or should do, in his spare time, follow with his mind the world around him.

This was the new role I found myself cast in when I joined the *Journal*'s editorial staff. I was, I must confess, attracted by the privilege of free-wheeling on public questions and I worked hard at it. If I proved any good at it, it was because I had good teachers. Grimes and Woodlock taught by example. But I owe a debt too to Webb Follin, all those years ago in Tennessee, who tried to instill discipline in writing by forcing me to write to a fixed word limit. There was also imbedded in my memory the dictum of Horace Williams at Chapel Hill that "opinions are a dime a dozen" (any cab driver any day has one on any subject); what counts is what supports the opinion. *Why* do you think what you think?

In retrospect my brief time in purgatory proved salutary. It forced me to think out what direction I wanted my career to take, and although I enjoyed political reporting as such I realized I would be unhappy just reporting the news with no license to comment on it. Within the shop, too, from my resurrection there was a gain. No longer was there any doubt about my status. I felt freer to speak up at the "coffee clatch" on things I thought the *Journal* ought to do.

One was that our "leader stories" could range farther afield than they did at that time. *Journal* readers were primarily interested in business and in news that affected it, but their general level of education (the demographics of our readership) was higher than the average of readers of general newspapers drawn from all levels of education and accomplishment. Because this fit nicely with Barney's concept of making a "national newspaper," he was encouraging, and so therefore were Kerby and Mac. We began to "brainstorm" story ideas on education or shifting patterns in society where the "business connection" was not immediately apparent. These ideas fit well with the talents of Henry Gemmill, the new managing editor.

A corollary to this, I thought, was that readers of the editorial columns might also like to read articles on such subjects as art, music, books, or theater. And why not longer articles on Washington or foreign topics which would not be editorials but would supply information and understanding of current events? We already had one outside contributor, William Henry Chamberlin, a former foreign correspondent for the *Christian Science Monitor*, whom we used sporadically. I found him a pedestrian writer, but he gave us something different for the editorial page. We might build up a stable of such writers, either in-house or from outside.

This idea met with less enthusiasm. Barney was sympathetic, but there were practical problems of cost, not just the pay of contributors but the cost of up to four additional columns to print the material in a newspaper averaging fourteen to eighteen pages a day, never over twenty-four. We would also need additional editorial page staff to solicit and edit such material. Progress was gradually made in this direction, but it was slow and the idea's full fruition was long delayed.

Besides, Barney had other ideas for expansion that would take capital. With New York and San Francisco plants we could efficiently service subscribers on both coasts. But yawning temptingly in the middle was the rest of the country. In 1948 he boldly launched a printing plant in Dallas—to serve the Southwest— over, I might note, Grimes's fearful objections. In 1955 came a plant in Washington, which put us in the nation's capital.

These plants, and others which followed, solved the problem of how the paper could reach a wider audience. But one of Royster's rules is that "every solution creates a problem," and this one proved no exception. Our circulation was fast outgrowing our advertising base. Heretofore our revenue came from financial advertising for brokerage offices and investment bankers offering new issues. These were remunerative and still are. But they weren't sufficient to meet our growing costs. We couldn't count on Bloomingdale's in New York, I. Magnin in San Francisco or Nieman-Marcus in Dallas to fill the gap. While our circulation nationally was large, it was relatively small in each region compared with the local papers. A new advertising source had to be found.

The man who wrestled with this problem, and ultimately solved it, was Robert Feemster. Another of that "Indiana mafia" and a contemporary of Barney's, Bob Feemster was what can only be mildly described as a "character." He was not just stocky; he was fat and sloppy. The social graces were not among his accomplishments. His office hours were eclectic. His eating habits involved mostly hamburgers and french fries, often eaten at his desk and their remains left on display until the nightly cleaners swept them away. I don't think Barney and he were personally compatible. But Feemster, like Barney, was a visionary genius and Barney knew it.

While those of us on the editorial side paid little attention, Bob set out to corral the kind of national advertising found in magazines. How he sold the *Journal* to them I don't know but he did, as you can see by opening any issue of the paper today. Since classified ads are a keystone of any local newspaper's revenue, he also set out to find a formula to sell them for the *Journal*. Run-of-the-mill job ads or those for apartments to rent obviously didn't fit us. So he developed something called "The Real Estate Corner" to match buyers and sellers of expensive houses for those moving between New York and San Francisco, or for holiday havens in Florida. Originally it ran once a week. For other days he created "The Mart" as a job exchange for high-priced executives or a marketplace for yachts and airplanes. He didn't scorn small one-inch ads, but he encouraged larger display ads designed for and aimed at businessmen. Today these "classified ads" are an important source of revenue.

Meanwhile, Barney's expansion plans raised technical problems. The newspaper business at the time relied almost entirely on "hot metal," type set by hand on Linotypes or similar machines. The printing trades were in the hands of tight, stubborn, short-sighted unions. Something different was needed if Barney's dream was to be fulfilled.

Enter here Joseph Ackell. Joe Ackell was a former printer, supervisor and *Journal* plant superintendent. He had little or no technical training but he was a tinkerer in the Yankee tradition. He put together a system of transmitting on punch tape the instructions to run distant typecasting machines automatically, and he adjusted existing machines to use the tape. The result looked like something from Rube Goldberg. But it worked. And it permitted the type in each *Journal* plant to be set by a single bank of punchers in headquarters. Today the Ackell system has been outmoded by electronic typesetting controlled by computers. But without our Yankee tinkerer the modern *Journal* would have been much longer coming.

Circulation sales also had to evolve. There simply weren't enough stockbrokers, bankers, big businessmen or market traders to meet

Barney's circulation dreams for that national paper. So, under Feemster's prodding, circulation sales efforts (much by direct mail) took aim at doctors, lawyers, small businessmen, union leaders, even housewives.

Most of us on the news and editorial side, sad to say, were little appreciative of any of this. We thought the paper's circulation was growing simply from our own brilliant efforts. But even without realizing all the causes of our changing readership we were responding to it. In the news columns we were writing for a wider audience. So were we in the editorial columns. Our mail told us that it was at least one whose interest was no longer so exclusively focused on the financial markets. Our readers wanted to be more informed on a wider range of subjects.

Looking back on these developments, I can see now how they all fitted together, the sales and the technical changes playing a major role in the *Journal*'s growth. At the time, that is in the early 1950s, I was too busy with my own preoccupations to pay other departments that much attention—or their just due.

*   *   *   *   *

My chief preoccupation, of course, was my own position, now that it had been reaffirmed, and how to advance it. I wasn't wanting in ambition. This meant my first task was to write about current events and to do so in a way to impress Grimes, Barney, my other colleagues, and our readers.

Politically and philosophically Grimes and I were compatible. My earlier skepticism about governmental postwar policies, especially its economic policies, increased as I watched the effects heavy spending and "easy money" had on inflation. I was also skeptical about the results of the growing intervention of government in the nation's affairs under the guise of "regulation." In foreign affairs I didn't share Grimes's isolationist instinct; I had felt since the late 1930s that the country could not stand aloof from world problems, including those posed by the obvious aggressiveness of the Soviet Union. I did feel, however, that as in domestic matters there was a danger the pendulum would swing too far and we would find ourselves over-committed around the world.

If I was successful in articulating my views, one reason was that I set out on a course of self-study on the issues we were writing about. Just as when I was assigned to cover the Supreme Court back in the 1930s I had prepared by reading up on constitutional history and past Court decisions, so I tried to educate myself on economics, having at Chapel Hill taken only an introductory course. I recall beginning with a book by D. D. Dillard on *The Economics of John Maynard Keynes*, Keynes then being the most influential voice. I followed this by readings from Keynes himself, though I found his *General Theory* hard going. I was also introduced to the views of his dissenters, notably Ludwig von Mises and Frederich von Hayek, spokesmen for what became known as the "Vienna School." Mises in particular was also hard going, but he helped as much as anyone to influence (and, I hope, clarify) my views.

In the same way as other new issues arose, whether in foreign affairs or whatever, I tried to come to grips with them by reading extensively. I gradually built up a personal reference library which has stood me in good stead over the years. Grimes, who was not a book reader, was often amused at what he thought an "academic" approach. His own thinking was inituitive, although no less perceptive for that, and I learned much from him of content as well as of style. My way was simply different. Fortunately I have always enjoyed studying new things, from economics to science to political philosophy.

I began writing more and more of the "lead" editorials, a situation abetted by Grimes's working habits. I was in the office early. He didn't get to the office before noon or thereabouts. Thus very often I had written on whatever was the major topic of the day before he arrived; consciously or unconsciously I was foreclosing him. And I can remember only two occasions when we had major editorial differences.

One was in April 1951 when President Truman fired General MacArthur. There were, I thought, two issues involved. One, military, was whether MacArthur was justified in arguing that if he was expected to defeat the Communist forces in Korea, which now included the Chinese, he had to be allowed to attack their bases north of the Yalu river; otherwise they would have a "privileged sanctuary." The other issue was whether MacArthur was justified in carrying his disagreement with the president into the public arena and whether Truman was justified in firing the general for so doing. The editorial I wrote said two things: that, militarily speaking, MacArthur was right; a general should not be asked for a victory and denied the means of winning it. And that, politically speaking, MacArthur was wrong to challenge the president publicly while holding his command under civilian authority. Therefore, I said, the president was justified in replacing the general.

Grimes felt that while military men must carry out orders, which MacArthur was doing, they should not be silenced. The public had a right to know of any difference of opinion. He also had reservations about the "on the one hand and on the other" tone of the editorial. It would satisfy nobody, he said, neither Truman's supporters nor MacArthur's. On the contrary, it would anger both.

Yet after lengthy discussions Grimes let the editorial stand. He was right, at least, about the reaction to it. The letters poured in, not in bundles but in mail sacks. We had to give columns to letters from irate readers on both sides. We got a foretaste of the passions that would sweep the country when MacArthur came home.

I was, to put it mildly, shaken by the response to that editorial, even though Grimes had warned me. I was also impressed. Never afterwards would I feel that what was said in our editorial columns were words adrift in a vacuum. It taught me also there was no such thing as a monolithic *Journal* audience. No matter what we said there would be disagreements among our readers. It would therefore be foolish, as well as dishonest, to tailor any opinion to the supposed prejudices of our readers. Practicality as well as duty dictated we simply say what we thought, hope we were right, and not worry whether the readers agreed.

As for MacArthur, I was to see him only once, briefly, in a small group at his Waldorf apartment later that summer. It wasn't an interview or even a visit; it was an "audience." I didn't find him a warm personality, but an impressive one. He was without doubt one of our greatest military leaders, deserving all the praise heaped on him on that account. He was also tragically flawed. I thought at the time, and still do, that tragedy is the only word for the ending of his career, the more so because he himself pulled down the pillars around him.

The other occasion when Grimes and I differed over an editorial position came in 1954 with the Supreme Court's decision in *Brown* v. *Board of Education* which held school segregation, common in the South but not unknown elsewhere, to be unconstitutional.

Grimes had doubts about the decision. For one, he thought the Court's opinion supporting the decision full of psychological mumbo-jumbo. He also felt that in abruptly overturning past judicial decisions the Court had unwisely injected itself into the political arena. Finally, he was fearful of what the decision would bring in terms of racial turmoil, even violence.

I had no quarrel with any of his observations. But I argued they were irrelevant. Segregation was wrong simply because all citizens should be treated alike by the state. I too regretted the Court felt it necessary to indulge in a lot of unsubstantiated psychology to buttress its opinion. I agreed with Grimes that when efforts were made to enforce the decision there would be trouble. I just thought the *Journal* should say in a straightforward way that the Court was right even if it gave the wrong reasons.

Once more Grimes yielded to my view. This time I think it was because he really agreed with me on the fundamental point. His reservations were largely because he foresaw the repercussions that would come not only from the decision but from that muddled opinion, and in that he was prescient. A factor in his yielding may also have been the fact that I was a Southerner, born into and reared under a system of racial segregation. That may well have added weight to my arguments supporting the decision to abolish it. In any event, while many major newspapers waffled in their first editorial opinions, some raising the same fears Grimes had, the *Journal* the next day was unequivocal in supporting the decision.

"The Supreme Court decision," I wrote straightaway, "was an inevitable one. If it had not come at this session, or from this Court, it would have come. . . . The philosophy of racial segregation under the law could not have survived because it does not comport with . . . the equity of government."

Nonetheless, I tried to take into account some of Grimes's fears and the foreseeable reaction. "There is a burden upon the Southern states to accept the principle of the Court and to work diligently toward a method of living with it. Of this burden we shall doubtless hear much, for the voices calling it to the South's attention will be very loud. But there is also an equal burden upon the rest of the country to recognize that this is not a change to be wrought by instant coercion upon a minority section of the country without consequences as bad as the ills it seeks to cure. . . . The quality of forbearance is not strained."

This plea for forbearance was not heeded even by our readers. Once more we were inundated by letters. The Court's decision proved as controversial as the MacArthur firing. Many of the writers were as angry with us as with the decision, some for our sympathy toward the South for what it now faced in the way of cultural upheaval, some for our endorsement of the Court's decision. But not all of them. A few, this time, agreed with us on both points. I was reminded again that *Journal* readers are not all of one mind.

Unfortunately, forbearance was also what the country would not have in the decade to come.

There was one other event in this period, however, in which the *Journal*'s editorial position has troubled me ever since. It was the Suez crisis of 1956.

Briefly summarized, what happened was that Secretary of State Dulles cancelled a promised loan to Egypt to build the Aswan dam. This provoked Lieutenant Colonel Nasser, leader of the junta that had ousted King Farouk, to seize the Suez canal from the Anglo-French combine that had built and owned it. "The annual income of the Suez Canal," Nasser explained, "is $100 million. Why not take it ourselves?" This seizure in turn provoked the Israelis, first, to attack Egyptian forces in the Sinai and, later, the British and French to intervene to retake the canal. The Russians thereupon warned that unless these forces were withdrawn they too would intervene.

It was a tangled situation and no doubt held the seeds of a possible Middle East conflagration. Our first editorial reaction, on October 31, was to criticize Nasser mildly and urge the others not to take "extreme action." The U.S., we said, should keep out of it. Eisenhower not only kept out of the situation but so severely criticized the French and British that their effort to retake the canal failed. It was a fiasco. On November 2, in an editorial for which I was responsible, we not only supported Eisenhower but praised him on both counts.

In the years since, I have not been so certain about any of this. Nasser's seizure of the canal was a blatant and illegal power grab. I find it harder now to blame the Israelis, the British, or the French for trying to block it. And there have been many times when I've wished the canal had remained in Anglo-French hands. If nothing else that would have kept it as a buffer between Israel and Egypt.

Subsequent Israeli-Egyptian wars might have been averted. Thus does time change one's perspective.

As an editorial writer, then, I had reached the point where I was not merely giving shape to another man's ideas. I was offering my own. I was in effect setting the paper's editorial policy on many issues. Yet there remained other areas in which Grimes and I continued to differ.

I had succeeded in getting on the editorial page reviews of theater, opera, books. For a time John Chamberlain, formerly of *Fortune Magazine* and later a syndicated columnist, served as a roving art critic, writing on everything from exhibitions at the Metropolitan Museum to new trends in architecture. Grimes thought this a waste of space. A Puritan at heart, he was incensed at some of the themes just beginning to creep into plays and novels. For example, he insisted that our theater critic, Richard Cooke, not mention the word "homosexual" even if that happened to be the theme of a Broadway play. On several occasions he simply killed reviews that thus transgressed, leaving me indignant. I could never explain to him I wasn't responsible for such thematic material or that we owed it to readers, planning a trip to New York for the theater, not to hide from them what a play was about. On the same grounds a story once proposed by Henry Gemmill on the condom business (a very profitable one and possibly of interest to investors) never saw print. Grimes sometimes also threw out letters-to-the-editor with the remark, "The man's a fool." Doubtless true, but we thus lost some interesting letters.

Fortunately, I had ways to escape his grumbling. I was getting more involved in other aspects of the paper through the "coffee-clatch." And I kept interest in political coverage.

As the 1952 presidential election approached it was clear that the Korean War, unresolved either by defeat or victory, would be a major influence. Both parties that year held their conventions in Chicago and, once more, I attended both. Although I attended every subsequent political convention through 1980, this was to be the last where I played any supervisory role in the paper's coverage. That happened because Joseph E. Evans, then chief of the Washington bureau, came down with appendicitis. Fortunately I could rely heavily on the political acumen of Albert Clark and Alan L. Otten, both later to be themselves Washington bureau chiefs.

Truman had eased the Democratic problem by announcing he would not be a candidate. The leading ones were Senator Estes Kefauver of Tennessee and Senator Richard Russell of Georgia, the Southern favorite. Standing in the wings, however, was Governor Adlai Stevenson of Illinois, whom I had met and who had impressed me favorably. He was intelligent, thoughtful, and remarkably modest for a politician.

Stevenson also showed what was to contribute to his eventual defeat, self-doubt and indecision. For a long time he couldn't make up his mind whether he wanted to be the nominee. Nonetheless, he won the nomination, in part because he gained Truman's support and in part because he made that rare thing, a well-written and well-delivered opening speech to the convention as the host governor.

Meanwhile the Republicans smelled victory from all of Truman's troubles. It was clear that if the convention delegates had voted their preferences they would have nominated Senator Taft. But his public personality was dull, he was too "conservative" for the so-called moderate wing of the party led by Governor Dewey, its two-time nominee, and his campaign was ineptly handled. His foes waged a campaign against him primarily on the grounds that he wasn't "electable."

The man who struck the party as being electable, if he would run, was General Eisenhower. He, like Stevenson, vacillated at first but was eventually persuaded by Dewey to put his hat in the ring. Once he had done so, Eisenhower campaigned vigorously and made strong showings in the later primaries. In the end the convention nominated him, though with sad hearts at abandoning the man justly known as "Mr. Republican."

Eisenhower I had seen briefly when he was Army chief of staff and met once at a luncheon when he was president of Columbia University. I respected the man, knew little of his political philosophy. It was only after the convention that in a well-publicized meeting with Taft he accepted most of the senator's conservative views. I'm not sure that Ike's political philosophy played much of a role in the election anyway. His strength lay in his personality and his war record. The latter he capitalized on by declaring that, if elected, he would "go to Korea." He didn't say what he would do, but the country felt he would somehow resolve that deadlock. I don't think the vice-presidential nominee, Richard Nixon, affected the election despite all the attention paid to his famous "Checkers speech" in which he defended himself against allegations of a secret campaign fund. The political pendulum was ready to swing, and it swung.

The *Journal*, as usual, endorsed neither candidate. Rereading our editorials I find them more pro-Eisenhower than otherwise, especially after he spoke strongly for a "drastic reduction in public spending." (How many times have I heard candidates issue the same call!) But we always treated Stevenson respectfully, even sympathetically.

After the election I wrote: "The supporters of Adlai Stevenson have nothing to be ashamed of and much to be proud of. No man could have better stated the cause of his party; no man could have so well demonstrated that his is a party that can claim allegiance from men of stature. . . . Adlai Stevenson was defeated because he was forced to go the wrong way on the tide."

It was better, I think, that the pendulum had swung. But he was a man I always admired.

*　*　*　*　*

So the decade of the fifties wore on. The newspaper Kilgore had built thrived as peace returned and the country prospered during Eisenhower's first term. Our circulation was growing both in numbers and its reach across the country. We had not yet achieved Barney's dream of delivering the paper everywhere on the day of publication, but that no longer seemed an impossible one. Both our news columns and our editorial voice were attracting more attention and with it more influence.

I too was gaining greater recognition, externally and internally, and I was beginning to enjoy life in the editorial sanctum. I found that a license to express my opinions was intoxicating. Outside recognition came in 1953 with a Pulitzer Prize for editorial writing, awarded not for any particular editorial but for the body of my work. Internally, my career got a boost when, on Barney's initiative, I was sent abroad to visit our bureaus in London and Paris and asked to suggest how we might improve our foreign coverage. My ambition to succeed Grimes seemed within my grasp.

But before that would happen there would be another period of frustrating uncertainty.

Grimes had by the late 1950s pretty much withdrawn from his

role as the *Journal*'s editorial voice, leaving that to me. He resurrected the old Woodlock column, changing the title slightly to "Thinking Things Over," to give himself an outlet for personal observations under his own name. In this he was much more informal than might be appropriate for an institutionalized editorial speaking the newspaper's official position on the issues of the day. He would often write about his dogs or the turkeys on his Duchess County farm, or recall some incident from his reporting past, using these to make some pertinent point. Since it was labelled an occasional column, he had no pressure from fixed deadlines. It was a well-written and a well-read addition to the paper. We had by this time begun to encroach on the whole editorial page, using the extra columns for more articles from the Washington or foreign staff as well as outside contributors, and we were always hungry for good copy. In the fall of 1957 Grimes moved to Florida, keeping only a pied-à-terre apartment in New York for periodic visits.

In any practical sense he was retired. Yet he kept the official title, certainly with the acquiescence of and probably at the insistence of Kilgore.

For Barney had a personnel problem to resolve. There were others besides myself who had legitimate claims to preferment. Kerby, of course, and McCormack, but also Robert Bottorff, another De-Pauw contemporary of Barney who had played a key part in the growth of the *Journal*. In earlier years he worked with Barney in San Francisco. Later he directed the buildup of our extensive West Coast news-gathering organization and was tapped to start the Chicago edition. In 1954 he'd been brought to New York as managing editor to succeed Henry Gemmill, who was moved to the West Coast, then to Europe, and finally to Washington.

Bob Bottorff was a wiry, sandy-haired bundle of energy with a gruff, no-nonsense manner. He proved an exceptionally strong managing editor and so often locked horns with Mac, at that time executive editor and his nominal superior. By 1955 the tension between the two was so great that once again Barney had to do some juggling. Mac became business manager and later vice-president. Bob was moved up to executive editor. Bob and I had long been good friends and we got along well, if for no other reason because our areas of authority didn't conflict. All the same, he too was ambitious.

On the surface there would seem to be no reason for all our ambitions to collide. Kerby, soon to be executive vice-president, was clearly marked as the company's number two man and Kilgore's successor. Mac was a corporate officer also in line of succession. Bottorff not only held the reins over the *Journal*'s news department but also oversaw *Barron's* and the Dow Jones News Service. Inside the company all had recognized positions of status. But in the outside world no title held the same prestige as the *Journal*'s editorship. Any man would covet it.

Barney's problem was complicated by the fact that we were all "his boys" and were all about the same age; five years would span the whole group, I being the youngest at forty-three in 1957. That made for a log jam. So all I could do was sit and wait to see how it would be resolved, a wait made more frustrating because I was now the paper's recognized voice, without the title.

I don't know how or why the resolution came, but in the summer of 1958 Grimes finally retired and I was appointed to his chair. In the years ahead I would myself become a vice-president, senior vice-president, and a director of Dow Jones, the parent company. But none of these promotions gave the same glow or have had for me the same meaning. In retirement I would never refer to myself as a former officer of the company but only as the paper's former editor.

My first reaction when Barney told me his decision was to ask, "Don't you think we could now make that 'temporary' job Grimes gave me a permanent one?" He laughed and replied, "Let's not be too hasty!" Neither then nor later did I have a formal, contractual relationship with the company, under Barney or his successors. But what began so casually in 1936 was to stretch into an association which, in various forms, lasted nearly half a century.

So it was that in the summer of 1958 I found, after some wanderings and many tribulations, that I had fulfilled the ambition that brought me to the New York office a decade earlier. I was the editor of a newspaper fast becoming truly national and already influential among politicians, businessmen, labor leaders, and others who, directly or indirectly, play major roles in the affairs of the country. What *The Wall Street Journal* said might provoke. It could not be ignored.

Neither, then, could the person who gave it voice. And I intended to make the most of it.

PART FIVE

New York, the Ending

Better is the end of a thing
than the beginning thereof.

—*The Book of Ecclesiastes*

NEW YORK, THE ENDING

n early January of 1961 president-elect John Fitzgerald Kennedy was using the Carlyle Hotel as his preinauguration headquarters in New York. The Carlyle was, even then, not the newest of the city's expensive hotels nor the most modern in its luxurious appointments. But it retained its air of quiet, civilized elegance. On normal days its small lobby would witness the comings and goings of well-dressed, well-mannered gentlefolk for whom it had long been a comfortable and familiar haven on their visits to the city.

On this particular wintry morning—January 5—all was bedlam. Police cars lined East Seventy-sixth Street before the main entrance. Inside were uniformed policemen, detectives in mufti, Secret Service agents being conspicuously inconspicuous. The doorman, reception clerks and elevator operators were overwhelmed by the army of security people, reporters, photographers, local politicians and the general hangers-on who follow power wherever it goes.

In the midst of this, two nicely dressed elderly ladies threaded their way through the throng and approached the elevators to find their way blocked by a stern Secret Service agent who asked for identification. One of the ladies, shocked, drew back in indignation and exclaimed, "Why, we live here!" That seemed to be a sufficient password, for they entered the elevator in voluble conversation. With that warning, I had my own identification ready. For I was there to have lunch with the man who was to be president.

This time, at long last, I could identify myself as editor of *The Wall Street Journal*. I had been such for nearly three years. And as years before I found that being chief of the Washington bureau gave me a little extra status in the capital, so I had already found that being editor of the paper gave me an easier entry to high places than being a senior associate editor. On this occasion, I had asked for an appointment and received a luncheon invitation.

I first saw Kennedy when he was a young congressman from

Massachusetts, newly elected along with another promising newcomer, Representative Richard Nixon from California. I knew him
as a senator. During the 1960 campaign, Barney Kilgore and I
spent an hour with him in Washington where he complained, fear-
fully, that he was handicapped in campaigning by the duties of the
senate while his opponent, Vice-President Nixon, was free to travel
the country at will. That did not prove an insurmountable handicap. Kennedy won, but by the narrowest of margins in the popular
vote. In the electoral college he had a comfortable majority but in
the popular vote he was, like Truman before him, a minority president because of those received by Senator Harry Byrd of Virginia
as an independent candidate.

Kilgore and I also had a visit with the newly elected vice-
president, Lyndon Johnson, at the Waldorf during the campaign
and found him surprisingly lukewarm about Kennedy, to whom he
had lost the presidential nomination in the Democratic convention. Though I had followed the usual *Journal* practice of endors-
ing neither presidential candidate I had been able to restrain my
enthusiasm for the youthful Kennedy. So I had both interest in and
curiosity about this meeting. What sort of reception would I get?

The bedlam continued as I arrived at Kenneth O'Donnell's suite
(he was Kennedy's appointments secretary). The first person to
greet me had never heard of either me or the luncheon date. I
waited some fifteen minutes before I could get to O'Donnell, who
sent me up to Kennedy's suite. Here I waited again. There seemed
to be two meetings going on in different rooms, very noisy, with
unknown people bustling back and forth between them. A pleasant young lady discovered that no one had thought to order lunch
and asked what I would like. I ordered steak (medium rare) for
both the president-elect and myself. Meanwhile Lyndon Johnson
walked by, stopped to chat a moment, and asked to be remembered to Kilgore. A few minutes later Kennedy passed by briefly,
shook my hand, and walked down the corridor with Johnson.

A small aside. As they walked away I heard Johnson sharply ask
Kennedy whether there would be a Johnson liaison man on the
National Security Council. I didn't catch Kennedy's reply, but then
I heard Johnson say, "But I want my own man just like Nixon
had." The vignette suggested all was not yet smoothly arranged be-
tween the two.

Kennedy returned and we went in to lunch. He didn't complain about my choice of menu. Indeed, the president-elect was most gracious. He managed to seem interested in seeing me and he recalled our last meeting. He had read (or been briefed on) my recent editorials, commenting on several of them, and even when he mentioned one he didn't like he did so with good humor. On only one *Journal* item did he display irritation. That was an article by Robert Novak, then in our Washington bureau, "about my brother," meaning Robert Kennedy, who was being appointed attorney general. Novak, Kennedy said, "had it in for me and my family." That piece evidently got under his skin, and I had some difficulty getting him off that subject.

The rest of the luncheon (we were alone except for occasional interruptions by a secretary with messages) was pleasant and relaxed. The "president" (for so I already called him) insisted he was not going to be "fiscally irresponsible"; he said the latest Eisenhower budget promised a phony balance because it depended on a postal rate increase and a rise in the gasoline tax. He said he'd endorse both of these revenue items, but that Congress might not grant them. Then there'd be a deficit and "it will look like my deficit."

On one or two other matters he sounded plaintive. He talked about the difficulty of getting good people for the many administration posts. "Everybody wants to be secretary of state." He said he was worried that matters in Laos, where the Communists were infiltrating, might come to a head just after January 20, which meant he would have to make any decisions, and "I don't have the confidence of the people the way Eisenhower does." He also said that one of his biggest problems in the postelection period was that he was "too busy to think."

Most of the conversation, then, turned on matters now only of historical interest. To me it was useful primarily because it gave me a better insight into the next president. I liked him personally and I found myself sympathetic about the problems he would soon be facing.

As I wrote in a memo to Kilgore immediately afterwards: "I think my chief impression is of a man who has suffered a shock in realizing that the job he fought for isn't as easy as he thought it was and who (momentarily at least) is harassed by uncertainties

and doubts. The closer January 20 comes the more oppressive become such matters as Laos, or the fiscal situation, where he may
have to make decisions fraught with all sorts of consequences. . . .
He hasn't yet learned to wear comfortably the mantle that must be
the garment of the president. Nonetheless, this is a very smart
young man."

In view of what was to come, from his unhappy encounter with
Khruschev in Vienna to the disaster of the Bay of Pigs, I think
this was not unperceptive. The tragedy was that he did not live
long enough to make full use of the intelligence I saw amid the
uncertainties.

*   *   *   *   *

That January lunch with a president-elect illustrates one of the advantages of my new position. Being editor of the *Journal* gave me
an easier entrée into government, politics, business, and to the
public world in general. Unlike Grimes, who was a social recluse, I
was trying to put this to use.

I also found that my status within the paper had altered, as two
incidents will show.

The first came early in 1959 after President Eisenhower's State
of the Union and budget messages. It seemed to me that in his second term he was yielding ground from his early positions, especially on governmental spending, and I wrote a critical editorial. I
was then barely six months in my new chair, and for the first time I
had no Grimes to read what I wrote or to whom I felt answerable
afterwards for opinions expressed in the paper. I was, I suppose,
still a little uncertain of how far to stretch the boundaries of my
new authority.

So on my way from my office to deliver the copy downstairs I
looked into Kilgore's office, noticed him sitting at his desk, and
walked over to lay the copy in front of him. After all, he was the
publisher. I told him I was being critical of the president and
thought he might want to look at it.

Barney picked up the typewritten sheets, waved them in his
hands without reading them, and handed them back to me. "I'll
read the editorial in the paper tomorrow," he said. It was a gesture
of confidence I would never forget.

The other incident was somewhat similar. The company's directors, except for Kilgore, were outside of management, most of

them lawyers and businessmen, not all of whom agreed with the *Journal*'s editorial policies. None dared quarrel with Grimes, given his age and seniority. But when I replaced him I suppose they saw new opportunities through influencing a young man. I began getting lunch and dinner invitations from several of the directors, and I noticed that the conversation always turned to arguments that the *Journal* was too conservative in its economic views, too little attuned to the "realities of the world." I enjoyed the attention, was amused by their transparent efforts, and ignored most of their views.

Sometime later Frances and I were invited to dinner at "21" by Jessie and Bill Cox, Bill being a member of our board and Jessie, along with her sister Jane Cook, being the controlling stockholders as granddaughters of Clarence Barron. I was seated next to Jessie and she asked me how I was getting along in my new job. I said fine, but I told her—in what I hoped was a light and bantering tone—of those invitations and what I suspected was behind them.

Jessie leaned over, put her hand on my arm. "Don't you pay any attention to them," she said. "They're only hired hands."

Of course I was only a hired hand myself while these were chief executives of major corporations. Now they were being casually dismissed! I thought it funny, but I took her meaning. And that, too, I never forgot.

Jessie Bancroft Cox was to be the dowager empress of her grandfather's company for years to come. Even after the company became publicly owned she retained control through shares held by herself, her sister Jane, and by family trusts which she voted. When her husband, Bill Cox, died she took his place on the board officially, representing the family. She was proud of the company, especially of *The Wall Street Journal*, and kept a proprietary interest in it. Several times she and Jane resisted offers to buy it. "The company's not for sale to anybody at any price." And they would allow nobody to tinker with it or those they trusted to manage it.

With such votes of confidence I never again felt threatened in my position.

* * * * *

The latter part of the Eisenhower administration, though we didn't know it, marked the beginning of a long period of social unrest that would last through the next decade into the seventies. It began

with the racial turmoil that Grimes had anticipated and was followed by that of the Vietnam War and finally by Watergate. If
we didn't foresee what was coming, it was because at first President Eisenhower brought the country a stability and tranquillity it
hadn't known since World War II. The peace he arranged in Korea
seemed to most people a reasonable substitute for victory. By ending wage and price controls he let loose a readjustment of the hidden realities of inflation which did mean rises in both prices and
wages, but the result of removing this artificiality was to usher in a
time of prosperity. Perhaps more important to the new mood were
some of the things he didn't do. He didn't send new American
troops anywhere in Asia, didn't embark on a policy of "liberation"
of Communist-dominated countries, though many of his party's
leaders urged these things. Take it all in all, in those early years
most people felt they were better off than before.

But not all. The first important ripple in the social tranquillity
came in 1957 at Little Rock, Arkansas. There dissatisfied blacks
had obtained a court order requiring integration of the public
schools to implement the Supreme Court decision in *Brown* v.
Board of Education. On the surface it seemed all would proceed
smoothly; the mayor had worked out an integration plan to carry
out the order. Enter then, however, Governor Orval Faubus. He
called out the National Guard, ostensibly to keep order, in reality
to keep blacks out of white schools in defiance of the courts.

Eisenhower, by all reports, shared Grimes's uneasiness about the
1954 Supreme Court decision; reputedly, he regretted appointing
Earl Warren as Chief Justice. His sense of constitutional duty,
however, was firm. He responded by putting the Arkansas National Guard under federal control and directing it to carry out the
court order, escorting the black children to school if necessary.

It was a historic moment. It was also, in a lesser sense, a sort of
turning point for the *Journal*. We of course supported the president editorially. We also, for the first time, sent a team of reporters
to cover a breaking news story of social importance. Heading the
team was Henry Gemmill. Henry was in the midst of one of the
many turns in his career which was to see him serve variously,
among other things, as managing editor, chief European correspondent, chief of the Washington bureau, and editor of the ill-
fated *National Observer*. Henry had his deficiencies as an admin-

istrator. No one surpassed him in ability to bring imagination to news coverage, in welding a group of reporters into a superb team, in helping make of their collective work well-written and exciting stories. We gave columns to the Little Rock stories, on the front page and elsewhere.

One of those, reported and written by Henry himself, set a pattern to be followed many times afterwards. While the events around the school were being covered by others—where in fact most of the attention of the press was directed—Henry went behind the obvious story. He went talking to the quiet citizens of Little Rock, especially those who could be termed community leaders. Among them he found a sharp contrast with the public bombast of the governor, an unexpected sense of moderation, a willingness to adjust to the new order between the races, however reluctantly. It was a significant, even a prophetic story, for it revealed the influence of the one group which could, and in time did, bring change to the segregated South. Faubus would disappear from history.

Little Rock didn't end racial turmoil; more would follow. It did, however, mark the beginning of the end, for thereafter it was clear that the orders of federal courts would be enforced by the national government. It also marked a broadening of the *Journal*'s news coverage in which more attention would be paid to social and other changes in the country even where their relation to business, our traditional field, was indirect.

Meanwhile, changes were also beginning in the editorial operation. Even before I was officially appointed as Grimes's successor it was clear we needed to strengthen the staff. If for no other reason, I would need trustworthy assistants unless I was to be anchored rigidly in the office, something I wished to avoid. A stronger staff was also needed if we were to break out of the limited two columns of editorials and use the whole page to provide more "intellectual fodder," in Barney's phrase, for our readers.

Grimes was aware of this. In 1951 he tried to hire a young man fresh out of Yale who had caught his eye with a book of conservative tone, brash and pungent style. We took him to lunch and Grimes made him a generous offer. Unfortunately, William Buckley had no need of a job and had different ambitions. He had the money to start at the top by founding his own magazine. Bill

would later become a famous personality as columnist, TV per-
former, and author of popular spy stories. But he had one of the
better minds of his generation and, to my way of thinking, never
lived up to the promise of his intellectual talents as fully as he
might have if he had spent a few years under the teaching discipline of someone like Grimes. I admire Bill immensely, and so have
thought that a pity.

Subsequently there would be an in-and-out parade of editorial
page staffers over the years. But the real solution to my problem,
an able and trustworthy lieutenant, lay already at hand in the person of Joseph E. Evans, whom Grimes had brought over from the
news side.

Joe Evans, a native of Iowa, had begun to write free-lance pieces
for us in 1946 after he was mustered out of the army in Europe.
He proved so prolific he was hired as a regular correspondent. In
1950 he was brought to New York as foreign editor. He impressed
everyone, and when Albert Clark left for *U.S. News and World Report*, Joe was named Washington bureau chief. Joe was another
whose forte wasn't in administration, but he was a perceptive observer of the Washington scene, a good and thoughtful writer. Inevitably he found his place on the editorial page.

Another who left an imprint on the editorial page was William
Fitzpatrick, who'd won a Pulitzer for editorial writing on the New
Orleans *States*. He left us in 1965 only to become editor of his
own paper in Norfolk. Still another who joined us, not as an editorial writer but for a newly created post of editorial features editor, was John Bridge, whom I succeeded in snaring from the news
department. These formed a nucleus of experienced people as others came and went. But Joe Evans became, and remained, the solid
anchor.

It was Joe, incidentally, who helped the paper catch the attention of President Eisenhower. I had not seen the president since
that long-ago luncheon at Columbia, Eisenhower not being particularly enamored of, or even comfortable with, the press in general.
So it was a surprise to get a letter from him in June 1960, complimenting me on an editorial Joe had written about our national
propensity for self-flagellation. "For some reason," the president
said, "I have never been a regular reader of your newspaper. But I
assure you that if it makes a habit of producing articles of this
value, I shall make it my business to see it regularly."

Thus Joe won me an undeserved honor. I could make recompense only by writing the president to give Joe the credit. Visiting Eisenhower later in Gettysburg I found that he was indeed paying more attention to the *Journal*, and once more I explained Joe's role. This brought a chuckle from him and the remark that generals, too, often got credit for the efforts of others.

I was often thereafter to get credit for Joe's work, as Grimes did at times for mine. But his greatest service to me was that his dependability gave me the freedom to make forays out of the office, to travel extensively, abroad as well as at home.

* * * * *

I took advantage of this in the presidential campaign of 1960, when as usual I attended both party conventions, leaving Joe to comment as he would on the platforms and key speeches. I was, once more, a supernumerary, as this time Al Clark was directing the news coverage. No matter. Political conventions have for me the same attraction as bullfights do for others.

Of the leading Democratic contenders I knew Lyndon Johnson best. He was a freshman congressman when I was covering the Hill before the war and had won a Senate seat in the Truman upset of 1948. More interestingly from my point of view, he was prominent in the "Southern Establishment" that dominated the Senate when I was Washington bureau chief. I had crossed paths with Hubert Humphrey but at this point didn't know him well. I'd watched Senator Kennedy maneuver unsuccessfully for the vice-presidential nomination in 1956. I'd had some conversation with him in the spring of 1960 and had been impressed with his skill in wading into the "Catholic issue" at that year's meeting of the American Society of Newspaper Editors.

By the time the Democrats met in Los Angeles Humphrey had dropped out; the Kennedy forces had outspent and so beaten him in West Virginia, which, because it was a predominantly Protestant state, was Humphrey's last chance. Up to balloting time Lyndon Johnson thought he might deadlock the convention. It was a forlorn hope. Kennedy won on the first ballot. After that came the convention's only real excitement. To the astonishment of many, and the anger of his own supporters, Kennedy asked Johnson to be his running mate because he knew he needed all the Southern votes the ticket could get.

I was with Johnson briefly between the Kennedy victory and the Kennedy invitation, and I wasn't surprised he accepted. Speaker of the House Sam Rayburn—fellow Texan, old Johnson friend and political mentor—advised it because he thought Kennedy would lose the election to Nixon, leaving Johnson a strong prospect for the 1964 convention. Kennedy wasn't the favorite candidate of the party pros. But unlike Kefauver before him or McGovern and Carter afterwards, he didn't run *against* the party. Rather, he wooed its leaders even while being a maverick. In person he reminded me much of his father, whom I had met so long ago at the Maritime Commission, though he had a softer, easier-going personality, a charm lacking in both his father and brother Bobby.

To the Republicans meeting in Chicago it also seemed that Nixon had the electoral edge. He had served for eight years as Eisenhower's vice-president, and if he lacked the general's personal appeal he had impressed nearly everyone as a man of ability. He had no serious rivals within the party, and he inherited the followers of the dead Senator Taft. Few foresaw the turns of the election campaign.

I too was impressed by Nixon, whom I knew better than any of the other candidates. I first talked with him during the famous Alger Hiss hearings. In 1957 I was president of the National Conference of Editorial Writers and invited Nixon to be our principal speaker. Frances and I gave a large reception for him at the Skirvin Hotel in Oklahoma City, which he appreciated as it gave him an opportunity to meet a broad spectrum of editorial page editors. Later that evening he and I sat and talked for an hour or more.

Nixon gave a virtuoso performance before this audience. Prior to the meeting he asked me if he could skip a formal speech, make only a few introductory remarks, and then answer questions. This he did for more than an hour, demonstrating both an articulateness and a remarkably detailed knowledge of national and international affairs. He even managed to win an accolade from John Oakes of *The New York Times*, neither then nor later a Nixon supporter. This was his first experiment with a format he was to use many times.

But Nixon made his first mistake on the morrow of his nomination. He promised to campaign in all fifty states, including the two newest, Alaska and Hawaii. Under the best of circumstances that would have been a reckless promise, taxing any man's physical strength. It turned out to be worse after he came down with a severe case of phlebitis in one of his legs, which put him in the hospital, and he exhausted himself in the effort. This exhaustion proved costly when he made his second mistake, agreeing to a series of television "debates" with Senator Kennedy.

I visited him during his stay at Walter Reed Hospital, where he was bedridden with his leg elevated. The question to debate or not to debate was much on his mind. He was uneasy about it but felt that to refuse would give Kennedy a continuing point of attack and concluded he had no choice. That was a mistake for two reasons. On the first debate he looked terrible, haggard of face (some of this was blamed on his makeup) and lacking his usual forcefulness. The general verdict was that he "won" the later debates, but he never overcame the impression left on the public by the first one. A more important factor, though, was that the debates gave Kennedy a public exposure he needed and could have gotten in no other way. He didn't have to "outpoint" Nixon. All he needed was a chance to show himself well-informed to overcome the handicap of appearing too youthful and inexperienced, giving him the recognition he didn't previously have.

The election itself was a cliff-hanger. Herbert Klein, an old friend of mine and Nixon's press secretary, invited me to the Waldorf that night for what was intended to be a victory celebration. As the night wore on and the returns came in, the celebration became a wake. By morning Nixon had lost. Kennedy won 34,227,096 votes; Nixon, 34,107,646. Nixon carried more states (twenty-six) than Kennedy (twenty-two), but the Kennedy states were larger with more Electoral College votes.

What followed was, in my opinion, Nixon's finest hour. He closeted himself at Key Biscayne, Florida, while his advisers urged him to contest the vote count in Illinois, where last minute votes from Mayor Daly's Chicago precincts put the state in the Kennedy column, and in Texas, where there was at least a suspicion that Lyndon Johnson's supporters had stolen some votes. By coincidence the directors of the American Society of Newspaper Editors were meeting there at the time and I was able to follow the discussion. In the end Nixon decided not to contest the election. He said it would mean a long period in which the country wouldn't know who was the next president, and he wouldn't put the nation through that strain. It was a decision, I think, that spoke well for Richard Nixon.

So the stage was set for the thousand days of John Kennedy. When I met with the president-elect that January day I could of course have no premonition of all that would happen to him and to the country in so short a time.

*   *   *   *   *

In memory the Kennedy days were a magic time, colored by the president's youth, his charm, and by the loveliness of his wife. At the time, however, they were not all bright and shining days. The racial troubles continued; so did the upward pressure on prices. In April 1961 came the disaster of the Bay of Pigs. In June followed the meeting between Kennedy and Nikita Khrushchev, which I was to witness.

Frances and I were in Italy when I received a cable from Joe Evans confirming the date. Once more Henry Gemmill would lead a news team from Washington assisted by Ray Vicker, our chief European correspondent. I joined the group in Paris, where the president and his wife enjoyed a brief triumph and from where Frances returned home. Then on to Vienna. A more perfect city could hardly be found for any kind of international meeting; it overflows with old world charm. Ray, who's a sort of journalistic Luther Billis, a fixer extraordinary, had preceded us and rented the top floor of a beer garden in the suburbs for our lodging, thus ensuring comfort while the horde of newsmen from all over the world were scrounging whatever space they could find. A vivid memory is of the lively music from below and of Henry, who had sprained his back en route, lounging in the bathtub while the rest of us gathered around swapping whatever information we had acquired.

Our State Department correspondent then was Philip Geyelin (later editorial page editor of *The Washington Post*) and his diplomatic contacts were important information sources. From these and other sources came depressing reports. Kennedy's staff was outraged at the treatment he received from Khrushchev, which was scornful—even vicious—toward the president in their private meetings. Publicly a good face was put on their encounter, but as we left it seemed clear that the youthful president was in a state of shock.

My own dispatches noted the "tough talk" from Khrushchev, adding that "President Kennedy should come out of his meeting a wiser and more experienced man." Whether or not that was true, the meeting between the two men was to have far-reaching consequences.

The first came before the summer was out. The Soviet Union boldly built its wall between East and West Berlin with no response other than words from the United States.

The following summer, 1962, I too had a visit in the Kremlin with Chairman Khrushchev as part of a small journalistic group to whom he gave an interview. (Included in that group, incidentally, was my old friend Paul Miller of the Gannett papers.) Khrushchev was no less belligerent with us. Among other things he accused the U.S. of clinging to West Berlin only "as a source of tension," and he insisted he would sign a formal peace treaty with East Germany unless the U.S. relaxed that tension. He also boasted of new Soviet weapons, among them a global rocket against which he claimed there was no defense.

My impression was of an arrogant man, for all that in appearance he looked like a simple dirt farmer back home. There was no polish about him; he didn't try to hide his irritation at what he took to be hostile questions. He seemed to me to know exactly where he wanted to go and, having survived all his enemies in the Kremlin, to be confident of his power to drive a Russian troika to get there. I had no trouble imagining the manner in which he reportedly talked to Kennedy.

On our return Paul Miller, Walker Stone of Scripps-Howard, Lee Hills of the Knight newspapers, and I reported all this to a subdued though cordial president. When the showdown came in October over the Soviet missiles in Cuba I wasn't surprised at either Khrushchev's daring or at Kennedy's aroused response.

But the most far-reaching consequence of that Vienna summit meeting would be felt in Vietnam. Eisenhower had restricted our role in that part of Southeast Asia to a handful of advisers to the South Vietnam government. Until Vienna, Kennedy had been equally restrained. Afterwards he seemed to feel that a U.S. show of weakness in that part of the world would embolden the Communists further. As Arthur Schlesinger, Jr., a Kennedy confidant, put it, "The president unquestionably felt that an American retreat in Asia might upset the whole world balance." The reaction began when Kennedy approved sending a detachment of Green Berets to Vietnam, the first American commitment to include troops. It climaxed with the assassination of President Diem in 1963.

There's never been convincing evidence that the Kennedy administration connived in that assassination. There's no question, though, that the administration had grown increasingly irritated by the leadership of Ngo Dinh Diem. I could understand why.

In 1959, as part of an around-the-world trip at Kilgore's instigation ("You need more education"), I had a three-hour visit with Diem, about par for the course with this nonstop talker. A nervous chain-smoker, Diem had all the airs of an annointed king or a hereditary despot. He was a firm and intensely dedicated anti-Communist, and so far as I could ever learn personally honest. He was also an equally dedicated Catholic in a country divided between Catholicism, the religion of the upper classes, and Buddhism, that of the middle and lower classes. Diem felt the Catholics should be privileged, and no amount of U.S. pressure was capable of making him modify his views. He would concede the need for reforms, but all the same his enemies—political, personal or religious—ended up in jail. For those three hours together he lectured me on the need to understand the need for strong, even ruthless, government if South Vietnam was to stand firm against the Viet Cong and North Vietnam.

"He is a strange man," I reported in the *Journal*, "disturbing and appealing all at once." I found in him "an almost mystical dedication to the independence of Vietnam. . . . So dedicated he does not hesitate to be ruthless against any he sees as enemies. . . . [Thus] the present government does not have deep political roots."

In Saigon I ran into old friend Henry Morgenthau, the former secretary of the treasury, and he asked me, "What are we doing in this country anyway?" Having travelled over as much of the country as was thought militarily secure, I had no satisfactory answer. I never found one, but I regret to say that it was a long time before I would let the *Journal* pose that same question publicly. I was too long intimidated by the idea of "responsibility" to support American foreign policy.

Anyway, by midsummer 1963 Ambassador Henry Cabot Lodge, a Republican, had in effect given dissident Vietnamese generals a green light for a coup d'etat, most of them being Buddhists who hated Diem. They struck on November 1, All Saint's Day, attacking the palace from which Diem fled. Captured, Diem and his brother were killed, whether or not the Americans acquiesced in this program in any part.

The coup d'etat was fatal not only to Diem but to any hopes that the U.S. could extricate itself from the Vietnam trap. Having let one government be overthrown, we had to accept responsibility for what came after. And that embarked us on a long road indeed.

Less than a month later, on November 22, John Kennedy was himself assassinated. The thousand days were over.

2

The shock of the Kennedy assassination was to be long with us. In time the Kennedy years were to grow into that legend that Theodore White dubbed "Camelot."

But the first shock produced a reaction bordering on hysteria. People found it difficult to accept it as the isolated act of a madman; the temptation to look for a conspiracy could not be put down. Neither could many avoid seeing in the event the reflection of some deep national malaise. The automatic first assumption among many was that the assassin must be a right-wing extremist, most likely a racist out to avenge Kennedy's civil rights efforts. When that proved not to be the case other causes were sought in the national psyche.

One senator put the responsibility squarely on "the people of Dallas." One of our highest judges said the president's murder was stimulated by "hatred and malevolence" that were "eating their way into the bloodstream of American life." A newspaper of great renown passed judgment that "none of us can escape a share of the fault for the spiral of violence." Similar charges, differing only in phrasing, were heard from commentators, from other public figures, even from the pulpit.

Our first editorials were a tribute to the fallen president and an expression of confidence in the new president, Lyndon Johnson. But as the public hysteria mounted so did my own indignation at this heaping of opprobrium upon the whole country. I felt it should not be left to pass unchallenged. So I turned from the assassination itself to this blind emotional reaction.

Under the heading "No Time For Collective Guilt," I said such statements could only come from those who had "neither paused to reflect how the event came about nor observed in what manner the whole American people have responded to the tragedy."

I noted that a president lay dead precisely because he moved freely among the people and because everywhere, as in Dallas, people turned out in great numbers to do him honor. "It is the fundamental orderliness of the American society that leads presidents to move exposed to all the people, making possible the act of a madman."

Negligence there may have been, I conceded, on the part of the police authorities not to search every window that might shield an assassin, even on the part of the president that he let his courage uncover him to potential assassins.

"In sum," the editorial concluded, "there is in all this—let there be no mistake—much to grieve, to regret. . . . But this is something different from the charge in the indictment. It is more than nonsense to say that the good people of Dallas, crowding the streets to honor a president, share a murderous guilt; or that the tragic acts of a madman cast a shadow on the whole of America. Such an indictment is vicious.

"Of reasons for shame we have enough this day without adding to them a shameful injustice to a mourning people."

It was an editorial to be widely reprinted, and I would like to think had something to do with the return to calmer, more sober judgment that marked later public comments. At least a few of those who gave way to hysterical words in the beginning came to feel shamefaced about them. It also expressed some thoughts that were to recur to me years later when another Kennedy was assassinated and another president was shot and also a pope, both happily to survive. On those occasions there was no repetition of the indictment for collective guilt. But then once again we were reminded of the terrible problem that faces leaders in a free society, one unknown to dictators who can refuse to move among the people. How can our leaders move freely without exposing themselves, and therefore the societies they lead, to unpreventable dangers? I had no answer to that after that day in Dallas. I have none now.

The grief that gripped the American people that winter would gradually lift, as grief for the dead must always do for the living who mourn, though none who lived through that time will ever forget it. In place of grief came a sort of consecration, with the dead president being enshrined in song and story.

I would not myself install Kennedy in any pantheon of great presidents. He made too many grievous mistakes, as with the ill-fated Bay of Pigs and his deepening of our involvement in Vietnam. I've been told that Kennedy for his part didn't like me; Pierre Salinger, his press secretary, once told Tim Wicker of *The New York Times* that he acknowledged me at a press conference because "the little bastard" was the only one he recognized. The phrase, at best, was probably only half in jest. Nonetheless, I saw more of President Kennedy before and in the White House than I had any of his predecessors, and I found him friendly and cordial in person. If I criticized his politics and policies, I also saw in him what Charlie Ross had seen in Truman back in 1936, the capacity to grow in the White House. Of the truth of that we will now never know.

But however the future may judge Jack Kennedy, that day in Dallas left a long shadow on the country and Lyndon Johnson began his presidency under it. He could not, or at least did not, at first surround himself with ministers of his own choosing. Like a king among sneering courtiers Johnson found himself scorned by those he was supposed to lead.

None of them were disposed to recognize that President Kennedy was in deep political trouble when he went to Dallas, which was in fact why he went there; he needed help from Vice-President Johnson. In their private conversations with me and others, those who had served Kennedy seemed to elevate him to a demigod— young, articulate, graceful, charming. President Johnson could only suffer by comparison.

There was another reason for his troubles. Johnson, like Nixon after him, neither belonged to nor was accepted by the "establishment." The word can only be used loosely and there are some who think it a myth. It is amorphous but it is real enough. It's composed of a group of people who went to school together— frequently at Harvard, Yale, or Stanford, especially their law schools—or who hold key positions in government, business, the major law firms, or foundations and who know each other. Some are Republicans, most Democrats. There are no membership requirements. Their common bond is a special interest in government and public affairs, especially foreign relations, and the time to devote to them. Rarely do they seek elective office, but they are in and out of government appointive office in the State Department, the Treasury, the Pentagon, and other agencies. They share a sense of noblesse oblige, and by osmosis they tend to share common viewpoints on many policy issues. They do not hold power. They do wield influence. Those Dow Jones directors with whom I clashed early in my editorship could be included. I could not.

Of recent presidents Herbert Hoover (Stanford and many public posts) could be considered a member; so could Franklin Roosevelt (Harvard plus family background). Truman won partial acceptance because he made use of them (Acheson). Kennedy, as a Boston Catholic, still had Harvard and Harvard friends and knew how to use them. Johnson, from the Pedernales by way of Southwest Texas State, was an outsider in background, education, and manners. What "the best and brightest" would accept from Kennedy they would not from Johnson.

All this drove Johnson to try to show them and the country he was a worthy successor to the dead Kennedy. He used all his political skill to carry forward Kennedy policies better than Kennedy could. Johnson succeeded because he was a man of the Senate while Kennedy was not. One result was a burst of social legislation, including that on civil rights, unmatched since the first Roosevelt years.

Another consequence, though, was that President Johnson could not retreat from our commitment to Vietnam, begun by Kennedy with the endorsement of those who thought themselves the best and brightest. He could only go forward. It was this, in the end, that brought his downfall.

But as 1964 began, little of this was apparent. Among the general public, if not among the former Kennedy advisers, Lyndon Johnson benefited from the same kind of goodwill as did Harry Truman after Roosevelt's death. People sympathized with him for the problems suddenly thrust upon him and they wanted him to surmount them. After all, in that phrase Johnson himself used repeatedly, he was the only president the country had. Within a year he would win election in his own right by a margin unmatched until Richard Nixon defeated George McGovern.

At the Republican convention that summer you could feel what would come in November. Barry Goldwater—tall, handsome, and affable—I would have to put down as one of the most likeable politicians I ever met, as well as one of the most sincere in the political philosophy he professed. It would never occur to him to tailor a political opinion to the political winds, and that stubbornness would contribute to his undoing. He was without any drive for the presidency; in fact, I believed him when he said, in public and in private, that he did not want to run. Like Adlai Stevenson earlier in the Democratic party, Goldwater had the Republican nomination thrust upon him.

Nelson Rockefeller's divorce and remarriage (including a bit of a mess about child custody with his second wife's first husband) had effectively eliminated him for that year. (Remember this was 1964, before a social revolution had made tangled marriage relations commonplace.) The only "moderate" Republican left in the fray by convention time was Governor William Scranton of Pennsylvania.

Earlier in the summer I had spent a Sunday morning with Governor Scranton and his wife in their official residence outside Harrisburg. I came away convinced that Scranton had no lust for the nomination either, although perhaps his wife did. He kept his hat in the ring more out of a sense of duty than anything else. And by the Sunday before the San Francisco convention, when I appeared with him on *Meet the Press*, it was clear the stop-Goldwater movement was motionless.

I doubt whether there was any way Goldwater could have won the November election. The times were out of joint for any conservative and would be for nearly another twenty years. Whatever chance there was, Goldwater threw it away before the convention ended. For running mate as vice-president he chose Congressman William Miller of New York, lifted from total obscurity and destined to return to it. Then in his acceptance speech Goldwater made not the slightest gesture of conciliation to the "moderates" in his party. Rather he flung down the gauntlet with the defiant words: "Extremism in the defense of liberty is no vice. . . . Moderation in the pursuit of justice is no virtue." Unexceptional thoughts, perhaps, but they made it easy to tag Goldwater as an "extremist," which is a pejorative term in American politics.

Meanwhile, back in Atlantic City, Lyndon Johnson was cavorting like a cowboy at a rodeo. He had no opposition whatever for the nomination. He could only enliven the convention proceedings by playing cat-and-mouse with vice-presidential hopefuls, after which he annointed Hubert Humphrey.

The campaign itself was a disaster for Goldwater, a triumphant march for Johnson. The country was still being torn by racial troubles, and fears over Vietnam had already begun to disturb people. Johnson turned both to advantage. He pushed hard on a new civil rights bill to woo minorities and their liberal supporters. He had earlier rigged a naval encounter in the Tonkin Gulf to make North Vietnam so appear the aggressor that he got a war-supporting resolution from Congress. Then while Goldwater was taking "strong" stands on the Vietnam War, Johnson scattered promises of peace like confetti. "We don't want our American boys to do the fighting for Asian boys. We don't want . . . to get tied down in a land war in Asia. . . . There can be, and will be, as long as I am president, peace for all Americans."

All this put me, and therefore the *Journal*, in a difficult position. As usual, of course, we endorsed neither candidate. But I liked Goldwater personally and thought it long past time for a more conservative president. I thought some of the propaganda against him outrageous. The "Daisy Girl" television commercial, for just one example, showed a child peacefully pulling petals off a daisy when suddenly the picture dissolved into a mushroom cloud, with the not-so-subtle suggestion this is what would happen with Goldwater as president. Yet for all my sympathy toward Goldwater I also felt he would be too rigid to succeed in the White House while Johnson, I felt, was a proven political leader. Rereading the *Journal*'s editorials of that time it's clear that on balance the leaning was toward Johnson.

Even today I cannot say I think Barry Goldwater would have been a successful president. It's clear, though, he could hardly have done worse. The next four years of Lyndon Johnson would turn into a shambles for the country, at home and abroad. As he enlarged the war in Vietnam, sending more Americans to fight for Asian boys, getting us deeper into this land war in Asia, all his campaign promises about "peace for all Americans as long as I am president" came to have a hollow ring. On that score the country might as well have elected Goldwater.

*   *   *   *   *

As the decade of the sixties wore on, there were also to be changes, and more pleasant ones, in my personal life, in my professional life, and in the development of my professional family, the newspaper I had now served so long.

Once Kilgore had rescued me from that purgatory to which Grimes briefly consigned me, Frances and I bought a house in Hastings-on-Hudson, a then quiet village up the river. There our children grew up, attending first the public schools and then the Masters School in Dobbs Ferry. There I spent some years as a volunteer fireman, Frances as a member of the Library Board. All of us made new friends. Then when Eleanor followed Bonnie to Wellesley, we moved back to the city in a comfortable, even elegant, co-op on East Seventy-second Street, where we spent some more happy years.

Within my professional family my career moved onward as I became a vice-president of the parent company, Dow Jones. This promotion was a mixed blessing. It did involve me more in larger corporate areas. It also cut into the time I could devote to my editor's role. Fortunately Joe Evans, as dependable as ever, grew in maturity and judgment, and I relied upon him more with each passing year. Others too were rising in importance in the company.

One was Theodore Callis, another Hoosier, who succeeded Bob Feemster when he retired as chief sales executive. Ted lacked Feemster's flamboyance but he shared the imagination while surpassing Bob in general executive ability. But the newcomer to make the most lasting impression on the company was Warren H. Phillips.

Warren, like Joe Evans, began as a foreign correspondent in our Bonn bureau and returned to New York as foreign editor. Unlike Joe, he was outgoing, driving, and ambitious beyond the ordinary. He wasn't as good a writer, but he was a competent reporter and more skilled as an administrator. He showed this talent when transferred to Chicago as head of all our midwestern coverage, and he was a natural to succeed Bob Bottorff as managing editor when, in the shuffle with McCormack, Bob became executive editor.

Warren is one of those rarities, a native New Yorker. After army service he graduated *cum laude* from Queens College, joining the *Journal* in 1947, a lanky young fellow at the time with tousled hair over a lean, dark face. Put a homburg on him and he could have passed for Anthony Eden. Put a burnoose on him and he looked like a delegate from OPEC. With his blond wife, Barbara, on his arm he has that distingué air of a jet setter out on the town, especially after he grew a mustache. That he ultimately became the company's chief executive officer surprised no one.

Among those even younger ones who caught our eye was Robert Bartley, who had been a reporter in both our Chicago and Philadelphia bureaus. There's a common feeling among young people in a large organization that those "higher up" hardly notice them. On the contrary, those in top management places—at least it's been so on the *Journal*—are constantly looking for bright and able youngsters, continually discussing the merits of this one or that one. It is upon them, after all, that the future depends.

Bright and brash are the words for Bob Bartley. Joe and I first took note of him when he offered some book reviews that were well and thoughtfully written. In 1964 we brought him to New York on the editorial staff and were immediately lectured, with the brashness of youth, about how we were too "conservative" and so out of touch with current political needs. Nonetheless, he plainly had talent, though yet undisciplined, and he proved an addition to the staff. Since his experience was limited, we sent him first on a trip to Vietnam and the Far East, from which he filed perceptive stories. Later we transferred him to Washington as a sort of supernumerary, attached to the editorial department, not the news department. Doubtless there's a lesson of sorts in the result that the experience made him in time appear more "conservative" than either Joe or I. Nonetheless, all this proved educational and good preparation for what lay ahead of him.

While these younger people were pushing upward, some changes were also taking place in my position outside the paper. In 1965 I was elected president of the American Society of Newspaper Editors, in which I had long been active, and presided over the Society's first meeting outside the United States, in Montreal in 1966. There I made so bold as to open the meeting in carefully rehearsed French as a gesture to our Quebec hosts, journalistic and political. (I read French well, write it passably, but it takes a lot of rehearsing to get Dixie out of my accent.)

This Canadian meeting gave me a better insight into some of Canada's internal problems from the language schism between French and English, to the causes of friction between Canada and the U.S. Thanks to the Dow Jones plane I took a Canadian-hopping preconvention tour in company with Creed Black of the *Chicago Daily News*, that year's program chairman. We were well received socially by local officials and newspaper people but we had a rather standoffish reaction to our invitation to Canadian editors to join us in Montreal. One, I remember, asked if there would be any "famous" editors present. The question cut Creed and me down to size, but I replied yes, and some "infamous" ones also. Our host didn't think that amusing.

Nonetheless, we did have a chance to meet Mayor Jean Drapeau of Montreal, Quebec Prime Minister Jean Lasage, and I had a chance to renew an acquaintance with Lester Pearson, the national prime minister. Drapeau and Lasage were frank in stating the resentment of French-speaking Canadians against the dominant English. From publishers we also met a thinly veiled hostility toward the inflow of "foreign" newspapers and magazines, particularly *Time* and *Newsweek*. Both of these issues would become more pronounced in the years ahead. I came away with a firm conviction that we at home were asking for trouble if we moved toward bilingualism. Having a common language, English, was vital to bind together our huge nation of many ethnic stocks.

That Montreal convention was also notable for an address by Robert McNamara, then U.S. secretary of defense, advocating a period of national service (military or otherwise) for all young people. He raised an issue that lingers with us yet.

* * * * *

If my own affairs, then, were progressing well, so much could not be said for those elsewhere, journalistically or politically.

Even as we met in Montreal the newspapers in New York were shut down by their third newspaper strike, and before it was over one more newspaper in our greatest city would disappear. The *Herald-Tribune* was forced to merge with the *World-Telegram* which had previously merged with the *Evening Journal* and the *Sun*. This hybrid, called the *World-Journal-Sun*, would also soon expire. The causes of this shrinkage in the city's newspapers since I first came to New York were many. Among them was the growing competition from TV as a news provider and as a competitor for advertising revenue. TV had already killed off such general circulation magazines as the *Saturday Evening Post* and *Collier's* as the public's reading habits gave way to viewing habits. Many cities were being reduced to one-newspaper towns. But an added factor in New York was the recalcitrance of the printing unions to any technological changes such as automatic typesetting or offset printing. Add to this the timidity of publishers in pressing for such changes. Publishing a newspaper became too costly.

The *Journal* was an exception. In 1963 Barney had already come around to abandoning New York City as a printing place. Moreover, he pushed hard on technological improvements, first with Joe Ackell's automatic Linotype, then with electronic typesetting and eventually with facsimile as a means of printing in outlying plants. The result of this was that we escaped New York's newspaper holocaust. We were not there to be shut down by strikes.

It was not newspapers alone that were the targets of militant unions. By 1966 strikes were becoming pandemic, especially in big cities. Earlier that year New York was closed down by a transit strike, halting all subways and busses and bringing chaos. The next year it would be the garbage collectors. Other strikes stretched across the country involving municipal workers, postal employees, teachers, and California grape pickers.

But none of these was as disruptive—or as destructive—as the racial troubles that burst out, North and South. They began quietly in Kennedy's last year with the black march on Washington which impressed everyone with its order and its nonviolent atmosphere, largely due to the restraining hand of Martin Luther King. That proved the quiet before the storm. Within a year came the riots in Mississippi, Alabama, Chicago and in 1965 the Watts explosion in Los Angeles. In the South the issue was clear— primarily that of voting rights for blacks, long denied. In the North, or in such explosions as in Watts, both the causes and the cures were murky.

I watched all this both puzzled and troubled. With the voting rights issue I had no problem. "The moral issue," I wrote in early 1965, "is indisputable. . . . For men of good will there can be only shame . . . at the way men have been denied their right to vote for no other reason than that their skin was black." Of the need for remedies, I said, "there can be no doubt."

About some of the remedies proposed, passing laws affecting only some states but not all, I was less certain. And I was opposed to the idea that would change the civil rights struggle from one to end all forms of segregation—in the schools, in public facilities, at the voting booth—into an effort to enforce integration of white and black society, the idea which would ultimately lead to forced bussing at no matter what cost. This effort, I felt, could only lead to more racial troubles, as indeed it did.

My puzzlement over the unrest lay in the fact that no president in all our history had worked so hard, done so much, to use government to improve the condition of the blacks, of the poor in general, as Lyndon Johnson. His early years saw an outpouring of social legislation of all kinds not even matched by the New Deal period. He persuaded Congress to pass the most sweeping civil rights bill in history. He launched Medicare. He established federal aid to education. He cut the people's taxes. He established the Department of Housing and Urban Development, a National Endowment for the Arts and Humanities. He declared "a war on poverty" with a new Office of Economic Opportunity. And yet from the public he received almost no credit at all. Nor did all this legislation, subsumed under the slogan "The Great Society," win approval even from those it was designed to benefit.

One reason was that shadow of Jack Kennedy. Johnson's natural supporters, liberal Democrats, credited everything to the dead president. But the most important reason was the Vietnam war, the deepening involvement in it, the means used to wage it, the perceived unfairness of the draft imposed to fight it, and not least its side effects on the economy, most notably inflation. It was all this, in the end, that would bring his downfall.

My own relation with Johnson, meanwhile, remained cordial for all that the *Journal* too was numbered among his critics on many matters. I was to see him several times in the White House both on social and journalistic occasions. Our elder daughter, Bonnie, accompanied Frances and myself to one reception and the president singled her out repeatedly as a dancing partner. Very early in his administration Alan Otten, then the *Journal*'s Washington bureau chief, and I spent an hour with him late one evening. He went to great lengths to impress us with his determination to "discipline the budget" and his willingness to close a number of military bases, which he and Secretary McNamara thought useless, despite the howls he would get from Congress. He

put considerable emphasis on his belief that the government ought
to encourage, not discourage, the business community, implying
that President Kennedy had unnecessarily antagonized it.

This was the political Johnson at work, saying the things he
thought these two from *The Wall Street Journal* would want to
hear. He reported that he had had a long talk with Eisenhower,
who had given him some thoughts to put in his first message to
Congress, and that he had called on former President Hoover.

Reporting on all this in a memorandum to Kilgore I noted a few
personal things: "In mannerisms Mr. Johnson is hardly changed.
He is all Texas and a yard wide. Like Kennedy he sat in a rocking
chair, but unlike Kennedy he hardly stayed put a consecutive five
minutes of the hour, popping up to ransack his desk for a copy
of a press conference statement, jiggling the buttons to call secretaries while hardly breaking stride in his conversation with Al and
me. . . .

"The Johnson ego is holding up quite well. . . . On this the chief
difference between Kennedy and Johnson is that Kennedy, being
more sophisticated, hid it a little better, whereas Johnson is as
open about it as a small boy who just got elected president of the
senior class. . . . In fact, there is a small boy quality about Lyndon Johnson."

But I concluded on a different note: "Johnson also gives the impression of being much more mature than Mr. Kennedy. He seems
to understand that politics is the art of getting things done and he
gives the impression of understanding the machinery of politics. In
this sense, if no other, he may prove a more successful president
than Mr. Kennedy. We will just have to wait before anybody can
decide successful to what end."

This meeting contrasts with another in the fall of 1967. The occasion then was a hurriedly-called White House luncheon of editors and those Johnson thought of as "influential" journalists to
talk about the Vietnam War.

I was boating on Long Island Sound when the ever-efficient
White House switchboard tracked me down. Turner Catledge of
The New York Times was called off the golf course. Altogether
about thirty of us were rounded up, including Walter Cronkite,
Otto Fuerbringer of *Time*, John Knight of the Knight newspaper
chain.

This time, as I jotted down in the usual memo, the mood was different: "The president is obviously a tortured man about this Vietnam business. It's quite clear he lives with it night and day and is getting desperate for some way out of it. It's a little bit embarrassing to see him do this in public. There is too much of the 'pity me, pity me' in everything he says about the terrible business of making decisions."

Different times, a different Lyndon Johnson.

A small footnote. Before the president began his remarks he presented McNamara and Secretary of State Rusk. But the vice-president, who was also there, was never even mentioned. Poor Hubert, I thought.

That occasion remains vivid in my memory for other reasons too. It would be the last time I wrote a memo to Barney about a visit with a president or any other person of public interest. I wrote such memos primarily to put down quickly an account for my own use. I had fallen into the habit of sending Barney a copy because he found them interesting; afterwards he would drop by to talk about them, sharing the visits vicariously. But now Barney was dying.

He had earlier given up his title of president to Bill Kerby, ostensibly moving to the sidelines as chairman of the board. His idea, often spoken, was that he would rotate the presidency of the company among that little band of those who had worked with him so long. That would be a reward for each of us in turn, although we all understood that no matter what title Barney carried his presence would be everywhere felt, his influence dominant on the company's affairs. He had already planned for Kerby, McCormack, and myself to join the board of directors. It was in the midst of these plans that he was struck suddenly, and without warning, by intestinal cancer.

Barney Kilgore died in November 1967, aged fifty-nine.

*   *   *   *   *

In my lifetime there have been three men who made original and lasting contributions to publishing. One was Henry Luce, who with Brit Haddon created the newsweekly. Another was Dewitt Wallace, who launched the *Reader's Digest*. The third was Bernard Kilgore, who dreamed of a national newspaper.

Of Barney's dream, where it started and how it became a reality, I have already written much. But for all who knew him there are other memories of the man besides his touch of genius. He was, strangely enough for so dynamic a leader, the gentlest of men. He was also shy, both with those who worked with him and among his peers in the publishing world. There was nothing flamboyant about him. There was a demon in him about what he wanted to create, an impatience in the creating of it, yet I never saw him lose his temper. Once when in my brashness I told him I thought something he proposed was "stupid" and then shocked by my temerity at using such a word to my boss started to stammer an apology, he merely grinned and said, "I'm the only one in this company who can't afford to get mad."

One secret, I think, was that he had the eye of a poet. Some men look at rivers and see them spanned by bridges. He looked at the nation and saw it crossed by a single newspaper. Though many tried, no one could persuade him it could not be done. It was because he believed in himself so firmly that he could be so patient with those who differed. When he made mistakes, as he did, he acknowledged them easily, with never a backward look or with any resentment against those who might have told him so beforehand.

One more thing. He had an unusual way of leadership. It was rare for him to call anyone to his office. His way was to walk through the building, floor by floor, stopping off to talk with department heads, reporters, clerks, or whomever. Sometimes to say something of importance, sometimes merely to pass the time. In the same way he would drop into our offices across the country, unannounced. Only the very newest employee ever addressed him as Mr. Kilgore. To everyone else he was Barney. The mantle of command, which everyone recognized, rested easily upon his shoulders. Outside the company his work was more famous than himself. He felt no need to build up his ego with applause.

To those who asked what manner of man he was, his friends could only say he had indeed a touch of genius and was to the full measure a gentleman.

So we all knew, that day in November, that an era had ended, without knowing what that would portend.

*   *   *   *   *

The White House luncheon in September sticks in my mind for another less personal reason. It was the beginning of a pleasant relationship with a man who was to be much maligned in public but for whom I came to have great respect, Dean Rusk.

After that luncheon, as the president was leaving, Secretary Rusk took me aside and said that later in the month he would be in New York, and if our editorial people were interested he would be glad to pay us a visit. I accepted with alacrity. We gave a luncheon for him and found him more thoughtful and articulate about Vietnam than the president had been.

Dean Rusk is a quiet, soft-spoken Southerner, a native of Georgia. He graduated from Davidson College in North Carolina, not far from Chapel Hill, and then went to Oxford as a Rhodes scholar. He first served in the State Department in 1946, then after a period as president of the Rockefeller Foundation was named secretary of state by President Kennedy. He proved to be one of the few holdovers who would serve President Johnson with equal loyalty. What his true feelings were about the conduct of the Vietnam war by Johnson I wasn't sure, except that he never doubted the president's motives. He had one characteristic not universal among secretaries of state. In private conversation he did not try to give the impression that he had somewhat different views on foreign policy from those of the president, in an effort to deflect any criticism from himself. He accepted criticism, of which he got plenty, with at least outward equanimity and the air of one who understood that on such issues as Vietnam reasonable men could differ.

At that *Journal* luncheon he gave as clear an explanation as anyone could have for the president's course in that far-off war. The real problem was that by 1967 no one could explain Vietnam.

No one can really explain it now. Contrary to many of those who have done postmortems, I don't believe our motives in involving ourselves in that far-off country are anything to be ashamed of. Here was a small country, South Vietnam, threatened with outright aggression by its northern neighbor. It's not to their discredit that "the best and the brightest" (among whom were many later to be most vicious in their denunciations of the war) should want to help this small country. The tragedy lay not in motive but in the nature of our response.

We began, of course, with some military advisers sent by President Eisenhower, who was willing to offer that much help but was opposed to any other military involvement in an Asian land war. After all, he had been through the experience of Korea. President Kennedy, without foreseeing the consequences, made the first real military commitment by sending in some of our Special Forces, better known as the Green Berets. Lyndon Johnson, then, inherited a situation where we were already involved with fighting troops. At that time, we ought not to forget, public opinion as well as the opinions of those best and brightest favored our support to the beleaguered South Vietnamese. We were imbued with the Truman-Kennedy doctrine that the U.S. had a duty to oppose Communist aggression anywhere. Had President Johnson done what he ought to have done, pulled back and accepted the fact that we were overreaching ourselves however worthy the cause, he would have been excoriated by the very people who later denounced him. Neither philosophically nor politically could he accept being the president who turned-tail and quit.

His first mistake thereafter was one that has lost many a commander a battle. He was unwilling to go all-out in the beginning. Had he done so while the North Vietnamese were still relatively weak, all might have turned out differently. Who knows? Instead, he committed forces piecemeal. Little by little he poured more into that quagmire.

His second mistake was to suppose the U.S. could fight a war thousands of miles across the Pacific Ocean, and against a determined foe, without changing anything at home. Though the war was costing billions he would subtract nothing from the billions to create his Great Society. He accepted a military draft but not an across-the-board draft as in World War II. The exceptions and exemptions in it, intended not to disrupt young people's education, meant in practice that the white sons of the middle class escaped. The poor, and especially the black poor, bore the brunt of it as they also bore the brunt of the growing inflation. The consequences of that, social and political, were inevitable.

By 1967, when I found Johnson so tormented, so was the whole country. Race riots, draft riots, the spread of drugs among the young by returning soldiers, the whole growth of a counter-culture like fungus on the body social, began to make everyone feel that the country was coming apart. Some feared we were on the edge of revolution.

I, too, was tormented. I was uneasy when President Kennedy sent in those first ground forces, alarmed when we acquiesced in the overthrow of Diem and more so as President Johnson continually escalated our military action. Even the military, as I was eventually to discover, was not as unanimously sanguine about the military prospects as it appeared to be in public. At the end of the 1960s I was at Pearl Harbor and the then Commander-in-Chief-Pacific, Admiral John S. McCain, an old friend from Navy days, arranged a briefing for me by senior officers of the Army, Air Force, Navy, and Marines. The briefing itself was the usual routine lecture before charts and maps showing our forces and North Vietnamese forces. But when over coffee afterwards I posed the blunt question whether there was a realistic prospect of "winning" the war I got no gung-ho answers. One general said, quite frankly, it wasn't a war he would choose to fight—"*but that's not my decision to make.*" My impression was of reluctant warriors doing their duty. That briefing didn't cheer me up.

But in 1967 I wasn't ready to join the chorus of those denouncing not only the conduct of the war as a blunder but our efforts to help the South Vietnamese as something immoral. One reason, I suppose, was my dislike for many of the voices in that chorus. Some were just general troublemakers, some were the very ones who had led us into the war. Another reason, no doubt, was a sense of "responsibility" to support my country in a time of troubles, or simple patriotism. Finally, there was a lingering hope that a way would be found, military or diplomatic, to end the agony.

By early 1968, however, I could no longer resist arguments that as a practical matter the war was a disaster. The editorial that appeared in February was largely Joe's work. Its form was a warning that the country had best reconcile itself to the prospect that "the whole Vietnam effort may be doomed." We had best prepare ourselves for the bitter taste of defeat.

The editorial attracted much attention. The wire services summarized it, a number of papers commented on it. Joe and I had to read often "Even *The Wall Street Journal* . . . ," a phrase that has always annoyed me with its implication that for us to say something reasonable was a rarity. Much of this attention came, I think,

from the fact that the editorial made good ammunition for the de-
nunciators of Johnson and all his works.

What was less noticed in that emotional atmosphere was that we
did not condemn the motives that led us into that war. "If it had
been possible to accomplish the original objective" of saving South
Vietnam it would have been "well worth doing." We also said our
failure would be "a stunning blow to the U.S. and the West . . . a
traumatic experience to have lost a war in which thousands of
Americans had died in vain." Our point was only that the war
"was not worth any price no matter how ruinous."

All the same, and no matter what qualifications we put on our
opinion, the editorial was one more voice opposing the continua-
tion of the war. That left few defenders of our deepening involvement on this distant shore.

So as the curtain rose on 1968 the stage was set for the most
tumultuous presidential election of my journalistic memory.

3

In February it was clear to everybody that President Johnson was
beleaguered. In the Far East there had been disaster after disaster.
A small navy ship the *USS Pueblo* had been seized by the North
Koreans in the Sea of Japan. In Vietnam the new year began with
the Tet offensive in which North Vietnamese and Viet Cong troops
infiltrated Saigon and attacked everywhere in the city, including
the U.S. Embassy. In the eventual postmortems we could claim
to have "won" since the Communist forces were repulsed. But at
the time the vivid reporting of the attack in newspapers and television gave the American public a picture of defeat; seemingly we
couldn't even protect the capital from Communist attack despite
the bombing of North Vietnam ordered by Johnson. Angry protests against the war had mounted. All this had been preceded by
black riots in Newark and Detroit which had to be quelled by national guardsmen and federal troops. The president was discredited within his own party.

On the far right domestically was George Wallace of Alabama
seeking to lead those opposed to the Great Society legislation and
especially white voters opposed to the president's civil rights program. On the left—these terms can only be used loosely—was
Senator Eugene McCarthy, handsome, gray-haired, spokesman for

the liberals in the Senate. He had been one of those toyed with by President Johnson in 1964 for the vice-presidential nomination which ultimately went to Hubert Humphrey. Less definable on the broad political spectrum was Robert Kennedy, but he was now to be classified as a "dove" on Vietnam though he had vigorously supported the war in his brother's administration. And once Johnson decided not to run there was, of course, Vice-President Humphrey.

Johnson's decision in March to withdraw was the better part of valor. In the 1962 off-year congressional election the Democrats had lost forty-seven House seats, three in the Senate, and eight governorships. This put the party pros in a mood to listen to a firebrand like Allard Lowenstein, former congressman (and Chapel Hill graduate), whose cry was "anybody but Johnson." It would be difficult for the Democrats to dump an incumbent president, but with Johnson heading the ticket the election prospect was grim. Lyndon Johnson could read political omens as well as anyone.

On the Republican side there was a covey of possibilities: Governors Romney of Michigan, Rockefeller of New York, and Reagan of California. Standing in the wings and now being noticed was Richard Nixon, undeterred by his defeat in 1960 by Jack Kennedy or by his subsequent failure to win the governorship of California.

Of the Democrats I knew Senator McCarthy least well; I had spoken with him and that was about all. Robert Kennedy and I were too well acquainted; I had gotten off on the wrong foot with him as far back as 1961. Newly installed as attorney general, he addressed the American Society of Newspaper Editors and I was called upon to introduce him. I meant to be humorous. Instead, what I said was taken by Kennedy to be insulting.

I began by noting that our speaker, unlike most of the others, wasn't yet listed in *Who's Who*. So I explained that the new attorney general was a graduate of the University of Virginia Law School, a place beloved by Southerners, and that at the Democratic convention the previous year he had come to the attention of a Southerner, now vice-president. That, indeed, at one point Lyndon Johnson had remarked he felt completely surrounded by Kennedys. I pointed out that while Kennedy had not yet had much legal experience he was sure to get it in the Justice Department, and that our highest elected government official (President Kennedy, of course) thought enough of him to see that he got some experience before he started practicing. I wound up by saying I felt sure he would soon make it into *Who's Who*, and we would hear a great deal more about him. Then I introduced him as a "fellow Southerner" by virtue of his Virginia background.

The audience was amused, but I was told later that Kennedy's expression was grim. Anyway, he acknowledged the introduction by saying he'd like to know where I filed my income tax, "and if I don't call on you personally on Monday I am sure you will enjoy the person who does."

I didn't escape from that bad beginning by later inviting him to lunch at the *Journal*. Unfortunately Joe Evans and some of the reporters present bore in on him pretty hard, to his evident irritation. When I escorted him to his car he took my proffered hand but returned not even a formal "thank you." With Bobby Kennedy, to my regret, I never recovered.

I found him abrasive, to be sure—but then I suppose he found me abrasive too. I also thought him smarter, or at least quicker of mind, than his elder brother. If he lacked Jack's polish or the ability to control an Irish temper, he could inspire fierce loyalty among those who knew him well. I never met anyone who had served closely with him who did not speak of him with affection. In the public eye, of course, he was the inheritor of the Camelot legacy. Had it not been for Sirhan Sirhan he would have been a formidable rival to Hubert Humphrey for the Democratic nomination. I wish I could have known him better.

By now I knew Vice-President Humphrey fairly well; twice he had been a *Journal* luncheon visitor where he proved as much a nonstop talker as Diem. Once, I remember, we got a chance to ask him only two questions, all the rest of the time being used up by his answers. Someone once remarked that there was a "puppy dog" air about Hubert, and that comment wasn't far off the mark. He was naturally friendly and always seemed to be trying hard to please. His liberalism also came naturally, I think, out of a sincere feeling that government had a responsibility to help the less fortunate.

On the Republican side, Rockefeller was an old acquaintance; Romney I'd known since his days as president of American Motors. Reagan I'd met a year earlier when Al Otten and I had a long visit with him. No one, not even the liberal Otten, could help being attracted to him. The ideas he expressed then were hardly different from those of 1980—the need for less of and less expensive government, for lower taxes—but the time wasn't yet ripe for either Reagan or his ideas.

Nixon I had come to know even better. After his defeat for the governorship of California he moved to New York to practice law. His office was near the *Journal* and we belonged to the same luncheon club. Though I did not see him frequently, when I did I found him far more relaxed than when he was vice-president or campaigning for the presidency. The informal Nixon is quite different from the public one. An introvert, a man haunted by a feeling of insecurity and of being persecuted by the media for reasons he doesn't understand, he cannot relax under the spotlight. When he tried it, it was an effort and the effect was artificial; in that respect he resembled Robert Taft, who also had no gift for informality. I liked the man and had much sympathy for him. His sense of persecution by the media wasn't all paranoia. From his campaign for the Senate against Helen Gahagan Douglas, a liberal liked by the press, through his prosecutorial role in the Alger Hiss case, he had been treated as "tricky Dick." This gave him the siege mentality that was to cause him so many problems later.

Some other things struck me. After 1962 I had thought his political future behind him—and with my prescience said so! But in New York it was plain he was determined to "show" his enemies and was using his time in the wilderness to build support for himself among the party regulars. His ambition was undiminished.

I also noticed that he seemed to be a man without close personal friends. He had grown up in a small town, Yorba Linda, California, and for his undergraduate education attended Whittier, a small college. Later he studied law at Duke University. He had been an active politician since 1946. Along the way he had acquired admirers and supporters. But there seemed to be none of the one or two enduring friends most of us acquire from our childhood or college days.

I'm not a psychologist, but I can't help thinking this was at least a partial clue to that Nixon tragedy. Even those who were close to him in early political days—Herb Klein, his first press secretary, William P. Rogers, a colleague of the Eisenhower years and his first secretary of state—were to vanish by the time of Watergate. In the White House he was surrounded by men who were no more than courtiers: Haldeman, Ehrlichman, Dean, Mitchell, all recent associates and all of whom—as courtiers will—turned on him with a vengeance after the fall.

The possible significance of the friendlessness of Richard Nixon escaped me in the 1960s. What was evident was his grasp of public affairs, about which he could talk knowledgeably and with perception. By 1968 it was also clear that a second presidential nomination was within his grasp.

The week before the Democratic convention I flew to Chicago for what would obviously be a tumultous meeting. What I found was something never seen before or since. A major American political convention was gathering in an armed camp.

The stockyards amphitheater was ringed by a high chain link fence topped with barbed wire. Around it were police equipped with riot gear. The Illinois National Guard was on alert and troops of the regular army had been brought up from Texas on President Johnson's orders. All this to protect Democrats from mobs outside. Near the downtown hotels unruly crowds packed the streets. Frances was with me but felt it wiser to stay in our own hotel. The cause of all this disturbance, at least ostensibly, was a spontaneous protest against the Vietnam War. In fact, the crowds included many who were just troublemakers or who were lured there by the prospects for excitement.

That Friday I got a call from Lawrence Spivak, creator and moderator of NBC's TV program *Meet the Press*. Vice-President Humphrey had agreed to be on the program if it was held in Washington rather than in Chicago. I was asked to be one of his inquisitors. So we flew back to the capital on Saturday. The questions and answers of that program are a blur in my mind. I remember only that most of them centered around Vietnam and that I, for one, felt so sorry for Humphrey I couldn't bring myself to push him hard.

After the program Humphrey offered Frances and me a ride back to Chicago on his chartered plane. The air aboard was oppressive. Hubert and Muriel sat alone together talking quietly. The rest of us knew he would win the nomination, which should have been cause for festivity, but all of us wondered whether the nomination would be worth anything. I remember just before we landed Humphrey got up, put on his jacket, let an aide powder his face in case of television cameras. Then, as the boarding ladder came alongside, he squared his shoulders, managed to smile, and stepped out jauntily to be greeted by only a handful of supporters. It would be the last time I would see him until after the election.

That election, to everyone's surprise, turned out to be another cliff-hanger. The Republican convention in Miami Beach had been relatively quiet, thanks in part to the fact that access to the beach could be easily controlled. Nixon won on the first ballot, Rockefeller having done his habitual on-again-off-again candidate bit. On March 1 he was "ready and willing" to be a candidate. On March 31 he said he wasn't an "active" candidate. He would accept a draft but would do nothing to encourage one. That shattered any hopes of a "Stop Nixon" drive. Then Nixon managed what had eluded Goldwater in 1964; as he made his acceptance speech he was surrounded on stage by all his challengers in the party. The smell of victory was in the air that night.

Considering the shambles of Chicago, that seemed reasonable. Although after the assassination of Bobby Kennedy there was no real challenger to Humphrey, there was no harmony in the Democratic party. Johnson's administration, of which Humphrey was a part, had been discredited. Senators McCarthy and McGovern, though garnering only a handful of delegate votes, led followers ready to desert the party. The television cameras had focused as much on the rioting outside the hall as on the party business inside, leaving a terrible impression on the home viewers. Humphrey came out of the convention in a nearly impossible situation. He could not renounce the president he had served for four years, yet he had somehow to distance himself from the Johnson war policies. Almost everyone thought him a beaten man before the election match began.

That he did as well as he did was a near miracle. In September, without criticizing Johnson directly, he announced he would stop the bombing of North Vietnam "as an acceptable risk for peace." This gave the militants a chance to come home. Meanwhile other segments of the party, notably the labor union leaders, remembered there were domestic issues too in the campaign. Nixon did not help himself with his choice of "Spiro Who?" as his running mate; Mr. Agnew added nothing to the ticket and alienated the so-called moderates of the party.

Election night 1968 was almost a replay of 1960, except that this time it was Nixon who squeaked by as the winner. This was before those magic computers that declare a winner before all the ballots have been cast, but the television networks were using electric scoreboards so the returns could be followed visually. Around midnight it was Humphrey in the lead. By dawn it was nip-and-tuck on the popular vote although Nixon seemed to have the edge in the Electoral College. There was talk that night that the election might be thrown into the House of Representatives—where the Democrats had the majority.

The final results, come morning, were Nixon, 31,770,222 popular votes; Humphrey, 31,267,744. In the electoral vote it was Nixon, 301; Humphrey, 191. As it was, less than one percent separated the two men in the popular vote.

Nevertheless, Nixon had won what he had so long sought. Because of the 9.8 million votes cast for Wallace, running as an independent, he was a minority president in popular votes as were John Kennedy and Harry Truman before him. He also failed to carry Congress for his party, the first time that had happened to a new president since Zachary Taylor over a century earlier. No matter. For all the disorder in the streets, order reigned in the political process. Richard Nixon was legitimately president of the United States.

*   *   *   *   *

It was now, that summer of 1968, over thirty years since I walked unannounced into Bill Grimes's office, ten years since my chief ambition had been fulfilled on that once small newspaper. Much had changed in those thirty years, much even in the past decade, in the country, in the newspaper, in my personal life.

Ten years earlier President Eisenhower had sent marines into Lebanon, an operation that proved quiet, peaceful, and short-lived. Now we were bogged down in a far-off war more searing to the country than any since our Civil War. A newly elected president had to deal with that war and something unheard of those thirty years ago, inflation. He, like his immediate predecessors, also faced a strange new world inherited from the peace plans of Franklin Roosevelt—a divided Germany, a divided Korea, a divided Vietnam; half of Europe under the sway of the Soviet Union, half of Asia dominated by the Chinese Communists. I could hardly subscribe to that nineteenth-century view, which I had once shared, that progress toward a better world was inevitable with the passing years. Yet I do not recall feeling despair that summer at the state of the world or the country. I had by now lived through too much. I am often a pessimist about the short-run; I remain an optimist about the long future. Somehow, I thought, we would survive even Vietnam.

My feeling, I'm sure, was colored by an egocentric viewpoint because for my newspaper, and for myself, the years had been kind. The *Journal* was touching a million circulation and still growing. The company itself was prospering. So was I. From our twenty-sixth floor apartment with its picture windows overlooking Manhattan, Frances and I couldn't help contrasting it with that third-floor walkup in Washington where the dinner dishes were washed in the bathtub.

There were also sadnesses. Barney I sorely missed both for his imagination and leadership in the office and for his personal friendship which had grown with the years. He and his wife, Mary Lou, had been newlyweds in Washington at the same time as Frances and I; the acquaintance that began then ripened with time. Even when I had my troubles in the office I kept my admiration for him and gained affection. But his other "boys"—Kerby, McCormack, Bottorff—remained. On us, too, time had worked its changes. The edges of friction had been worn down. We all by now shared much social life as well as a common interest in our enterprise. If Bill Kerby, the new company president, was no Kilgore, he had been a superb lieutenant and would be a safe caretaker of what Barney had built.

So I could look back, especially on the last decade, with satisfaction. Part of that, of course, was the new vantage point I had to observe the country's politics and politicians. There was also the opportunity I had to see other countries, other men, and take their measure.

On our family room wall I keep a map of the world dotted with pins, each to mark some distant place visited. Some come from the war years, marking forgotten places like Eniwetok or Ulithi, or never-to-be-forgotten places like Nagasaki. But most of them I owe to *Journal* travels.

The around-the-world trip in 1959 introduced me to the Far East; only the People's Republic of China then closed its doors to me. The Russian journey in 1962 in which I encountered Nikita Khruschev also covered some eight thousand miles of the Soviet Union, from Leningrad in the west to the depths of Central Asia where Genghis Khan and Tamerlane once reigned. It included also the beaches of the Black Sea and the countryside of Georgia and the Ukraine. I came back with some views I have not changed.

Khruschev convinced me the Kremlin, no matter in whose hands, will never abandon Russia's ambitions, which reach back to the days of the czars, for an enlarging empire. I found it a land of immense potential, rich in physical resources and with many able and vigorous people. I also acquired the conviction that the Soviet Union is, at bottom, a feudalistic society, a backward country whether the test be industry, agriculture, technology, labor skills or the people's standard of living. If the economic system "works" it does so only by brute strength and awkwardness. The source of Soviet power, its ruthlessness in bending 200 million people to a central will, is weakened by the very thing it feeds upon. As I would remark to an inquisitive congressional committee, "I came back an advocate of the Communist system—for the Russians!" With a better economic system they would be an even greater threat to the world.

The paradox of Russia is matched by the puzzle of India. Because it is huge in size (a "subcontinent," in the usual phrase) and huge in population (700 million plus), and because it sits athwart the route from Europe to Western Asia, there is a mystique about its strategic importance. The U.S. has lent or given huge sums to support it as the "largest democracy in the world."

But a visitor there goes through a cycle of moods as ordered as the seasons. The first is despair born of shock at the human degradation of poverty. Can this truly be so important a country? This is followed by hope for India as the visitor encounters able men and women educated on the model set by the British raj. Then once more depression as a journey from the model city, farm, or factory shown with such pride brings you again to the primitiveness of a millennium past.

In 1966 I went through all these cycles, once having them compressed into a single day in the presence of Indira Gandhi, the prime minister. A handsome woman of statuesque proportions, she appears at first very British in accent, manner, and political style, much of which she acquired as a student at Oxford. She talks like the leader of a true parliamentary democracy. But as the questions press her, you get a glimpse of the authoritarianism of an oriental despot. Then once again graciousness. And finally, when she begins to talk about her plans for India, you begin to wonder whether she is really intelligent beneath the educated patina. It was disturbing to hear her talk of plans for steel mills, locomotive factories and auto plants when the country so desperately needs to spend its money on flood control, irrigation, and fertilizer to make the land fruitful. You leave doubting if the gap can ever be closed between the western and the semi-oriental mind.

A visit to Israel, by way of contrast, makes you realize what can be done to make a poor land flourish. A journey from Dan to Beersheba shows that the Israelis have, as they claim, made the desert bloom, a fact made more impressive when you step from Israel to, say, Jordan, where much remains as it must have been a thousand years ago. You are also struck by the contrast between Madam Gandhi and another woman political leader, Golda Meir, not yet the prime minister in 1968 but soon to be. Mrs. Meir too had iron beneath her motherly manner, but if she lacked the educated sophistication of Madam Gandhi she made up for it in common sense. Furthermore, though Israel has an astonishing number of political crosscurrents for so small a country, I had no feeling it was only a make-believe democracy. I felt right at home listening to people freely denounce the government for things done or undone. The wonder I felt there was that the little country had managed to survive and whether it would continue to do so.

On that visit Frances and I got some glimpses of the pressures under which the Israelis live. One came at a northern kibbutz below the Golan heights where we spent a night. There we could see the marks remaining from the shellings that came intermittently from the Syrians on those heights, and the underground shelters to which the Israelis had to flee until the 1967 war removed that danger. We had another view from what came to be known as the "one-day war," an excursion by Israeli tanks and troops across the Jordan River to clear out reported camps from which Palestinians made guerrilla raids into Israel. We had a chance to watch it from the hills of Jericho which overlook the river valley. We also, though, saw some of the other side of the story among the refugees

in the Sinai Peninsula. What I didn't see was any solution to the
Middle East problem. Neither has anyone since.

Other travels, other feelings.

I concede I feel more at home in the countries of Western Europe. If the French can be as puzzling in their way as any peoples
(especially under de Gaulle), their politics are still in a familiar
mode. At one time or another in repeated visits I had some hours
with politicians in or out of office there and in Britain, West Germany, and elsewhere. With due allowances for differences in language, history and culture I found them not much different from
their counterparts at home. I might despair of Britain's economy,
feel frustrated by France's foreign policy, or marvel at the miracle
of West Germany, but at least I felt on familiar terrain. For that
reason, perhaps, the visits to other parts of the world are more
vivid in memory and did more to broaden my own political
horizons.

Yet some of the European personalities stick in my mind. Ludwig Erhard, solid in appearance and stolid in conversation, yet
with a sure grasp of the economic needs of West Germany; his real
contribution was as economics minister rather than later as chancellor. Couve de Murville, de Gaulle's foreign minister, suave, articulate, gifted with the skill to state outrageous propositions and
make them sound like truisms. Guido Carli, a man of solid good
sense who managed to remain head of the Bank of Italy while governments toppled to the right and left of him in that politically dis-
ordered country. Harold Wilson, whose policies as Labor prime
minister contributed to Great Britain's present sad state but who in
person had that English polish an Oxbridge education can give
a man.

But if the *Journal* let me roam, and though I enjoyed all of it, the
focus of my interest remained at home, with our own troubles and
with our politicians' efforts to deal with them.

4

The year 1969 was not a propitious one for any man to be installed as president of the United States. In some ways he faced
more difficulties than Franklin Roosevelt in 1933, for though FDR
had to deal with the depression the country was not then in an
explosive mood.

It was on Richard Nixon's inauguration day. The Vietnam War

had provided the spark to ignite turmoil everywhere. Blacks were angry at what they saw as the failed promises of government and of white society despite all that Lyndon Johnson had tried to do. Working people, white collar as well as blue collar, were angry at the mounting inflation the war had let loose. In the previous year there had been two assassinations to stun the country, those of Martin Luther King and Robert Kennedy. Crimes of violence were rampant in city streets and suburbs. The draft had unleashed violence among the militant young on the nation's campuses. To many people the very order of society appeared to have broken down.

Of all these signs of disintegration the most disturbing to me were the campus eruptions. Labor strikes and race riots were at least familiar; I had seen both before. Moreover, their causes were understandable, and however grave their consequences they were remediable. If the new president could return hope to the black community, if he could get hold of the government's economic policies to check the inflation eroding the people's money, these grievances would diminish. With the militant young all was baffling.

The shock of student violence was felt across the country, from Berkeley in California to Columbia in New York. The militants took over buildings, seized university presidents, vandalized offices, laboratories, even libraries. The explanation that all this was a protest against the draft struck me as unpersuasive. Because of the exemptions for college students most of these campus young had little to fear from it. Besides, opposition to the draft didn't alone explain other forms the rebellion was taking. The drug culture, the new sexual mores, these were forms of revolt against all authority, any authority, including that of traditional morality.

Equally baffling to me was the response of faculty and administrators to the student uprisings. With a few exceptions, such as S. I. Hayakawa at San Francisco State, college presidents simply abdicated. They made little effort to assert the discipline of the collegium, in or out of the classroom. In quite a few cases faculty members encouraged the student militancy. It was as if we were seeing a form of hysteria known as the madness of crowds.

As a commentator I found all this frustrating. The revolters were not among my audience. What was the point of a comment if no one was listening? Anyway, the whirlwind swept away all calming or cautionary words no matter by whom uttered.

But this gave me sympathy for the man who was the new president. Extricating us from Vietnam would be difficult enough. The task of restoring social tranquility was staggering.

Nonetheless, Richard Nixon made a good beginning. In Washington that inauguration day his cabinet, some of whose members I met for the first time, seemed to me uninspiring but competent. Of those I already knew, William Rogers didn't promise a forceful secretary of state but he was an old Nixon friend, and the president would likely be his own foreign policy creator anyway. Melvin Laird, former congressman, I thought would make an able secretary of defense; so should David Kennedy, Chicago Banker and former staff member at the Federal Reserve, as secretary of the treasury. John Mitchell, newly met, struck me as a humorless but experienced lawyer who might be a strong attorney general. All in all, it seemed no better but no worse a cabinet than other presidents had begun with.

Nixon himself would be the key. I had no illusions that he could or would be a charismatic president in the way of Roosevelt or Kennedy. I did think, and said so at the time, that he would prove a more able president than Lyndon Johnson. Experience had given him a good grasp of public affairs, though less so on economics than on foreign policy. He did not shy from responsibility. On Vietnam, his most prickly problem, I thought he would grasp the nettle boldly. On such social issues as civil rights I saw him as following the Eisenhower path; not an innovator but an upholder of the law and a defender of the gains the blacks had thus far made.

I was not far wrong in the beginning. During the campaign Nixon had implied he had a "plan" for ending the Vietnam War. In his inaugural he said the greatest honor history could bestow on a man is "the title of peacemaker." Not long afterwards he was telling newsmen, "Peace in Asia cannot come from the United States. It must come from Asia. The people of Asia, the governments of Asia—they are the ones who must lead the way."

Whenever Nixon spoke, publicly or privately, it was clear what he had in mind was an American withdrawal from Vietnam. Or put bluntly, an American retreat, a word a president dare not use. His words were soon backed by his deeds, for he did in fact begin the process of "reducing American involvement"—i.e., withdrawing U.S. troops. In time he invented a euphemism for the defeat he was accepting by this withdrawal: "Vietnamization." That is, turning the fighting over to South Vietnamese troops while we supplied the guns, ammunition and other supplies.

So I became persuaded that President Nixon was, with considerable courage, grasping the thorns of the overriding problem before the country. That would at least open the way for dealing with the other two major ones—relations between the races and the economic problem of inflation.

I approved of this. "The hope of anything approaching victory in that weary war has long since vanished," I wrote in the autumn of 1969. "The turn in American policy has already come. . . . We are now in the process of liquidating that war. More, the end is going to come faster than the hawks fear or the doves hope."

I also said, however, the winding down of that war would not be the totally unmixed blessing it might appear to those who so vociferously claimed that all we had to do was quit and all would be well.

"The question 'After Vietnam, what?' is neither academic nor rhetorical. And we will be foolish to blink its possible torments.

"The other countries of Asia will draw the justified conclusion. They will put less trust in both our intent and our ability to shield them from aggressive neighbors. There is no use pretending, either, that then our country will stand as tall in Europe and the Middle East. . . . Failure in Vietnam will do more than cost us 'face.' It will make friend and foe reassess the power balance of the world, with consequences unknown."

For once, at least, I think I may claim some foresight. It was to be longer than I thought before our withdrawal would be complete, but when it came it would leave in its wake the wreckage of the American foreign policy followed since World War II. The Truman Doctrine, the Kennedy Doctrine, would disappear into the wastebin of history. The consequences of Vietnam—of our defeat there—would haunt many presidents to come.

"What we have to face as a country," I said, "is what men sometimes have to face in their private lives, an agony for which there is no balm. We are going to withdraw from the war in Vietnam not because it is a good solution but because we cannot do otherwise."

I concluded that it wasn't too soon to prepare ourselves for what would follow—"which means among other things not being gulled into supposing the torments will be ended when the last soldier comes home." As it turned out, the torments wouldn't be ended, either for the country or for the president who brought that last soldier home.

These observations of mine in the *Journal*, I might note, didn't appear in an editorial. They were in the signed column begun long ago by Tom Woodlock, continued by Bill Grimes, and now resurrected by me. The reappearance of "Thinking Things Over" was a reflection of the way my role on the paper was again changing.

*   *   *   *   *

As early as 1964 I began to realize Joe Evans was doing the same thing to me I had done to Bill Grimes, usurping—if that's the word—the position of being the chief author of the *Journal*'s views. Some of this may have been by design; often he would appear in the morning with at least a rough outline of an editorial on whatever was the main topic at the time. I could still modify his ideas, suggest different phraseology here, add a thought there or, sometimes, reshape the whole editorial. Because Joe was a polished writer and because our minds ran in the same channels, there was less and less of this "editing" as time passed. But much of the alteration in our relationship was due to changes in my position within the company because the company itself was changing. With our growth, with the multiplication of printing plants, with the beginnings of expansion into new areas, we had outgrown the simplicity of the "coffee clatch." Barney tried to keep as much of its informality as he could but gradually it outgrew a newsroom desk with the addition of top people from other departments and moved to a regular conference room. Later Barney formed a more formal management committee. This led to more formality in titles. In the early 1960s I was named first a vice-president and, as other officers were added from the business and production side, the senior vice-president. In 1970 I was elected to the board of directors of Dow Jones, the parent company. All this inevitably took up more and more of my time.

Before Barney died he asked Bottorff and me to work with an outside investment consultant, Brad Mills, on possible acquisitions which would fit into our existing operations; he had no intention of creating a conglomerate with shoe stores and grocery chains. This led to a joint venture with the Richard D. Irwin Company,

publishers of textbooks on business and economics, and ultimately
to acquisition of that company. We had also started on our own a
weekly newspaper, *The National Observer*, largely because Barney
was growing restless.

As he often said, the *Journal* now pretty much ran itself with
able people in its various departments. It was also so successful
that he couldn't "tinker" with it as he had in the beginning. For
mental stimulation he had already purchased for himself the
weekly newspaper in Princeton, where he lived, and with the *Observer* he envisioned a national weekly of general news resembling
the *Journal* in format but not in content. It would have a cost advantage, he thought, because it could be printed in existing *Journal* plants where the presses were idle on Saturday.

It proved not to be one of Barney's better ideas. It was an attractive, well-written and edited newspaper liked by its subscribers. Its
problem was finding an advertising niche in competition with such
magazines as *Time* and *Newsweek.* As a consequence it continually lost money.

After Barney's death Bill Kerby asked Donald Macdonald, inheritor of the Feemster mantle as our chief marketing officer, and
me to see what we could do to make the *Observer* financially viable. Don is a tough, hard-driving Scotsman who sparks a dozen
ideas a day, one of which may be very good indeed. I learned much
from him and have for him much respect. For over a year we gave
it the "good college try," surveying readers, consulting with advertising agencies, examining and re-examining everything from its
editorial concept to its budget. All to no avail. In the end I had to
tell Bill that I saw no way the figures of cost and revenue could
make it profitable. It might have died then except for Bill's loyalty
to Barney's dying wish that he try not to let it die.

What all this did was make it impossible for me to be any longer
a daily editor. Joe was named "editor of the editorial page" and
officially recognized internally as the paper's daily voice. The trouble for me was that I still thought of myself as primarily a newspaperman, not a businessman, and so in frustration I began that
occasional column for personal reflections on passing events.

I came to like it very much. Because in both style and content it
could be more personal than an institutional editorial, I felt free to
offer observations not only on such major issues as inflation or

Vietnam but also on anything else that came to mind. If I wished to comment on the state of education I did so, and made it personal by drawing on my memories of my own anachronistic education at the Webb School or incidents from the educational experiences of my daughters. To illustrate the Johnsonian manner of sermonizing to visitors in the White House rose garden I might compare it to the preaching of Tom Sawyer's Uncle Silas. The modern presidential press conference might stir memories of that first one I attended of Franklin Roosevelt back in the thirties.

I didn't think either that in such a personal column every thought had to be earthshaking. I looked upon the column as a way to have a conversation with our readers. I would often invite the reader to let his mind wander, often far afield from the great issues of the day. A small observation can be interesting without being the final answer to anything. Personal experience, too, can spur a reflection as it will in conversation; if I felt like writing of my feeling on seeing my first grandchild I did so. I was to find that many times these personal thoughts, tinged no doubt with sentimentality, would spark the most interest among readers, bringing in far more letters than a more "significant" column on a major political issue.

The format too was more flexible. I could begin here, wander over there, and end up at a place as surprising to me as to the reader. I was, then, using lessons from Grimes as well as Woodlock. Writing to a fixed space, one *Journal* column, also had its advantages. At first I would overwrite in the first draft and then have to cut it back to fit, resulting in tighter writing if not better thinking. With time I came to have a "feel" for the space, and here I found the merit in that madness of Webb Follin, those years ago, who assigned school papers of a certain number of words, no more, no less.

Happily these little essays were well received by the readers. Alfred Knopf, for one, took notice of them and persuaded me to collect a few in a volume published as *A Pride of Prejudices*.

In a logical world I might have then given up the title of editor. But I wasn't ready to yield up all responsibility for the *Journal*'s editorial viewpoint even to Joe, and I continued to write editorials on major issues when I felt it important to get all the nuances exactly as I wanted them, though these diminished in number. Kerby, I'm glad to say, concurred and so did the directors.

Besides—and this was vanity—in the outside world a corporate title, no matter how important, didn't have the same prestige among either journalistic colleagues or the major actors in either business or politics. With a Manhattan apartment suitable for entertaining, and with our daughters now off making their own way in the world, Frances and I enjoyed living in New York. I was serving on the Pulitzer Advisory Board, I was a past president of the American Society of Newspaper Editors, so it was natural for us to gather visiting editors when they came to town. We could also be on more friendly terms with local colleagues as well as business friends. John Lindsay, the city's mayor, could drop by for a late evening drink after a frustrating day.

There were also national affairs afoot, and being editor of the *Journal* helped open doors in Washington more easily.

* * * * *

Vietnam was not the only problem with which the new president had to deal. Lyndon Johnson had left behind him not only a going war but an on-going economic problem. President Nixon also had a political one because the Congress, both houses of it, was controlled by Democrats. There remained all the social troubles which had so marred 1968: the labor strikes, the unrest in the black community, the continuing militancy on the campus. For one reason or another, I spent a lot of time in Washington in 1969.

My relation with the president was very friendly if not intimate. But for a journalist who wishes to follow the direction of an administration, an acquaintance with cabinet officers, White House staff and officials on the second or even third tier is frequently more fruitful. For that I lacked the advantage of the *Journal* reporters or others who had actively covered Nixon's 1968 campaign. For instance, I knew the White House staff hardly at all.

H. R. Haldeman, when I came to know him, struck me as a bright young man who would be useful to have around, having the qualities a corporate chief executive might like in an administrative assistant but not as a man of larger scope. John Ehrlichman didn't impress me at all. He was a pudgy fellow with a somewhat pompous manner who seemed to be trying to give the impression he was smarter than he was. Neither of them had much political experience. I might have used the word naïve to apply to both. I never dreamed that they would become the powers they did within the White House and that Nixon would rely on them for advice on important matters.

As a domestic adviser Leonard Garment, a quiet, soft-spoken man whose field of attention was civil rights, did impress me as having both common sense and some political savvy. Early on it seemed clear that Henry Kissinger, a former Harvard history professor whom Nixon had "inherited" from Nelson Rockefeller, would emerge as the strongest voice on foreign policy because Secretary of State Rogers was out of his depth, nice fellow though he was. Herb Klein, my old friend and long-time Nixon press aide, had more political sense than any of them; it was unfortunate for Nixon that the Haldeman-Ehrlichman duo gradually squeezed him out of the inner circle with a high-sounding promotion to "Director of Communications," which put his office in the Executive Office Building, not in the White House. Ron Ziegler, who got the press secretary job in the White House, was an ex-advertising man with no newspaper experience, which probably explains a lot.

The Democrats, meanwhile, were in no mood to roll over and play dead just because they had lost the White House. As a parting gift to the new president, Lyndon Johnson proposed a government budget for fiscal 1970 which promised a surplus (!) of $3.4 billion. No one, least of all President Johnson, really believed that would happen, as indeed it didn't, but it put Nixon on a fiscal spot. In Congress the Senate rejected successively two of Nixon's nominations for the Supreme Court, both already federal judges, both Southerners. The House took a Nixon proposal for tax reform and so tinkered with it that it was unrecognizable and moved me to call it "the accountants and lawyers relief act of 1970." Even Wilbur Mills, chairman of the Ways and Means Committee, conceded he didn't know exactly what it provided.

It was remarkable, then, that a midyear Gallup poll reported that 57 percent of the populace approved of President Nixon's conduct of office thus far. I thought this partly Nixon's doing, partly luck.

The president helped himself by giving number one priority to Vietnam, laying down a schedule for withdrawing American troops, and by making foreign affairs in general his second priority, an area in which people thought Nixon experienced and competent. Two major overseas trips, one to the Far East, one to

Europe, were seen as successful; the president even managed to gain approval from General de Gaulle, something that escaped both Kennedy and Johnson.

The luck came from two directions. One was Neil Armstrong's walk on the moon in midsummer. The credit for this space program success belonged to Nixon's predecessors, but he benefited from the lift it gave to American spirits which he skillfully exploited. The other piece of luck was less dramatic, more subtle, but I suspect equally important in 1969.

That was a shift in the public attitude—call it a backlash, if you will—toward student militancy. In the beginning people had been shocked, of course, at the campus eruptions, the behavior of the young, but there had been an air of resignation or at least a bafflement. By late spring it was clear people thought "something ought to be done about it."

The first sign of this was the applause that greeted Governor Reagan's asking the California legislature "to make it perfectly clear higher education in our state colleges and universities is a privilege not a right." The governor wanted troublemakers expelled. Then University of Illinois trustees voted to expel students participating in campus demonstrations and agreed to prosecute a dozen of them who had been arrested for violence the preceding September. But the most influential action came from the Reverend Theodore Hesburgh of Notre Dame, a universally respected academician and liberal of impeccable credentials. Father Hesburgh announced a "get tough policy" toward militants on his campus. This drew wide publicity and a letter of praise from President Nixon.

But I read too much into these signs of a changing public mood. The campus disturbances broke out again, and in March the anti-Vietnam war demonstrations reached a peak. Some 250,000 protesters marched on Washington. This was accompanied by the revelation of the Mylai massacre in which a young army officer led his troops to a ruthless slaughter of South Vietnamese. The incident had occurred the previous year while Johnson was president, though he had nothing to do with it. No matter. The public reacted in shock and inevitably the reaction was directed toward President Nixon, the incumbent. I also mistook the signs that seemed to point toward a more "conservative" view in domestic matters, particularly economic. Perhaps they were shifting, but any real shift was a long time coming. It would be another decade, after Vietnam, before Ronald Reagan would ride a new political wave into the White House.

Still the president, or so I thought, was proving the Nixon-haters wrong. He gave every sign of moving forcefully, and probably successfully, in finally extricating us from Vietnam with a minimum of stigma for "defeat." His economic and social policies weren't so impressive in ending inflation or in mollifying the black community. But I could understand his attitude of "first things first," which meant Vietnam.

As a people we always expect too much of our presidents, especially when they first come to office. We suppose that with a few commands, as by some magic wand, they can cure all the ailments of the country at once. The truth is otherwise, the presidency being in fact an office of limited powers. If the incumbent has the wisdom of Solomon, he still needs time, patience, and political skill to change much of anything. This is doubly true when the national government is divided between the two major parties, as it was for Nixon. No matter what the president proposes, the other party will oppose or at least try to modify it. A president must work little by little, with the hope that little by little ends in a lot. It seemed to me President Nixon's "good beginning" was as much as I or the public could reasonably expect.

The hopes of 1969, however, faded in 1970. Once more the change came partly from Mr. Nixon's actions, partly from events he could not control. The campuses continued to erupt, though less now from spontaneous sparks than from nonstudent outside agitators. In April a bank near the University of California at Santa Barbara was set fire; so were buildings on the University of Kansas campus. The governor of Ohio had to call out the National Guard to quell rioters against the ROTC program on the university campus. Arson destroyed many books in the Yale University law library. Then in May came the events at Kent State.

There a large crowd of young militants, some students, some not, confronted national guardsmen, most of whom were equally young. Some excited guardsmen opened fire. Four young people were killed. Nixon had nothing to do with it. Nonetheless, public anger fell on him.

One reason for that was that on April 29 Nixon had ordered American forces to invade Cambodia. The problem there was a repetition of the situation in Korea which brought the clash between McArthur and Truman. Cambodia, technically neutral, provided a sanctuary on the borders of South Vietnam for marshalling North Vietnamese troops. Nixon sent American forces to remove the sanctuary, which they did, but at the cost of angry denunciations from congressional Democrats, many in the media, and much of the public. The president was pilloried for being "trigger happy." My own view, unchanged by time, was that it was a sound tactical decision (the Cambodians, incidentally, made only token protests) to protect our own forces in South Vietnam. It was a political mistake, though, because it made indelible the picture of Nixon as a wild "hawk" which was to haunt him so much later.

On the domestic front he did propose in 1969 the Family Assistance Plan based on a premise he stated, "What the poor need to help them rise out of poverty is money." That struck me as on a par with Cal Coolidge's remark that unemployment results when people are out of work. Obviously, having the government give them money would keep the poor out of need as long as the money came. It wouldn't lift them out of poverty. The first year cost of the FAP was put at two billion dollars. Its prime political purpose, I thought, was to appeal to liberals, a way of showing Nixon was compassionate to the poor. As he said, "predictably" conservatives (presumably like the *Journal*) opposed it. The irony was that it won him no Brownie points with the liberals. They viewed it with suspicion and it died in Congress. Poor Richard.

In 1970 he got a chance to replace William McChesney Martin as Federal Reserve chairman because his term expired. He appointed Arthur Burns, his long-time economic adviser, thinking that Burns would be more amenable to White House guidance. I liked Burns and respected him, but Bill Martin was one of my oldest political acquaintances, a man I admired, and so I was sorry to see his time run out. I had first seen Martin (but not met him) when he was the youthful president of the New York Stock Exchange, met him later when he headed the Export-Import Bank after the war, and got to know him better as assistant secretary of the treasury. At the Fed Martin wanted to counteract as much as he could the inflationary pressure from continual government deficits, which I suspect was why Nixon was happy to see him leave.

In the spring Frances and I attended a White House dinner to

honor the outgoing Martin and welcome the incoming Burns.
Nixon said the appropriate things about Martin but reserved his
main praise for Burns. (Frances, incidentally, had Bill Buckley as
her dinner companion and somewhat to her surprise found him
"charming"; Bill reserves his curmudgeonly personality for his
public appearances.) But the upshot of that changing-of-the-guard
was that before long Burns and Nixon crossed swords on the Fed's
policy. Once in that post with its fixed term Federal Reserve chairmen are as unpredictable in performance as Supreme Court judges.

*   *   *   *   *

I must note, though, that in that spring of 1970 I didn't give my
full attention to what was going on in the world. I was distracted
by some health problems, which I was assured were transient, and
also by the fact I was now deeply involved in the problems of *The
National Observer*. I was leaving to Joe Evans more and more the
task of commenting on public affairs.

In the summer of 1970 I had been editor of one of the major
newspapers of the country for a dozen years, and I was content.
Thanks to Joe and others, things within the office were well enough
organized so that I could occupy myself with other matters while
retaining ultimate control of the *Journal*'s publicly spoken editorial policies. I knew I was sufficiently established, that I could
remain so until the years forced retirement. Beyond that, I had reasonable prospects that in time, and in my turn, I might become
president of the company I had so long served. Kerby, it seemed to
me, was preparing me for it by assigning me wider duties, as for
instance with *The National Observer*.

On the level of pure vanity, if I was hardly famous I was respected among my peers in my craft. My position was such that I
had entrée to those in business, government, or elsewhere who
played major roles in the affairs of the country. The incumbent
president was one I knew better, or thought I did, than any of his
predecessors. I anticipated at least two more years, perhaps more,
of good relations with the White House. I could even suppose that
from time to time I might have some influence on the country's
course. Every man, without exception, has his vanity and I apolo-
gize not for mine.

I had every reason, then, to look forward to the coming decade,
that of the 1970s, with excited anticipation. Midway in it I would

celebrate the fortieth anniversary of that journey northward from Dixie that had taken so many unexpected turns. What I couldn't foresee was that fortune had one more surprising turn in store for me.

*   *   *   *   *

The surprise, and what came of it, can be briefly told. One winter morning in 1969 I found blood in my urine. It is, I assure you, a sight to shock. This began a long period of on-and-off-again symptoms while two teams of urologists tried to diagnose the cause. By midsummer the verdict was that I had a tumor of the left kidney. It was removed by Dr. Victor Marshall, chief urologist at New York Hospital, and the pathologist said I had a carcinoma.

My reaction was, I hope, understandable. To have a carcinoma gives one to think. The long convalescence gave time for thinking. Barney had died of cancer three years earlier; Mac had cancer of the prostate, soon to prove fatal. While I could remain editor of the *Journal* as long as I wished and could hope someday to be president of the company, a look at the calendar and Bill Kerby's age told me that couldn't happen until I was well into my sixties. Bob Bottorff, reading the same calendar, had already retired to California.

The question was, what did I want to do? Did I *want* to be company president, spending the waiting time doing what I had been doing for a dozen years?

In the midst of this uncertainty came a proposal from the chancellor at Chapel Hill, an old friend of mine, Lyle Sitterson, that I consider a chair to teach at the University. I doubt if any man fully understands all the reasons that impel him to make a major change in his life; some of them, I'm sure, spring from the deep subconscious. In my case the precipitating cause was the cancer; the final push was the opportunity to return home and begin a new life.

In any event, in January 1971 I decided to retire as editor and as senior vice-president, although I would remain a director of the company. I assumed, with some regret but with much satisfaction over all that had happened since I came to New York thirty-five years before, that I was ending my journalistic career. Frances and I sold our apartment, left New York, and embarked on a new journey.

But that journey, too, would take an unexpected turn. Within a year I would once more be a journalist of sorts, this time as merely a contributor to my old newspaper. But that would soon have me flying off again to faraway places abroad and at home, seeking out presidents—and would-be presidents.

PART SIX

Dixie Again

Now will I move on, go home . . .
giving thanks to the gods
who led me forth
and brought me back again.

        —Aeschylus,
          The Libation Bearers

lains, Georgia, lies some hundred miles south of Atlanta, about nine miles off the main highway to Albany, and in the early autumn of 1976 the tranquility of this small village was just beginning to be ruffled. It hadn't yet been overrun by the outside world, but already it was attracting curious tourists and inquisitive journalists.

To get there from Chapel Hill, North Carolina, I flew from the Raleigh-Durham airport to Atlanta, changed to another plane for Albany, and rented a car to drive to Americus, the closest place I could find a motel to lay my head. On the road I passed through Leesburg and Eagle Pond and Smithfield, small Southern towns with good Southern names. Along the roadside were the farm houses of the rural South, watching over orchards or peanut fields or clumps of cutover pine woods. As I made the journey that September afternoon, I was struck by a feeling of déjà vu. I had seen these towns before in North Carolina under names like Leesburg and Eagle Springs and even Smithfield. Indeed, I had grown up among them.

So I made this journey with mixed emotions. Once more I was on my way to visit a man who would like to be president. But this time with a difference. Four decades as a journalist watching and writing about public affairs, including national politics, cautioned me to remain detached when I sat down with Jimmy Carter. I had known all the sitting presidents and their rival candidates since Franklin Roosevelt, when I first went to Washington forty years earlier. Although I had liked some more than others, I had tried to be dispassionate about them all. Yet here I was, a Southerner born and bred, going to see the first Southern presidential nominee of a major political party since the Civil War. Could I keep my journalistic detachment?

Woodrow Wilson, true enough, had been born in Virginia. He was nominated and elected, though, after being governor of New Jersey. Lyndon Johnson, a Texan, was already a sitting president when his party nominated him. Jimmy Carter was the first to gain his nomination from the Democratic party directly from one of the states of the former Confederacy. He had won it from Georgia, a state through which a century earlier Sherman's troops had cut a swath of destruction. It was this that made his nomination remarkable.

Another thing might make my detachment difficult. Not only were we both—Carter the candidate and I the journalist— Southerners by birth, we were also from small towns. We were both from families who had lived for generations in the land. We had both left to make our way in the outer world. We had both come back again. We even shared a naval background, he as a peacetime regular officer in submarines, I as a wartime reserve commanding an escort destroyer. And we had both lived our adult lives under the shadow of that tradition which said no one from the deep South could ever be president. All that explains why I confessed to myself as I approached Plains that I would be hard pressed to keep the journalistic distance I so much valued.

My appointment, according to Jody Powell, his press secretary, was for one o'clock the next afternoon. Arriving early, I took a few minutes—it took only a few minutes—to drive around the town. There was one block of stores on the left going in, across the rail- road tracks. Nothing on the right except Billy Carter's gasoline station, already famous. An abandoned railroad station had a sign reading "Carter Headquarters," though it wasn't really. It was a place for tourists where Miss Lillian, Carter's mother, handed out campaign literature. A few tourists were already in evidence, tak- ing pictures and buying the souvenirs for sale everywhere.

The highway from Americus to Columbus formed the main street, a few blocks long with comfortable-looking clapboard houses set back from the road. There were about a half-dozen cross-streets leading to two other streets parallel to the highway. On the north one was a Baptist church, a white frame building with a steeple, typical of the rural South. On one of the cross- streets, its entrance blocked off by the Secret Service, was Jimmy Carter's house, an unpretentious one story ranch-type of non- descript design. It was down this street, a little before one o'clock, that I was taken by a young aide. Standing in the driveway was Rosalyn Carter, who chatted a moment and told me I was expected.

I had met Jimmy Carter briefly once before at a luncheon in New York where the conversation was no more than politeness. So thus far in trying to assess the man I had to rely on second-hand impressions from *Wall Street Journal* reporters and others. I had found these sometimes contradictory, always puzzling. Now I could look forward to a quiet visit with this obviously unusual man.

The road from New York to Plains had been a winding one. When at age fifty-seven I had retired from the *Journal*, Frances and I had at first stored our furniture, and told Lyle Sitterson I would accept his offer to teach at the University the next January. Meanwhile we took off to live for a year on our boat. This boat, the latest of three, was a fifty-foot deep-draft trawler type, built in Hong Kong of teak and other oriental woods. She was a beautiful boat, roomy (three double-staterooms), designed for the open sea and equipped for it with heavy duty diesels, large fuel tanks, autopilot, and radar. I had named her the *Covenant* because years before I had made a pact with myself that someday I would have a seagoing boat large enough to live on. The pull of the sea had never left me. While living in New York we were limited to weekends and vacations. Now in "retirement" I could fulfill a dream. We spent months cruising offshore along the coast and in the waterway, New York to Florida, and then out through the Bahamas. For me it was heaven. Fortunately I had no further physical problems and the sea gave me back my spirits.

In 1972 I began teaching both in journalism and in political science, which I enjoyed. Later that year after a Dow Jones board meeting Bill Kerby was kind enough to say the paper missed my writing. How would I like to restart the column "Thinking Things Over"? I was uncertain how well I could do it cut off from the accustomed surroundings of a newspaper but said I would try it on a once-a-week basis.

This made me again a journalist, at least of sorts. From that beginning I wound up four years later in Plains, Georgia.

* * * * *

Once inside the house I found myself immediately comfortable with Jimmy Carter. For all that he was plainly an unusual man— from junior naval officer to small-town farmer to governor to nominee for president, the record marked him so—in manner, in speech, in bearing he was familiar to me as if he had been a neighbor in the days of my youth.

We sat alone in the living room and talked for more than an hour. He was dressed in open sports shirt, jeans, and farmer's boots. At first he seemed surprised that I had no tape recorder; I suppose he expected another of those Q and A interviews. Once he realized I didn't intend to make "news," only to have a visit, he relaxed, reminisced about the past, and spoke in general terms about why he wanted to be president and how he expected to use the office. He struck me at once as a different kind of Southern Democratic politician.

Like me he had grown up in a segregated world, black and white, and had taken it for granted. Like me his ideas on race relations had changed. There was no trace in him of the Wallaces or Faubuses railing against a changing world. That alone made him refreshing.

For the South, at long last, had changed in this respect. Coming home in the 1970s I had been impressed by the signs of change after the turmoil of the fifties and sixties. It was not only that formal segregation—in restaurants, hotels, busses, shops, even schools—had vanished. It was also that better educated blacks had risen in the economic and social scale and were being accepted by white politicians, lawyers, doctors, college professors, and businessmen. I had myself met many. There were now blacks as students at the University and a few on the faculty. To the mass of uneducated or unskilled blacks, and certainly to the more rabble-rousing black leaders, these were doubtless viewed as "tokens" or, worse, as "Uncle Toms." To many the progress seemed glacial. To someone like myself coming back after forty years the change was startling. There was everywhere evidence that the South was adapting itself to the new race relations better than much of the North. There was still to be some turmoil, violence in places, but it seemed to me the progress of change hereafter would be relentless.

That on this old issue Jimmy Carter represented the "New South" would become clear in the coming election. In Dixie he would get large numbers of white votes as well as an overwhelming majority of black votes. Southern voters would not split along the familiar racial lines.

On other matters I found Jimmy Carter more puzzling. He accepted the description of himself as a "populist," a political stance with deep Southern roots. On the one hand he said he believed the country suffered from too much government; on the other that he believed in a strong government. He favored more spending on such things as a national health plan and on direct government aid to the unemployed. Yet he also pledged a balanced government budget by 1980.

He professed to find nothing incompatible between his goals of more government spending, as on a national health program, and of a balanced budget by 1980. They were to be reconciled by tax reforms, unspecified, and by actions to stimulate the economy, also unspecified. Beyond that he spoke of the need for better government ("a government as good as the people") which he thought beyond the reach of the old, established political leadership in either party.

So I described my puzzlement once the conversation went beyond generalities. "You go seeking his political philosophy," I wrote, "and no matter how you rephrase the question it slips away from you." Yet I noted that despite these ambiguities, and beneath his courteous manner, "there's the self-confidence marking a man who's bold, afraid of no gamble, deterred by no obstacle. He's smart, able and vigorous, and he knows it. If there is also a touch of steel in his eyes, that is just another sign of determination in a strong-willed man." I also found him likeable personally.

As I went out into the Georgia sun, I knew I had met an extraordinary man; his stern-willed dedication to winning the nomination against all odds was proof of that. What I didn't know was what he expected to do with the presidency if he won it. I concluded he was an enigmatic man and confessed "we may have to wait until he's elected—if he's elected—to solve the puzzle locked in that enigma."

That evening back at the Americus motel I ran into Marquis Childs, the syndicated columnist and friend from Washington days, who had also seen Carter that day. As we exchanged impressions Mark asked me, as a Southerner, to explain this Jimmy Carter, this man from Plains, population 683, stuck away in rural Georgia, who might well become president of the United States.

It was a question I could not answer. Among the many things

that made Carter whatever he was, one surely was the fact that he was born and grew up in the South, bred from a long line of those who had lived and died there. So had I. Yet, I had to confess to Mark, a Midwesterner from Iowa, that didn't help me explain what puzzled him.

In the event I was never able to solve the enigma of Jimmy Carter, even after he was elected. Nor, I think, did the country.

*   *   *   *   *

At this time, of course, I was only a part-time journalist. I had found the weekly column not as difficult to do as I had feared. For one thing, a university community is itself a resource. Not only was there a splendid library at my disposal, there was hardly any subject area in which there was not someone on the faculty with special knowledge who was willing to share it with me. Be it a sought-for literary allusion, clarification on some point of history or economics, background on the politics of a foreign country no matter how unfamiliar, I had only to lift the telephone. Another help was that the *Journal* did not begrudge me travel funds, to New York, to Washington, to political conventions or wherever, and travel from Chapel Hill was easy since the airport (twenty minutes away) is on a main north-south track.

Another aid, this one unexpected, was the classroom, which was now my main occupation. Since I drew students in only two areas, journalism and political science, I can't generalize about the whole student body, but I personally encountered none of the rebelliousness, sullenness or bad manners I had heard so much about. Most of my students were advanced undergraduates (juniors or seniors) or graduate students, and I found them inquisitive intellectually and no less diligent in study than my own college generation. They were ready to dispute any statement I made about anything, of course, sometimes vehemently, but never with anger or boorishness. The brighter ones forced me to think through statements better than I might otherwise have done. I would tell my friends back in New York concerned about the new generation that these young would make no bigger mess of the world than their fathers had— which gave them a lot of leeway.

Still, there were some surprises. No brash young student would have occasion to confront authority over laundry-torn socks as I had done years before. The fashion was to be shod sans socks. There were some older faculty members who wore ties and jackets, but for most the open shirt, with or without sweater depending on the weather, was common attire. After a few weeks I too succumbed. One day a male student (they didn't like to be called boys and girls) showed up without socks *or* shoes. I was advised by a dean to make no issue of it as that might involve me in a "judicial" hearing of a faculty-student panel if the young man appealed. I eventually weaned him away from such informality only by addressing him, when called upon to recite, as "the barefoot boy with feet of tan." The female students were almost equally informal. Jeans, old sweat shirts, straggly hair were commonplace.

There were more disturbing shocks. In spite of everything I had read about how "Johnny can't read" I was surprised to find how really unprepared the average student—the average, that is, not the better ones—was in the basic tools of language, spelling and grammar, and the form of the simple English sentence. The Journalism School was forced to require the students to take and pass a spelling and grammar test designed for high school graduates. About half of them failed on the first attempt and had to take a remedial study to pass. And these, mind you, were juniors in a major university, since it was not until their third year they could register in the Journalism School. This had nothing to do with their intelligence, as I would quickly discover. It was not a failure of their minds but of the education they had received—not only at the high school level but during their first two college years.

There was also, at least for me, surprise in the gaps in their general knowledge of history or of literature. Teachers in other areas told me they had like problems, as in mathematics for example.

I was equally surprised to discover the changes that had taken place in the University curriculum since my antique days. It was possible for a student to get a bachelor's degree in liberal arts (and even make Phi Beta Kappa) with no courses at all in a foreign language—any foreign language, never mind that Latin bit. Or without any courses in mathematics. A student had the option of one or the other, as if the two were interchangeable. For the rest of the credit requirements outside his major a student could choose from a sort of smorgasbord, some of this and some of that, which might or might not make a coherent whole. In all this Chapel Hill was not unusual. Some years before, Harvard had abandoned the idea of a basic curriculum necessary to make an educated person, and all over the country universities had followed like sheep. The result, so I thought, was to leave many students floundering with a smattering of ignorance. Such thoughts naturally marked me as an anachronistic man, although I was to find many colleagues on the faculty who shared my uneasiness about the unstructured under-graduate curriculum.

I should say that none of this formlessness (as I saw it) prevented a student at Chapel Hill from getting a fine education if he or she sought it. The University had excellent departments in foreign languages, including classics, and in history, English, mathematics, philosophy, and the physical sciences. The faculty included many who were outstanding as both scholars and teachers. With a number of them I formed warm friendships even though I was an anomaly, a full professor without an earned doctorate.

I should also say that in teaching I learned the truth of the observation "by our pupils we are taught." To conduct a semester's seminar with bright students on, say, the relationship between the press and the society in which it functions, I was forced to study the history of the press in Western society, to examine the philosophy underlying that society, in a more formal way than I had done. In a similar fashion, teaching a course in modern politics from the New Deal period onward I began to see things I had not noticed before.

I had for years been both observer and commentator on American politics, especially as they were reflected in our quadrennial presidential elections. But perforce I had taken each election as it came, observed and analyzed it as an event in itself. When I had tried to link one election with another my views of the latest one were colored by my preconceptions from the previous election. The result, I came to realize, was a sort of myopia. I now had both the time and the inspiration to look back on the whole period. I began to see a pattern which surprised me. It did not fit with the traditional view, which I had shared, that for nearly four decades the country had been firmly in the grip of the so-called Democratic (or Roosevelt) coalition which had made the nation's politics essentially liberal in outlook. At the very least this long-span view suggested crosscurrents of unexpected strength.

*   *   *   *   *

What I noticed, first of all, was the declining force of the Roosevelt coalition from 1936 onwards. In 1936 Roosevelt won reelection by a landslide, winning 62.5 percent of the two-party vote and carrying all but two states in the electoral college. He would win twice more. But in 1940 against Wendell Willkie, a political Johnny-come-lately, his margin of the two-party vote dropped to 55 percent and the Republicans carried ten states with eighty-two electoral votes. In 1944 Roosevelt had the advantage of being the incumbent president in the midst of a global war, yet his percentage of the two-party vote dropped again and the Republicans carried twelve states with ninety-nine electoral votes.

It was the 1948 election, however, that in retrospect marked a turning point, although I wasn't aware of it. Everyone (myself included) expected Harry Truman to lose. So when he won, any evidence of an erosion in the old New Deal coalition seemed discredited. The sheer surprise of that Truman win drew attention away from the fact that the old coalition was shattered. The New Deal Democrats, for the first time since 1932, were a minority in a presidential election. That old coalition splintered on both ends of the spectrum. The States Rights party—or Dixiecrats—polled nearly 1.2 million votes; the left-wing Progressives led by Henry Wallace almost exactly the same. Of a total popular vote of 48.8 million, Truman received 24.1 million, or slightly less than half. True, that was more than 50 percent of the *two-party vote*, as between Republicans and regular Democrats, but by then the two-party vote was by no means the whole of the matter.

When Eisenhower was elected in 1952, winning also Republican control of both houses of Congress, it appeared to many (myself included) that the pendulum had fully swung. Not so. Ike did get reelected but Congress returned to the Democrats. In 1960 Nixon lost to Kennedy, and Goldwater to Johnson in 1964. Then Nixon won in 1968, but he too was a minority president.

So as the 1972 election came, a look back could be summarized this way: With the single exception of Lyndon Johnson, no Democratic president after 1944 won by a true majority of the votes. Since then the presidency had seesawed between the two major parties. There had been three Democrats (Truman, Kennedy, and Johnson) and two Republicans (Eisenhower and Nixon). Three of those presidents (Truman, Eisenhower, and Nixon) had at least one house of Congress controlled by the opposition party. Three of them (Truman, Kennedy, and Nixon) were minority presidents in the popular vote, two of them Democratic, one Republican.

What sense could anyone make of such a political seesaw?

Prodding my students, and being prodded by them, I came to two conclusions. The legend of the enduring power of the Democratic or Roosevelt coalition was plainly that, a legend. That coalition lost its firm grip on the electorate somewhere in the 1940s and had not been the controlling force in American politics for the past twenty-five years. Equally plainly, the theory of an emerging Republican majority, so much discussed, could only be given a Scotch verdict, not proved. The Democrats managed to control Congress under each of the Republican presidents.

The 1972 election, the first I would follow as part-time journalist, looked like it might break this zigzag pattern. In 1970 the Democrats had retained control of Congress, but the next year in some state and local elections there were surprising conservative wins. The Republicans captured the Virginia and New Jersey governorships, each for the first time in many years. Barry Goldwater, Jr., almost as conservative as his father, was elected to Congress from, of all places, California. Two mayoralty elections, in Minneapolis and Los Angeles, should have sent a shudder through the ranks of liberal Democrats. An ex-policeman won in Minneapolis on a strong law-and-order platform, and in Los Angeles voters returned Sam Yorty, who on the race issue was nearly as reactionary as Wallace or Faubus. In the face of those omens the Democrats nominated the liberal Senator George McGovern at a convention even wilder, though in an entirely different way, than that of 1968.

George McGovern of South Dakota had been a relatively obscure senator prior to 1972, but he had chaired a commission to revise the Democratic party rules on delegate selection. The new rules would gain him the nomination and help him lose the election. A quiet, soft-spoken man, thoroughly decent, he would come out of that convention seeming as much an extremist of the left as Goldwater had appeared of the right in 1964.

That Democratic gathering in Miami Beach, which I attended, looked like no political convention I had ever seen. First off, few of the delegates were party regulars. Only about 30 elected congressmen (out of 255) were on the floor. Eight of every ten delegates were newcomers, a third were women, some 15 percent were black, about 20 percent under thirty. The new party rules setting quotas for various minority groups had taken the convention out of the hands of experienced party professionals, making it a whole new ballgame. Quotas for minorities may have seemed like good politics. In fact, they alienated the regulars, many of whom would sit out the ensuing campaign. The behavior of many of these new-comers, and of the hangers-on drawn to it, made a bad impression on the audience at home as gay liberationists and other noisy fringe groups demonstrated on TV. It was these amateurs, heady with a sense of power, who rejected all the more orthodox Demo-crats and nominated George McGovern. Only in a technical sense was he the nominee of the Democratic party.

This inauspicious beginning was followed by other troubles. McGovern had selected for his vice-presidential running mate Sen-ator Thomas Eagleton of Missouri, not quite so obscure as Gold-water's choice of Representative Miller or Nixon's of Spiro Agnew but still relatively unknown on the national scene. Within two weeks it became known that Eagleton had previously undergone electroshock therapy for psychological problems. McGovern de-cided to drop him from the ticket, substituting Sargent Shriver, a Kennedy in-law with no experience in an elected office. The drop-ping of Eagleton came on the heels of a McGovern statement that he was "a thousand percent behind him." This left a bad public impression of vacillation.

McGovern never recovered. His campaign simply fell apart. As my friend Mark Childs remarked, it was one of the "most un-happy campaigns in American history."

Meanwhile President Nixon won a routine renomination from the Republicans. Although his public support had sagged badly in late 1969 and 1970 he had recovered much of it by 1971. He hadn't charmed the populace but he had impressed people as a man of ability. In 1971 he had launched a sweeping economic re-form program, including a wage-price freeze which however disas-trous in the long run was popular at the time. Early in 1972 he had electrified the country and the world with his visit to Peking which opened the way to new relations with the People's Republic of China.

Given the time, the circumstance, and the man, it was a stun-ning move. Ever since World War II Communist China had been an anathema in American public opinion. After Mao ousted Chiang Kai-shek and forced his Nationalists to flee to Taiwan, there were bitter recriminations over who had "lost" China, that is, mainland China, and how. The careers of many honorable public servants were wrecked because they had warned early that Chiang had no real hold on Chinese allegiance, that he was an arrogant and misguided man. As Taiwan, not held in the straitjacket of Communist economic doctrine, became prosperous and one of our major Asian trading partners, our policy was to treat it as if it were China itself. We treated mainland China, huge in area and with a billion people, as if it didn't exist. That made no sense. Yet as late as 1971 it seemed no American politician would dare recognize the absurdity.

Probably no politician could have except Richard Nixon, who had a long anti-Communist record. Even for him it was a bold, daring move with large political risks. He was sure to be denounced by the old rigid, right-wing "China lobby," as indeed he was. Yet the instant it was done, as the American people saw on television the president meeting with "Communist" leaders in Peking, the political mood changed overnight. Nixon appeared even to the strongest of Nixon haters as a man of vision. More than any other single thing, I think, this gave Nixon world stature and contributed greatly to his overwhelming victory in November.

For overwhelming it was. The combination of the impression of the "new Nixon" and of the ineptitude of McGovern won Nixon more than 47 million popular votes to barely 29 million for McGovern. Worse, the Democrats carried only one state, Massachusetts; Nixon had outdone Franklin Roosevelt, who had lost two states in 1936. In state and local elections there were shocking losses for them.

So sweeping was the Nixon victory that both politicians and journalists began comparing it to 1936 and predicting a long period of Democratic decline. I thought not. For one reason, the Democrats retained control of the Congress despite the burial of Senator McGovern and the numerous upsets in old Democratic strongholds. For another, preelection polls predicting the Nixon sweep also noted the oddity, or apparent oddity, that the voters nonetheless "trusted" the Democrats more than they did the Republicans.

"As long as that feeling prevails," I wrote immediately after the election, "the Republicans will not be a true majority party. Voters will think them a handy alternative when Democrats are out of step; they will be inclined to return to the Democratic fold when the aberration has passed." I could not see the election as a transfer by the electorate "to a new and durable allegiance to the Republican party."

I advanced this at the time as a "tentative conclusion" drawn on the morrow of Nixon's sweeping victory. I might have stated it more firmly if I had paid more attention to a seemingly minor break-in that had occurred just before the election at the Democratic headquarters in the Watergate office-apartment complex overlooking the Potomac River.

2

Until it reached its climax in mid-1974 I followed the Watergate affair mostly from afar. In both years I was mainly occupied with my new role. Much of my attention went to the challenge, and for me a new one, of learning to teach in an academic setting and of building a place for myself in the collegium of a university.

I found teaching more challenging, more work, and more interesting than I thought it would be. I was teaching two courses in the Journalism School and one in the Political Science Department. I varied the journalism courses from semester to semester, ranging from reporting and writing to an advanced seminar on the role of the press in American society. Any idea I had that because I had dealt with and thought about these topics for years teaching would be easy proved an illusion. You cannot lecture for an academic hour, or preside over a two-hour seminar, "off the top of your head." If the secret of an impromptu speech is careful preparation, then this is equally true of classroom lectures. Perhaps it grows easier for someone teaching, say, the English romantic poets (neither Byron nor Shelley has written anything lately), but I found that each semester I had to reorganize my material, change the student reading list, and in general prepare anew. This was particularly true in teaching modern American politics, for while I began each time with the New Deal period I came forward each time to the current political situation. This meant even the earlier material had to be revamped and abridged to leave time for later developments. I came to have more appreciation than before for my academic colleagues. Happily I enjoyed it all, especially the stimulation I got from the brighter and more industrious students.

Naturally I followed avidly the news about Watergate from the first hints there was more to it than a simple burglary by overzealous Nixon supporters. My first comment on the Watergate developments was in a column in March 1973. "Here it is nine months later and the Watergate affair is no longer an amusing caper, or escapade, the administration can lightly brush aside."

This premonition, for at the time that's all it was, gave me a troubled mind because earlier I had been impressed by the beginning of Nixon's second administration. He had brought the North Vietnamese to the conference table, and by February our prisoners of war were on their way home, their return a moving experience which the nation shared on television. I, anyway, got an emotional lift from the first remarks of Navy Captain Jeremiah Denton upon setting foot on American soil. "We are happy to have had this opportunity to serve our country under difficult circumstances." How oddly these understated words sounded after all the turmoil at home over the war. Happy? Difficult circumstances? I thought, and I said, that our country was blest to have such men as these, who could suffer so much and come home without recriminations.

But Watergate, of course, would not go away. By April I was saying the confusion about the president's role, if any, was "especially dangerous for President Nixon because . . . he has raised high the banner of probity in government . . . In order to tarnish Nixon it will only be necessary to dangle suspicions and have those suspicions unallayed."

It's hard now to recapture all my thoughts of those months except those I wrote. Like most of the American people at the time I was disturbed by the news from Washington, but I clung to the belief, or at least the hope, that the president himself was not personally involved. What had puzzled me much, however, from the beginnings of Nixon's presidency was his choice of lieutenants and advisers. Long before many of them wound up in disgrace, and some of them in jail, it seemed to me too many of them were of dubious ability and of doubtful character, men chosen mainly because they would be loyal courtiers.

There were exceptions, to be sure. Henry Kissinger, national security adviser and later secretary of state, was and would remain a controversial figure, but you recognized him as a man of intellectual capacity. Elliott Richardson wasn't so intellectual, but he was a man of New England probity who had served several administrations in various positions. As Nixon's attorney general he would resign in the "Saturday night massacre" because he would not fire Archibald Cox, the special prosecutor appointed to investigate Watergate. Unfortunately, there were all too few such men among those around the president.

Of the White House staff I had only the briefest contacts with John Ehrlichman. John Dean I never met at all. Bob Haldeman I saw several times. With his close-cropped hair and his brusque manner he reminded me a bit of a marine in appearance. His loyalty to Nixon was obvious; his qualifications beyond that of henchman were not so clear. Given what happened, it's embarrassing to say that I rather liked Spiro Agnew, but I did. He was easy to talk to, lacking that uptight appearance of those in the White House inner circle, of which the vice-president definitely was not. I even agreed with much of what he had to say when he criticized the press (or the "media" in the modern phrase). I've never shared the feelings of many of my colleagues that anyone criticizing the Fourth Estate is, ipso facto, a villain. It turned out, of course, that Mr. Agnew had some hidden villainies, but even villains sometimes speak some truth.

Now that I lived at a remove from New York and Washington I had less contact with cabinet officers than formerly. Nonetheless, I knew and respected John Connally even though at the Treasury he sometimes acted like a bull in a china shop. Maurice Stans was an able man and in any event couldn't suffer by comparison with past secretaries of commerce, Herbert Hoover being the only one to make any impress on his times. Among others, Herbert Stein, chief of the Council of Economic Advisers, was able, thoughtful and stimulating.

Anyway, I had made an interesting discovery. In my role as commentator it didn't make as much difference whether I visited those in high places, including presidents, as I thought it had. The sources of information available to anyone in this country who wishes to follow public affairs are so great he really needs no personal contact with high officials to form judgments on the state of public affairs. Indeed, I began to suspect that much of my past effort to visit with politicians, up to and including presidents, was largely ego building. It fed vanity to be able to drop casual remarks about what Secretary So-and-so said to me or to refer to "my visit with the president." Its usefulness beyond that was limited. I wish I could say this discovery cured me of such vanity. I was to find, however, as what follows will show, that I was far from cured. Or, if it wasn't vanity, it was at least curiosity that drove me to break out of the quiet of academia and again take to the road of an active journalist.

*   *   *   *   *

By January 1974 it was clear the Nixon administration was falling apart. Vice-President Agnew had resigned the previous October one jump ahead of the sheriff, to be succeeded by an appointed vice-president, Gerald Ford. Earlier Nixon's former appointments secretary, Alexander Butterfield, had revealed to the Ervin committee that the president had an automatic taping system to record all conversations in the Oval Office; this startling revelation was ultimately to bring the president's downfall as it launched "the battle of the tapes." The so-called Saturday night massacre in which Attorney General Richardson resigned, followed by his assistant, William Ruckelshaus, had also come in October. With all these fireworks exploding everywhere I was getting restless. All I knew was what I read in the newspapers, which was plenty but also confusing.

Haldeman and Ehrlichman had by this time both departed in disgrace. I had no longer any entrée to the White House staff. Ford, whom I had met, knew little and wished he knew less. Judge Sirica, presiding over the key court battles, was properly aloof. My one possibly useful contact from former times was Senator Sam Ervin, chairman of the Special Investigating Committee.

Up to this point Senator Ervin was little known to the public. Such attention as he had gotten from the press was as a conservative Southern senator resisting integration. A big, jowly man, he affected a slow, drawling manner reminiscent of all the caricatures of the "country bumpkin." He himself frequently said he was "only a country lawyer." Few expected much from an investigating committee headed by Senator Ervin.

I thought otherwise. A North Carolina native, he'd done his undergraduate study at Chapel Hill (where my father taught him Latin) and gone on to the Harvard Law School. Before reaching the Senate in 1954 he served in the state legislature, in Congress as a representative, had been a state Superior Court judge, and associate justice of the North Carolina Supreme Court. All that "only a country lawyer" bit was an act, self-written to help him with rural constituents, as was his cultivation of folksy storytelling to illustrate a point. Tucked away in his pocket wherever he went was a copy of the U.S. Constitution, and he was probably one of the few men in the country who could quote copiously from it verbatim. I thought Senator Sam would fool everybody, as indeed he did.

In his office he would lean back in his big swivel chair and allow as how he thought President Nixon had surrounded himself with some very strange people, but that he also thought Nixon too smart to have involved himself personally in any misbehavior by underlings. Anyway, he said, he'd have no part in any "lynching" of a president of the United States, whatever some of the partisan firebrands on his committee might want to do. He intended the committee's work to be done with decorum—but thoroughly. That last word was the key, as Nixon and the television-watching audience would discover.

The Ervin committee was not, technically speaking, the instrument of Nixon's downfall any more than were the much-vaunted "revelations" of *The Washington Post*. The latter were largely reports of what was being testified by witnesses before the federal grand jury which would have eventually become public anyway. The real battlefield was Federal Judge John Sirica's courtroom. It was Judge Sirica who subpoenaed the Nixon tapes, an action to go all the way to the Supreme Court where Nixon lost.

What the Ervin committee did through its televised hearings was to keep the public attention riveted on Watergate. In the beginning the Nixon people thought Ervin would be a soft opponent; after all, he was a conservative who had supported Nixon on many issues. What they forgot was that Ervin was also a conservative on the Constitution and in his belief in defending the law even against a president. What they overlooked was his innate toughness. By the time those hearings were over Ervin had been affectionately dubbed by the public as "Senator Sam" and was something of a hero to Nixon opponents. The committee's effectiveness was enhanced by Senator Sam's insistence on thoroughness and his care to restrain the committee from an appearance of demagoguery.

I'm not sure when I realized that President Nixon would have to go. In retrospect it's easier to seem prescient early. But as disaster to him seemed to follow disaster I began to think more about Gerald Ford and the likelihood he might be president.

As early as February 1974 I started trying to set up an appointment with Vice-President Ford, whom I had met when he was House minority leader. My first request for an appointment went unanswered. In May, after the first (and incomplete) publication of the Nixon transcripts I renewed it, moved by a feeling that, impeachment or no, a climax was approaching. As it happened, I finally got an appointment for August 7. The account of that meeting appeared in the *Journal* the morning of August 9, the day Richard Nixon announced his resignation as president.

For that reason, some of that interview may be worth recalling.

On the day we met, Alexander Haig, Nixon's chief of staff, had told Ford of the resignation decision and that he should prepare to assume the presidency. Given that situation, Ford might well have cancelled our meeting. He didn't, although he set a ground rule that he wouldn't answer any questions about Watergate or Nixon's intentions. I was convinced, however, that it was only a matter of time before Gerald Ford would be president, and so I groped for clues to Ford as president.

I began the *Journal* article this way: "Gerald R. Ford, president of the United States. As all week the expectations grew that he soon would be, the questions came tumbling after. What sort of man? What sort of president?"

He would be, I noted, the first president-by-appointment in our two-hundred years, because not until the adoption of the Twenty-fifth Amendment had there been any provision for filling the office of vice-president when it was vacant. It was the fortunate adoption of this amendment that made possible now a smooth transition in what might otherwise have been a constitutional crisis. Ford had been confirmed only the previous December.

"Inevitably, then, there are things to wonder about," I wrote. "What is his grasp of foreign policy? How deep is his understanding of economic problems; can he grapple with inflation? And beyond such specific questions, the intangible questions about the general quality of leadership Jerry Ford will offer the country."

An afternoon's private conversation, I conceded, hardly sufficed to answer them. "But when the conversation is wide-ranging . . . it surely offers some clues as to what manner of man this is. And so what sort of president he might be."

Then: "Mr. Ford says publicly that the number one problem is inflation [but] privately thinks that it is matched by the problem of regaining confidence in government in general and the White House in particular after the shocks of Watergate. As president he clearly intends to devote his energies to both. . . . His approach is not thoughtless in either case.

"On inflation, for example, he feels that for years the U.S. has simply tried to do too much, spending money without regard to the resources available. And he thinks the process must be reversed. The government must put its own house in order. . . .

"He claims no expertise in foreign affairs and until recently his involvement in it has been limited to that of a congressional leader supporting administration policies. . . . Yet he is, in his own phrase, a 'reformed isolationist,' the reform coming as much from his intuitive feeling that the United States cannot withdraw from the world as from any profound analysis of the world's troubles. . . . His instinctive feelings show when he discusses the need for, and the problems of, detente. He knows that the world will be better off if it can be achieved—that true success in the second round SALT talks can ease world tensions and save the U.S. billions in defense appropriations. He is wary, though, of unilateral concessions in the name of detente. His instinct is that we can only negotiate with the Soviets from a position of strength."

I observed that his positions on other current issues seem to derive from similar instinctive feelings—"from what some of his critics have called 'off the top of his head reactions' and what his friends prefer to call commonsense."

Because this was the first occasion in which Gerald Ford had spoken as a prospective president rather than as a subordinate leader, I devoted much space to his comments on current issues. But since he was so little known outside of Washington I also set down many of my own impressions.

First of all, he was a man who did not easily "get uptight." I noted that while this particular day had been a frantic one for him, one of turmoil all over Washington, he could still take time for an hour's visit with a journalist, speak freely and easily with no signs of tension. I agreed he was not going to appeal to the intellectual elite once they had recovered from their relief at being relieved of President Nixon. He might have no honeymoon at all with liberals and only a brief one with doctrinaire conservatives. I also suggested that many people would be misled by "that air of the All-American Boy, well-scrubbed and clean-cut, heritage of his football and Navy flying days."

"But make no mistake," I added. "This is not a man wanting in intelligence or in the varied experiences that shape political leaders. His law degree is from Yale, he has served under every president from Truman to Nixon. . . . He sufficiently impressed his peers so that in due time they chose him for party leadership. Today, when you talk to him on any subject, you may not find profundity but you find a wide range of knowledge."

It had been a long interview and a hard one to write under the pressure of time and circumstance. I had, I knew, lucked out on a journalistic coup by this talk with a man on the eve of his assuming the presidency amid unprecedented events. How could I sum it up?

The only thing I could think of was to add one final impression: "In the best of all possible worlds, the country might do better than Gerald Ford of Michigan. In the world as it is, we could surely do worse."

I would not change that conclusion today.

* * * * *

The controversy over Watergate didn't end with Richard Nixon's resignation. For almost thirty years, from his first campaign against Helen Gahagan Douglas for a seat in Congress, he had been a man who stirred great passions. While there were many who admired him, some for the enemies he had made, those enemies were venomous and had been since his role in convicting Alger Hiss for perjury. These passions dogged him throughout his up-and-down career and played a role in the Watergate affair in two ways. For one, they had given Nixon a persecution complex, a feeling that he could not win over his enemies no matter what he did, and this accounted much for his "hunkering down" when the Watergate attacks began. Herb Klein, long-time and loyal Nixon associate, once told me that if Nixon had been elected in 1960 instead of 1968 he would have been an entirely different president. There wouldn't have been, in Herb's view, the same retiring behind a stone wall of silence and stubbornness. At the same time those hate-Nixon passions accounted for much of the doggedness with which the Watergate investigation was pursued.

President Ford stirred the passions again with his pardon. I don't think he acted too precipitously. His pardon spared the country a long and bitter time, dragging out Watergate endlessly with a former president of the United States in the dock. I do think, though, Ford did it ineptly. He made his announcement abruptly on a Sunday morning with no public preparation, with no chance to explain to the country why he had done so. The first reaction was that the pardon was part of some kind of a "deal," an accusation that was to haunt Ford throughout his term even though he hadn't done it for Nixon's sake but for the country's sake.

In spite of this new controversy I had the feeling that Ford as president would have a calming effect on the public mood. He made a modest and appealing first appearance before the country on TV. He was so evidently himself a nice man. Nobody could hate Ford no matter what anyone thought of his politics. This proved to be the case. Of the presidents of my time no other left office, even in defeat, with so much public goodwill. Eisenhower in retirement was venerated. Ford in retirement simply remained likeable.

It would be a long time before I could sort out my feelings about Richard Nixon and Watergate. But the immediate feeling that the country was regaining its calm after all the turmoil gave me a chance to turn my thoughts to other, more personal matters.

* * * * *

One of these was the affairs of my old newspaper and its parent company. When I retired from the *Journal* in 1971, I had the feeling that, with Joe Evans, I had left its editorial voice in capable hands. But in December 1971 Joe had a sudden, fatal heart attack. He was only fifty-two. This left the paper with an unanticipated problem. Who was the best man to replace him? By this time Warren Phillips had risen to vice-president and general manager, with

the additional title of editorial director. Because Buren McCormack was ailing (he would himself die the following year) this
meant Warren was the effective officer under Bill Kerby to resolve
the problem. Under Joe there had been able assistants, good and
thoughtful writers, but neither Warren nor I felt they had the
wide-ranging interests or the flair the paper's voice needed. One
who did, in both our opinions, was Bob Bartley, still a young man
not yet thirty-five, and then in Washington. But he was also still
brash and had no experience in an executive capacity. Warren decided, rightly, to bring him back to New York as an associate editor and let it be known informally that he would be in charge but
under the supervision of Warren himself, who though not writing
would take the responsibility for the paper's editorial positions.
This meant Bob was one of several associate editors, none of whom
had an editor to be "associate to." It was at first an awkward arrangement. It worked because Bob grew in judgment and in the
respect of his peers. Within a year he was named editor of the editorial page. In 1979 he became officially the paper's editor. In
1980 he would become the third *Journal* editor in succession to
win a Pulitzer Prize. The judgment of 1972 would be vindicated.

Warren's role in this shows how rapidly he was rising within the
company. It also shows how he would step into any power vacuum
when the need arose and was willing to make decisions he thought
best while knowing they would not be everywhere well received.
It was that way with this Bartley appointment; Bob was years
younger than his colleagues, and naturally there was some disgruntlement. Theoretically the decision wasn't Warren's to make;
the selection of anyone to fill that important a post on the paper
should have been Bill Kerby's. Warren, of course, cleared it with
Bill, though there was no real consultation. He just did it. The fact
that he "consulted" with me was more a courtesy than anything
else, just as when later in 1979 he telephoned to ask if I would "object" to his giving Bartley the editor's title. I had by now acquired a
sort of unofficial status as "elder statesman" or whatever. But had I
objected on either occasion I'm sure Warren would have made his
decision anyway.

For Warren was not only ambitious; he was unafraid of responsibility. He also, as it happens, has good judgment. This was fortunate because long before he became the company's chief executive

officer (not until 1975 at the age of forty-nine) he was the operating head of the enterprise. As events would show, that turned out to be to the company's good fortune.

But in late 1974 I had other things on my mind besides the affairs of the paper or the company. In the thirty-eight years I had by then been writing for the *Journal* I had filed stories with datelines from all over the world; my wall map was sprinkled with its dotted pins of foreign travel. But I had never served as a foreign correspondent; that is, one resident abroad rather than just passing by. That was a lacuna in my career I had long wanted to fill.

Now I saw the chance. Watergate had had its denouement, if not its ending. President Ford would have his problems, but I felt sure they would not be as turmoil-producing as Vietnam or Watergate. It would be two years before the next presidential election. Meanwhile, at sixty, I was getting no younger. If I was to have the experience of living abroad, time was growing short.

One nice thing about academia, as someone once said of baseball umpiring, is you can't beat the hours. Another is that academia tends to be very liberal with leaves of absence, especially for full professors, so long as the university doesn't have to pay their salaries. (True sabbaticals, that is a year off with full pay every seven years, have become fond memories on most campuses.) I applied for and received a leave of absence for 1975. I also talked Warren into picking up part of the travel tab. Since my contract for the *Journal* column would continue, there would be no great financial sacrifice.

So in January 1975 Frances and I took flight for London to seek new adventures.

3

London was a logical place to establish a base. For one thing, it was the headquarters and communications center for the *Journal*'s European coverage, having a direct teletype line to New York. For another, it was a city we knew and loved, having visited it often. There are many exciting cities in the world to visit—Rome, Tokyo, Hong Kong, Singapore, New Delhi, Moscow—but my three favorites for repeated journeys are San Francisco, Paris, and London. Of London and Paris we had fond memories of a trip with Bonnie and Eleanor when they were teenagers. Bonnie, in fact, had celebrated her eighteenth birthday in London, including an invitation to a party that day at the ambassadorial residence when John Hay Whitney held that post. A perennial family joke is of the time Eleanor, having crossed with us on the old *Queen Elizabeth*, was a dinner guest at the Hotel Crillon Grill in Paris and being asked if she would like some caviar, replied "I'm tired of caviar!" It seemed to all assembled a delightful expression of sophisticated world-weariness coming from a thirteen-year-old.

London also had the advantage of being a travel center. From London a trip to any place on the continent is no greater journey than from Chapel Hill to New York or Chicago. Frances and I could, and did, make easy and frequent trips to Paris, Brussels, West Berlin, or wherever fancy or journalistic usefulness suggested.

No luxury hotel in London this time. We took a furnished flat first in Chelsea and later on Curzon Street in the middle of Mayfair, overlooking Shepherd's Market. Since my commitment to the *Journal* was still only for the once-a-week column, there was time to enjoy the city itself, wandering byways we had missed before. I could also spend some time in the British Museum doing research on a subject that long interested me, the origin in England of many of a citizen's civil rights, including those of free speech and freedom to publish, that were embodied in our own constitutional Bill of Rights.

By now the *Journal* editors and readers were accustomed to (or at least inured to) my habit of writing sometimes on less consequential topics than the world's great events. So I had the fun of writing occasionally about the London theater and other offerings of the city. My very first column from there, in fact, was on the discomforts and annoyances of trans-Atlantic air travel as compared with the pleasures and comfort of the vanishing ocean liners. I've always viewed air travel as about on a par with a stagecoach trip from New York to Boston. (It hasn't improved with the years.)

But politics fascinates me in every country, not just my own. We happened to arrive in the midst of turmoil within the British Conservative party. The back-benchers in Parliament had grown weary of Ted Heath, the party's leader and a former prime minister, and a struggle was underway among other aspirants to leadership. These included a lady, Margaret Thatcher, daughter of middle-class parents, who had won a scholarship to Somerville College at Oxford. From there she emerged in 1951 as a research chemist, an occupation she followed for a couple of years. Then she was "called," as the British put it, to Lincoln's Inn and shifted to a legal career. In 1959 she was elected to Parliament.

Obviously, she was an unusual woman, or rather I should say "lady," for along the way she had acquired the accent and manners of the British upper-class. She had also acquired a husband, Dennis Thatcher, a successful businessman, and two children. But the most unusual thing about her was that she decided to contest the party leadership, for centuries a man's domain. When to the country's astonishment she won, the shock reverberated through the Carlton Club, traditional haven of Conservative party leaders but heretofore a men-only preserve. If the Conservatives should win the next election, that would mean a lady prime minister. Unheard of! A queen for sovereign, yes. But the prime minister's is not a ceremonial office. He—or she?—holds the chief power of the realm.

I found the lady fascinating. Whether she had the ability, the iron will to control Parliament and the government's machinery I could not tell on short acquaintance, although there was nothing self-effacing about her speeches, nothing timid about her attacks on the Labor party's mismanagement of the nation's affairs. What she did have, at least to me and to much of the country, was charm, that mysterious bloom on a woman. In Barrie's play *What Every Woman Knows* charm is described by Maggie Wylie, the woman of the title, as something which if a woman lacks, it doesn't matter what else she has; whereas if she has it she doesn't need anything else.

So it was hardly surprising that Margaret Thatcher quickly became Maggie Thatcher to one and all, and remained so after she did in fact become prime minister of Great Britain.

"With her blonde good looks and well-tailored clothes," so I wrote, "she still looks every inch the lady. And along the way she has acquired self-assurance and an unflappable poise." Badgered by a foreign journalist, she skewered him with the remark, "You chaps do not like a direct answer. Men like long, rambling answers."

This moved me to recall the line about the power of a woman, known to Barrie's Maggie Wylie long before the *Ladies Home Journal* used it as a slogan: "Never underestimate."

If I couldn't foresee Maggie Thatcher's future, I could see well enough that she had returned excitement to the nearly moribund Conservative party. At her formal investiture as party leader, if that's the word for it, she was greeted with tumultuous applause from all the Tory MPs. A few days later a Gallup poll showed the Conservative party as well as its new leader soaring in popularity. When she shortly thereafter took to the hustings, she was greeted in Edinburgh with bagpipes playing "A Man's a Man for a' That."

I could also see well enough that if the Conservative party needed revitalizing, so did the country itself. Both were in sad estate. Living there and shopping from day to day, we didn't need statistics to tell us the British inflation rate was twice ours at home, at least in 1975. The large unemployment was visible. So were the labor troubles. We had to check each morning to see whether the railroads or busses were running. "Wildcat" strikes were routine.

What this could mean to British industry was driven home to me one day on a visit to a British-Leyland plant, the auto company, near Oxford. It was shut down because some twenty-five workers who installed doors on the cars were having their own private strike. All the rest of the plant workers were also thrown out of work because you can't make cars without doors. As far as I could tell, the nonstriking workers didn't complain about the handful of strikers who had put them all out of jobs.

That wasn't the only plant problem. The manager, a man who seemed to know his job, told me wistfully that he could make cars "as good or better than General Motors" but not as efficiently or cheaply. He blamed only part of that on such wildcat strikes and other labor troubles. Just as much, he said, was because he had to work with antiquated machinery, worn out and wearing out machine tools. In his years on the job there had been very little investment for modernizing the facilities.

This summed up Britain's woe. An "I'm-all-right-Jack" attitude on the part of labor (title of a marvellous Peter Sellers' movie) which means work as little as possible, take what you can get and be satisfied as long as you have tea and beer. Confiscatory taxes with a top rate rising to 90 percent, which cruelly squeezed the middle class, leaving no savings to provide investment. A government that nonetheless had to print money to "pay for" its extravagant spending made necessary by its efforts to provide cradle-to-the-grave welfare. A government whose bureaucracy laid its heavy hand everywhere—as on this auto plant, owned and mismanaged by government-appointed executives. All that makes a vicious circle, or rather a spiral leading ever downwards. For me it was sad, especially so because there was—and is—so much in British life and culture, so much in British civility and manners, to admire and to inspire affection.

It was painful to write about much of this. For it remained true that a visitor still found in London superb theater, ballet, and concerts as well as that other form of the performing arts, pageantry. The English remained civilized; rare was the taxidriver trying to cheat the foreigner, and at a neighborhood pub the regulars welcomed the stranger to try a game of darts. The pain was in writing about the 20 percent inflation, the noticeably dirtier streets, the long queues awaiting those needing hospital surgery, the breakdown of major services such as the post office. At one point, after having written of the pleasures that remained in walking the streets so full of history, I expressed the feeling that "what I am enjoying is the pleasure of being in a vast museum of the way things were."

Of course living in Britain wasn't the whole point of this residency abroad. A trip to West Berlin (the second for me, the first for Frances) reminded me anew of the grim contrast with that other city just across the border. I also found there a more discouraged spirit among the West Berliners than on my previous visit. I was frequently asked whether the U.S. would come to their aid in case of another Soviet blockade, as President Truman had done those years ago. In the aftermath of Vietnam on the American mood I could not reassure them with any confidence.

I found a similar question posed by the French, from the man on the street to the functionary at the Quai D'Orsai, the French foreign office. "Is the United States—militarily, economically and politically—now a declining world power?" In the eyes of Europe, I was moved to write, "the United States is no longer . . . the power in the world it so briefly was. The American hegemony (in European eyes) is over . . . an era has ended." The one encouraging note was sounded by Giscard d'Estaing, at that time the president. He no longer felt it so necessary, as had de Gaulle, to be anti-American, perhaps because the apparent decline in the American world role gave France less the feeling of occupying a subordinate position.

In Brussels a day at the headquarters of NATO didn't increase my confidence in the military effectiveness of that supposed shield against the Russians. Staff officers trotted out all the usual charts and maps showing how the allied forces would meet any invasion. These were impressive, but they left me with that same uneasiness I felt at Pearl Harbor seeing the same sort of things about our war in Vietnam. NATO headquarters was a babel of languages and uniforms, representing different nations with different aims, different ideas. I couldn't help recalling the remark attributed to General Eisenhower when he commanded NATO that it was "a can of worms."

Setting all this down now may give the impression of nothing but depression on our year abroad. This is misleading. We found many pleasures in our travels and I found cheering things to write about. On the thirtieth anniversary of V-E day in May we were touring by car on the backroads of France, and we stopped for lunch in a small village. The *anciens de la guerre* were having a reunion, and when they found I too was a veteran of that long-ago war the cheers rang out to cries of "*vive l'Amerique!*" All was not forgotten nor old friendships abandoned everywhere.

In fact, wherever we went, and no matter how pointed some of the questions posed about America after Vietnam and Watergate, I found no discourtesy either among political officials or ordinary people. Their reaction to Watergate, incidentally, was more puzzlement than anything else. Europeans couldn't quite understand why we got so excited over President Nixon and his alleged misdeeds. By their standards, I suppose, he had done no more than what they expected from their political leaders. I was never able to explain adequately the excitement about it at home.

I remember two such occasions particularly. One was a visit with Huw Weldon, then head of the British Broadcasting Company, the other with Raymond Aron, the distinguished dean of French journalistic commentators. Neither quite understood why the Watergate "scandal" was sufficient to drive a president out of office. Elliot Richardson, at the time our ambassador to Britain, told me he had encountered similar difficulties explaining Watergate to those who questioned him.

I found myself equally puzzled sometimes by the public attitudes in Europe. I would have thought that in such countries as Belgium or France, twice overrun and devastated in this century because of blindness about their defenses, there would be strong support for NATO. What NATO had at most was lip service. France had withdrawn its army and thrown NATO headquarters out of the country. Belgium balked at every suggestion that it strengthen its military contribution. As best I could judge, the people in both countries supported the policies of their governments in this regard.

In their small country the Belgians were still preoccupied with quarrelling over their ethnic and linguistic differences. The French, I suppose, were just being French, asserting their independence no matter at what cost. The West Germans talked more of their thriving economy, of which they were justly proud, and of the dangers of inflation from government overspending, the memories of that terrible inflation of the 1920s not yet extinguished. As for Italy, trying to understand its politics would drive anyone into a nervous breakdown. Whatever government was in office on Monday might be out on Tuesday. Altogether, I wound up my continental tours with little hope for those dreams of a united Europe beyond superficial forms. A "Parliament of Europe" might exist, but it would be handicapped by too many centuries of quarrels among peoples.

In Britain, our home base, we stayed long enough to make some new and lasting friends, and they were most hospitable to us. Here we felt the most at home, not only because of the shared language but the shared outlooks on life. From Britain we inherited our political system and much of our culture. For me personally there was the fact that in imagination I had served under Drake's flag, grown up with Clive of India. At the Old Cheshire Cheese I could imagine myself chatting with the good Sam Johnson. In the House of Commons gallery I could almost hear Edmund Burke or Winston Churchill. In my mind's eye Britannia still ruled the waves.

The reality I found was something different. Those I actually heard in the Commons, with a due nod to the spunk of Maggie Thatcher, were dispirited voices. In fact, everywhere I turned it seemed to me the spirit had gone out of the people and so out of the country. The two great wars, the second of which had taken the last ounce of strength to survive, had left exhaustion. Among the friends and acquaintances I made the manners remained, as did the civility, but confidence was gone. This was, it seemed to me, not just the result of the welfare state complex that gripped the country but also a cause of it. Frances and I enjoyed our stay there, but it was therefore overlaid with sadness. I had, moreover, a haunting feeling that I might be seeing my own country a generation or so in the future. There is nothing immutable in the greatness of nations.

That feeling was to lead to a final episode that would be amusing if not for its sadness. As a wrap-up piece on departing I wrote a column on "the British lesson on how to ruin a country" by creating such a welfare state that it put intolerable burdens on the economy and sapped a people's vitality. I said it offered a model study on what not to do in the United States.

To my astonishment these observations were reprinted in a front-page story by the *Times* of London. This led to an interview by the BBC. The tone of the interviewer was definitely unfriendly. At what luxury hotel had I stayed? What had I seen of the country beyond its famous restaurants and the changing of the guard? Why was I so "hostile" to Britain? My explanation that it was not hostility but melancholy affection that moved me didn't take the sting out of it.

All these adventures made the prospect of a return to Chapel Hill seem rather humdrum.

4

The return to the home country proved not to be as humdrum as I expected. For one thing, I had a lot of catching up to do. Reading foreign newspapers, even the British ones, gives a peculiar view of affairs in the United States. They cover the major events (such as the resignation of a president, major policy utterances of a sitting president, riots and disturbances), but the American resident abroad is left with some frustrations about more general affairs in his own country unless he's interested in scandal or titillating gossip. The Paris-published *Herald-Tribune* is of more help as are the news magazines, though the editions of the latter are not the same as those published for domestic audiences. My own newspaper is also a help, but in 1975 it was not easily available outside the major cities. It would be 1983 before it published an edition in Europe. In addition, 1976 was a presidential election year, which is never humdrum.

My initial thought, nevertheless, was that I would not be drawn into presidential politics until convention time rolled around. The impression I had was that, on the whole, President Ford was doing well enough, and I saw no rivals on the scene other than those who had been around the track before. I had enough to do, I thought, in preparing to teach again. In all this I was mistaken.

In November 1975 Nelson Rockefeller, our second vice-president-by-appointment, had announced that he would not run again. This was the first surprise, although perhaps it shouldn't have been.

I had never been enthusiastic about Rockefeller's politics. Years ago my father told me to beware of men of inherited wealth in politics. Unlike someone who has earned his own wealth, a person born with money has little appreciation of it; he thinks it is simply for spending. I remember a time when Governor Rockefeller, on a luncheon visit at the *Journal*, was advocating an increase in New York State income taxes. He remarked that he couldn't understand the opposition because the bill would increase the average family's tax bill by "only a hundred dollars." It struck me then that the governor could understand the problems of the poor, which were visible to anyone visiting poverty areas, but he didn't understand those of a middle-class family with a mortgage and with children to support and educate. To Rockefeller, after all, a hundred dollars wasn't very much. I think this had a great deal to do with his spending proclivities as governor and his liberal attitude toward the federal budget.

In other ways I had to admire him, and indeed the whole Rockefeller clan. With their wealth they could all have been jet-set playboys, and his brother Winthrop had been for a time. But somewhere along the line they acquired a sense of noblesse oblige, the idea of public duty. Winthrop changed enough to become governor of Arkansas. David earned his doctorate at the University of Chicago, served as secretary to Mayor LaGuardia, and wasn't handed the chairmanship of the family-owned Chase bank merely out of nepotism. John devoted much of his time to philanthropy, at which he worked hard. Nelson didn't need to enter the political fray in order to "be somebody." He too got into politics from a praiseworthy sense of obligation.

Yet I also felt that simply being a Rockefeller had taken some of the drive out of his on-and-off-again presidential attempts. I suspect he took the vice-presidency for the honor of the thing but that he couldn't accommodate to being "number two" under a plain person like Jerry Ford. After all, in or out of office he was still a Rockefeller. He didn't have to put up with all the slings and arrows flung at him by his vocal critics within the party.

Whatever the truth of that, his withdrawal meant the end of the Rockefeller political career. And it couldn't help but create a fissure in the political armor of President Ford. It left him with the tricky problem of picking another running mate.

I quickly discovered Ford had some other problems. His efforts to "talk down" inflation with all those WIN buttons had turned into a joke. The purchasing power of the dollar declined in both 1975 and 1976, although by a small amount (about 5 percent) compared with what came later. When Ford tried to exercise some fiscal restraint by vetoing a $45 billion appropriation for welfare and manpower programs, the Democratic Congress overrode him. He also got himself tangled up (unnecessarily, I thought) in the abortion issue.

Meanwhile, presidential rivals were cropping up in both parties. Ronald Reagan, former California governor, decided to contest Ford in his own party. Senators Henry Jackson and Frank Church both announced for the Democratic nomination, and out on what seemed to be the fringes there was the emerging unknown, Jimmy Carter of Georgia. With my usual political acumen, I didn't think Reagan would prove a major problem for the incumbent Republican, and I didn't think a small-town Southerner would succeed against the Democratic establishment.

I was wrong on both counts. The turning point for Reagan probably came in the North Carolina primary in March, which he won with the active support of Senator Jesse Helms. Previous to that, Ford had topped Reagan in four successive primaries. Jimmy Carter had by then drawn the attention of all the media, especially television, first by stealing a march on everyone in the Iowa caucus and then by "winning" the New Hampshire primary, always viewed by the press as more important than its real delegate strength warranted.

Suddenly I felt my political juices flowing again. In late April I had another interview with President Ford. Naturally much of this was devoted to politics. At the time he thought Senator Jackson or, somewhat to my surprise, Hubert Humphrey would be the Democratic nominee. This was just a few days before the ailing Humphrey tearfully announced that he would not be a candidate. As for Carter, Ford thought that as an outsider his fortunes would turn on the Pennsylvania primary where Senator Jackson had the support of most of the state party leaders as well as of the labor unions. Without Pennsylvania, Ford thought, Carter would have no chance. With a win there he would have.

Carter did win the Pennsylvania primary two weeks later, followed by wins in Tennessee, Arkansas, and Kentucky. On May 1 Jackson quit. And with that it was all over for the Democratic convention. It was only from habit that I bothered to attend.

But that April conversation with Ford wasn't just about politics. I've often wondered whether for those who achieve it the presidency turns out to be what they expected, how closely the reality matches the dream. In that long-ago talk with President-elect Kennedy I had intimations that as the office bore down on him it looked more formidable than it had been when he was striving for it. So I asked Ford in what way he thought the presidency differed from his previous experiences in Congress.

"One of the most dramatic changes," he said, "is that you have to make definitive decisions. You get a bill sent down, you either veto it or you sign it. . . . In the process of working on legislation you can compromise a little bit, you can vote for an amendment or not vote for an amendment. It is rather extended give and take, pretty much."

He went on to say that he had enough previous experience with presidents to know the job requires definite decisions, yea or nay, but "you don't really get the impact of it until you do it yourself . . . I guess Harry Truman had the right phrase—'The buck stops here.'"

Another requirement of the job, he said, is that "you have to be a good listener. . . . It's a very time-consuming job where you have to cover a wide range of subject matters dealing with literally hundreds of highly technical people who have very frequently diverse views."

Then he added, "The immensity of it descends on you when you take a look at some of these problems that come across your desk, and I think that it is probably greater than I anticipated. But you get used to it and begin to take it in stride."

I recalled the oft-made observation that the presidency always changes those who occupy it, and asked in what way he thought his twenty months in office had changed him.

"My instincts are the same," he replied. "I don't think I'm any different in any way other than the responsibilities as an executive are different from the responsibilities as a legislative leader. . . .

"The first several months, as you can well imagine, were very difficult months. We were thrust into the breach, so to speak, under the most unusual circumstances in the history of the country. . . . I went from the position of vice-president, where you really make no decisions at all, to a job where decisions had to be made every day in great numbers. Yes, there was a period of some transition where things were not as smooth, not as well organized."

The natural next question was whether he thought any experience could prepare anyone for being president, or whether the person would have to find his way after he got there.

He replied that obviously it depended on the individual. "I do think it is helpful to have had a great deal of exposure with the problems of the federal government. That does not mean you could not have someone [without] it, but it would be my impression that a person coming from the federal government knows the issues . . . better than someone who comes from a different circle, so to speak."

I took this remark as a dart at Reagan and Carter, both former governors, neither with any experience in the federal government, especially since it was delivered with a grin.

Finally, I got nerve enough to ask him what could be an embarrassing question. How would he react if perchance he would be defeated in the coming election? It must be crushing, I thought to myself, to have risen so high and then be toppled over, as had Johnson and Nixon.

There was a pause while the president puffed on his ubiquitous pipe, and for a moment I feared I had overreached courtesy. But Ford's answer showed clearly that he had thought about that possibility.

"A lot would depend upon who was elected," he began, "and the kind of Congress that would be elected at the same time. If a person was elected who had completely different ideological, philosophical views, I would be very concerned." As for his personal

feelings, "You never like to lose. . . . I would probably be sad-
dened and very disappointed but not crushed, and I would certainly not take it as a personal matter. I have lost some ball games
before. As long as you do your best, as long as you have belief in
what you are doing, it is always a gamble that you are going to
lose. When you do, you have to be man enough to take it."

In sharing the president's thoughts with *Journal* readers (he was
not quoted directly at the time) I thought I should add my own
impressions. I began by observing he had "grown accustomed to
the seat of power . . . today he sits comfortably there."

I also said something that, I think, helps explain the election's
outcome: "Gerald Ford doesn't exude the commanding presence
of a Franklin Roosevelt or a Dwight Eisenhower . . . or the fiery
cockiness of Harry Truman. He lacks Jack Kennedy's wit, and you
don't detect a sense of humor that might make him laugh at what
the turn of fortune has done to Gerald Ford."

This want of "presence" hindered him in the contest with Reagan for the nomination, which he almost lost, and certainly was a
handicap in the campaign against Jimmy Carter, which he did
lose. Not since Kennedy had there been a presidential candidate
with as much personal attractiveness as the strange man from the
South.

But I also wrote something else about Gerald Ford: "If there is
in him any of that inner insecurity that haunted his two immediate
predecessors, Richard Nixon and Lyndon Johnson, it's not apparent to a visitor." It was the last time I would see him as president.
By autumn I was on that winding road to Plains, Georgia.

*　*　*　*　*

It's a curious thing. Except for his Camp David conference with
Begin and Sadat which led to peace between Israel and Egypt, I
have trouble remembering the four years of President Carter. For
the first time in writing any of this I have had to look back at the
record not merely to confirm details but simply to recall what happened and what I was writing about at the time.

I would put this down to advancing age, which supposedly dims
recent recollections, except that the events of the 1980 election
and the excitement of President Reagan's beginning are still vivid
in memory. But I'm not alone in that forgetfulness. Not since Her-

bert Hoover did a president, once out of office, vanish so quickly from the public eye. Six months afterwards it was almost as if Carter had never been. Both the country and the media ignored him. It was left to history to resurrect him.

One thing the history of the 1976 election did, at least to my mind, was to confirm my feeling that the nation was still on a political seesaw, unwilling to give any party or political leader a true mandate to govern. Though Carter won, it was once again a close election. It was also, in an unprecedented fashion for modern times, a sectional victory. Draw a line on a map from North Dakota and Minnesota in the north southward to the border of Oklahoma and Arkansas. Ford carried everything west of that line except Hawaii, the island state. In fact, Ford carried more states than Carter. The Carter victory rested entirely on his native South. He carried every state of the old Confederacy except Virginia, every border state except Oklahoma. Without these he could not have won.

Moreover, Carter didn't win the South because of overwhelming personal popularity. Many white Southerners voted for him for the same reason the preponderance of Catholics voted for Kennedy in 1960. They wanted to put to rest the idea that no Southerner could be elected president of the United States. That legend put to rest, as was the "no Catholic president" one in 1960, Southern white voters redivided by their political inclinations as did the rest of the country.

Even with all that Southern sentiment working for him, I'm not sure Carter would have won—or Ford lost—without some other factors. One was the damage done to Republican solidarity by the Reagan-Ford battle for the nomination. At the Kansas City convention there was bitter feeling between the more conservative Republicans, mostly for Reagan, and the Ford loyalists. The two principals did little to heal the breach after the issue was settled. The night when Ford and Reagan made a joint appearance to perform at least the obligatory courtesies, I remember thinking what a pity it was that Ford didn't pick Ronald Reagan as his running mate, or couldn't persuade him to accept. The vice-presidential choice Ford made, Senator Robert Dole of Kansas, was no help; he proved an inept campaigner. Then President Ford didn't help himself with a major slip-of-the-tongue in the TV debates; he sounded as if he thought Poland was not behind the Iron Curtain. Bumping his head on airplane doors didn't help him either; it made him the butt of jokes.

There was another interesting thing about that 1976 election. Carter ran as an "outsider," free of the taint of too much a Washington view of the country's problems. Over and over again he promised a balanced budget and with it a diminishing of the size of federal government and its heavy hand of bureaucratic regulation. "And you can count on that," he said time and again. Few people disliked Gerald Ford; a majority liked Carter for what seemed the freshness of his political views. What makes this especially interesting is that four years later Reagan defeated Carter with the same political appeal and philosophy. Carter's problem as president was that almost none of his preelection promises were fulfilled; had they been, Reagan would have had much less ammunition. Had politicians and those of us who follow politics paid enough attention we could have seen in 1976 the nation's shifting mood that caused a political earthquake in 1980.

Between 1976 and the 1980 election a great many things went from bad to worse, both for the country and for Carter's political fortunes. Despite his talk about reducing the size of government, President Carter did nothing to shrink even the size of the executive office; the Executive Office Building next to the White House overflowed with staff, many with unclear duties. In 1977, six months in office, Carter created a whole new department, the Department of Energy, appointing as its secretary James Schlesinger, a man of some abilities but with no gift for explaining energy policy to either Congress or the country—if indeed anyone could have explained it. This department burgeoned rapidly but with no diminution of the confusion over energy or with relief from the energy shortage (or at least a shortage of oil, gasoline, and natural gas at accustomed prices). In 1979 Carter split the former Department of Health, Education, and Welfare into two departments, each with its own secretary and secretariat. The cabinet table in the White House was getting crowded.

Spending went up accordingly. In 1976, Ford's last year, the federal government spent $365 billion; by the 1980 fiscal year, embracing Carter's last budget, it was estimated at $579 billion, an increase of close to 60 percent. Inflation, or the decrease in the dollar's buying power, matched it. In 1976 the consumer price index rose 5.8 percent. In 1978 Carter signed the Humphrey-Hawkins bill calling for a reduction of inflation to 4 percent. But in 1979 consumer prices rose 11.5 percent, and the rate increased as the 1980 election approached.

Tax receipts went up too, of course, which kept the deficit from being worse, but this was no help to Carter politically; the steep rises in Social Security taxes hit lower and middle income earners particularly hard. This led to the first "tax revolt," in California where a referendum demanding a 57 percent cut in property taxes ("Proposition 13") passed overwhelmingly. A recession also hit business, particularly the auto industry. Chrysler had to be rescued from bankruptcy by the federal government (as did New York City) while unemployment increased.

Carter was also plagued by other troubles, not all of his own making. In 1979 the Shah of Iran was toppled and fled to the United States for medical treatment; that November militant Iranian students seized the U.S. embassy and sixty-three American hostages who would remain prisoners until Carter's last day in office. Then the Soviet Union invaded Afghanistan and a war broke out between Iraq and Iran. If President Carter could have halted none of these things, they nonetheless provided ammunition for his critics. The impression the public had of him, rightly or wrongly, was of a president who abandoned his campaign promises, zigzagged in his policy courses, vacillated on decisions. His earlier effort to reduce defense expenditures, for example, was blamed for "emboldening" the Soviet Union, and in his last year he had to reverse himself on the arms budget. His embargo on grain exports to Russia and against American participation in the Moscow Olympic games were attacked as feeble gestures.

Looking back on what I wrote for the *Journal*, I find that I was rather sympathetic to President Carter in the beginning. I didn't join the howling over Bert Lance, his budget director, which eventually drove him out of the administration. I thought Lance's alleged malfeasances as a banker mostly a teapot tempest brewed by the media. He was eventually acquitted of all charges. His departure, I thought, was a loss to Carter, since Lance was one of the more intelligent of the Georgia crowd. His levelheaded common sense would have been a counterweight to some of Carter's other advisers.

Nor did I join the voices decrying Billy Carter. In the first place I don't think presidents are responsible for their kinfolk. I also liked Billy and could understand that some of his wilder actions and statements were reactions to having a brother as president while he remained a small-town figure of fun. It must have been galling.

I didn't even blame the first slight rise in the inflation rate (to six percent) on the president, noting that it resulted from the accumulation of past policies and that in no way could any president brake it in three months.

I also find, looking back, I wrote more columns devoted to "peripheral" issues, or just to idle thoughts. I got entangled in a long controversy with women's rights militants over such trivialities as not using "she" as well as "he" when speaking generally, or for using "mankind" when referring to the whole species. At least that was amusing.

One reason, I suppose, for writing less about politics or public policy was that I felt the country had decided on a leader for the next four years and that he deserved a chance to settle on a course without endless carping on every move. Others were more personal. I was ready for an excuse to think of other things.

For one, the gaps on my wall map where there were no red-headed pins, or where there were places to revisit, stared at me. Time was getting short for more travel. In 1977 Frances and I took a long freighter voyage with Chapel Hill friends, Phyllis and Gerry Barrett, across the northern Pacific to Taiwan, Singapore, and Hong Kong. In 1978 we took our two granddaughters, Heather and Shelley, to Europe as we had our daughters years before. Eleanor, their mother, was living in Dallas with her biochemist husband and working on her master's degree. Bonnie had decided to return to school for a doctorate in drama after a dozen successful years as a community-theater director. With the daughters thus settled our attention shifted to the next generation. An account of that granddaughterly journey drew an astonishing number of letters, some from grandparents who had done it, some from those who now said they would. I was reminded anew that sometimes a sentimental column provoked more interest than my profound comments on taxes, inflation, or the Middle East.

In that same year, 1978, I finally got a chance to visit the People's Republic of China, this trip as a journalist and at *Journal* expense. Much of what I saw and wrote about has been altered by time, but I did come away with the feeling that the long-sleeping giant was awakening and that the U.S. had better pay attention. Later Frances and I circumnavigated South America through the Straits of Magellan, and afterwards cruised the South Pacific as far as Tasmania, with stops in New Zealand and Australia. At least I was adding more pins to my map.

That China trip, though I enjoyed every moment of it, convinced me that reporting was a young man's game while I was becoming a Senior Citizen. I was hard put to keep up with my younger colleagues on a schedule that began at six, filled the day with trips to farms or steel mills or long visits with political figures over endless tea, and then continued with banqueting until a late hour. I realized I would have to leave that kind of journalism to younger, more energetic members of the craft. I had done enough of that. Hereafter I would be an observer from a distance.

It was at this time that I first found my thoughts, as those of old men will, dwelling on all I had seen and done since those brash young days in New Deal Washington. That was the beginning of these recollections.

*   *   *   *   *

For all these reasons I was much less active as a peripatetic journalist throughout the late seventies and the 1980 campaign. There were a few trips to Washington, mostly out of habit, to see Secretary of the Treasury Blumenthal, Secretary of Commerce Juanita Kreps, Arthur Burns at the Fed, or a few old friends on Capitol Hill like Senators Harry Byrd of Virginia, Henry Jackson of Washington, or Jesse Helms of North Carolina. There were fewer congressmen I knew from former times outside of those from North Carolina; the years had thinned their ranks. The new Speaker Thomas "Tip" O'Neill, I never really knew at all.

In reality I found visits with these less rewarding than a day spent with Norman "Mike" Miller, the *Journal*'s Washington bureau chief, and his staff. Since my day newcomers had come to the fore, notably James Perry, Albert Hunt, Arlen Large, and Karen Elliot House. All were well-informed and Karen was becoming one of the most respected diplomatic correspondents. Alan Otten, with whom I had worked for years, was now the "gray eminence" of the bureau. There were also other Washington reporters known from the past, David Broder and Haynes Johnson of the *Post*, Mary McGrory of the *Star*, "Scotty" Reston of *The New York Times*, Robert Novak, formerly of the *Journal* and now teamed with Rowland Evans as syndicated columnists. A half-hour with these or a few others would give me a better insight into administration politics and policies, as well as Republican counterviews, than I could have gathered myself in a week.

Meanwhile my uneasiness about, and therefore my criticism of, President Carter increased. He didn't seem to me to have any insight as to the causes of inflation or the energy shortage, the two chief domestic problems, and certainly no grip on a solution for either. Nor did he have a firm posture on the government's attitude toward the Soviet Union or on the related issue of national defense. He waffled on all of them. On inflation he swung from cutting the government's budget to increasing it, from advocating a tax cut to opposing one. On energy, from restriction to relaxation. Toward the Soviet Union he vacillated between a "soft" attitude and a belligerent one, as he did between cutting defense spending and increasing it.

As 1979 opened I saw it as "the year of testing," particularly with regard to inflation, which I considered—and had long considered—our number one priority. Failure to solve it, I wrote, "will undermine our economic prosperity. It will cost us our position in the world. It will weaken our ability to defend ourselves against an enemy from without the gates. It . . . will fall heaviest on the poor and the middle class, strain the social contract which binds us together."

On this, I said, President Carter had floundered. "We begin [1979] with a nagging doubt whether we will meet the challenge, and with a haunting question: If not this year, then whenever?"

I wasn't the only one nagged by doubts. By midsummer Carter's "approval rating" had sunk in the polls to a record low (less than 30 percent) for incumbent presidents. What I couldn't see, or any of the polls show, were the viable political alternatives to Carter either in his own party or among the Republicans. I had heard too much about the "emerging Republican party" to put too much credence in it.

There were two things I could and did note. One was that the Republican party, over which many funeral orations had been preached, had 41 members in the Senate, 189 in the House. "Not a majority," I remarked, "but not a remnant band either." I also recalled that eighteen months before Carter was inaugurated as president the country had hardly heard of him. Eighteen months before Nixon it was generally thought his political career was over. Eighteen months before Kennedy's election he wasn't taken seriously by his party or by political observers. So a great deal could happen between the summer of '79 and the election of 1980.

*   *   *   *   *

What happened was Ronald Reagan. He had been a perennial candidate since his first term as governor of California in 1967. His closest approach to national political success was in 1976 when he tried to take the nomination from Ford and failed. In 1980 he would be sixty-nine. His political profile was as a spokesman for extreme conservatism which for half-a-century hadn't been very saleable. Cartoonists caricatured him as an actor playing *Bedtime For Bonzo*. Not a record to inspire gamblers to lay wagers on his chances.

Ten years earlier, as mentioned, I'd met Reagan. I found him personable and much more thoughtful than his reputation, which was that he was a lightweight who got elected governor only because of his Hollywood exposure. That was belied by his gubernatorial record which got him reelected. His abortive presidential try in 1976 showed at least a widespread respect for the man and his ideas, the same ideas he had been expressing for a decade. Yet I didn't begin to take him seriously as a presidential candidate until well into 1980.

My doubts were about his realistic chances for election, and I suppose by then I had become cynical about the willingness, not to mention the ability, of any president to do what Reagan promised to do. I had too often heard the refrains, only to see them drowned out in the Washington clamor for more not less government. After all, Carter had promised too—"and you can depend on that"— and look what happened to him.

My first column treating Reagan seriously as a candidate, in April 1980, was sparked by a flurry of stories saying the Democrats thought him the easiest candidate to beat. They kept saying they hoped Reagan would be the Republican nominee. It reminded me of the fable of Brer Fox, Brer Rabbit and the briar patch. "Brer

Fox, whatever you gonna do with me *please* don' throw me in that briar patch." Brer Fox does and Brer Rabbit laughs and laughs and laughs. The moral I drew from that was "he who gets the other fellow to follow his suggestion gets to laugh last." Or, turning it around, the Democrats wouldn't sneer at Reagan unless they feared him most.

"Indeed," I went on, "you begin to suspect that Mr. Reagan in fact has the Democrats biting their nails." He had clobbered all his Republican opponents in the primaries and had drawn many independents and former Democrats to switch to Republican ballots. "That hardly suggests the voters think of him as some kind of ogre."

The Democratic fears seemed justified. Carter was sinking deeper every day and the polls were showing what Anthony Lewis of *The New York Times* called "a sharply conservative trend in the country." I wasn't sure whether "conservative" was the word, but there was clearly a reaction against so many years of reckless spending, mounting inflation, and our weakened position in the world.

I went to both conventions that year simply because they were there. Conventions, though, weren't what they used to be. The nominations were settled before they assembled. The Democrats couldn't dump Carter; Reagan had the GOP delegates. I found myself skipping the long nights in the halls, watching proceedings on a hotel television set. I might as well have stayed in Chapel Hill.

It wasn't an election, it was a political upheaval. The Democrats managed to hold a small majority in the House. They lost the Senate. In a three-cornered race (John Anderson, Republican turned Independent, polled 5.7 million votes) Reagan won nearly 44 million, Carter less than 36 million. Reagan swept the electoral college 489 to 49. In the South, the land where he was born and whence he came, Jimmy Carter carried only his native Georgia of all the states in the old Confederacy. The winds of change had swept all else away.

*   *   *   *   *

Now it remained to see whether President Reagan, aged seventy on his inauguration day, would try to do what he promised. And whether he could. A half-century of political history augured against it.

Yet six months later he had pushed a reluctant Congress into agreeing to wholesale budget cuts, many of which bit into once sacred social programs, and to commit the nation to a three-year tax cut. Although every income level would benefit from the tax cut, much of it was aimed at an almost forgotten group of society, those of middle-class incomes, and even at the rich, always thought of by politicians as safe targets for milking. I was moved to compare this twin victory over the Democrats to that most famous military "double envelopment," the battle of Cannae where Hannibal turned both flanks of the Roman army and drove it from the field.

As if all this was not astounding enough, the new president held his lines against an onslaught from a major union, the nation's air controllers. When they struck despite presidential pleas and warnings and in the face of an explicit law against strikes by government employees (passed before Reagan), the president fired the strikers. He acted like a throwback to Calvin Coolidge, who as governor told striking Boston policemen there was "no right to strike against the public safety."

Reagan thus surprised everyone because he set out to do what he said he would do and, initially at least, succeeded. He succeeded because he was resolute and skillfully used the presidency for a "bully pulpit" as no president had done since Franklin Roosevelt. The actual powers of a president, contrary to the popular view, are limited. He cannot order the government's budget or the level of taxes, or himself pass or repeal laws. His chief power is that of persuasion.

In the past two hundred years only the means of persuasion have changed. FDR proved himself master of the radio. Reagan was the first to fully understand television, which requires more than technique taught by a TV adviser. Other presidents had practiced before the camera, experimented with different formats. None had avoided the impression of artificiality. Reagan, perhaps because of his acting experience, perhaps because it came naturally to him, understood the medium is best adapted to an easy, conversational style. He made a good impression in the living room where most of his audience watched. The reason the Democrats had defectors in the House on both budget and tax bills was that Reagan had persuaded their constituents the time had come for both, and the congressmen heard from them.

Yet if people had not been already attuned to the message Reagan preached they would not have heeded him and he would have lost. If people hadn't felt that "enough was enough" on strikes that threaten basic services, of which air service has become a major one, they would not have supported him in his stand against the air controllers' union. A political leader cannot swim against the tide.

So what struck me forcibly, that summer of 1981, was that I had now lived through a full cycle from political revolution to counter-revolution. Roosevelt, president when I began, launched the revolutionary idea that government should take the responsibility not only for the state of the economy but for much of what had formerly been left to people's own responsibility, caring for themselves in unemployment, sickness, and old age. The idea that a government is best which governs least died in the 1930s.

However needed that revolution—and I happen to believe that much of it was needed—it had outrun those who began it and turned into excess, as revolutions are wont to do. Now half-a-century and eight presidents later the country had grown weary of that revolution road and was ready to try another, one just as revolutionary.

The next question, then, was where the new road (or an old one retravelled) would lead. Would the economic policy of less government spending and less government taxes (the new phrase for it was "supply-side economics") revitalize the economy or lead to new woes? For with his victories President Reagan had given hostages to fortune both for himself and the country. If his program reduced inflation, increased capital investment, opened new job opportunities, he would be hailed by the multitude. If not, he and his ideas would get the blame.

The answer to that question would have to wait the decade of the '80s, which was beyond my vision. But I felt that whatever the answer it might at last take the nation off that political seesaw on which it had rocked for more than a generation. If the Reagan philosophy won the day, then those who offered it would gain a mandate to govern which might last through the next generation. If it failed to win the people, it would be discredited. The mandate would go elsewhere, and this time there might be no restraining those who held it.

With the approach of that three-score-and-ten milestone I could not expect to follow whatever the future held with the same vigor and excitement as I had the past. My thoughts inevitably grew retrospective. There remained only to seek what instruction I could find from my own and my country's time.

PART SEVEN

Retrospective

A man's real possession
is his memory,
in nothing else is he rich,
in nothing else is he poor.

—Alexander Smith,
*Of Death and the
Fear of Dying*

RETROSPECTIVE

ll men's lives, and women's too, differ in details, but where they share a common time they also share a common history and so common memories.

Those of us in America for whom the 1980s mark our senior years have in a lifetime lived through four of our country's wars. Two of them great world wars. One of them the most searing for our country since the Civil War.

We have lived through the greatest economic depression of modern times.

We have lived through four periods of inflation robbing us of the benefits of our labor and troubling our dream of security in our age. We have seen inflation threaten the very social contract which binds people together in common endeavor.

We have seen riots and disturbances everywhere, from the labor riots of the 1930s to the race riots of the 1960s. We have seen violence grow everywhere, in the streets of our cities, in the schoolyards of our young, even creeping behind the once sheltering walls of our homes.

Between our youth and age we've seen changes unimaginable in the mores of society, in its manners and customs, in the relation between the sexes, in the role of the family, in the rearing of the young, in the caring for the old.

In that time we watched our country grow to a preeminent place in the world, only now to fear its fading as our economic strength wanes, to see our once great cities decay, to feel our once accustomed confidence in the future diminish.

But if there is much in this to trouble the spirit, we have also seen in our time the greatest leap of knowledge the world has ever known. We've seen poverty disappearing if not yet vanished, disease reduced if not yet conquered, the life span of our species stretched beyond the imagination of our forebears.

We were born in the time of the horse and buggy when a motor car was still an object for children's curiosity. We've lived into the age of space to watch men walking upon the moon.

Politically the changes have been equally astounding. There are only dim memories of the years between Wilson and Coolidge. But the ways in which we govern ourselves in the time of Ronald Reagan are far different from the time of Franklin Roosevelt, as his time was from that of Hoover. In our adult years we've seen the political pendulum swing in great sweeps between opposing poles.

These were the years of my own, my country's time, and the measure of them can't be taken by those of lesser years. These decades are the private domain of those who shared them. So startling have been the changes in so short a span that we ourselves can hardly grasp them. But all of us, however varied our lives, have one thing in common. We survived it all.

Now we can only seek in memory something to bequeath to those who do not remember.

* * * * *

My own memories of the first Great War are small. There's that recollection of a railroad platform lined with cars of crowded soldiers where my mother in Red Cross uniform, long black tresses showing beneath a tailored kerchief, served them coffee and sandwiches. To boys far from home and off to war she must have seemed a ministering angel, as she did to me. I can also remember, with some amusement now, lying awake in bed while joyous bells rang out celebrating Armistice day and wondering why they named the celebration after my neighborhood friend Armistead Maupin.

In after years I would learn that my father, spared from the war for family reasons, was haunted by the fact he had not served while so many friends and contemporaries had. That sense of regret would grow as others held reunions to swap reminiscenses of Chateau Thierry or the Argonne Forest. In time he could talk to me about it and out of that, I am sure, grew my own feelings about what to do when my war came.

That First World War had many effects on the country. It's been said it ended America's age of innocence. But the first reaction, after all the hopes from victory were shattered in the peace, was to turn the country once more inward. In a different kind of innocence we thought nations could agree to no more war; the 1920s were the decade of disarmament treaties. If they failed, so we thought, America would nonetheless never again embroil itself in a distant war.

My college generation told itself war was made by the greed of armaments makers, whom we would abolish. We pledged ourselves against "war and fascism," seeing no contradiction in the phrase. Abroad, our contemporaries at Oxford swore nevermore "to fight for King and country." Well into the 1930s neither President Roosevelt nor the Congress would give thought to rebuilding the ramparts fallen into disrepair.

So history repeated itself. In reading of the years before 1914 I've always been surprised that people and their leaders could not see, or would not believe, the gathering war clouds until the guns of August sounded. The Kaiser, his ministers, and his generals made no effort to hide their aggressive intent. In recalling the years before 1939 it amazes me that the same blindness recurred. Except for a few lonely men, such as Winston Churchill, statesmen and people refused to believe what Adolf Hitler so plainly told them. Even after he swept up Czechoslovakia people clung to the hope of "peace for our time." Even after war broke out, after Hitler's Germany and Stalin's Russia agreed to partition Poland between them, complacency was bred by the illusion of a "phony war." Even after the Nazis, using the same war plans as the Kaiser's army, swallowed up first Belgium and then France, my country thought it a war that could not involve us. President Roosevelt, like Woodrow Wilson before him, proclaimed our neutrality. Not until 1940 would my country accept a "peacetime" draft. Not until Pearl Harbor, in 1941, would we accept that once more we were in a war of worlds.

To remember Pearl Harbor is to remember how unprepared we were. We could have equally been surprised at the Panama Canal, where I was that day. To send that ancient destroyer on which I served to fight a war was to send a popgun against the foe. Not at sea only were we unprepared. Others newly called to arms drilled with pretend-weapons, trucks pretending to be tanks, shouldered broomsticks pretending to be rifles. It was impossible to think so at the time, but the disaster at Pearl Harbor was a hidden stroke of fortune; it shocked us awake as nothing else could have. Had the Japanese been more clever and launched their war in more distant places, had Hitler not been so quick to join them by declaring war upon us, that war would have lasted longer because without the shock we would have been slower to gird ourselves as we did.

As in every war there were those who tried to shirk it, those who thought only of how to profit from it, but they were few among our total numbers. Of my childhood friends there were many who did not await the draft. I can name a dozen who wore uniforms before Pearl Harbor, one of them my brother who was before me. Those who went to later wars in Korea, and more so in Vietnam, must find it hard to believe with what willingness, though not with eagerness, my generation went to its war. Nor did those at home escape the burdens. Wives left behind, parents seeing their sons leave for battle, bore with remarkable patience the rationing of food, of gasoline, of clothes. My Frances was not alone in taking up the burden left by a departing husband, many of them destined not to return, as Tommy did not.

The reason, I think, is that as a nation we had no doubt about our purpose, a conviction missing in Korea and Vietnam. It wasn't that we feared our own shores would be invaded. Rather it was a belief that it would be a tragedy for the world if the Nazis conquered all of Europe, bringing darkness everywhere, or if the Japanese were left free to swallow all of Asia. It's not an exaggeration to say that we believed civilization was at peril, whether that belief was true or false.

It is often said, and with much truth, that Vietnam left an indelible mark on its generation precisely because it was a war of unclear purpose, one in which the whole nation was neither involved nor committed. If we had won it, that would have settled nothing. If we lost it, as we did, the result would be disaster neither for our own country nor the world. I have no doubt that this want of believed purpose was responsible for the woes it brought. I can only say that the war of my generation also left its indelible mark. None of us escaped it. It had its effect on our thinking ever afterward.

The mark was left not only by the war itself but by its aftermath. For with a mighty effort, at the cost of millions of lives, the new world once more came to the rescue of the old. We vanquished all our enemies. Yet having done so, we found the hopes of victory once more turned to dust. Europe was left split asunder, a full half of it engulfed by the Soviet Union which we had done so much to save from being conquered. In Asia, Korea was partitioned, Southeast Asia left prey to chaos, the Communists free to do what we would not let the Japanese do: conquer all of China. The disillusionment was deep and lasting.

If it had not all happened, no one would believe it.

What has all this ancient history, you ask, to do with present days?

My generation is in no position to give lessons. In our time we made too big a mess of things. But we cannot avoid a sense of déjà vu seeing another aggressor eager for conquest and making no secret of it. Our problem is that we remember the twin perils of too much complacency, giving faith to talk of disarmament among nations, and of the mistaken pride that our arms alone could defend all. Others will have to find their way, as we did not, between these two: on one side the siren song of Scylla promising peace and on the other the whirlpool of Charybdis which can entrap those who too much venture. We remain astonished, all the same, at hearing so many voices say again that because war is "unthinkable" it cannot come and that we therefore need not arm against it. It was because our times would not learn from history that in 1939 we were doomed to repeat 1914.

If my generation has an excuse, and we sorely seek one, it was that the 1930s found us already beaten down by the Great Depression.

* * * * *

The Great Depression arrived just as we were coming of age.

The 1920s spanned our adolescence and few of us were aware that they were boom times or that shadows already lay over them. I can't recall paying any attention to business or economics. Insofar as I thought about family finances at all it was to think us "comfortable," not so rich as other families with expensive cars and mansions but certainly not poor. I was more interested in Babe Ruth, Big Bill Tilden, doing the Charleston, winding the Victrola to play "I scream, you scream, we all scream for ice cream," listening to Amos and Andy on the radio, looking at short skirts and bobbed hair. Even my mother bobbed hers. When the stock market crashed in October 1929, I was in that monastery of Webb School. If I heard anything about it, I paid no attention.

For many the depression really began about 1933. That year, my second in college, Roosevelt closed the banks. That caught our attention, but I must confess it was more exciting than worrisome; it was fun to just "write chits" for meals at the New Deal cafe or even for the movies, none of us having any money. But the University at Chapel Hill was no monastery. It was at the time one of the most liberal and intellectually stimulating in the South. Professors awakened our interest in the world beyond and gave us the awareness that much was awry. The early New Deal stimulated that interest and, like many students, I came to have many "radical" ideas about the mismanagement of the economy, flirting with the promises of socialism. Others were even more radical, tempted by Marxism. After I graduated and found my Phi Beta Kappa key got me no more than a busboy's job, the word "depression" became tangible.

I was luckier than many and there's a temptation in age to romanticize youthful adventures (I could be a busboy or a bank messenger with no loss of pride), but for others, especially those of middle age, there was nothing romantic about any of it. That depression, be it noted, lasted until the outbreak of World War II. Despite all the economic experiments of the New Deal there had been little improvement by 1939.

As I look back on those years, my surprise is not that there was some radicalism but that there was so little of it. The flirtation with Marxism was largely confined to intellectuals, academics and journalists. There were, as we learned later, a few who succumbed to the allure of Russian communism to the extent that they secretly plotted to aid it, the Alger Hiss–Whittaker Chambers affair being the most notable. But you might have thought communism would catch hold of many among the people, especially the young and the dispossessed who were numbered in the millions. It didn't, even among the blacks who had the greatest cause for despair or among the unemployed in industry who had cause enough. I can't explain it except to say that people in general had more faith in the American experiment than some of those whom we might have expected to have it most.

That depression left its scar on all my generation. It explains, at least in part, our early reluctance to recognize the gathering war clouds or to get involved once again in foreign entanglements. Our eyes were fixed on the economic struggle here at home. Ironically, that depression, as I could see in hindsight, helped us when at last we were in the war. The country had a large reservoir of underutilized capacity which we could quickly put to use. An economy stretched taut or in the grip of inflation would have found the task more difficult.

That depression experience, it also seems to me, played an enduring role in American politics.

Just as generals are said to "fight the last war," so economists and politicians kept looking backward at other times. They have clung to economic policies aimed at warding off another depression and thus in time have brought on new and different economic woes. The word "inflation" did not appear in the political vocabulary until after the war was won. We would hear it many times in the years ahead.

*　　*　　*　　*　　*

Those of us returning from the war met it in 1945–46. When I was rehired by the *Journal* my pay was increased from $75 to $125 a week, an increase of over 60 percent, and seeming to me a fortune. I was quickly disillusioned when I went to buy food and shelter. A small example of the change from my own experience: the 1939 Chevrolet Frances and I had bought for $850 we sold in 1946 for $800, but its replacement cost us nearly $2,000.

Now that I have read much on the origins of that depression I find that some blame it on the Federal Reserve's monetary policies, swinging from "easy money" to restriction. Some on the carelessness of the banking community which overextended itself in making loans. Some on the overoptimism that the 1920s spurred in industry. Some on the public's mood for speculation in the stock market, in real estate and elsewhere. The whole country seemed to be imbued with the idea that everything must grow ever upward and onward. What's worth noting now, it seems to me, is the common denominator in all of these various explanations. The word "excess" applies to all. And with it the very human belief that "what is will continue to be." Everyone knew there had been panics and depressions before. Almost everyone was convinced they couldn't happen again. It was, in general, the same sort of psychology that made people, despite World War I, turn a blind eye to the coming of World War II.

There must be something deep in the human psyche that makes it difficult for people to retain old lessons. The idea that "something will make it different next time" will not be downed. The country suffered an inflation after World War I (the "boom"), after World War II, after Korea, after Vietnam. It became especially virulent in the late 1970s, carrying over into the 1980s. And always for the same reason—the idea that the government can in effect print money (to fight a war or whatever) and we can escape the consequences.

Does anyone remember when in the 1950s the whole world was supposedly suffering from a "dollar shortage" and learned economists told us it would be permanent unless the U.S. did something about it? We did; we pumped out dollars all over the world as well as at home. And the next thing we knew there was a worldwide inflation sparked largely by the huge pile of "Eurodollars" floating everywhere, beyond control or even of reckoning. This was not what was intended by the Marshall Plan, a worthy effort of the new world to come to the aid of the old in peace as in war. The difficulty arose because it worked so well, did so much to restore the economic health of Europe to the benefit of all, that we began to think from our limitless resources we could do the same for the whole world. We recklessly poured out dollars in foreign aid everywhere. The crunch came when we found out our resources weren't limitless after all. And we did little by way of increasing savings and new investment to improve and enlarge our industrial resources.

Not all of this was the fault of government which was, after all, responding to what politicians thought the people wanted done. When I returned to the *Journal* in 1946 one of the first series of articles I wrote for it was an account of how the steel mills, the shipyards, and other industrial plants of Japan had been levelled by our bombings, and I noted that as they were rebuilt they would be perforce new, modernized with the latest technological developments. The same applied to Germany, although I had no such personal evidence to cite. Meanwhile we would enter the 1950s and beyond with industrial plants of the 1940s. I think today this had much to do with the rapidity with which the industry of Japan and Germany caught up with ours and in some areas surpassed us. Anyway, there is surely irony in the fact that the defeated nations emerged rather quickly with some gains from their total defeat. It was a long time before the managers of American industry awoke to the fact that they had new competitors better equipped. Imported steel from Germany, to use one example, became the modern equivalent of shipping coals to Newcastle.

If for the past forty years we have lived under the shadow of another world war, this time with the terror it could be more destructive than any before, it has also been for want of learning from past lessons. In Korea, and especially in Vietnam, we wasted our strength on what in global terms were skirmishes. Then we paid the price of the revulsion from that. We not only let our arms deteriorate. We also as a people fell into a mood not unlike that my generation can remember before 1939. We grew enamored of the idea that the Soviet Union would be reasonable if only we would proffer gestures of peace, just as before we thought Hitler and Tojo would be. By 1980 the country would no more tolerate the idea that the young should be prepared to defend it than it did in the days of my youth.

Of course I cannot say that history will again repeat itself. I fervently hope not, for the next global war, if it should come, is too terrifying to contemplate. I would myself join the marchers crying "ban the bomb" if it were possible to do so, but knowledge once released from Pandora's box cannot be stuffed back into it. What those marchers really cry for is for us alone to ban the bomb, which would truly leave us defenseless before our enemies. My generation did learn that when that happens, history can repeat itself, and we paid a huge price for the lesson.

* * * * *

Depression and war, however, were not our only shared experiences. In our time we saw much change in our country and in the world, some felt with foreboding, much with gratitude.

We are most grateful for, and proud of, the changes wrought in our time in the relation between the races, black and white, which had so long been a haunting shame upon the country. That change, as everyone knows, did not come easily, nor has it been complete. But a younger generation can hardly grasp what a revolution has been wrought.

I recall one day recently flying to Atlanta when my seat companion in the first-class section was a young black man, well-dressed, well-mannered, and obviously well-educated. He told me he was a computer programmer for IBM. Then as our conversation became relaxed he also talked of the plight of blacks in the country which he thought had basically changed little. My first impulse, I'll admit, was to respond by saying that I could remember when he would not have held his present position, that in fact he and I would not be travelling together, and that this was surely a measure of both change and progress. I restrained myself after thinking that we both were right. I for seeing so much change, he for thinking so much left to change.

What has happened, I think, is that the race problem has taken a different shape. When I was growing up in Dixie, white and black were two societies living closely together but separate and unequal. When the members were personally close there was mutual respect and affection, as my relationshps with Mamie, Lucinda, and most of all Skibo were typical. A few blacks with enterprise made successful businesses, mostly in insurance or retail sales. Few, though, were doctors, lawyers or other professionals. For the most part their schools, and not in the South only, were inferior. Blacks rarely voted or had much influence in the affairs of their communities.

When I came back to Dixie the situation was hardly recognizable. As with my airplane seat companion I met many who had "made it" in business, in politics, in the professions. Chapel Hill had a black mayor, the University black professors and black students. On the whole they were accepted and respected by their peers. There were also by then a number of first-class black schools—or "predominantly black schools" as the euphemism had it—including St. Augustine's College which I served as a trustee. The change would have astounded anyone of my father's generation.

All the same, my airplane acquaintance had a point. What was happening was the emergence of an elite group no longer handicapped by (and perhaps even benefiting from) being black. But beneath this level of the successful there were many blacks who had benefited little, some not at all. Every society, including white America, has its underclass, those who for one reason or another do not, or cannot, fit into the larger society. For the blacks this underclass has been relatively more numerous, living at or below the poverty line, dependent on welfare in one of its many forms. It struck me as early as the late 1970s that the white-black race schism was being replaced by internal black separation, a class differential. The black lawyer, doctor, or university professor had no more in common, socially or in political outlook, with the semiliterate black than his white counterpart in white society; less, perhaps, because this difference was a new one in black society. Meanwhile the older and outmoded close personal relationship which had existed in the South between black and white was fast disappearing. The relationship might be formally correct but it was as distant as in other parts of the country.

I must leave it to the sociologist to explain all this, to the future to show whether the growing class consciousness among blacks will lead to a new kind of race problem. I only set down what I observed.

I found other differences, too, between the old South and the new. When I was growing up, North Carolina was primarily a rural state of farms and small towns. The few industries, mostly textile mills, were in the Piedmont area, a narrow strip in midstate. By the 1970s many industries were moving southward and a new phrase had entered our vocabulary, the Sun Belt. The change was mainly due to technology, the development of air conditioning. A common habit of my childhood summers was for the whole family to get in the car after supper, drive around for an hour or so just to cool off, ending up usually with ice cream for the children, Cokes for the elders. Then home to try to sleep in temperatures ranging into the high nineties and beyond, the electric fans swirling helplessly against the heat. I remember many restless nights abed wearing only shorts with the perspiration rolling down. The climate, not any innate qualities, gave rise to the traditional image of the "lazy Southerner" or the "shiftless black." Air conditioning, when it came to homes, offices and factories, changed all of that. The South became a pleasant place to live and work.

Air conditioning was not the only technology to alter the South. Despite the example of Birmingham, the South was not well adapted to such heavy industries as steelmaking. It adapts well to what are called "light" industries, such as those made possible by electronics. They opened all manner of new job opportunities. That in its turn helped improve the position of blacks, quite apart from the social changes, and it accounts for much of the reversal of migration, which once saw blacks fleeing to the north and now sees the tide reversed. A lot of things have interacted to make the New South.

Thus the plight of blacks in the South as the nation entered the 1980s was not as bleak as in the crowded Northern industrial areas. They were not as dispossessed by unemployment as in, say, Detroit when the auto industry had to layoff thousands of workers. The South had its racial clashes during the civil rights struggle. But the more dreadful violence occurred in such places as New York's Harlem, Los Angeles' Watts area, and other places where unemployed blacks were packed together in hopelessness.

I do not mean to say that the South has become a paradise for blacks, particularly the ill-educated who make up an underclass, but the changes I found were nonetheless immense. There were equal changes even for the white population. To my generation the greater opportunities for the ambitious seemed to lie elsewhere, which is why I fled Dixie in 1935. This is no longer so true. In the South today the lawyer will find firms as prosperous and prestigious as elsewhere. There are many great teaching hospitals for doctors, universities offering opportunities for recognition to scholars. The horizons in business are wider for those of entrepreneurial or managerial bent. The South today is not losing its best young, black or white, to other parts of the country. There is no longer a "brain drain."

All of this, quite apart from the nostalgia of coming home, explains the satisfaction I found in returning to the land of my youth.

2

Some years ago on a television program an interviewer asked whom I would name as the "greatest" presidents of my journalistic days. Caught unawares, I answered without much thinking, Roosevelt and Eisenhower. This caught the interviewer by surprise. He had expected Roosevelt. He was puzzled by the other choice. At that time President Eisenhower was thought of in the intellectual community, and among those who took themselves to be members of that community, as a sort of hero father-figure the country might have needed but neither a forceful president nor a man of any intellectual perceptions. So the interviewer asked me, with obvious curiosity, why I named him.

This time I had to pause to ask myself why, a rather long pause for television which abhors nothing so much as silence on a talk-show. Finally I said, "Because he did the least damage of any president, left behind the fewest problems for his successors."

Since then, of course, the publication of Eisenhower's letters and diary have altered his public image. They show that he was indeed a man of perception who saw rather clearly the men and issues of his time, had given them much thought and rendered reasonable, if private, judgments. There was more depth to the man than anyone gave him credit for.

But I still like my impulsive assessment. For I have been struck by how often presidents come to office to wrestle with problems left by their predecessors and then, even if they are successful with those, leave behind other problems for the presidents who come after.

Franklin Roosevelt inherited the depression from Herbert Hoover. Despite all his experiments he never solved it; the "recession" (a nice euphemism) of 1937–38 disappointed and depressed his supporters. But FDR did for the country what Winston Churchill was later to do for his; he held up people's spirits in a time of trouble. Roosevelt's oratory was no match for Churchill's, but his inaugural phrase "we have nothing to fear but fear itself" served notice that he would never surrender to the economic foe. He never did, although he swung violently from budget cutting to bigger budget deficits, from the cartelism of the National Recovery Administration (NRA) to even more vigorous trust-busting than his cousin Teddy Roosevelt. FDR injected the federal government into the nation's life as never before, where it was to remain even in the administration of Ronald Reagan.

If only for his maintenance of the national morale in the 1930s, Roosevelt deserves the appellation of a great president. He was also, when the time came, a superb wartime leader. From Pearl Harbor onward the nation had no doubt it would emerge victorious no matter how long it took. Roosevelt will remain, then, a towering figure in the history books.

But he also left Harry Truman a burdensome inheritance, a world divided by the peace plans Roosevelt insisted on. The tragedy of FDR lay in hubris, the self-confidence that grew into overweening pride. He thought he could "handle" Joseph Stalin. That hubris also proved a tragedy for the world.

Truman met his inherited challenges with courage, clear eyes as to Stalin, and with bold action. He didn't hesitate to use the atom bomb to end the war in Asia, saving millions of lives thereby for the thousands who died at Hiroshima and Nagasaki. After Okinawa I was privy to our plans for invading Japan and had no doubt of their cost. Those who afterward blamed Truman for ushering in the nuclear age, or took upon the whole country the burden of that guilt, mistake the relentless history of science. The nuclear age would have come anyway.

Truman also met the Soviet challenge at Berlin with boldness, defying the efforts to blockade that island city set by Roosevelt in the midst of a Communist sea. The Marshall Plan testifies to Truman's vision of the need to resuscitate even our former enemies. He made both West Germany and Japan a beneficiary of magnanimity. None of this can be taken from his credit.

Unhappily, President Truman didn't recognize the limits of boldness. Once he proclaimed the doctrine of resisting Communist aggression everywhere a Korea somewhere became inevitable. So did a Vietnam when President Kennedy not only accepted but broadened that doctrine. Kennedy, cut off in midstream, thus left the country mired in a bog from which Lyndon Johnson couldn't extricate it.

Also unhappily, President Truman didn't recognize that the Keynsian economic policies of spending a nation into prosperity, even if they made sense during the depression, made no sense in the postwar world. We already had the inflationary pressures built up from World War II spending. Truman added to them with his spending for a "welfare state" and for the Korean war. The consequences of that would be long with us.

Which brings us to Eisenhower. Imagine, for a moment, any new president being inaugurated. What would the country hope from his days in office? First, surely, no war. If we were in one at his beginning, that it would end; if we were at peace, that it would not be broken. Beyond that, some years of economic stability with a minimum of inflation and, if there must be recessions that they would be mild at worst. That this new president would give the country confidence in its government and in itself. Finally, that when his time passed his successor would not find the country faced with huge new problems.

This, in my opinion, is what Dwight Eisenhower did for his country as president. He ended the Korean War and brought on no other. He could not eliminate the effects of wartime inflation, but by boldly ending the wage-price controls he permitted the country to adjust to past inflation. He met the racial troubles at Little Rock with firmness, and though that did not spare us further racial turmoil it set a precedent that would keep the turmoil from being worse.

During the 1960 campaign Senator Kennedy did try to blame a "missile gap" on Eisenhower, but once in office President Kennedy admitted it never existed. Indeed, it was Eisenhower, the former general, who did most to keep a tight rein on the military and its budget. He left office with the country reasonably prosperous, suffering a minimum of inflation and facing no new problems ahead.

It's been fashionable in some quarters to put all this down to "luck." But I've noticed that in his long career Eisenhower seemed always to be credited with luck, from the Normandy landing to the Battle of the Bulge, with little credit for what he may have done to create it. However that may be, the Eisenhower years in retrospect were "the best years of our lives" from Roosevelt through Carter. As for Reagan, it will be a decade before we can take his measure.

The country surely had no luck with those after Eisenhower. Kennedy left Lyndon Johnson embroiled in Vietnam, despite Eisenhower's warnings against a land war in Asia. Johnson dug us deeper into that mire, and by trying to have "both guns and butter," launched the virulent inflation that would plague us into the 1980s. Nixon, inheriting all this, added Watergate to the Gerald Ford inheritance, from which Ford never escaped. Jimmy Carter, man of good will, left an even more fierce inflation to his successor and to a discouraged country.

So even after time for reflection I will stick with my impulsive answer to that inquiring TV interviewer.

* * * * *

Each of these presidents, Roosevelt through Reagan, had different personalities, different perceptions of their office and of the country's needs, different abilities and different frailties. They make a study in contrasts.

The essence of Roosevelt was his aristocratic lineage. Not only had he a kinsman who had been president before him, the whole

Roosevelt clan had deep roots in America and by virtue of "old money," by education (mostly Harvard) and by tradition came as close to being an aristocracy as we have. FDR was deeply marked by a sense of family and public service. He was ambitious, yes, but it was an ambition to fulfill what he felt was a destiny.

He was not a man of great intellectual capacity. He came to office with no clear idea of how to deal with the depression, as his early zigzagging showed. But he was bothered by no uncertainty as to who he was and no hesitancy brought on by fear of mistakes. Probably the best phrase for his quality was a feeling for leadership, almost in the military sense. Like a good general he sought to surround himself with those who had more expertise than he without ever yielding to them the responsibility for final decisions. It's a quality great leaders have always had. Lincoln had it, so did Churchill, so did de Gaulle.

In time that very same quality would lead Roosevelt to his blunders. Too much success can entrap all but the wisest men, and that kind of wisdom was not among Roosevelt's qualities. Put him down, all the same, as the man for his times. His personal tragedy was that he lived beyond his times, was old and sick when he had to make his final judgments.

Harry Truman was entirely different. He came out of nowhere, a failed haberdasher whose only path to rising in the world was that of politics. He entered it not as an aristocrat but as a protegé of the Pendergast machine in Kansas City. It was an accident of politics that brought him the vice-presidency, where he was left by Roosevelt outside the councils of state and even in ignorance of what went on there. It was fate that put him in the White House at a fateful moment.

But Harry Truman had other qualities. One was a deeply ingrained love of country and with it a sense of the majesty and obligation of its presidency. He also had a shrewd common sense, a rarer quality than we may suppose. All this served him well when "the sun and the moon and the stars" fell on him one day in 1945.

Some say his common sense deserted him in his too-quick dismantlement of the armed forces. That was a mistake, I agree. But I doubt if Truman could have halted it; the country after four years at war was insisting that he "bring the boys home." It did desert him, in my opinion, in his later dealings with General MacArthur in Korea. Given the snap decision to fight in Korea, he gave the general too loose a rein; probably after the Inchon landings he should have halted MacArthur's northward advance at the fortieth parallel, accomplishing our initial "war aims." Thereafter he couldn't possibly rein-in MacArthur without trouble.

Other Truman troubles weren't altogether his own making. He could hardly be expected to abandon the Roosevelt economic policies. He was right to push his civil rights program, but for that the political times were out of joint; having to resist even more liberal programs from his left wing he was caught between two nether stones. His basic problem was that the country expected him to be Roosevelt, which he wasn't and couldn't be.

Nevertheless of all the presidents I found Truman one of the most "likeable." There was a down-to-earth quality about him that was appealing. As for his scrappy, sometimes belligerent manner, his need to always insist "I am the boss," I always felt this masked a feeling of insecurity in the job he had been thrust into. He tried to do the best he could, which was all the country had any right to expect from him. And his accomplishments—the Berlin airlift, the Marshall Plan, the magnanimity toward Japan—outweigh his mistakes in the long run.

Eisenhower, like Truman, was a poor boy of undistinguished family. But, like Roosevelt, he had acquired self-assurance, a feeling of his own merit, not from lineage but from his army career, especially from his command of the greatest army ever assembled. I never got close enough to him to think of him as likeable. What I felt for him, as did the country, was enormous respect.

If Eisenhower's military career gave him self-assurance, it also affected his personality in other ways. While he had a keen political sense in many respects, it always seemed to me he had little appreciation of the role of party in American politics. In fact, he disapproved of it. He had a marvellous opportunity to rebuild the Republican party of which he was the nominal leader, but he never seized it. Consequently he left the party no stronger than when he came to office. The rebuilding of a viable two-party system, so important in our political system, would have to await another time. This aspect of his personality, I'm convinced, contributed to the narrow defeat of Vice-President Nixon by John Kennedy.

President Kennedy, for all his charisma, wasn't in office long enough to acquire the self-confidence of either Roosevelt or Eisenhower. At that long luncheon at the Carlyle Hotel on the morrow of his election victory I could sense an inner insecurity. Kennedy's family was as wealthy, or more so, as Roosevelt's. It was "new money," however, without the patina of generations to give it an aristocratic mien. And in his time his Boston Irish ancestry gave no assured social position as that enjoyed by Roosevelt. He hadn't had, either, the Eisenhower advantage of long previous command responsibility. Intelligence he had, as well as charm, which might in time have built self-confidence. Who knows what he might have become but for that day in Dallas?

A feeling of insecurity also marked his immediate successors, Lyndon Johnson and Richard Nixon, somewhat surprising in both. It accounts, I think, for much of their failures. Johnson, though a superb man of the legislature, never felt comfortable in the White House. Neither did Nixon, for all that he may have been our most "intellectual" president since Wilson. Both reacted to it by overassertiveness. With Johnson this led to the disaster of Vietnam. With Nixon it contained the roots of Watergate.

Nonetheless, it should be noted that in chancelleries abroad few presidents have been as highly regarded as Richard Nixon. Years after his downfall he was still welcomed by high officials abroad whom he visited. His reconciliation with Communist China redounds to his credit. At home, though, he remained a continuing source of controversy unforgiven by many, as the turmoil at Duke University, his law school alma mater, over accepting his papers would illustrate. All in all, I have to put down Richard Nixon as the strangest, most puzzling of the presidents of my time. I liked the man in many ways, admired him in others, but even now I cannot explain him.

Gerald Ford was the most placid of those presidents. When I had my first formal interview with him, on the eve of his becoming president, his composure amid all the drama swirling around him was astonishing. He retained that calm all through his administration. Whether he was being attacked for his Nixon pardon, ridiculed for his ineffectual anti-inflation program (remember those WIN buttons), made the butt of jokes for bumping his head on airplane doors, or being assailed by Reagan on the right, Carter on the left, he remained unruffled. Of all our presidents he became also the best adjusted to being "ex." In many ways he was just "an ordinary man," but his very calm served the country well in the turbulence of Watergate wake.

Jimmy Carter was, to me, an enigma from my first meeting with him until the end of his White House years. Personally appealing, he seemed in his campaign to have clear ideas of what he wanted to do as president, but when he became president he set no clear, consistent course. He zigzagged repeatedly from being economy-minded to being a spendthrift, from advocating a strong military to curtailing it, and back again. There was an ambivalence in all his policy positions, even in his view of the presidency itself in which he began trying to be "just folks" (carrying his own luggage, abolishing "Hail To The Chief") and ended by relishing the trappings of office as much as any White House occupant. His only real success was the Camp David agreement between Begin and Sadat, and even that had begun to fray before he left office. My own feeling about Carter was that he was a very nice man who wanted to be president but never really decided what he wanted to do with the office after he won it. He was, take it all in all, simply ineffectual.

About all I can say about Ronald Reagan, while we await the verdict of time, is that he came to office with more thoroughly developed ideas of what he wanted to accomplish with the office than any of his predecessors. Those ideas were controversial, possibly mistaken, but at least on domestic policy clearly thought-out and firmly believed. He also had a charm peculiarly his own, unlike that of Roosevelt or Kennedy but equally appealing.

It was these qualities—the consistency and persistency of his political ideas and his "likeability"—that finally put Ronald Reagan in the White House. By then the political pendulum had swung so far hardly anyone was surprised. What surprised nearly everybody (myself included) was that within six months he won from a reluctant Congress at least formal acquiescence to huge budget cuts. He ran over Democratic opposition to enact a three-year tax cut of unprecedented proportions. It was a performance unmatched since Roosevelt. And even when, as inevitably happened, the bloom was off his political honeymoon and his critics grew bolder, Reagan retained his good humor. I had the impression he was the first president since Eisenhower to feel comfortable in the Oval Office, or at least not awed by it. In his case I put it down to the maturity of age—he was seventy when he took office—and to the fact that he was confident of his own political ideas.

Altogether, then, a fascinating group of men to have led the country during my journalistic years. I defy anyone to draw from them a pattern of what it takes to become president of the United States or of what it takes to be successful in that office. Personally, I'm glad to have known them all, if not intimately at least well enough so that for me they aren't vague figures in the headlines or the history books.

3

The changes in the country between the time of my childhood and that of my age weren't limited to politics. The alterations in society in its behavior and attitudes have also been profound. To my generation many of them are astounding, and we cannot avoid being affected by them.

One has been the changing attitude toward education. I found myself at war with the "educationists" long before I returned to Chapel Hill to teach myself. It began with that discovery, when our daughter Bonnie was in high school, that in teaching Latin the New York approved textbook eliminated all those subjunctives from Caesar's Latin, that even Dickens's language had been "simplified." With this background I shouldn't have been surprised later to find many college juniors floundering in the English language. It was not their fault. Many from the public school system had simply never been taught spelling, grammar, or how to use those tools to express themselves. Teaching at the elementary and secondary level had come to be viewed as a matter of "technique," having only a remote connection with what was taught. To assign lessons in, say, spelling or arithmetic or the facts of history (as, for instance, dates) and demand they be memorized and recited to the teacher was thought to stultify the children. "Learning by rote" was a pejorative phrase in the new educational philosophy, a misinterpretation of the ideas of John Dewey.

Yet there is no way to learn spelling or the multiplication tables without learning by rote. A child who has to think out for himself every time the product of eight times five instead of knowing the answer from memory is ill-equipped for the world he must live in. So also if he does not know by rote the varied spellings of "two," "too," and "to" and by authoritarian rules the proper use of each.

At the root of the new attitude toward education was the idea that young people shouldn't be *required* to learn anything. Put in the requisite number of years in high school and you were "entitled" to a diploma. One consequence was the devaluation of a high school diploma; it couldn't be trusted to mean anything. The loss was both to the person himself, ill-prepared to make his or her way in the real world, and to society. This did particular injury to those underprivileged in their home environment, as was the case with many young blacks. The schools thus failed to make up for the handicaps of those not raised in families where reading is a habit, where learning is a family tradition.

Accompanying this was a breakdown in all forms of discipline, in behavior as well as study. By the late 1960s the phrase "blackboard jungle" had become familiar as a description of pupil behavior in public schools, especially those in the cities. It was not unusual for school authorities to have to call in police to patrol the corridors. Although the new ideas about education cannot escape some responsibility for this breakdown in order, it would be unfair to blame it all on teachers and principals. Much of it was both a symptom and a consequence of a general breakdown in former restraints on societal behavior. These were the years of "anything goes," when adults as well as the young proclaimed the right "to do your own thing."

The signs of this breakdown were visible in many areas. One of the most noticeable was what came to be called the sexual revolution against old mores. It would be seen in the rising divorce rate and its effect on family life, in the wide acceptance of sexual promiscuity and casual "living together" as a norm of behavior, in the swelling figures on illegitimate births and the ready availability of abortions which were its consequence. Teenage pregnancies became commonplace. So did venereal disease, which once we thought we had conquered. It was a revolution that crossed all "class lines" of education or family tradition.

I shan't pretend that I welcomed that revolution and its accompaniments. A society that is not bound by some socially accepted restraints on behavior stands always at risk of disintegration. But I think it futile to repeat the cry *O Tempora, O Mores* that has rung down the years since old Cicero first uttered it. Not misplaced necessarily, but futile surely.

For I think much of the sexual revolution, if not its accompaniments, was probably inevitable. The barriers against divorce, legal and social, had been crumbling for a century under the relentless pressure of a new role for women. Modern medicine freed them from endless childbearing. Modern technology freed them from household drudgery with clothes-washers, dish-washers, and vacuum cleaners. Job opportunities became wider; the fractional horsepower motor made it possible for them, if they wished, to drive heavy trucks. Education opportunities opened the professions to the ambitious. Laws made divorce easier. What all this made inevitable was that more women left the confines of home, and as more did so the social barriers against divorce and sexual freedom came down also. How much this reflects a real change in marital stability is uncertain. When childbearing was a woman's main role, when few ways to earn a living were open to her, when divorces were difficult, there were naturally few divorces. But that only disguised many marriages unhappy for both partners; it also made for furtive sexual relationships. Present divorce statistics, which seem so alarming, could thus be misleading. The present situation may provide a better relationship between men and women because it puts both on an equal plane.

Yet that conceded, I have no doubt that the sexual revolution found a parallel in the breakdown of other mores. A danger of any revolution is that it may not remain within its borders. Once one restraining barrier, political or social, is broken, others become vulnerable.

By the decade of the 1970s I could see little consensus in the country as to what was acceptable or not acceptable in social behavior short of murder and rape. Inhibitions against the use of drugs, from pot to cocaine, were diminishing if not vanishing. Violence had become endemic, crime in the streets flourishing in the cities and creeping into towns and hamlets. Peaceable folk walked warily and barred themselves at night behind double-locked doors. The sale of burglar alarms and electronic surveillance systems had become a booming business. On my university campus women students did not move alone after dark. Cheating in the classroom may not have been more prevalent than in my student days (how do you measure it?), but in contrast with my time it was accepted by both students and faculty without any great stigma attached to it. All this I could not, in my anachronistic way, view with equanimity.

Yet put me not down as a Jeremiah bewailing all his times, with only wormwood to eat and the water of gall to drink. There are other ways to measure the quality of life.

Had I been born a generation earlier I would never have approached the three-score-and-ten. I have lived to see the tuberculosis sanitoriums become antiquarian memories, smallpox and the plague conquered, and a host of other infectious diseases, including many forms of pneumonia, nearly so. My maternal grandfather died of "an inflammation of the bowels," known now as appendicitis, which for both Frances and myself was a ten-day inconvenience. My mother and father died of cancer. I have now survived a decade after my own carcinoma. Year by year the mortality statistics have reflected the stretching of our life-spans. The hazards of sickness, to be sure, have not been obliterated, but a person of seventy, or even eighty, is no longer a curiosity to be remarked upon. If this aging of the population has brought problems to which society has not yet fully adjusted, as for example with the Social Security program launched in the 1930s, for those of my generation—make no mistake about it—it's a boon unimagined in prior times.

There is also the simple fact that poverty in my country, though yet much talked of, bears no relation to that of those prior times or to that known still in other places. The county "poorhouse" is no more. The soup kitchens of the 1930s have shrunk. Unemployment remains among the unhappiest of burdens but it is, nonetheless, not the scourge it once was; Charles Dickens would be astounded. If to many "the affluent society" remains a hyperbole of a hyperbolic writer, it's a reach that doesn't exceed our grasp, which is more than can be said of other times or other countries. This too has brought its problems, social and economic, one of them being the insidiousness of inflation. Few of the survivors, nonetheless, would swap them for the pains of that Great Depression.

In fact, everywhere you look—if you will pause to think about them—are contributions to the quality of life newer generations are hardly conscious of. In my childhood a trip from Raleigh to Chapel Hill, a distance of some thirty miles, was an all-day journey. Most people would spend their lives within a circumference of a hundred miles. Few were those who ever glimpsed a foreign country; travel was the province of the rich and those with the leisure time to spare for it. The technology of modern transportation has shrunk not only the expanse of our country but of the world. First the movies and then television have brought to people not only a wider range of entertainment but also an awareness of other cultures, other peoples, once beyond their reach. When I first attended that Roosevelt press conference I was a privileged person indeed. Today the whole country can, if it chooses, see its president in action. The same technology, of course, makes people witness to terrible and upsetting events, from a massacre at an olympic village to assassination attempts on presidents and popes. But for better or worse modern transportation and communications help bring the whole world within our ken.

Everywhere I look I find the effects of technology on culture to be immense. It is, of course, a mixed blessing. The nuclear age threatens terrible destruction; it also holds promise of great advancements in medicine, much already visible, and in enlarging the world's energy resources, as yet more promise than fulfillment. So with the space program. It began as a tool of the military. It remains that, but it has also given us the magic of computers whose promise taxes our imagination. Its satellites in the sky offer another huge leap in global communications. All of this, blessing and curse, affects our politics, our social attitudes, our very vision of the future. Technology, put simply, has reshaped our lives.

There is another reason why I am not a Jeremiah, or a Miniver Cheevy praising every century but his own. I have lived long enough to learn that pendulums swing both ways. I have seen the swing dramatically in our politics, but not in politics alone. The pendulum has swung as well, or at least begun to, in social attitudes that both affect and reach beyond politics.

The swing back in education is already pronounced. In North Carolina, as in other states, there is a move backward in the primary schools to more stress on the fundamentals of reading, writing and arithmetic. The idea that everyone is "entitled" to a high school diploma regardless of accomplishment has been abandoned. There's a return to recognition that different children should be taught differently; for those with different talents there are now within the publicly supported school system special schools for the arts, for mathematics, for mechanics and other fields. In 1980 my own university reinstated its older requirement that its undergraduates must study both mathematics and a foreign language, giving up the idea that one is a substitute for the other. Chapel Hill is not alone in this. Verily a revolution! Or more accurately, I suppose, a counterrevolution.

This change in educational views, if it holds against its critics, is bound to bring many other changes in our societal attitudes. It could even begin a counterrevolution in manners, morals and behavior. A change here can be detected in the rising influence of what's been called (and denounced in some quarters) as the "moral majority" with its emphasis on marriage and family, on ethical and moral teaching for the young. I confess that for my own part I am put off by the stridency of some of this moral majority with their rigid religious fundamentalism. I understand, though, what has brought it about and I can at least sympathize with the yearning it represents.

The yearning is for society to recapture some of the older attitudes once held to be virtues. Among them are a sense of duty, honesty, loyalty, obligation, even chastity, words almost vanished from the common vocabulary, while such once-honored words as "gentleman" or "lady" have lost their meaning. The yearning, put simply, is for a renewal of common belief in the qualities once embodied in the "copybook maxims."

Whether the future will bring such a renewal I will have to leave to the future. But such a renewal cannot come from any kind of authoritarianism, that of religious dogma or any other. It can only come, if it comes, from within ourselves. Meanwhile, my generation has had to learn to live in a country far different from that of our childhood and youth. For my own part, I find in those changes some to cheer for, some to weep for. And I am not always sure which is which.

For such ideas on the society and politics of these later years I've been labelled as a "conservative" or something called a "nineteenth-century liberal." I don't think either label fits. I'm certainly not a conservative if the word means, as it so often seems to, an opposition to change for opposition's sake. I think of myself, rather, as a radical for there is much I would like to see change in both society and politics. I have no desire to return to the nineteenth-century romanticized in memory as the pinnacle of an enlightened age. Yet I do believe that our heritage from the past contains values worth conserving as we approach the end of the twentieth century. I also happen to believe those values will be rediscovered, for as mankind time and again does forget old lessons it always relearns them, as children do those of their fathers.

I think that makes me an optimist, or at least a romantic. Anyway, my regret is that I won't live long enough to see how the pendulum swings in the twenty-first century.

4

In the garnering of memories from so long a time there are many all my generation share, those of our wars, of economic troubles, of social upheavals, of shifting mores, of political change both here and in the world around us. There are other memories, though, personal to each of us, the private ones that differ by circumstance. My own seem especially rich.

I don't mean only those from having a ringside seat to observe presidents and politics. Because of my newspaper I had the opportunity to meet people from varied walks of life, some famous, some not. These included colleagues in journalism, most of the leading business executives of the time, and an assortment of those best described as "colorful."

The richest of my journalistic memories, all the same, remain those of watching the *Journal* grow into a place of eminence and of knowing those who made it happen. Not long ago a young journalist (he said he was twenty-nine) called from Washington to say he was doing a magazine article on "the modern *Wall Street Journal*" which, as he put it, "has in the last few years become a national newspaper." He remarked in complimentary fashion on the usefulness of its daily "What's News" summary of world events. On the reporting depth and writing skill of the front-page stories known around the office as "leaders." On the general high quality of its Washington and foreign coverage. On the vigor of its editorial columns. On its reviews of books, theater, opera and ballet which he found surprising in such a newspaper. On the marvelous fact that the paper is simultaneously printed every night in plants across the country and so can be delivered everywhere in the country. He wanted to interview me, as an old-timer, on how all these recent changes came about and how the "new" *Journal* contrasted with the old.

I started to tell him about Barney Kilgore, Bill Grimes, Bob Feemster, Joe Ackell. He'd heard something about Kilgore, nothing about the others, and he was a little incredulous when he heard me say his "modern" *Wall Street Journal* had been born forty years ago.

There's no doubt whatever that the *Journal* today is bigger, more successful and a better newspaper than it was even a decade ago, never mind that ancient time of 1936. When I joined it then, it had a tiny circulation and its influence, while not inconsiderable, was confined to a narrow area. When I retired in 1971 its circulation had grown to 1.2 million, making it second only to the tabloid New York *Daily News*. Today with a circulation of more than two million it's the largest in the nation. With that growth has come prosperity; with prosperity has come a bigger paper and larger resources to devote to the improvement of what it offers the reader. Because it can afford more reporters worldwide its news columns are broader in their coverage. It can devote more space to cultural affairs, literature and the arts, as well as to reporting on social changes. The vigor and the influence of its editorial columns are measured on a wider scale. Using satellites it is now printed each night in more places and therefore reaches far more readers, which in turn has made it an outstanding advertising medium. There are few places left where a Tuesday paper can't be delivered to readers that same day. No other newspaper in the country can match it.

Yet fundamentally there is very little "new" in any of this. Much of the content of today's *Journal* would be familiar to Charles Dow, who founded the company a century ago; its very first issue carried page one news about the Jake Kilrain–John L. Sullivan heavyweight fight as well as corporate and stock market news. The expansion of company and newspaper wouldn't surprise Clarence Barron, who acquired them early in the century. He first began the practice of offering his news by printing in different cities. He inspired the first corporate expansion with *Barron's Weekly*, which still flourishes.

As for the "modern" format and the broadening of the *Journal*'s coverage of government, politics, cultural affairs, and international news, that began in the 1930s and sped up with the arrival of

Barney Kilgore first as managing editor and then as company general manager in 1941. Bill Grimes made its editorial page a voice to be reckoned with and won the paper's first Pulitzer Prize in 1946. (Three successive *Journal* editors have won Pulitzers, which as far as I know is unmatched by any other newspaper.) In fact, by 1950 all the basic elements of the "modern" *Wall Street Journal* were in place.

A comparison of a *Journal* issue in, say, the 1950s with one from the 1980s will show a vast extension and improvement in all of this; the earlier one would be for today's reader less bulky in appearance (the paper then ran twenty-two to twenty-four pages on most days) and perhaps strike him as of lesser quality. The news staff was smaller in number; no more than two or three editors supervised those front-page "leaders." One senior copy editor rode herd on all the "spot" news inside. The whole editorial page staff at one time consisted of Bill Grimes, Joe Evans, and myself, responsible not only for all the editorials but for the other articles on the page, many of which we wrote ourselves. The multiple printings then were all done with hot-metal type which gave a less polished appearance to the published paper.

The point of these recollections is simply to note that all that came thereafter has been a process of evolution, not revolution, and one that continues to this day. That evolution has been made possible by a brilliant young editor, Bob Bartley, by a succession of able and imaginative managing editors, by an advertising, sales and production staff who could build on the solid foundations laid by Bob Feemster, Joe Ackell and others. And most of all by Warren Phillips, the one-time young foreign correspondent, who has made his way to the chief executive's office.

My pleasure in these recollections is that I had the privilege of being present at the creation; that is, at the time when Barney first saw the potentiality of the *Journal* as a truly national newspaper. And that, as one of "Kilgore's boys," I shared the struggle to make that vision a reality. Bill Kerby, Buren McCormack, and the rest of us didn't always know how to do what we wanted to do, because it had never been done before. Inevitably, as strong-minded people, we differed with one another and so at times there was friction among us. But with Grimes providing the leavening of experience (sometimes squelching our overenthusiasm) and Barney goading us to try things differently, we somehow succeeded. And by the time we did, that shopworn phrase about "a band of brothers" would not be amiss. The *Journal* had become a national newspaper when that inquiring young reporter was still in knee pants.

Yet he can't be faulted for his misperception. A familiar phenomenon among new *Journal* readers is that as each becomes one he thinks himself a discoverer. This newspaper, which accords so little with the image conjured by its name, comes to him as a surprise. It must surely have suddenly started doing things differently in recent days. The letters of surprise from each new generation of readers delight the editors; they herald readers who will become the faithful.

My memories are full of all of this. And as, one by one, the ranks of those who made up that little band have been thinned by the years, I find the memories of them and of their time more in my mind than memories of more famous people, presidents included, met along the way. For one thing, many of those encounters seem now no more than ego-building of the kind that fades with time. Who remembers today, except for the presidents, the names of many once in the national spotlight and so sought out by journalists, equally forgotten? Besides, I know that without the *Journal* I would have met none of them. It was that newspaper built by old friends that gave me my entrée.

Many have made their way into these pages. Others will be familiar only to older readers. Some labored in anonymity, ungraced by bylines or names upon the masthead: Oliver Gingold, who joined the paper in the days of Charlie Dow and continued daily at his desk as editor of "Abreast of the Market" well into his eighties; Sammy Lesch and Bill Kregar, supervisors *seriatim* of the inside of the paper; Richard Cooke, a reporter who doubled in brass as our theater critic; Sidney Self, our pioneer writer on science and medicine; Ted Callis, along with Feemster the architect of the *Journal*'s sales success; Eddie Costenbader, my first boss, who introduced me to "boilermakers," bourbon with a beer chaser; Joe Guilfoyle, former copyboy who rose to succeed Costenbader as editor of the Dow Jones News Service. Most of them are gone now. None of them will ever be nameless to me.

Then there are other, more personal, memories not without present meanings.

* * * * *

Our first daughter, whom we call Bonnie, was born in March 1941. Nine months later I left to go to war. For five years we saw each other only on my few and fleeting visits between ships, every time in a different port under different circumstances. When I look at her now, a grown lady, with pride and love, I still cannot escape knowing that those lost bonding years are irreplaceable.

Eleanor, born of one of those fleeting home-leaves, arrived in March 1945 while I was at sea in the Pacific readying for what would become the invasion of Okinawa. For weeks I did not know she had been born, though we had agreed to name a girl after Eleanor Badger, Tommy's widow, so there would be an Eleanor Royster in the next generation. But I did not see her until she was six months old, and her first greeting was a cry of fright at this stranger who rushed to pick her up.

During those war years I was twice eighteen months at sea away from Frances. Had the commitment between us, and the love and trust upon which it rested, not been forged beforehand we too would have met as strangers that autumn.

Our experience in those war years differs from others only in its details. In 1945 and 1946 there were thousands of soldiers and sailors returning to children they knew not, to wives who had become strangers. Many were marriages made on short acquaintance, as in every war. So it is not surprising that with the return to peace many of them foundered. Put them down among the casualties of war my generation knew. But Frances and I were not unique. There are many friends now who share our times and our experience and who are growing old together. None of us can escape a sadness at seeing new generations, some among them being our children, abandon commitments to one another for what—at least to us—seem often trivial reasons. Much of that, I think, comes from the new belief in "doing your own thing" regardless of any pain to others.

My feeling, I suppose, is one more to mark me down as an anachronistic man. How much out of touch with these times I am was driven home to me a few years back when Frances and I watched an NBC special billed as a report on the new ways of men and women. It was an interesting program, but nowhere was there a hint that there could be anything else between men and women except an unrequited searching, coupling and uncoupling. If there was a marriage its inevitable end was divorce. Or at least there was not a single couple interviewed who had stayed married a space of years. Even the septuagenarians we met, still reporting pleasure in their sex lives, were all survivors of previous marriages.

Perhaps that was understandable. Tolstoy thought only unhappy marriages made a story because all happy marriages were alike. Putting a happy one on stage or television poses the difficulty of giving dramatic interest to what may seem dull. That's why novelists and fairy-tale tellers don't know what to do after the line "and they lived happily ever after." Yet with a little imagination, a little probing, a playwright might find, here and there, a tale to tell.

Begin with a boy of seventeen, a girl of sixteen. Have them meet, romantically, on the Fourth of July. Follow them through the torments of adolescence, groping with the wonders of emerging sexuality, rebelling against the constraints of parents, exploring the world to find out who they are—separating, returning, quarreling, reconciling.

Set them down, married, in a third-floor walkup with a bathtub for a kitchen sink; she earning more than he, and neither much, in times of depression. Bring on a baby and then a war, giving him an excuse to run away to sea, answering who knows what yearning for adventure and escape from domestic responsibility.

Follow them through the war. He repeatedly absent, she left to work and raise a daughter, with only brief meetings in drab and distant places. Afterwards, with no money and two children, watch them try to put their lives back together; he restless at the return from high excitement, she fighting to submerge recriminations. Uproot them several times.

Since this is the after-part of a fairy story, let them grow slowly prosperous—entering the dangerous years when a husband finds new excitement in success, a wife needs to find a new way of life with her role as mother passed.

Give them grandchildren—two granddaughters, Heather and Shelley, will do—and if that seems just a sentimental touch it's also a part of real life because grandchildren are the vital connections in the lifestream.

Do not pretend that for the once boy of seventeen and the girl of sixteen all of this passed without hurts, without days of strain. That is not life. But let it finally come to pass that the days of strain are any days apart, that the two are only whole in the same bed, at the same table, beside the same hearth.

A banal tale, too dull for television? Perhaps. But I think it would be so only in the hands of a dull tale-teller. For it did happen once and there was nothing dull about it. I know. And can we be sure the story would not speak for others also, or that it has nothing to say about the human condition?

*   *   *   *   *

Of all such things are my memories compounded. All of them, sad and happy, have made me rich, and none of them would I relinquish. If there is any melancholy in my days now it is only from the awareness that sometime all of them will be washed away as if they never were. To be left without memories is the true tragedy of life's end.

When that hour comes the memory I will most weep for will be that of my Frances, who shares so many of them and has no need of a book to tell her how it was.

Index

THE AUTHOR

VERMONT ROYSTER IS EDITOR EMERITUS OF *The Wall Street Journal* and continues to contribute a weekly column on public affairs to that newspaper, on which he began as a reporter in 1936.

In his long career he has received every major journalistic award, including a Pulitzer Prize (1953) and the Fourth Estate Award from The National Press Club (1978) for his lifetime contribution to journalism.

He was formerly a regular commentator on the CBS radio-television program *Spectrum* and has appeared frequently on public affairs programs such as NBC's *Meet the Press*. His writing has appeared in magazines ranging from *The American Scholar* to *TV Guide*. He is the author of *Journey Through the Soviet Union* and a book of essays, *A Pride of Prejudices*.

He now lives in Chapel Hill, North Carolina, where he has taught both journalism and political science at the university there.

THE BOOK

The book was composed in Mergenthaler Linotron 202 Sabon, a typeface designed by the late Swiss typographer, Jan Tschichold.

The book was composed by G & S Typesetters in Austin, Texas, and printed on 60 lb. Warren's Olde Style by Kingsport Press, Kingsport, Tennessee.

Bound by Kingsport Press, Kingsport, Tennessee.

Designed and produced by Joyce Kachergis Book Design & Production.